Copyright and Multimedia Products

A Comparative Analysis

Multimedia products have recently experienced tremendous market success. Yet too often they are given inadequate protection under existing national and international copyright schemes. Irini Stamatoudi provides one of the first comprehensive, comparative treatments of multimedia works and copyright protection in this clear and concise volume. A detailed introduction outlines the nature of multimedia works, as well as the scope of existing legislation; separate chapters consider collections and compilations, databases, audiovisual works and computer programs (video games are here treated as a 'test case'). Stamatoudi then analyses issues of qualification and regimes of protection, and offers a model for a European legislative solution.

Copyright and Multimedia Products will interest academics and students, as well as practitioners and copyright policy makers.

IRINI A. STAMATOUDI, Faculty of Law, University of Leicester

Cambridge Studies in Intellectual Property Rights

Series editor
Professor William R. Cornish, University of Cambridge

Advisory editors
Professor François Dessemontet, University of Lausanne
Professor Paul Goldstein, Stanford University
The Hon. Sir Robin Jacob, The High Court, England and Wales

As its economic potential has expanded rapidly, intellectual property has become a subject of front-rank legal importance. *Cambridge Studies in Intellectual Property Rights* is a series of monograph studies of major current issues in intellectual property. Each volume will contain a mix of international, European, comparative and national law, making this a highly significant series for practitioners, judges and academic researchers in many countries.

Copyright and Multimedia Products

A Comparative Analysis

Irini A. Stamatoudi

CAMBRIDGE UNIVERSITY PRESS
Cambridge, New York, Melbourne, Madrid, Cape Town, Singapore, São Paulo

Cambridge University Press
The Edinburgh Building, Cambridge CB2 2RU, UK

Published in the United States of America by Cambridge University Press, New York

www.cambridge.org
Information on this title: www.cambridge.org/9780521808194

© Irini A. Stamatoudi 2002

This publication is in copyright. Subject to statutory exception
and to the provisions of relevant collective licensing agreements,
no reproduction of any part may take place without
the written permission of Cambridge University Press.

First published 2002

A catalogue record for this publication is available from the British Library

Library of Congress Cataloguing in Publication data
Stamatoudi, Irini A.
Copyright and multimedia products: a comparative analysis / Irini A. Stamatoudi.
    p. cm. – (Cambridge studies in intellectual property rights)
Includes bibliographical references and index.
ISBN 0 521 80819 7 (HB)
1. Copyright.   2. Copyright and electronic data processing.   3. Multimedia
systems – Law and legislation.   4. Audio-visual materials – Law and legislation.
5. Intellectual property.   I. Title.   II. Series.
K1441 .S73   2001
346.04'82–dc21   2001025805

ISBN-13 978-0-521-80819-4 hardback
ISBN-10 0-521-80819-7 hardback

Transferred to digital printing 2005

To the memory of my grandfather, Kostas

Contents

Acknowledgments	*page* xi
List of abbreviations	xiii
Introduction	1
1 Placing multimedia products within the scope of copyright	3
1.1 General introductory comments	3
1.2 History of copyright and redefinition of the term	6
1.3 The choice between patent and copyright protection	10
1.4 Notions relating to multimedia	14
2 The scope of multimedia works	16
2.1 Definition of multimedia works	16
2.2 Layers of protection	26
2.3 Project participants in the creation of a multimedia product	32
2.4 The differences between multimedia products and existing copyright works	36
3 Traditional literary works	42
3.1 Literary works as works of language	42
3.2 Depurification of copyright	45
3.3 Fixation of literary works	63
3.4 Multimedia products and traditional literary works	64
4 Collections and compilations	71
4.1 Traditional approaches to collections and compilations	71
4.2 The notion of works as components of a compilation	79
4.3 The bond between literary works, compilations and multimedia works	80
5 Databases	88
5.1 The database framework	88
5.2 Beyond copyright	94
5.3 Multimedia products as databases	96
6 Audiovisual works	104
6.1 'Audiovisual works' as a generic term	104

x   Contents

6.2	Composite characteristics of audiovisual works	111
6.3	A comparison between audiovisual works and literary works, compilations, databases and computer programs	116
6.4	Distinctive features of the regime of protection of audiovisual works	119
6.5	Multimedia works as audiovisual works	126
6.6	Multimedia products and the regime of protection of audiovisual works	146

7 Computer programs   152

7.1	A multimedia work as a computer program	152
7.2	Multimedia works and the regime of protection for computer programs	157
7.3	Summing up	164

8 Video games as a test case   166

8.1	Video games as multimedia works	166
8.2	The case-law on video games	167
8.3	Video games as a model for other multimedia works	179
8.4	Conclusions	184

9 Multimedia products and existing categories of copyright works   186

9.1	Originality and qualification for copyright protection	186
9.2	Qualification of multimedia works according to the type of co-operation of the contributors (the French paradigm)	196
9.3	Qualification of multimedia works according to their nature	203
9.4	A hybrid product in need of a *sui generis* copyright classification	206

10 A regime of protection for multimedia products   211

10.1	A copyright regime for multimedia products	211
10.2	A 'database-style' *sui generis* regime of protection for multimedia products	249
10.3	Collective administration and unfair competition law	256

11 Conclusions   270

11.1	A regime of protection for multimedia products: a mixture of the regime for films and the *sui generis* right for databases	271
11.2	Wider implications for copyright	276

Postscript   282
Bibliography   283
Index   315

Acknowledgments

This book became possible thanks to financial support from the University of Leicester and the Training and Mobility of Researchers Marie Curie Programme of the Commission of the European Union.

The comparative research for this project was conducted in the libraries of the universities of a number of European countries, as well as in the USA. Most significantly I am grateful for the hospitality which I received at the University of Athens, the University of Oxford, the Institute of Advanced Legal Studies, Leuven University in Belgium, George Washington University and Georgetown University in Washington, the Library of Congress, the Max-Planck-Institut in Munich and in WIPO in Geneva. Special thanks in this respect are due to Mr Woodliffe, Dean of the Faculty of Law at the University of Leicester. I would particularly like to thank him not only for financial support in order for this research to be conducted in the most comprehensive way possible, but also for his moral support during my stay in Leicester.

I would also like to acknowledge the assistance which I received from Ms Sue Smith of the library of the University of Leicester in tracking down even the most untraceable documents in the area and from Ms Wendy Addison in preparing the final version of the manuscript.

I would like to thank all the people who devoted time to talk to me on the topic of multimedia and especially Professor A. Dietz, Dr M. Ficsor and Professor A. Strowel. I am also deeply indebted to Professor John N. Adams and Professor Hector MacQueen for their detailed and helpful comments on an earlier version of the manuscript.

Special thanks are also due to Professor G. Koumantos, whose inspiring example made me aim for a career in intellectual property, to Professor A. Chiotellis for allowing me to start achieving that aim by working with him and for helping me to choose the subject of my current research, and to Professor W. R. Cornish, the editor of the Cambridge Studies in Intellectual Property Rights series, for his continued encouragement.

Most importantly, I would like to thank Paul Torremans. I really appreciated his sharp comments, encouragement and patience when discussing the finer details of this project.

It would be a significant oversight if I did not mention the one person who assisted me most both morally and intellectually, in bringing this project to an end. Professor M. Stathopoulos taught me how to think legally and dialectically, analyse legal problems and pursue my ideas. It was he who introduced me to academia.

Last, but not least, I would like to thank my parents and my sister for making it possible for me to pursue my dreams. I can never thank them enough.

The law is stated as at 1 April 2001.

Abbreviations

AFTEL	Association Française de la Télématique Multimédia
AIDAA	Association Internationale des Auteurs de l'Audiovisuel
ALAI	Association Littéraire et Artistique Internationale
All ER	All England Law Reports
ASLIB	Association of Special Libraries and Information Bureaux
Ass. Plén	Assemblée Plénière
ATRIP	Association for the Advancement of Teaching and Research in Intellectual Property
BGHZ	Entscheidungen des Bundesgerichtshof in Zivilsachen
CA	Cour d'Appel
Cass. Ass. Plén.	Cassation Assemblée Plénière
Cass. Fr.	Cassation Française
Cass.	Cour de cassation (Supreme Court)
CERDI	Centre d'Etudes et de Recherche en Droit de l'Informatique de l'Université Paris Sud
cess.	cessation
CDPA 1988	Copyright, Designs and Patents Act 1988
Ch	Law Reports. Chancery (alternative title: Chancery Reports)
Cir.	Circuit
Civ.	Civil
CMLR	Common Market Law Reports
CML Rev	Common Market Law Review
Col LR	Columbia Law Review
concl.	conclusions
CR	Computer und Recht
D.	Dalloz
DA	Dalloz Analytique

DB	Der Betrieb
D.C. Cir.	District of Columbia Circuit
DEE	Dikaio Epihirisseon ke Etarion
DG	Directorate General of the European Commission
D. Mass.	District of Massachusetts
D. Neb.	District of Nebraska
D. Somm.	Recueil Dalloz Sommaires
Doc. Parl.	Document of the Parliament
Dr. Inform.	Droit de l'Informatique et des Télécoms
EC	European Community
ECJ	European Court of Justice
ECLR	European Competition Law Review
ECR	Reports of Cases before the Court of Justice and the Court of First Instance (Alternative title: European Court Reports)
EIPR	European Intellectual Property Review
EL Rev	European Law Review
Ent LR	Entertainment Law Review
EU	European Union
F	Federal Reporter
F 2d	Federal Reporter, Second Series
F Supp	Federal Supplement
FSR	Fleet Street Reports
FT	Financial Times
GATT	General Agreement on Tariffs and Trade
Gaz Pal	Gazette du Palais
GRUR	Gewerblicher Rechtsschutz und Urheberrecht
GRUR Int	Gewerblicher Rechtsschutz und Urheberrecht Internationaler Teil
HMSO	Her Majesty's Stationery Office
HR Rep	House of Representatives Report
ICC	International Chamber of Commerce
IIC	International Review of Industrial Property and Copyright Law
IJLIT	International Journal of Law and Information Technology
Ing. Cons.	Revue de Droit Intellectuel – L'Ingénieur-Conseil
IPQ	Intellectual Property Quarterly
IPR	Intellectual Property Reporter
IRDI	Intellectuele Rechten – Droits Intellectuels
ITR	International Trade Reporter
JCP	Juris-classeur périodique (La Semaine Juridique), édition G, parties jurisprudence

JT	Journal des Tribunaux
LJOS	Law Journal Reports (old series, nineteenth century)
LQR	Law Quarterly Review
LR Eq	Law Reports – Equity
LT	Law Times
MLR	Modern Law Review
N.D.	North Dakota Supreme Court Reports (1890–1953)
OJ	Official Journal of the European Community
Pas.	Pasicrisie
Qd R	Queensland Reports
Rec. Sirey	Recueil Sirey
RIDA	Revue Internationale du Droit d'Auteur
RPC	Reports of Patent Cases
SACEM	Société des Auteurs, Compositeurs et Editeurs de Musique
S Ct	West's Supreme Court Reporter
SDNY	Southern District of New York
SI	Statutory Instrument
SO	Session ordinaire
TGI	Tribunal de Grande Instance
TRIPs	Trade Related aspects of Intellectual Property
UFITA	Archiv für Urheber-, Film-, Funk- und Theaterrecht
UNSW Law Jo	University of New South Wales Law Journal
USC	United States Code
US CAN	US Code Congressional and Administrative News
USPQ	United States Patent Quarterly
Vand LR	Vanderbilt Law Review
VARA	(United States) Visual Artists Rights' Act
WCT	WIPO Copyright Treaty
WIPO	World Intellectual Property Organization
WPPT	WIPO Performances and Phonograms Treaty
WLR	Weekly Law Reports
ZUM	Zeitschrift für Urheber- und Medienrecht

Introduction

Mr Richard Lehrberg, executive vice-president and managing director of Interplay Productions in California, said, in an attempt to define the notion of multimedia at a conference in Cannes in 1994 on 'New technologies and their influence on international audiovisual law':

> It appears that [once] there were some blind men who had never seen an elephant before, so they were taken to the circus in order to examine one. They all gathered around the elephant and they all touched it in order to get a feeling of what the elephant was like. They were then asked to describe their experience. One said that the elephant was like a rope, another said that the elephant was like a tree trunk, another said that the elephant was like a wall, another said that the elephant was like a big palm leaf, another said it was like a boa constrictor. The fact is that all of them were right because they had touched different parts of the elephant. The one who had thought it was like a rope had touched the tail; the one who had thought it was like a tree trunk had touched a leg; the one who had thought it was like a leaf had touched an ear; the one who had thought it was like a boa constrictor had touched the trunk. They were all correct but they were also all wrong because they were unaware of the totality. Certainly, an elephant is greater than the sum of its parts. Multimedia is like the elephant and we are blinded by our past.[1]

Multimedia is even more a phenomenon than a product or service, although we are concerned only with the product or service here. Nowadays it is one of the most popular and widely used words, which describes many different things at the same time. However, very few people really understand what multimedia is all about. This is largely because technological developments in the area have been extremely rapid and most of the time people approach them only through the experience they already have as publishers, film directors or producers, computer manufacturers and so on. This approach is not entirely wrong if we consider that multimedia is essentially an extension of what already exists on the market, i.e.

---

[1] R. Lehrberg, 'Blind men and the elephant: what does multimedia really mean?', ICC Conference on *New technologies and their influence on international audiovisual law*, Cannes, 1994, Proceedings, at 9.

books, films or television. At the same time we have to bear in mind that it can also be something very different from its predecessors, in which case it will necessarily demand a very different form of protection, particularly in the field of intellectual property. It is this form of protection which constitutes the focus of this book.

Multimedia will be considered from the point of view of intellectual property and specifically of copyright.[2] The central question will be whether multimedia products constitute products which are different from those already in existence, and, if they do, whether these products require different legal protection. The examination will be limited to the copyright protection afforded to such products, this being considered the closest and most appropriate form of protection for them.

Before we enter into a discussion of the substantive issues of copyright protection in relation to multimedia products, we should perhaps try and describe the very complex and diverse course of production and marketing of multimedia products. At present, multimedia works are often commissioned by software houses. As soon as all the elements that make up a multimedia product are brought together by the team of authors that has been commissioned to create the image of the work, as it is presented in the interface with the consumer or user, the software house fits them in with the required operating software and, in the vast majority of cases, it also supplies the trade mark under which the multimedia product will be marketed, as well as the distribution system. However, it should be noted that although this is the customary way of producing and marketing multimedia products it is by no means the only way.

The description of this process could lead to the suggestion that trade mark law may provide the appropriate tools to protect multimedia products. Whilst a registered trade mark may be a valuable tool of protection, it is submitted that it can by no means protect the whole product. As will be shown in more detail later, the real value of a multimedia product is often found in its content. That content is not in all circumstances protectable through the use of trade mark law. The public may be attracted to a certain content even if it is offered in a plagiarised version to which another trade mark has been affixed. Trade mark law would in those cases not be able to prevent a substantial loss being incurred by the producer of the original multimedia product. Legal protection for multimedia products must therefore go beyond the confines of trade mark law, and it is to the appropriate format for this wider protection that we now turn.

---

[2] There are, of course, other legal fields of protection for multimedia according to the national jurisdiction being considered: for example, passing-off, unfair competition law, economic and other torts, contract, criminal law, and so on.

1 Placing multimedia products within the scope of copyright

1.1 GENERAL INTRODUCTORY COMMENTS

A book dealing with multimedia can only reach a certain level of scientific accuracy in relation to new technology products. The reason is obvious. 'Multimedia' is a newly evolved term, which brings with it the imponderables every newly evolved term brings: vagueness and uncertainty.

Multimedia products have introduced new forms of expression by combining the existing ones with new technologies, thus creating a new concept. Many experts in the field state that multimedia has signified the commencement of a new era in relation to communications. Its essential ingredient is not solely interactivity, as one would expect (although interactivity still is the key feature for this kind of communication), but the amount of data multimedia products carry. Information as such has become extremely important. The more information you possess, the more power you have. The possession of information is the key to the successful creation and marketing of a multimedia product. The information contained in it is the crucial factor when consumers decide to purchase. The need for a free flow of information around the world is the ultimate reason for the financing of communication industries. The ability to distribute such information is the parameter by which financial success in the international market is measured. Information has to do with development, evolution, culture, civilisation and state power. Interactivity is valuable in so far as it facilitates the manipulation of information and responds to the needs of the user with regard to that particular information.

In the present era multimedia is bound to be at the centre of developments because the advantages of multimedia applications are so great. The public's access to information and its concept of communication will change the face of communication as a whole. There will also be an impact on inter-human relations and on social structures. Space and time will become more readily available and accurate and comprehensive information will become a possible target. Creators will be afforded more opportunities to create as a result of the great demand for creative content in the new technology products. Communication and intellectual property industries will be given more opportunities for exploitation and thus the convergence of existing technologies will lead to the emergence of a new breed of product. This will provide a substantial push for technology. Boundaries will be pushed out. Cultures and ideas will work more closely together. It is time we started seeking solutions at an international rather than at a national level.

If we want to put the fast-growing commercial importance of multimedia products on the European market in figures, we should refer to those most recently available. In 1989 the multimedia market had a global turnover of US $3 billion. This turnover increased fivefold in 1995 and 1996.[1] Other statistics show that the multimedia market, excluding video games, was worth US $1.4 billion in 1989, whilst in 1997 it was expected to reach US $23.9 billion.[2] Multimedia products in CD-ROMs, which is the most popular form of distribution, have increased their market turnover forty-five times between 1990 and 1995, with the USA and Europe being market leaders. The statistics show that the USA led the pace until 1993, when Europe seems to have taken over. Of course part of the reason why these statistics look impressive is that the spread of the new technology took place mainly in this period. Before then this form of computer technology was not widely available, and, even if it was, the cost was in most cases prohibitive. By now most households in the developed world will have become equipped with CD-ROM devices and will have subscribed to an on-line service, either for domestic or for professional use. After the 'big bang' of this period, increases in market figures will stop being so dramatic. However, multimedia products will still occupy a substantial part of the market. People who have already bought the relevant equipment will become regular clients of the technology industry.

Apart from the trends in technology and information culture, law is bound to play one of the most important roles in the area. The obvious regime for the protection of these works is intellectual property. Works which possess any kind of creativity, originality and intellectual effort come within the scope of the national intellectual property laws and international treaties in this area. At some time in the past the law, apart from regulating the social and technological evolutions that had already

---

[1] See G. Vercken, *Guide pratique du droit d'auteur pour les producteurs de multimédia*, commissioned by the European Communities, DG XIII (Translic) from AIDAA, 1994, at 16ff.

[2] M. Radcliffe, 'Legal issues in new media: multimedia for publishers' in D. Campbell and S. Cotter (eds.), *International intellectual property law. New developments*, J. Wiley & Sons, Chichester, 1995, at 181.

taken place, also had an educative role, foreseeing developments and problems and introducing legal solutions even before the occurrence of such problems. Nowadays, it is evident that the law has long been left behind, especially in the area of technology. That is partly due to the fact that lawyers are not always so familiar with technical issues, much less high-tech issues, and that they prefer those kinds of problems to find their natural solutions in their natural environment. It seems in this sense that as well as the natural law in legal history and theory, there may also be a natural law in the self-rescuing sense in technology. Later in this book, we will see that perhaps this is not always very far from the truth.

Although multimedia products are of such great economic importance, there is no direct legislation to protect them. That, of course, does not mean that there is no protection whatsoever in relation to these products. The protection afforded to them is essentially an amalgam of the existing regimes of protection for other similar intellectual property works, and they are the subject of protection in other branches of law, such as contract and tort, etc. There is also some part of the literature which claims that in fact no differentiation is to be found in terms of protection between the traditional categories of intellectual property works and the new technology products. Yet many initiatives have taken place on both a national and an international level, not directly relating to multimedia products, but to digital rights and rights in databases. Here, and especially in the recent EU Directive on databases, the introduction along with copyright protection of a *sui generis* regime of protection for compilations of data is indicative of the need for separate treatment of the intellectual property products of the new generation.

With regard to intellectual property the regime of protection which seems more appropriate for multimedia works is that of copyright protection. Multimedia works, though sometimes functional and utilitarian, are in most cases considered to be works within the scope of the Berne Convention and therefore of most of the national laws of states. Moreover, there are only rare cases where they can also be covered by other regimes, for example patent protection. We will consider this possibility in section 1.3.

In the course of analysing the copyright protection of multimedia products we will examine issues such as the legal definition of multimedia products, their regime of protection under current national, European and international laws, clearing rights in contents and competition issues. We will also propose the most convenient solutions from the point of view of the author.

Before we get into the main body of this book, it is important to make clear that we will deal with multimedia products essentially from the point of view of copyright. The fact that we refer to them more as products and less as works might already look peculiar. This, however, accords with the latest changes in the area of intellectual property. The immediate question is whether 'works' and 'products' are interchangeable concepts. In general they are not, but in this book it is considered that they are by reason of the fact that intellectual property today encompasses works in which the functional aspect is prevalent rather than the creative one. In such a situation the concept of product rather than work is more appropriate. But this is not the main reason since in order for a work to qualify as such, it has also to come within the scope of the definition. If the work is merely of a functional and utilitarian nature this definition is bound not to cover it, apart from certain cases in common law countries. The essential reason for calling multimedia works 'products' is the fact that the actual focus of their creation is economic. Multimedia works acquire their significance partly from their creation and the new methods of communication they represent but substantially more from the market value they command. They are basically commodities and are treated as such. Any intellectual property right protection is aiming at this target. This is, of course, not very different from the existing traditional intellectual property works. But in the latter case their market value is less considerable than that of multimedia products. Perhaps less relevant are rights other than economic rights. Because of this new intellectual property platform immediate legal solutions are needed.

The key approach of this book is less to describe what the situation is at present, rather more to look into the future, albeit short term. Are the existing intellectual property laws capable of accommodating multimedia products? If not, what is required: transformations in the existing regimes of protection or *sui generis* legislation? How well has copyright survived the test of time and technology? Where are we heading in this respect if present and forthcoming developments in the area are bound to change the face of copyright?

1.2 HISTORY OF COPYRIGHT AND REDEFINITION OF THE TERM

Intellectual property provides a clear case where law follows developments. Its function is post-regulative rather than one forming the rights and obligations in relation to intellectual property products. The history of technological change shows that new forms of expression have invariably led to new types of creative works.[3] The invention of the printing

---

[3] M. Turner, 'Do the old legal categories fit the new multimedia products? A multimedia CD-ROM as a film' [1995] 3 *EIPR* 107.

press technique by Gutenberg was an essential push to the emergence of copyright law. Then the photograph, film, radio and television appeared.[4] It took quite some time for these forms of expression to be considered media in their own right, with an independent regime of protection adjusted to their own needs. It was not until 1956, for example, that a separate regime for protecting films was introduced into the UK's Copyright Act.

Today we are facing the same process of inventing multimedia. We have both the general feeling that we know what it is all about and the strange feeling that we are still not completely familiar with the full technology and reality. This is due to the following reasons. First, the more multimedia products enter our lives, the more we familiarise ourselves with them and gain the feeling we understand them. Secondly, it is too early to trace and understand the full set of problems multimedia products are bound to present. In this respect we are blinded by our past. We can only appreciate things and problems with the knowledge we possess, which is inevitably restricted to the problems traditional intellectual property works present. Foreseeing the future with regard to this is not easy. The technology progresses so quickly that any solutions are outdated before people even become familiar with them.

Existing intellectual property rights present an advantage. They are established worldwide rights, long practised and well known. Lawyers can deal more easily with a situation where they know both the ally and the enemy. It is hard to admit that new rights are called for because any new right or development creates uncertainty and awkward situations.

All the above explain the different reactions of people to new technologies, depending on which angle they view them from. 'Book people see talking books. TV people see interactive game shows. Movie people see either choose-your-own-ending movies or a way to film some cut scenes or set-ups and slap in an arcade action sequence.'[5] Yet, the technological evolution has already called, if not for *sui generis* solutions in the area of intellectual property law, then at least for substantial transformations.

It is evident that, since copyright is supposed to be the intellectual property law closest to multimedia products, its stretching to include new technologies has touched on its original concept. Copyright works

---

[4] At first people tried to fit the new phenomena into existing categories. For example, films were treated as talking books and sets of pictures. They were only given protection in their own right once their commercial exploitation became sizeable enough to demand proper protection to avoid losses from copying.

[5] R. Lehrberg, 'Blind men and the elephant: what does multimedia really mean?', ICC Conference on *New technologies and their influence on international audiovisual law*, Cannes, 1994, Proceedings, at 9.

were always held to be works which involved some kind of creativity (mostly for continental law countries) or some kind of original effort (for common law countries). Copyright, as a substantial and concrete form of protection, has been stretched to cover a large variety of works which were not originally considered as coming explicitly within the scope of international conventions and national legislation. A recent example is databases, which have up to now only been explicitly covered by the TRIPs Agreement and recently by the WIPO Copyright Treaty. By using copyright protection to protect works other than the ones which were originally considered to be literary or artistic, the essential components of copyright have been stretched.

One of the ways in which copyright has been revised is by the inclusion of new works which are at most works of a functional and utilitarian nature and by reason of this particular nature involve only a low degree of originality, if any. Secondly, until recently any work required some kind of fixation on a material support with a degree of permanence in order to be protected. Now, however, copyright protection has been extended to intellectual property services or to works which are not fixed or not fixed permanently on a material support, as for example the memory of a computer. It also covers works with a life of some seconds while being transmitted through the cable of a network. These changes have placed the importance on the work as such, as an immaterial good, and less on what it looks like. Moreover, the works which copyright has been extended to cover are not the outcome of the effort of a single person or of a limited number of persons. Usually there is a sizeable team of persons involved in their production. Thus, there are also many individual works included in such a work. These works are regarded as information rather than the artistic creation or expression of the personality of the authors. The aim of the new intellectual property works is not to entertain an audience. It is more to educate an audience in the sense of informing it. These works are essentially of an informative nature with the direct aim of being comprehensive, efficient and functional, rather than original, different or new.

Thus works of this kind are less often considered works in the original sense of the word. Technology sets its own rules. These kinds of works are approached from their commercial point of view. They are commoditised and mainly called products. It is not only the technological reality, however, that makes the rules. There is a more immediate force leading technology. This is the market reality. No matter how important something may be from an educational or technological point of view, if it cannot be marketed successfully, or if there is no market at all for it, it is bound not to survive. Multimedia products are important and pose important questions of law because of their market success and their influence on communications. Of course, what we are almost saying is that the market successfully accommodates only useful and worthy products, but because the market can be somewhat unpredictable and does not respond to such simplistic evaluations this cannot be the case.

Thus, the notion of copyright has been partially adapted to the new reality. In common law countries such as the United Kingdom there has been no great transformation. Copyright there was rather more economically orientated from the start. The degree of originality is also very low, involving only skill and labour. In other words, works which are not merely copied and involve the previously mentioned prerequisites are copyrightable. The common law countries' approach is a limited one compared to the rest of Europe where copyright has become increasingly market orientated and any alleged moral right infringement is decided on the grounds of the types of work involved. Reasons to justify strong copyright protection are sometimes lacking.

If we are to describe the latest trends in copyright we could say that it has become more utilitarian in nature. The originality criterion appears to have been lowered. The forms seem to have dematerialised. Information has taken the place of works and the author's role has been redefined. It is no longer purely creative. But even in the original creative model, the author's role should not be allowed to impede the evolution that is taking place in this area. Either way that evolution should be accommodated, albeit not automatically. As with any transformation, it has many repercussions. The moral rights of authors will be revised and competition law will be relaxed to allow co-operation of industries which would be forbidden in another context. Clearing rights techniques will call for collective administration and remuneration, and the rightholders will essentially be rewarded through the payment of a lump sum. How far the evolution will go is unpredictable. For example, will compulsory licences be introduced? Will multimedia products come within the scope of copyright with the same term of protection and the same bundle of exclusive rights or will a *sui generis* regime of protection be introduced? How much are we to expect from intellectual property law? As a substantial part of the literature suggests, where technology sets problems it is technology in most cases which has to find the solutions as well.[6] Yet, the imposition or facilitation of these solutions might be an issue for intellectual property law.

---

[6] C. Clark, 'The answer to the machine is the machine' in B. Hugenholtz (ed.), *The future of copyright in a digital environment*, Kluwer Law International, The Hague, London, Boston, 1996, at 139.

1.3 THE CHOICE BETWEEN PATENT AND COPYRIGHT PROTECTION

If we are to limit their protection to the ambit of intellectual property protection, multimedia works, by reason of their hybrid nature, can form the subject matter of protection of many intellectual property rights. The categorisation and the choice of regime of protection are subject to the following issues: first, it depends which part of a multimedia product we are seeking to protect, and secondly, it depends on the structure and the whole manufacturing process of this particular product. In other words, it depends on whether this product is linked and in what sense it is linked to its operating computer program and whether it meets the requirements of more than one set of intellectual property rights.

For the purposes of this book we will make the distinction between the various parts of a multimedia product and we will distinguish any rights on the operating software of this product from the multimedia work itself. The multimedia work will be defined as a compilation of pre-existing or commissioned works or other data. We will also point out that this kind of distinction, though logical and coherent at this stage of technological evolution, cannot be considered to be watertight for the future. If more and more technical devices incorporate more and more technical functions, it is very likely that we will end up with comprehensive regimes of protection for the full device, whether this is a computer program or anything else.

As intellectual property stands today, both at national and international level, it is essentially a bipolar system. This means it is divided into the two broad categories of industrial property (mainly regulated by the Paris Convention for the Protection of Industrial Property, 1883) and literary and artistic property (mainly regulated by the Berne Convention for the Protection of Literary and Artistic Works, 1886).[7] The dominant paradigms in these two regimes of protection are patents and copyright respectively.

Although the rationales behind these two intellectual property rights seem at first glance diametrically opposite, serving different functions and therefore bringing with them different economic and social premises in relation to the works protected, more and more deviant cases arise which blur the borderline between industrial property protection and copyright. This underlines the need for a different regulation (which is neither patent

---

[7] TRIPs (1994), in the context of GATT and the World Trade Organisation, also plays a very important regulative role both for industrial and for literary and artistic property, as does the WIPO Copyright Treaty (hereinafter WCT) which essentially brings international copyright up to date with recent technological developments.

nor copyright) or a mixed regulation (which is both patent and copyright) or a hybrid regulation (which generates a *sui generis* right encompassing basic characteristics of both types of protection). These products are almost entirely new technology products which combine technical devices with traditional design of works, as identified in the Berne Convention. The debate as to whether certain kinds of new technology products come within the scope of one or other regime of protection, or if they require a *sui generis* treatment, is also not a new one. It essentially started when the discussion about the protection of computer programs began in the 1980s.[8]

If we are first to examine the issue of how close multimedia products are to patents, we have to see to what extent multimedia meets the criteria for qualifying for this regime of protection. TRIPs, which clarified and improved upon the Paris Convention in respect of the criteria for patentability, provides that an invention is patentable when it is new, involves an inventive step and is capable of industrial application.[9] In relation to a multimedia work, as long as we are dealing with the compilation of information as such, irrespective of the technical devices that have manufactured it and that run it, there is nothing to advocate inventive step or industrial application. Even the notion of an invention itself is non-existent in this case. Invention is linked to the idea of a technical device. The multimedia work is not a device but a work and from this point of view it seems to come closer to the definition of the specific subject matter in the Berne Convention.

Even if we were to consider the multimedia work in conjunction with its operating program, the software tool that runs the application, and if we were to consider that the latter is the dominant part which has to be protected and whose protection covers the protection of the whole compilation, the multimedia work would still not, in most cases, qualify for patentability. TRIPs, in article 10.1, provides that computer programs, whether in source or object form, shall be protected as literary works under the Berne Convention.[10] This, of course, does not exclude cases where computer programs can constitute the subject matter of

---

[8] See also J. Reichman, 'Legal hybrids between the patent and copyright paradigms' (1994) 94 *Col LR* 2432.
[9] Art. 27(1). A footnote in this article indicates that '[f]or the purposes of this article, the terms "inventive step" and "capable of industrial application" may be deemed by a Member to be synonymous with the terms "non-obvious" and "useful" respectively'. Thus, the wording of TRIPs covers also the wording of the requirements of the US patent law which provide for novelty, utility and non-obviousness. 35 USC §§ 101–3, 271 (1988).
[10] See also the European Patent Convention at art. 52.2c, s. 1(2)(c) of the English Patents Act 1977 and art. 5 of the WCT.

patent protection. However, these cases have to be a computer program and something else which goes beyond the computer program itself. A possible example of such a case would be a computer-program-related invention.[11]

Applying this train of thought to multimedia, it is perhaps clear up to now that even the assimilation of the multimedia work into its operating software would not be enough to make it qualify for a patent protection. But if what we are dealing with is an invention run by some kind of software which functions interactively, or which has a multimedia application closely relating to the invention as one of its functions, then the whole invention is very likely to qualify as a patent. However, if we can still distinguish the multimedia work as an independent part of the invention, holding its separate and distinctive value, then this multimedia work is not patentable. Although these cases may at present look extreme and rather unlikely, there is nothing to prevent inventors in the future from coming up with such kinds of inventions, especially in the area of robotics. The rule at present though remains that multimedia products, as well as software, are outside the scope of patents.

The area which seems to fit better with multimedia is copyright. Multimedia products do not come explicitly within the scope of works under any international or national legal instrument relating to copyright protection. This, however, is not due to the fact that they constitute subject matter which is excluded from the scope of copyright. It is rather due to the fact that, firstly, this kind of work could not have been foreseen at the time that most international instruments were drafted, and, secondly, it is too novel for the legal literature to decide where to put it. Thus, any legal solution relating to multimedia is necessarily the outcome of treatment analogous to existing regimes of protection.

The notion of a 'work' under the Berne Convention is quite loose. It includes a large number of works which, if they possess some kind of originality and are expressed in one or other form, qualify for copyright protection as literary and artistic works. Copyright seems to be the most appropriate regime of protection for many reasons. First, although multimedia works are not as such protected by copyright they come very close to traditional copyrightable works such as compilations, films, computer programs, etc. Secondly, if multimedia works possess something it is more likely to be originality rather than any kind of novelty or inventive step. Although they are meant to be marketed, they are not meant to be industrially applicable and confer on their rightholder any kind of

---

[11] E.g. *IBM's application* [1999] RPC 563. See C. Reed and J. Angel (eds.), *Computer law*, 4th edn, Blackstone Press Ltd, London, 2000, at 115ff.

absolute exclusive patent-like rights which will justify the investment that has to be undertaken for their creation.

The economic and social premises which underlie patents are essentially different from those relating to copyright. The former confer a kind of protection on the rightholder that will permit him, for a limited period in time, to exploit exclusively not only the functional expression of his invention but also the idea itself, so as to have the incentive to produce it commercially and possibly invent further devices in the future. From this point of view, patent protection, though shorter in time, is stronger. This is also the very reason why many companies producing new technology products strive for the patentability of their products more than for any kind of copyright protection. Copyright is by definition a looser right, as it aims to prevent the copying of the whole or a substantial part of the work. The idea as such is not protected; only its expression is protected. In the end the idea itself can be as precious as its expression in the market of new technology products, especially if the products at issue come close enough to functional and utilitarian works possessing the minimum requirements for copyright protection.

An issue which arises here is how much the scope of copyright can be extended to accommodate new technology works, especially when these works depart substantially from copyright's traditional requirements. First, the notion of dematerialisation outweighs any notion of fixation, especially in permanent form. Secondly, the originality criterion is defined on the grounds of structure and arrangement rather than of the originality of the work itself. We mentioned that structure and arrangement are also subject to the use and presentation by the user of the compilation on his screen, an issue which points to how absurd and ill-defined such a criterion can sometimes be. Moreover, the importance of the originality criterion as such comes substantially down the list. The more the new works involve data and the more they involve it in a comprehensive way, the more these works become functional and utilitarian. The problem is where are we to draw the line of originality in order to accommodate these products? We run the risk of either affording more protection than is needed to certain works, or not affording adequate protection to others. Even the design of a *sui generis* regime presents difficulties in so far as it derogates from the common established and known principles of the traditional intellectual property laws. But it is also a decision of policy whether we will continue to stretch a notion such as that of copyright so far as to, in fact, revise it. The question remains as to what extent this is advisable. Multimedia constitutes a characteristic example of such a situation. This book will consider to what degree the existing legislation is capable of providing such products with an adequate level of protection.

1.4 NOTIONS RELATING TO MULTIMEDIA

As will be explained in more detail in chapter 2, multimedia is held to be a term which includes anything from enterprises to networks and means of distribution, from sources to material supports and from products to services. This, however, is likely to cause confusion not only about what we mean when we refer to the notion of multimedia, but also to what degree this notion is the same as or related to notions such as the Internet, the information superhighway, virtual reality, hypermedia, hypertext and so on. For the sake of clarification it is perhaps advisable to define the scope of these terms.

The information superhighway and the Internet are somewhat interchangeable terms. An information superhighway is an international digital network into which interactive multimedia networks serving the interests and needs of multiple users and services are integrated. The Internet is today's version of the information superhighway. It is an (unstructured) interconnection of a vast unknown number of computers worldwide. It is in fact a network, which is accessible by any computer linked to it at any place or time. The Internet was initially set up in 1969 as a system of networked computers (originally four) of the US Department of Defence, known as ARPANET. It was designed in such a way so as to withstand the loss of numerous key computers and interconnections and still function in the event of war. The Internet can serve today as a means of distributing multimedia services, in the same sense as any other on-line distribution service.

One form of distribution of multimedia is virtual reality. Virtual reality is a 3-D multimedia product or service. It is a way of enabling users to interact in real time with a computer-simulated environment by entering this environment with their own human senses by means of special equipment, i.e. gloves, helmets, glasses, etc. A computer is used to map their body and senses directly into the digital world. Virtual reality, though still at a primitive stage, presents the most advanced form of multimedia applications and is used in entertainment, health and science. The creation of 3-D computer-generated environments is limited only by the multimedia software designed to generate them and the computer processing power available to bring them to life.[12] Virtual reality requires immensely fast and powerful computing and apparently also poses metaphysical questions in addition to questions of technology and law.

Hypertext is an underlying structure in multimedia design. It is an 'interlinkedness' between different elements of information which allows

---

[12] For further details see T. Feldman, *Multimedia in the 1990s. BNB Research Fund Report*, British Library, 1991.

the users to follow pathways in order to access that information, in the order in which they wish to do so. 'Hypertext' makes this non-sequential approach to information possible by offering the very connections needed to jump instantly to other locations in a database or at any other site where one finds related information of interest. The multimedia version of this technical concept is called hypermedia. Here the information elements may be text, sound, images or a combination of the three. Hypermedia really amounts to an environment of interconnected multimedia elements. However, in practice the terms 'hypertext' and 'hypermedia' are used interchangeably.

Common to all the above notions, whether these are underlying multimedia technologies or distribution systems, is that they are only able to function in a digital environment, that they combine more than one different kind of expression and that they provide interactive services. A lot more could be said about technical notions and technology. It is submitted though that this brief outline of the environment in which multimedia operates is sufficient for the purposes of this book.

2 The scope of multimedia works

2.1 DEFINITION OF MULTIMEDIA WORKS

As previously mentioned, multimedia means many different things to different people. For example, it can mean enterprises, types of communication, products or services. It is rather an amorphous term. People understand it as encompassing interactive television, interactive guides in museums, product catalogues in electronic malls, schedules in train stations, on-line databases which can be retrieved worldwide from networks such as the Internet in the form of virtual reality, simple video, computer games, and so on.[1]

As we will see in more detail later on, all these products share characteristics that come within the definition of multimedia products and therefore belong to the same generation. However, they are also somewhat different from one another by reason of the particularities they present and the different purposes and functions they serve. The large and vague variety of products[2] that exists in the market constitutes the reason why multimedia is more of a phenomenon than a product which can be pinned

---

[1] Multimedia and similar terms 'are more and more used by different sets of people, in different circumstances for designating different kinds of applications based on different technologies and standards'. EC Commission, DG XIII, *Report on Multimedia*, 30 September 1992, at 1, as referred to by U. Loewenheim in 'Multimedia and the European copyright law' (1996) 27 *IIC* 41, at 42.

[2] In this book, by 'products' it is intended to include both products and services (on-line and off-line products) for reasons of economy and avoidance of repetition. However, wherever a different treatment is intended, products and services will be distinguished. Moreover, throughout this book multimedia works will occasionally be referred to as multimedia products. That will be so for two main reasons. First, the customary term for this kind of work is established as multimedia products and secondly, this term puts the emphasis on the market value and significance of these works. We cannot disregard the fact that if it were not for their market success, multimedia products would not occupy such an important place in both the legal and the economic literature. In fact, because the market success of intellectual property products is increasing significantly, they are valued and approached from this point of view more and more. In many cases it is the market reality and the transactions that necessitate efficient legal solutions. Multimedia underlines this. The contents of multimedia will be referred to as information or data for the purposes of this book. Once works have been digitised and can be freely circulated

The scope of multimedia works 17

down to certain particular functions and characteristics, remaining stable over several years.

Because multimedia is a comparatively new term, inextricably linked with technology and its progress, it is also a fast-evolving term, which inevitably brings with it the characteristics of every new term: broadness and ambiguity. Broadness has a positive connotation in so far as it signifies the capacity multimedia has to accommodate a vast range of things. Ambiguity has a negative connotation in so far as it signifies a reservation as to what it finally accommodates. Thus, multimedia is a notion both rich in content and at the same time vague. In the light of this, this book will deal with multimedia in a broad sense so as to encompass legal solutions which will not soon be outdated by reason of the development of technology in this area.

Multimedia cannot be categorised in one of the existing categories of media. It is rather a descriptive word for computer-based works (in which many technologies are combined) and media which were formerly used separately.[3] In this sense multimedia is a category in itself. In broad terms it is used today as a generic concept, which encompasses new services of communication linked to digital techniques.[4] New services are not, however, 'new' in the literal meaning of the word. In fact, multimedia is a hybrid of heterogeneous technologies, which were formerly used separately and which now permit the exploitation of existing or newly created works in different formats and media.[5] It is a convergence of video, audio and telephony technologies.[6] This convergence signifies new co-existing types of communication, which separate the known material supports

---

around the world in vast numbers, their function is mostly regarded as informative rather than anything else. This principal role is mirrored in the terminology. It also clearly describes the need for users of such products to possess and access as much information as possible. The accumulation of vast amounts of information in a particular field is the reason that multimedia is successful. Even if this information is works, it is still regarded as data, since it no longer performs the function a traditional work performs.

[3] See R. Raysman, P. Brown and J. Neuburger, *Multimedia law: forms and analysis*, Law Journal Seminars-Press, New York, 1996, at 1–2; and Loewenheim, 'Multimedia' (*IIC*), at 42. Multimedia has also been described as an information system of audiovisual communication with the public which permits a user to consult even from a distance a database comprising text, images, sound or messages of any nature and to receive in response up to the minute information. J. Boyle, 'Aspects contractuels relatifs à l'informatisation' in *Droit de l'informatique, enjeux, nouvelles responsabilités*, Jeune Barreau, Paris, 1993, at 236.

[4] G. Vercken, *Guide pratique du droit d'auteur pour les producteurs de multimédia*, commissioned by the European Communities, DG XIII (Translic) from AIDAA, 1994, at 14.

[5] See Loewenheim, 'Multimedia' (*IIC*), at 42; and M. Radcliffe, 'Legal issues in new media: multimedia for publishers' in D. Campbell and S. Cotter (eds.), *International intellectual property law. New developments*, J. Wiley & Sons, Chichester, 1995, at 181.

[6] J. Cameron, 'Approaches to the problems of multimedia' [1996] 3 *EIPR* 115.

from the information they carry and store it in a digitised manner in PCs or create new information, irrespective of any material support.[7]

However, whatever may be the different definitions we give to multimedia, by natural assimilation between the object and its material support, multimedia is essentially used today solely to mean the marketed product, the commercial carrier of the work (often a material support), i.e. the CD-ROM (compact disc – read only memory), CD-I (compact disc – interactive), DCC (digital compact cassette), Data Discman, mini-disc, DVD (digital video disc), interactive database on-line, and whatever other form its commercialisation might take.[8] And it is in this sense that we will use the term multimedia in this book.

2.1.1 Definition

The main distinctive characteristic of multimedia is that its technology is meant to combine, in a single medium, diverse types of works or information. In order for this combination to become possible a digital environment is required. The information has to be digitally processed, stored and accessed by a computer. Computers are the only media capable of performing such tasks in a digital environment. In addition to the conversion of the data to a digital format, this format also has to offer, again with the aid of a computer, the option of interactivity, in other words the possibility of a dialogue between the user and the system.

Even though, as mentioned above, a single medium can technically be the combination of many different types of technology, the fact that an essential feature of a multimedia product is the convergence of multiple elements (works) on a single medium has led many commentators to think that the term itself is a misnomer.[9] 'Multi-media' literally signifies the existence of many (multi-) means of communication (media) rather than the multiplicity or mixture of many types or categories of works.[10]

---

[7] M. Marinos, 'Nomiki prostassia vasseon dedomenon. To idiaitero (*sui generis*) dikaioma tis odigias 96/9/EOK' [1997] 2 *DEE* 128.

[8] Vercken, *Guide pratique*, at 14.

[9] The term 'multimedia' was first used in the 1980s to designate the enterprises which were originally printing, publishing and advertising companies, though later they turned their interests to the audiovisual market after the deregulation of public audiovisual monopolies in Europe. They thus became multi-media companies. A. Strowel and J.-P. Triaille, *Le droit d'auteur, du logiciel au multimédia (Copyright, from software to multimedia)*, Bruylant, Brussels, 1997, at 332.

[10] The term 'mixed media' is sometimes used as an alternative in the USA. Like 'multimedia' this term is a misnomer. See B. Lehman and R. Brown, 'Intellectual property and the national information infrastructure', *Report of the Working Group on Intellectual Property Rights*, US Patent and Trademark Office, Washington D.C., September 1995, at 41.

From this point of view a term which has been suggested by Koumantos[11] as being more appropriate is the 'unimedium multiwork' (*multioeuvre unimédia*),[12] or, perhaps, a simpler abbreviation of it, 'unimedium'.[13] The latter term puts the emphasis on the single medium with which consumers are confronted. Yet it does not exclude the significance of the contents that are included. In the final analysis it is the contents that make a multimedia product sell. The technology only makes it easily and readily available and perhaps commercially more attractive.

However, the term 'multimedia' is by now a well-established term in the area of information technology and, as is often the case with law, it is the trend (or technology) that comes first and the law that follows. Since technology has imposed its terminology in practice, it is the 'multimedia' term that will be used for the purposes of this book as well.

As we described earlier, multimedia is an ill-defined notion by reason of its polymorphism.[14] The vast number of products (on-line and off-line)

---

[11] G. Koumantos, 'Les aspects de droit international privé en matière d'infrastructure mondiale d'information' [1996] *Koinodikion* 2.B, 241, at 243.

[12] See also M. Ficsor, 'New technologies and copyright: need for change, need for continuity' in *WIPO Worldwide Symposium on the Future of Copyright and Neighbouring Rights*, Louvre, Paris, 1–3 June 1994, 209, at 227.

[13] See also Raysman, Brown and Neuburger, *Multimedia law*, at 1–2, footnote 1 referring to Lehman and Brown, 'Intellectual property and the national information infrastructure'. This discussion has also been joined by other scholars in the area of information technology. Apart from the term 'unimedium', they also propose the terms 'monomedium', 'plurimedia', 'mediamix', 'hypermedia', 'polymedia', 'interactive integrated media', etc. Strowel and Triaille, *Le droit d'auteur*, at 331 and 334. In relation to the term 'interactive integrated media' see D. Monet, *Le multimédia*, Flammarion, Paris, 1995, at 8.

[14] It is interesting to note that in France, three official documents referring to multimedia have defined it in rather contradictory ways. The 1994 Théry Report (*The Information Superhighways*, at 14, quoted in N. Muenchinger, 'French law and practice concerning multimedia and telecommunications' [1996] 4 *EIPR* 186) defined multimedia as 'a set of interactive services using solely digitised media, for the processing and transmission of information in all of its forms: text, data, sound, still images, animated real or virtual images'. Decree 93-1429 of 31 December 1993 relating to the obligatory legal deposit of certain works at the National Library (Official Journal, 1 January 1994, at 64) defined it as 'a document which regroups two or more media (of the ones mentioned in its previous chapters), or which associates, on the same medium, two or more documents which are subject to the obligation of deposit (according to this Decree)'. Lastly, an order of the French Ministry of Industry, Post, Telecommunications and External Commerce (Official Journal, 22 March 1994) described the term as a concept which associates several modes of representation of information such as text, sound and image. Muenchinger, who was the source of this information ('French law'), points out that 'the latter definitions do not make any reference to digitisation, processing or transmission of data, interactivity or services, nor do they refer to digitisation as a medium... [T]he three official references to multimedia which exist thus far in France may in fact be contradictory.' This is indicative of the confusion that reigns in this area. Multimedia is a term which, apart from the inherent difficulties its definition presents, also suffers from the difficulty of any definition which is subject to technological evolution in the area.

it comprises makes it difficult to limit this notion to a specific and rigid definition. However, there are certain elements that characterise multimedia and that can therefore be found in any product coming within this category. *Multimedia is a product or service which combines and integrates in a single medium, in a digitised form, at least two*[15] *of the following elements: text, audio, still or moving images, computer programs and other data. It requires a software tool that allows for a substantial degree of interactivity and which allows for the retrieval and presentation of the above information.*[16] It is clear that the concept of interactivity (or even full integration) is a key one in this debate and one to which we will have to return at a later stage.

Text, audio and images form, in fact, what we call the contents of a multimedia product. By *text* we mean any material in written form, such as literary works, magazines, newspapers, databases, data,[17] or even entries, instructions or guidelines, as these appear on the screen to assist navigation through the multimedia work. The last three, of course, are regarded

---

[15] Some scholars would argue that even the inclusion of a single type of work in combination with a software tool suffices to create a multimedia work. Strowel and Triaille, *Le droit d'auteur*, at 335. Yet by stretching the definition that far, one risks the inclusion in the notion of multimedia of even traditional compilations of works, for which, no matter how many works they incorporate, a separate legal treatment is not needed in most cases. One of the characteristics of a multimedia product should be the combination of different kinds of works in one single digitised format on one medium. The software tool that operates the multimedia work should in this respect be distinguished from all the other works that are included and it should not be counted as one of them. If multimedia does not include more than one type of work, even the simplest database or compilation will amount to a multimedia work. Yet, there is nothing in such a work to warrant a treatment different from the one that traditional copyright affords.

[16] The Commission of the European Union refers to multimedia products as 'combinations of data and works of different kinds such as pictures (still or animated), text, music and software. These services are linked together by a common factor: the concept of interactivity, which will allow the contents themselves to be changed. The degree of interactivity necessary has still to be determined.' The Commission adds that '[m]ost of these services will be generated by means of databases. Another characteristic of the new services will be that the consumer will probably be charged for their use.' Green Paper on copyright and related rights in the information society, COM (95) 382 final, at 19. According to the US White Paper on intellectual property and the national information infrastructure, 'The very premise of a so-called "multimedia" work is that it combines several different elements or types of works (e.g., text (literary works), sound (sound recordings), still images (pictorial works), and moving images (audiovisual works)) into a single medium (e.g., a CD-ROM) – not multiple media', at 41–2. See also B. Wittweiler, 'Produktion von Multimedia und Urheberrecht aus schweizerischer Sicht' (1995) 128 *UFITA* 5, at 6, who emphasises the importance of digitisation, the combination of more than one medium and interactivity.

[17] Data is mentioned separately in the multimedia definition because many scholars do not consider it to be part of text. Mere factual data can consist of figures or other information, but this would be a very restrictive definition of text.

more as multimedia product operating materials and less as contents.[18] By *audio* we mean sounds (natural, instrumental or electronically generated), songs, speech and music. By *images* we mean any kind of still images, such as photographs, graphics and artwork, or animated works and moving images, such as films and videos, plus any kind of computer-generated pictures.

So far there are three key features which distinguish multimedia products from traditional or conventional works. These are *digitisation, combination* (or rather integration) *of different kinds of works or expressions* and *interactivity*, and they have to exist cumulatively.

It should be noted that the degree of interactivity is capable of introducing differences in quality between the various multimedia products found on the market. Multimedia works with a primitive form of interactivity (such as electronic encyclopaedias or interactive databases) can still be adequately protected by the existing copyright legislation. This is the *first generation* of multimedia products. However, multimedia works with an advanced level of interactivity (and a sufficient degree of integration of their various elements) constitute the *second generation* of multimedia products. In this book we will primarily focus on the second generation of multimedia products.

2.1.2 Digitisation

2.1.2.1 General observations

The importance of multimedia derives from the underlying technology of digitisation, which is the necessary prerequisite for any seamless combination of materials. Digitisation is not a new technological development. It appeared more or less when computers appeared and its function, though using many media to circulate its signals, has been inextricably linked with computers. Without the intervention of a computer at some stage, digitisation would not have been possible.

Digital technology should be distinguished from its traditional counterpart, analogue technology. Analogue technology is the technology which has dominated the market up to now. Almost all audiovisual media, such as radio, broadcast television, audio and video cassettes, are paradigms of analogue technology. Analogue technology stores information in the form of a continuous signal, which recognises changes in the

---

[18] Some examples of these materials would be entries or indexes to the multimedia product which also offer pathways for browsing such a product and whose structure, whether simple or not, contributes to their market success.

information by modulating the amplitude (AM) or the frequency of the signal.[19] Digital technology stores any kind of information in a computer memory, after having translated it into binary code (a sequence of zeros and ones) with the help of a computer program. Because the digitised information is stored in a single format, with only two possible means of expression (0s or 1s), the quality of the information is less prone to errors or deterioration in comparison to its analogue counterpart.

Distribution of digitised material can take place in two ways: through physical storage media or independently of any physical storage media. The first category, also known as off-line or non-linear media, includes CD-ROMs, CD-Is, DVDs, Data Discman, floppy disks, and so on. The second category, also known as on-line services, encompasses all kinds of multimedia services which are independent of any material support and which are transmitted by fibre-optic cables, telephone lines and wireless personal communication systems, such as (broadcast) television and integrated digital networks. The Internet is an example of the latter.[20]

In on-line services the information itself becomes independent of any material support or carrier on which it was previously stored or kept. The material support is separated from the data it carries; the data is 'repurposed'[21] in a digitised format and is put on-line. We have, in fact, a dematerialisation of information. In this context, information is important as such, irrespective of its presentation on any hard copy, and it also becomes the object of regulation. This is indicative of the fact that fixation, and even more permanent fixation, of works is a notion that is losing ground very quickly as it stands and is in need of being redefined.

2.1.2.2 Special features of digitisation

In relation to digitisation the following points are worth stressing at this stage:

(1) Digital technology, which is indispensable for the creation of a multimedia product, is inextricably linked with computers. Software tools

---

[19] See A. Williams, D. Calow and A. Lee, *Multimedia: contracts, rights and licensing*, FT Law and Tax, London, 1996, at 5–6.
[20] These forms of transmission are also thought to constitute the 'information superhighway'.
[21] According to Raysman, Brown and Neuburger, *Multimedia law*, at 1–5, footnote 3, 'within the industry, when a particular work which has existed in a traditional form becomes "content" in a multimedia application, it is said to be "repurposed"'.

are used to translate the information from its conventional form into a digital format ('repurpose' it), store it and create the capacity to retrieve and manipulate it. The digital language is a uniform language which can be comprehended only by computers. Its transmission, distribution or presentation is, of course, due to the other mediums' compatibility with the particular primary computer that has stored this information in its memory. In this context, multimedia products are in essence computer-based products.[22]

(2) Digital technology offers information which can be accessed worldwide (borderlessly) easily, quickly, accurately and with stability. This is also so regarding reproduction, transmission and distribution of this information. Copies can be produced with great ease in infinite numbers, all possessing the same quality as the original.

(3) Digital compression techniques abolish the existing constraints regarding the manipulation and circulation of information: data compression techniques abolish (a) any physical constraints regarding the storage and content of the information, and (b) any physical constraints relating to space and time.[23] In this way vast amounts of data can be stored on physical or non-physical distribution systems which are available worldwide. Data is no longer territorially based and it is portable.

(4) The convergence of all kinds of works and data into the contents of a multimedia product in a digital format that is seamless renders obsolete any traditional distinctions between literary and audiovisual works. Once digitised, all works form part of a single format (which is the same for all kinds of works) and they are essentially regarded and referred to as information or contents rather than works.

(5) Digitisation offers more opportunities than analogue technology for on-line communication of information. Thus, dematerialisation of information is a concept which has started gaining particular ground. The traditional notions of fixation and permanent fixation on some

---

[22] Note that the notion of a computer-based product does not necessarily imply that multimedia products are computer programs. Whether or not multimedia products are computer programs is an issue which will be discussed in chapter 7.

[23] Vercken, *Guide pratique*, at 14. There are different kinds of compression techniques relating to each kind of work. For example, there is MPEG for audiovisual works, JPEG for fixed images, MUSICAM for phonograms, and so on. These techniques (referred to in a French textbook) multiply the space and capacity of any network and support by up to 100 times. Thus, an almost infinite amount of information can be stored. In addition, compatibility and interoperability between national and international networks facilitates the effective, comprehensive and quick transmission of data. Strowel and Triaille, *Le droit d'auteur*, at 335.

kind of stable carrier[24] seem no longer tenable as necessary prerequisites for the qualification of a work as an intellectual property work.[25]

(6) Digitisation and storage of information do not present any structure and specific arrangement in the sense in which the average person would understand the notion of structure and arrangement. The records containing the information, which are found in the computer memory, are standard normalising entries (data put in the right boxes) which do not represent any special selection or arrangement. The result, however, which is produced on screen under the command of a user, may eventually be an original one. This is important to note with regard to the authorship and originality problems that multimedia poses.

2.1.3 Combination and integration of various forms of expression

Another distinctive feature of multimedia is the fact that it can hold a vast number of a wide range of communications, such as text, sound and images. The convergence of these kinds of expressions requires a digital environment and PC-processed technologies. All data is transformed into one format: the digital format.[26] This enables it to be seamlessly integrated in a single medium, in such a way as to construct a single information resource.[27]

2.1.4 Interactivity

Interactivity is an equally important feature of multimedia. Although digitisation constitutes the enabling technology for the creation of a multimedia product and for the combination and convergence of different kinds of works (content), this being the main reason for its purchase, it is interactivity (a technique for 'reading' such a product) which makes

---

[24] Interesting at this point is the debate about whether a copy in the RAM memory of a computer forms some kind of reproduction if considered as being a storage medium, though a temporary one.

[25] As E. Mackaay mentions, 'the information has become less dependent on the vehicle through which it is conveyed; it has become "purer"'. 'Economic incentives in markets for information and innovation' (1990) 13 *Harvard Journal of Law and Public Policy* 867, at 868.

[26] This constitutes the reason for a separate remuneration for the authors of the contents of a multimedia product, since digitisation may be considered another kind of reproduction (use) of their work which is not covered by, for example, traditional contracts of publishing and is not within the notion of the conventional use of the work.

[27] See T. Feldman, *Multimedia in the 1990s. BNB Research Fund Report*, British Library, 1991, at 9.

multimedia different from conventional media and existing intellectual property works. It is the particular feature that makes it appealing and answers the various needs of the users.

Interactivity cannot be seen in isolation. It can only be seen in conjunction with the two previous prerequisites: digitisation and combination of different kinds of works. A work cannot qualify as a multimedia work unless all three features are met. Digitisation and interactivity are inextricably linked. There is no interactivity without digitisation, although digitisation can exist in a non-interactive form. Computer technology allows the user to interact with the information contained in a multimedia work by selecting the pathways that will eventually lead him to the bits of information that will serve his particular needs. He is also offered the freedom to organise this information as he wishes by manipulating its arrangement, re-arrangement, selection, combination, inputs or outputs on his screen.

Interactivity, however, is subject to two inherent limitations. First, the user's choice regarding the selection, arrangement and presentation of the information is necessarily limited by the choices already made by the producer and the developer of the product. In other words, the user has to limit his choice to the data available in the multimedia product or service, which, however vast, might not be comprehensive or exhaustive. In all cases the work represents the advance selection made by the initiator of the multimedia product. The user has to make his choices from the pathways and commands available in the system and, though they might be great in number, the user is still limited by the capacity and design of the computer system which runs the particular product. It should be noted though that these limits are not narrow and may eventually allow the user to produce a result in which the original material can hardly be recognised.

Secondly, the constructive and operating computer software of the multimedia product may also limit the degree of interactivity available, even though it is only over a certain degree of interactivity that a product qualifies as a multimedia product.

Five standard levels of interactivity are said to exist:

(1) *No interactivity*, e.g. in the case of a film, where one watches it from the beginning to the end without the ability to intervene in the sequence of the images
(2) *Manual interactivity*, e.g. commands such as those usually found on a video cassette player: slow or quick motion, freeze frame, scan, etc.
(3) *Limited interactivity*, e.g. pre-programming or downloading instructions through an onboard microprocessor in a video player

(4) *True and versatile interactivity*, e.g. interfacing a video player with an external computer, or allowing a user to control graphics, animation and video images

(5) *Full interactivity*, e.g. authoring and delivering with a complete hardware and software package[28]

Multimedia products are thought necessarily to be able to provide the fourth or fifth level of interactivity in order to be considered as such. The user must be provided with the ability to morph (digitally blur and alter images beyond recognition) and sample (sample and blur any kind of works to an unlimited degree). In other words he must be able to initiate newly created works using existing material. The fourth and fifth levels of interactivity are those that offer to the user a real dialogue with the contents of the product. Anything less than that would come close to, if not totally qualify for, one of the conventional existing categories of intellectual property products, but would not be considered as a multimedia product. In this sense, multimedia products are different from the traditional categories of works.

Yet interactivity, as such, is not new. Only its latest and more developed forms are. Interactivity is undoubtedly the evolution, or else an advanced form, of the first search and retrieval software of the early electronic databases.[29] What, however, is the novel (or better, innovative) aspect of it is that it offers to users the possibility of a full direct dialogue, a multifarious interference with the vast amounts of data provided. This it does quickly and efficiently with literally all kinds of expression in a single medium. In view of this, the search and retrieval facilities have to possess two essential characteristics: (1) they have to be complex enough to deal with all the encompassed elements in an efficient and competent way, and (2) they have to look simple, user-friendly, powerful and compelling in order to be marketed successfully and thereby to secure the continuity of their existence in the future.

2.2 LAYERS OF PROTECTION

A multimedia product is a complex product in so far as it incorporates many traditional works in a single medium that can only be manipulated by a computer. This alone indicates that many different elements are involved in the creation of a multimedia product and they cannot all

---

[28] J. Choe, 'Interactive multimedia: a new technology tests the limits of copyright law' (1994) 46 *Rutgers Law Review* 929, at 935. Depending on the degree of interactivity, users can also become creators in relation to the work they create by using the materials available in the multimedia product. *Ibid.*, at 976.

[29] See Feldman, *Multimedia in the 1990s*, at 8.

come under the same category of protection. Thus, inevitably, different layers of protection exist.

The three essential[30] layers of protection with regard to a multimedia product are: (1) the protection of the contents of a multimedia product, (2) the protection of the multimedia product itself (as a compilation of the works it includes, but not necessarily protection as such from the point of view of intellectual property), and (3) the protection of its technical base. Although this distinction of parts in a multimedia product is theoretically possible, in practice it is not always clear. For example, there is often an overlap between the multimedia product and its technical basis, especially if we consider that whilst a multimedia product might not be a computer program itself, it cannot be accessed unless a computer is used. With such rapid technical progress in the area of information technology leading to computers performing more and more tasks, any distinction might be even more difficult to make in the future. Solutions will eventually need to be somewhat different from the ones that are reached now. This is undoubtedly an area which stresses the need for flexibility as far as legal regulation of information technology is concerned. Moreover, any problems regarding the protection of any one of these three layers will inevitably have repercussions on the other two. All three layers have to co-exist in regulative harmony in order for the creation and proper functioning of the product not to be impeded.

The first layer of protection, that of the contents of a multimedia product, consists either of contents of pre-existing works or of works commissioned for the creation of a particular product. Since the works that are included in the multimedia compilation are independent, they are also the object of a separate and distinguishable protection. This protection is afforded to them by means of copyright, patents, trade marks or any other kind of intellectual property rights. This, of course, does not exclude the possibility that the works included are also protected by other areas of law, i.e. by contract, tort, confidentiality, etc.

If composite works, such as films, videos, live performances, sound recordings, etc., are included, the whole bundle of rights (both economic

---

[30] There are also non-essential layers of protection in case a multimedia product is accompanied by leaflets, manuals or other documentation. These can be the object of a separate protection if they are found to qualify as 'works'. However, if they are reproduced digitally on the screen of the computer they are very likely to come under the same scope of protection as the contents of a multimedia product. This is the case even if they are considered to be operating materials for the multimedia product. See also in this respect Recital 20 to the EU database Directive (96/9/EC) on the legal protection of databases, [1996] OJ L77/20.

and moral) of the rightholders have to be taken into account. The inclusion of these works in a multimedia product does not affect the existence of any of these rights, nor does it alter in any respect the regime of their protection. These rights accompany the works in each inclusion in new products. Inevitably the creation of a new multimedia product will take place in a 'multilegia' environment, i.e. one where the laws and the rights corresponding to the particular elements constituting the parts of the multimedia product have to be respected and taken into account by any person dealing with them, from the producer to the end user.[31] The newly evolved rights of the producer, developer or maker of the multimedia product, or any other person involved, are additional to the original rights. Thus, the chain of rightholders becomes ever longer. The rights existing in the works that form the content of a multimedia product are important in so far as they have to be cleared in order for the emergence of such a product to take place. If these rights are not cleared, or are not cleared properly, or are not cleared in relation to all the works needed for inclusion, then the creation of the multimedia product is impossible or, in the last case, its success will be dubious and conditional on possible litigation. Contents are always considered to be the essential marketing features of multimedia.

The second layer is the protection of the multimedia product itself. Putting together a number of works in a digitised format with potential interactivity does not assimilate existing rights in the works, but creates new rights in the compilation itself, which now serves a separate and distinctive function. The emerging multimedia product or service produced in the course of an independent idea and plan has an autonomous value. This value is in most cases greater than the value each of the works has on its own. Yet this value should not be confused with the value of a genuine literary work by reason of originality or artistic input in the continental sense.[32] The value of a multimedia product is judged more on market and economic terms than on any other terms.

The third layer of protection is that afforded to the technical base of a multimedia product:

(1) The *platform* is divided into two parts: (a) the hardware on which the multimedia application runs, e.g. IBM/PC, Macintosh, etc., and (b) the operating software which is used for the running of a

---

[31] See T. Hoeren, 'An assessment of long-term solutions in the context of copyright and electronic delivery services and multimedia products', European Commission, Brussels, Luxembourg, 1995 (vol. 4, Copyright on electronic delivery services and multimedia products series, EUR 16069 EN), at 53.
[32] Though this is not impossible in a multimedia context.

multimedia application on a particular piece of hardware, e.g. Windows 2000, etc. The operating software has to be compatible with the hardware, otherwise no application is possible. In any case, the platform is something clearly distinguishable from a multimedia product. The platform is the compatible environment in which a multimedia work runs in the same way any other application runs.

(2) The operating or making program technically creates the multimedia application. This program, which is the authoring program of the newly constructed work, is a separate program and does not accompany the work itself onto the market.

(3) The software tool, known as the *driver*, *runtime* or *engine*,[33] allows the user to access, display and manipulate the information available on the multimedia product created. It is the same tool which technically permits the user to interact with the product, by selecting, arranging or transforming the data available. The driver is a component of the multimedia application itself and is embedded in it in object code form.[34] The driver has to be compatible with the platform in order for the multimedia application to be able to run.

(4) The *operation materials* for the multimedia product, also known as the *command procedure*, are the commands, pathways, entries, indexation systems, thesaurus, crossroads and other means of tracing, arranging and selecting information in the multimedia product. These are the commands which the operating program obeys, in order to perform its function.

(5) The *distribution media* carry the multimedia product. They have the form of either a physical or a non-physical (on-line) medium.[35] The most popular distribution media in the first category are CD-ROMs, floppy disks, CD-Is, DVDs, etc. On-line distribution (or better, transmission) can take place on practically any network which possesses the technology for transmitting vast amounts of data. However, although distribution media incorporate the multimedia work and represent, in the eyes of consumers, the product itself, they are something separate which is protected on its own merits. The technology of the manufacturing of these media is distinct from the technology of the multimedia work. From the point of view of a multimedia product, they can only be regarded as its carriers, which in practice add nothing

---

[33] See Raysman, Brown and Neuburger, *Multimedia law*, at 1–5.
[34] The term 'multimedia application' is wider than the term 'multimedia work or product' in the sense that the former also incorporates the technical basis which is needed for its use. However, they are essentially used interchangeably.
[35] In this case we are talking about transmission rather than distribution.

to its value apart from the fact that they make it easily available to the public.[36]

From the foregoing it can be seen that it is not easy to distinguish between the different parts of a multimedia product in all situations, and this is going to be even more difficult in the future given that computer programs perform more and more tasks every day. The command procedure is an obvious example of a case where distinction is not always possible. The command procedure and the data contained in a multimedia product are linked. Any structure, selection or arrangement of the data is subject to the command that is chosen or inserted by the user. The functions it performs may be functions which are computer related, but the commands themselves as they appear on the screen can still be viewed as data. In this sense the command procedure can be regarded as 'contents' and can therefore come under the same regime of protection as the one applied to contents.

However, there will be cases where the command procedure is particularly sophisticated, especially where the multimedia product is sophisticated as well. In such a case it is very likely that the formal language of the command procedure in terms of syntax, structure and range of expressions will closely resemble a conventional high-level computer language, if not a computer program itself. Thus, the command procedure might also come within the scope of the EC software Directive and qualify for separate protection.[37]

---

[36] A considerable problem in relation to the marketing of multimedia products is that they are not technically compatible with all kinds of platforms available on the market. This is due to a lack of standardisation. It is said that lack of compatibility seriously impinges on the successful commercialisation of multimedia products and therefore is regarded as a hurdle. Nevertheless, there are also some regulating advantages to be found. (1) Although sales are kept at a low level in certain areas because users cannot buy all the products available on the market due to the fact that they are not compatible with the hardware they possess, a balance is still kept between information technology industries. Monopolies and the emergence of dominant undertakings are controlled. If this were not the case, one or two giant companies would be likely to sell all their products to the detriment of those who did not possess equal publishing material in the area. Moreover, in view of the competition retrogressions with regard to joint ventures and mergers, regulation is increasingly needed so as to facilitate the co-operation of new media industries and the emergence of new technology products. (2) Rightholders are remunerated separately for each piece of information technology in their works. They will therefore be more willing to give out licences for the digital exploitation of their works as they will be less fearful of being blocked by a single obsolete technology. Of course, at this stage we also have to take into account the fact that the emergence of too many rights makes clearing of contents difficult in relation to the creation of a multimedia product, though this is compensated for by rightholders being more willing to license under these circumstances. (3) Standardisation is becoming less significant in so far as on-line transmission is becoming an increasingly popular form of distribution.

[37] [1991] OJ L122/42.

This will also be the case, but from another point of view, when the command procedure itself is embedded in the computer program that designed and constructed the multimedia product. This might happen in cases where the making program has to perform 'classic' or non-sophisticated tasks in relation to the multimedia product. Then, of course, the solution of theoretically including the command procedure in the contents is no longer appropriate. Neither is the solution of considering it as a separate computer program. In this case the one protection afforded to the making program will also apply to the operation of the materials. This will also be so in the more likely case of the command procedure being part of the driver, when the protection afforded to the driver will be the same as the protection of the command procedure. This protection will obviously be a protection of computer programs.

It is clear from the above that only a case-by-case decision is possible on this point. As long as operation materials form part of, or constitute by themselves, a computer program there will be no problem, since an autonomous protection for computer programs is available, irrespective of the legal status of the work these programs operate. Yet problems will arise when such a protection is not possible due to the lack of such a qualification.[38]

A possible solution is found in the sole legal instrument which partly regulates such issues: the database Directive.[39] Recital 20 to the database Directive states that 'protection under this Directive may also apply to the materials necessary for the operation or consultation of certain databases such as thesaurus and indexation systems'. It follows from this that if a database does not qualify for protection under article 1(2) of the Directive, the command procedure is not protected either. The problems which such regulation presents are not discussed here as they fall outside the scope of this book.[40] The problems they present in relation to multimedia products, however, are relevant.

First, in the database Directive the command procedure does not qualify for any kind of protection unless the database itself is protected. The individual merits of the operation materials therefore remain insignificant, in so far, of course, as they do not qualify individually as literary works or computer programs. If this line of thought is followed, the operation materials in a multimedia product, if anything, qualify for the

---

[38] See S. Chalton, 'The amended database Directive proposal: a commentary and synopsis' [1994] 3 *EIPR* 94, at 96; I. Stamatoudi, 'The EU database Directive: reconceptualising copyright and tracing the future of the *sui generis* right' (1997) 50 *Revue Hellénique de Droit International* 436, at 446.
[39] EU database Directive, [1996] OJ L77/20.
[40] For further details see Stamatoudi, 'EU database Directive'.

same kind of protection as the one afforded to the compilation. They do not follow the fate of the 'contents'. However, they do follow the fate of the driver, if they form part of it. Although this issue appears to be an important one, not too much practical significance should be given to it, because in most cases the driver itself is bound to contain the command procedure as well. In addition, reproduction of the command procedure is less important if the contents of the particular multimedia product cannot also be reproduced at the same time. If the command procedure is to be used for a similar multimedia application to the one from which it was originally taken, if no originality is attached to it, it will not be worthy of protection as such and thus its copying by a competitor can cause little damage to the original owner.

This book will focus on the second layer of protection, i.e. on the protection of the multimedia work, irrespective of its contents and its technical base. The problems presented by the contents or the technical base will be taken into account in so far as they have direct repercussions on the multimedia compilation itself and on its independent regime of protection. Relevant issues are, for example, the clearing of rights in the contents, the ability to distinguish between the technical base and the multimedia work in new technological developments, and so on.

2.3 PROJECT PARTICIPANTS IN THE CREATION OF A MULTIMEDIA PRODUCT

Usually many people are involved in the creation of a multimedia product. This poses a number of problems which will be discussed later in this book. The most important questions are who the author or authors of a multimedia product are and who qualify as rightholders in relation to which rights.

The persons usually involved in the creation of a multimedia product are:

(1) The *authors of the works* which form the 'content' of the multimedia product.[41] These persons are either authors of pre-existing works who have agreed for their works to be included in the multimedia product or commissioned authors who have created works, either independently or in the course of an employment contract, which are to be included in the multimedia compilation. At this point we should note, of course, that other rights, apart from the classical ones an author

---

[41] For the purposes of this book, the authors of the contents of a multimedia work will be called 'contributors'.

The scope of multimedia works 33

possesses, exist in many cases in the works that form the contents of a multimedia product. For example, rights in performances or other neighbouring rights are involved, as well as *sui generis* rights. These rights accompany the intellectual property work in any use and, if clearing proceedings are to take place, clearance will be required in relation to all these rights.

As previously mentioned, there might not only be copyright works forming the contents of a multimedia product. Patent, design and trade mark rights may also be involved. The laws relevant to their protection will apply in these cases.

(2) The *rightholders of the works of the authors* mentioned in the first category. Rightholders of the works which form the contents of a multimedia product can be any natural or legal persons. Usually rightholders are publishers, producers of phonograms and audiovisual works (generally employers), collecting societies, and so on. If holders of the rights to a certain work are not the authors themselves but other parties, these other parties do not possess all the rights to a work. They possess the economic rights to the work or a part of it. Any moral rights are non-assignable and they remain with the author until (and in certain jurisdictions even after)[42] the expiry of the copyright in the work. A further layer of rights is the 'secondary copyrights' in the fixation of a work, i.e. the right in the typeface and in the recording. Usually this layer of rights is possessed by the rightholders of the second category, since in order to publish or record a work they also need some if not most of the economic rights in the work at issue.

(3) The *producer*[43] of the multimedia product (or a *provider* if it is a multimedia service) can be either a publishing company or an individual (publisher).[44] The producer is the architect of the project. He is the one to select, acquire, bring together and combine the works of all the contributors. He conceives the idea and from him originates the concept for the product. He designs the project and develops the plan of the compilation. When this part of the job is done by a separate person, he or she can be called the *editor*.[45] The producer also produces or supervises its realisation in terms of production and sinks into it the necessary investments. For example, a CD-ROM is published in

---

[42] E.g. the moral rights provisions in French copyright law.
[43] The producer of a multimedia program should not be regarded as equivalent to the producer of a film. Both finance the creation of the project, but the producer of a multimedia product resembles more the director of a film with regard to the rest of his tasks.
[44] It is usually book publishers or software companies which undertake the production of a multimedia product.
[45] In practice this will often be the case.

the same way as a book, apart from requiring larger investments. The producer usually undertakes the distribution of the product either under his trade mark, if it is considered to be commercially effective, or under the trade mark of the maker of the multimedia work.

The producer should also be the rightholder of those rights that are required for the digital use of the authors' works that will be included in the product. These rights are acquired either through the authors or through other rightholders such as collecting societies.[46] In cases of commissioned works the economic rights of the authors will automatically be transferred to the producer by means of some kind of contract. In the case of employees, that will be done by means of the employment contract, if the particular employee's job is the creation of works that will form part of the contents of a multimedia product.

An issue which is problematic is the moral rights issue. Moral rights are non-assignable. However, in common law jurisdictions, as for example in the UK, they are waivable. Where they have not been waived or where they cannot be waived, they form a separate layer of rights that have to be respected in any use of the copyright work. The producer cannot possess any moral rights in the works he is to use digitally and the same moral rights will apply whether the work is digitally disclosed or not. Therefore the producer has to be very careful not to supersede the limits of normal use of the product and the limits of the use he has been assigned. The users' conduct forms a separate issue.

The producer has important creative and production roles.[47] This notion of creation does not have anything to do with producing highly original material. It is creative in so far as he brings various works together, after having selected them and after having put them in a particular structure and arrangement. The more commercialised and commodified the works are, the less original and the more functional they are. His important production role lies not only in the development of the project as such but also in the fact that he adds economic value to the compilation by turning it into a multimedia product: 'The product has distribution and exploitation rights which are worth considerably more than that of the individual elements going to make up the program.'[48]

---

[46] It is a highly contested issue whether the conventional contracts between collecting societies and authors also include digital rights.
[47] M. Turner, 'Do the old legal categories fit the new multimedia products? A multimedia CD-ROM as a film' [1995] 3 *EIPR* 107, at 107.
[48] *Ibid.*

The combining elements of a multimedia product are included in a way which enables them to be used in more than one traditional format, e.g. alphabetically. Usually many pathways (or crossroads) are designed, which permit the user to browse the contents in several different ways according to his own needs. The user is given the opportunity to include or exclude information on his screen at any time, as he wishes. This is also the reason why the whole is greater than the sum of its parts.[49]

(4) The *maker* or *developer* of a multimedia product. The developer of a multimedia product has to be distinguished from the producer in so far as he is not involved in the planning and structuring of the product as a work. The maker is responsible only for the physical development and technical organisation of the product. He designs the operating computer program (driver), the screen displays (the functionality displayed on the screen elements and the positioning of the individual screen elements)[50] and he digitises and stores the information. He may also design the look of the multimedia work as a product, i.e. its form and packaging, etc. The multimedia product is usually produced under the trade mark of the developer if it is decided that his trade mark is capable of contributing to its market success. However, apart from the very technical issues for which the maker is responsible, in most cases the maker and the editor share responsibility for the creative aspects of the product. Depending on their respective roles, they can be considered as co-authors.[51]

(5) Lastly, there are the *users*. The users do not have any creative role in the multimedia work. The only control they have over the product is that, because of its interactivity, they can manipulate the display of information on the screen of their computer. They can change the outcome of their searches as they wish by selecting or re-arranging the information that is already available in the product but only through the pathways that are available.[52]

Although users of multimedia products are not just passive spectators like film and TV viewers, and although they are given rich forms

---

[49] *Ibid.* See also Strowel and Triaille, *Le droit d'auteur*, at 334–5; Koumantos, 'Les aspects', at 243.
[50] Turner, 'Old legal categories', at 107.
[51] Raysman, Brown and Neuburger, *Multimedia law*, at 1-10–1-11.
[52] Koumantos, 'Les aspects', at 243. There can be more project participants: for example, the manufacturers of the platform on which multimedia applications run, the manufacturers of the material supports and modes of transmission (CD-ROMs, televisions, video recorders, video games, etc.), the operators of the networks, the access providers, the designers and makers of instruction leaflets, and so on.

of interactivity, as for example hypermedia (or hypertext), they are still not deemed to be creators. They are turned from spectators into users and from passive into active users only by the multimedia products which enable them to edit the information provided. Whether they have copyright in the edition of their work is a matter judged on its own merits. The creation of a new visual, artistic or literary work that is original and attracts copyright protection in its own right is probably an extreme and rare case, but it may take place if there is enough creativity involved and if the work is independently created and fixed in some kind of permanent form from which it can be retrieved.

The issue of who, from the above project participants, qualifies as the author or the co-author of a multimedia product will be considered separately in chapter 10.

2.4 THE DIFFERENCES BETWEEN MULTIMEDIA PRODUCTS AND EXISTING COPYRIGHT WORKS

Multimedia works are said to have some unique and distinctive features in relation to conventional copyright works. These features are not new. They are in most cases the combination and evolution of pre-existing, but less developed, characteristics, as was also demonstrated with regard to interactivity. However, their evolution in certain cases has become so significant that it is no longer a change in quantity but one in quality. In this respect some multimedia characteristics can be regarded as new.

Whether or not the particularity and individuality of the multimedia products' characteristics merit a different regime of protection adjusted to their needs is highly disputed and is under investigation. Even if the existing intellectual property laws have to be adjusted to the reality of the new technologies, how far this adjustment has to go, what alterations have to take place and how far these alterations are capable of transforming the original established notion of intellectual property rights, remains uncertain.

The particularities of multimedia products include the following features.

2.4.1 Combination of different forms of communication

Various works which are traditionally classified in different categories are combined in a single medium. Such works existed for centuries in the form of a combination of text and images, for example, an illustrated book

The scope of multimedia works

or newspaper. Audiovisual works are also a good example of combinations of sound and images.[53] The term 'multimedia' has recently become popular as a description of computer-based products or applications.[54] However, some particular features have developed which make it unique.

(1) All the works included, irrespective of their nature, are integrated in a single format: a digitised one.
(2) There are no physical limits as to the quantity of the works included, because new technologies, such as digital compression techniques, can store almost infinite amounts of data. As Koumantos argues, the quantity of the various elements involved in a multimedia product is such that any quantitative modification becomes necessarily a qualitative one as well.[55] Here, quantity and quality are closely interrelated. Thus, any physical constraints on the storage, the kind of work, the space or time have been abolished and, as a result, information gains value. It becomes portable, quick and easy to access, and capable of been carried by both off-line and on-line media.
(3) In relation to on-line transmission of data, no territorial limits exist. Information can be picked up in any place in the world at any time as long as one possesses the necessary technical equipment.
(4) The digitised format of the work allows the work to be copied quickly, easily and cheaply. On top of that an infinite number of copies can be made without any loss of quality.

2.4.2 A single material support

Although in the past combinations of different kinds of works existed, such as text and images, these combinations were based on the combination of the different supports that carried the works, i.e. recordings, pictures, etc. In the case of multimedia products we are no longer tied to any kind of *emballage* which regroups the different material expressions of the various works under one name, for example a film. Multimedia is a single product which incorporates different kinds of works which have been integrated in this single medium in a single format. The 'Livre blanc du Groupe Audiovisuel et Multimédia de l'Édition' states that: 'on ne devrait pas appeler multimédia un produit regroupant sous un même

---

[53] Strowel and Triaille, *Le droit d'auteur*, at 334.
[54] Raysman, Brown and Neuburger, *Multimedia law*, at 1–2; B. Isaac, 'Intellectual property and multimedia: problems of definition and enforcement' [1995] 12 *Canadian Intellectual Property Review* 47, at 51. Isaac also points out that the interactive nature of a multimedia product is a result of the underlying computer program and that is itself covered by copyright.
[55] Koumantos, 'Les aspects', at 243. See also Strowel and Triaille, 'Le tout n'est pas réductible à la somme des parties' in *Le droit d'auteur*, at 335.

emballage, mais sur des supports différents, des éléments textuels, sonors ou visuels'.[56]

The practical significance of such a differentiation in storing information with regard to copyright will be considered later.

2.4.3 Originality

The value of multimedia products does not necessarily lie in the originality of the works included. If any originality is to be found, it usually consists of the appearance of the product and its userfriendliness rather than the works it incorporates. In these cases multimedia products are valuable because they are comprehensive in terms of information and because their contents are primarily functional and utilitarian in nature.[57] In other cases though, multimedia products can be very creative works. Their creativity is found in the combination and integration of the various components.

2.4.4 Computer-based product or service

A multimedia work's function is computer-based. Although a multimedia product is a work, it cannot as such perform any task unless it is computer aided. That renders it dependent on a computer program but does not necessarily render it a computer program itself.

2.4.5 Combination of information technology and communications technology

The main technologies that a multimedia application combines are digital video, electronics, informatics and digital communications.[58]

2.4.6 Fixation

One of the most important aspects of a multimedia product, and perhaps the one that determines its market success, is its content.[59] Although

---

[56] 'We should not call a product "multimedia" which combines as part of the same package, but on different material supports, textual, sound and visual elements.' Groupe Audiovisuel et Multimédia de l'Edition, *Questions juridiques relatives aux oeuvres multimédia* (Livre Blanc), Paris, 1994, at 65.

[57] A. Lucas, 'Droit d'auteur et multimédia' in *Propriétés intellectuelles, mélanges en l'honneur de André Françon*, Dalloz, Paris, 1995, 325, at 326.

[58] By digital communications we mean digital telecommunications and audiovisual communications.

[59] After standardisation, information will become even more important. Raysman, Brown and Neuburger, *Multimedia law*, at 1-5, footnote 2.

The scope of multimedia works

content is found at the heart of a multimedia product or service, it is alleged it is not fixed, at least not according to what fixation is considered to mean traditionally, and in relation to conventional intellectual property works. The basis on which lack of fixation in relation to multimedia products is advocated is twofold. Principally, it is based on the fact that information which can be retrieved interactively can circulate and will probably circulate even more in the future as on-line services (lack of fixation in the broad sense). The information will be accessed irrespective of any material carrier. It becomes a valuable commodity on its own without needing to be fixed on some kind of medium. Here the notion of *dematerialisation* of information is relevant again. In cases where some kind of fixation exists, there is a factual assimilation between the carrier and the data it carries.

Claims which are based on the fact that storing information in the RAM memory of the computer is a form of fixation, though not permanent,[60] add little value to the arguments against dematerialisation. It is the information which counts and its placing in the RAM memory is rather less significant. Interesting in this respect is the draft EU Directive on the harmonisation of certain aspects of copyright and related rights in the information society.[61] This more or less solves the problem regarding the status of temporary reproduction. According to article 2 of the Directive, the reproduction right also covers temporary copies (e.g. RAM). Article 5 provides for an automatic exemption for temporary acts of reproduction 'which are transient or incidental, which are an integral part of a technological process whose sole purpose is to enable: (a) a transmission in a network between third parties by an intermediary or (b) a lawful

---

[60] 'The RAM memory of a computer constitutes a difficult problem. A program that exists only in the RAM memory of the computer exists only in the form of electrical currency and when the power supply is interrupted the program disappears. At first sight this does not involve the required degree of permanency, but the conclusion may be different if such a program lives in the RAM or a similar memory of a computer network and if it is quite unreasonable to expect the network to be shut down in the foreseeable future. The example of software made available via the various bulletin boards of the Internet comes to mind.' P. Torremans and J. Holyoak, *Holyoak and Torremans' intellectual property law*, 2nd edn, Butterworths, London, Dublin, Edinburgh, 1998, at 499. *Triad Systems Corporation* v. *Southeastern Express Co.* (US District Court for the Northern District of California) 31 USPQ 2d 1239 and *MAI Systems Corporation* v. *Peak Computer Inc., Vincent Chiechi and Eric Francis* (US Court of Appeals for the 9th Circuit) F 2d 511, 26 USPQ 2d 1458.

[61] See Lexis, 'Draft EC Directive strongly protects online content; ISPS placed at risk' (1997) 14 *ITR* 1954; 'Draft EU legislation to update copyright law ready by year's end' (1997) 14 *ITR* 1910. See the Common Position adopted by the Council with a view to the adoption of a Directive of the European Parliament on the harmonisation of certain aspects of copyright and related rights in the information society, Brussels, 14 September 2000.

use of the work or other subject-matter to be made, and which have no independent economic significance'.[62]

The second aspect that is contradictory to the notion of fixation is interactivity (lack of fixation narrowly defined). Interactivity offers the facility to users to revise, re-order and re-organise their data according to their specific needs. They can skip information, reform it and use different pathways to retrieve the data they need. This aspect can be found in both multimedia products and services, whilst the first one is inherent only in the provision of services. Although information is contained on a material support, there is no specific and stable order to which this data is subject. Rather we find information in a 'loose' form as elements and a box of tools, which can be combined when necessary. Up to now fixation has been synonymous with a permanent and stable form; not just the tools and elements needed to be fixed, but also the work itself. New technologies have rendered this notion obsolete. Fixation has become broader in a sense. No order is required, no stability, no permanence. Perhaps the fact that data can be carried in whatever form suffices. If that were not the case, interactivity would not have been possible. Users are the only persons responsible for any potential structure. Of course, as we made clear earlier, users do not create. They select and arrange from what is already available. Their true creative role can be very limited. Often no originality or even effort and labour are invested.

2.4.7 Ease of manipulation and copying

Up to now, apart from intellectual property laws, there have also been physical barriers which prevented large-scale copying of copyright works. As technology has advanced, the problems of volume and time, which constituted the essential barriers against copying, have disappeared. More than ever before digital technology provides users with the ability to manipulate and transform, sometimes to an unrecognisable degree, the data available in the multimedia product.[63] It also allows users to make as many copies as desired or possible, easily, quickly and without any loss of quality. This undoubtedly poses new risks of unauthorised exploitation especially if it is coupled with the fact that copying equipment is now readily available privately (e.g. PCs, etc.). Moreover, it poses risks

---

[62] In general reservations have been expressed with regard to the exceptions introduced by the Directive in so far as they impede real harmonisation in the area of copyright and allow wide margins of discretion to Member States which are bound to exercise or keep implementing their own differing traditions in the field.

[63] I.e. morphing and sampling. Later we will consider the degree of manipulation offered and allowed to users and its possible repercussions on the moral rights of the authors involved.

of infringement of moral rights (as well as economic rights if the copies are to be put on the market and take the place of originals) without any opportunity of tracking down trespassers. More than ever before a more effective and consistent regulation is called for. Copying, which has been the plunder of the last decades, has taken on new dimensions due to the new technological ease with which it can take place. Technological devices to safeguard rights are becoming increasingly necessary. The new draft Directive outlaws the manufacture of any devices that facilitate circumvention of copyright protection technologies.[64] It is a battle which will definitely not be played solely on the field of law. The view that technological devices are to prevent technology inefficiencies in the area is gaining ground. Law can only play a post-factum regulative role. Classical theories of educative and pre-regulative function of the law have been left behind by the new reality.

[64] Art. 6 of the EU draft Directive, Brussels, 14 September 2000.

3 Traditional literary works

Originally copyright was meant as a regime of protection for literary works. Literary works, seen as a generic term, really refers to most oral and written works of the mind, which are expressed by means of language and which can be literary, scientific or of any other nature.[1] To take two examples only, Belgian copyright law refers to literary works as *écrits de tout genre* (writings of any kind), and as *manifestations orales de la pensée*[2] (oral expressions of the mind), whilst the Swiss Act refers to them as *créations de l'esprit*[3] (creations of the mind).[4] The UK's Copyright Designs and Patents Act 1988 refers to a literary work as simply 'any work...which is written, spoken or sung'.[5]

What we usually understand as literary works are books, articles, pamphlets, lectures, sermons and other works of the same nature.

3.1 LITERARY WORKS AS WORKS OF LANGUAGE

3.1.1 The concepts of 'language' and 'words'

The key feature of literary works is the fact that they are conceived in language. The final format can be written, recorded or oral. In other words, genuine literary works are, in their original format, either spoken or written, and are created in order to be listened to or read. If their primary aim were not this one, but were for visual or musical performance, or display, they would strictly speaking not be literary works, though they

---

[1] See art. 2(1) of the Berne Convention.
[2] Art. 8 of the Law on Copyright and Neighbouring Rights of 30 June 1994, as amended by the Law of 3 April 1995.
[3] Art. 2.2 of the Swiss Copyright Act of 9 October 1992.
[4] Most jurisdictions refer to literary works as works of the mind. See also art. 101 of the American Copyright Act, art. 2.1 of the German Copyright Act, arts. L112-1 and L112-2 of the French Copyright Act and art. 2(1) of the Greek Copyright Act. See also A. Strowel and J.-P. Triaille, *Le droit d'auteur, du logiciel au multimédia (Copyright, from software to multimedia)*, Bruylant, Brussels, 1997, at 354; A. and H.-J. Lucas, *Traité de la propriété littéraire et artistique*, Litec, Paris, 1994, at 108.
[5] Section 3(1).

would still come within the category of literary works in the broad sense.[6] This includes dramatic, musical, pictorial or artistic works.[7]

To narrow down the category of literary works even further, we could argue that oral works, such as lectures, addresses or sermons, which indisputably attract copyright in most jurisdictions, have to be fixed. This is indeed the case in certain jurisdictions, such as the UK one, where copyright protection is subject to some kind of permanent fixation of the work.[8] A work cannot qualify for copyright protection in these jurisdictions unless it is written, recorded, or otherwise fixed in some form. The right to make any copyright protection dependent on a fixation requirement was given by the Berne Convention in its article 2(2), after pressure was put on the drafters of the Convention by the delegations of common law countries, particularly the UK delegation. In section 49(9) of the UK's Copyright Act 1956 it was stated that the role of fixation is to create certainty in the subject matter of copyright, or more precisely in the scope of the monopoly, copyright being a monopoly in nature, in order to avoid injustice for the rest of the world. This means that simply the expression of language is sufficient to create a literary work. In addition, materialisation provides the means of both proving its existence and communicating the work to third parties. The materialisation of the work in hard copy (irrespective of being off-line or on-line), quite apart from an economic right, is also considered to be a moral right in many continental law systems, known as the right of divulgation of the work. This has a broader meaning and scope than the concept of fixation. Fixation of a work does not always require publication or communication of the work to the public, even though no communication to the public can take place unless fixation has preceded it.

Thus, literary works in the narrow sense are essentially text. Text is inextricably linked with language and has the ability to be communicated and understood by third parties (it should be noted that whether or not the author had the intention of communication is of no relevance). In judging whether a text is copyrightable or not it is essential that the text is expressed in a language which is living or has been alive in the past (e.g. Latin) and which is consequently understood. However, that language does not necessarily have to make sense to a majority of people.

At this point we should distinguish between the concepts of language and words. Language does not necessarily require a text composed of

---

[6] See, for example, 'literary and artistic works' as used in art. 2(1) of the Berne Convention.
[7] The CDPA 1988 reaches a radically different conclusion when it stipulates in s. 3(1) that any dramatic or musical work is by definition excluded from the category of literary works.
[8] Section 3(2) CDPA 1988.

words. A text can also be composed of figures or signs since they can be expressed in an oral or written way with the use of words, the classical means of communication for which the human tongue is used.[9] Thus, the concept of words is narrower compared to that of language. Words are a vehicle for language not the language itself. In common law systems copyright protection is afforded to works which are presented in figures (e.g. mathematical tables,[10] football fixtures, hieroglyphics, Chinese characters,[11] etc.). In all copyright systems copyright is also granted irrespective of the national origin of the language[12] (e.g. a tale written in a rare Indian dialect). The notion of language does not necessarily mean 'our' language or a language which is well known and understood by a large number of people. That would unnecessarily restrict any notion of language, as it would leave outside its scope anything that would not fall within the definition of a 'word'. Language can be any language with which you can communicate messages to people, no matter how small this group of people. The only acceptable limitation is that it has to be a living language (or one that has been alive in the past) through which people can conceive and send messages.

3.1.2 Natural or artificial language?

A question arises whether the notion of a 'living' language implies only a natural language or whether an artificial language would qualify as well. In the early 1990s, when the market for new technology products was flourishing and the need for legal regulation was consequently growing and becoming more pressing, the category of literary works was stretched substantially to include new technology products. Computer programs were the first type of such products to be included within the ambit of literary works.[13] Examinations carried out at that stage, as to whether computer programs were in fact coming even close to the definition of a literary work, were rather loose. Dominating the debate was the need for a legal environment that had already been mapped out. Detailed rules that were internationally accepted and applied were required, and the issue of whether a computer program could really be seen as a literary

---

[9] In this sense sign language for deaf people, for example, is not protected as a literary work as such, though it is called language, since no use of the tongue is made.

[10] *Bailey* v. *Taylor* (1824) 3 LJOS 66; *Express Newspapers plc* v. *Liverpool Daily Post and Echo plc* [1985] 3 All ER 680, [1985] FSR 306.

[11] Since it is signs and symbols that are used in writing.

[12] H. Laddie, P. Prescott and M. Vitoria, *The modern law of copyright and designs*, 2nd edn, Butterworths, London, Dublin, Edinburgh 1995, at 30.

[13] Council Directive (91/250/EEC) on the legal protection of computer programs, [1991] OJ L122/42.

work was glossed over. Computer programs were thus brought within the definition of works of language. Yet, it was only the presentation of the information they carried which was in conventional language, and which could therefore be communicated to people. The means for creating and constructing a computer program constituted an artificial language, a language conceived and used only by technicians and other experts in the area of software. The inclusion of computer programs within the ambit of protection of literary works extended the definition of literary works to works in both natural and artificial language.

This extension of the notion of language to include artificial language in relation to literary works qualifying for copyright protection did not come on its own. A number of practical consequences followed from it. Primarily the notion of communication has taken on different meanings compared to its traditional one. Communication is no longer seen as two or more people understanding each other through the transmission or exchange of information, thoughts, feelings or emotions, but also the capacity to understand the functioning of a machine at an intermediate stage, before this machine transforms the information it carries into text, which can in turn be understood by someone (as is the case of literary works in their original sense). Artificial language acknowledges the need for the intervention of machines in the communication between people. The communication between people and machines, or between machines alone, is also held to be an acceptable form of communication, forming a work, and qualifying for copyright protection under the world's Copyright Acts.[14]

Artificial language was meant to facilitate communication between experts rather than between ordinary people. The latter would only enter at the stage when computer language was transformed into normal language, text or images, in their traditional format.

3.2 DEPURIFICATION OF COPYRIGHT

3.2.1 Computer programs

The inclusion of computer programs within the ambit of literary works was, as explained earlier, more a policy decision than a decision on the grounds that literary works and software were works which were closely related. The convenience and ease of squeezing a work into an already well-established and internationally acknowledged regime of protection,

---

[14] It is generally understood that high-level computer languages such as Cobol, Pascal, etc. are artificial languages. The same cannot be said about binary code, as it cannot be understood by the ordinary person.

such as the copyright regime, was tempting and presented considerable advantages. The drafting of any new *sui generis* legislation, which would have to undergo much discussion and involve many compromises, was considered not to be an option. Conflicting interests would no doubt have resulted in a much watered-down regime of protection, whereas copyright offered a relatively strong existing regime, which was internationally accepted and which could be adopted for computer programs on a 'take it or leave it' basis. On top of that no valuable time would be lost at the expense of the protection of products already widely used on the market. The need for instant protection of software products constituted an important factor that had to be taken into account.

Fitting a new product within the scope of an existing legal regime means applying the rules of this regime *in toto* to the product newly included. Yet, traditional conduct with regard to certain issues was difficult to continue. To take but one example, investigation in cases of copying in relation to computer programs could no longer take place in the traditional way by comparing the works at issue (the original and the copied one). Comparison of software demanded other kinds of equipment, both practical and intellectual. The literature on copyright moved from the notion of literary copying to the notion of comparing the 'look and feel' of computer programs.

The inclusion of software within the ambit of copyright was thought to render obsolete the boundaries between patent law and copyright, and between machine and work. Software was found to possess characteristics of both patent and copyright law, which at that time would normally have excluded it from protection under the copyright rules, these being orientated towards protecting only cultural creations, such as books, paintings, etc. Software was both a work and an item linked to a machine as far as it constituted a written text of commands and a part of a machine (PC, hardware) to which these commands had to be linked in order to become functional. Computer programs were held to be works of function defined as 'works that use information to describe or implement a process, procedure or algorithm'.[15] Copyright has traditionally rejected functional, utilitarian and technological works which were not at the same time functioning as supports for some form of expression of the information they carried.[16] If some creative, literal or artistic features were not there, apart from the prominent technical features of the work, there was no way that such a work could be justified as being capable of being protected

[15] OTA Report, *Intellectual property rights in an age of electronics and information*, US Congress, Office of Technology Assessment, Washington D.C., 1986, at 78.
[16] M. Marinos, 'Nomiki prostassia vasseon dedomenon. To idiaitero (*sui generis*) dikaioma tis odigias 96/9/EOK' [1997] 2 *DEE* 128, at 129.

under copyright. Any inclusion of software into copyright would jeopardise and render useless in the future any distinctions between patent law and copyright. That was also combined with the fact that a copyright work was meant to be communicated to other people and not to be used. If a work could only be used and did not convey messages, feelings or emotions, then it was a work coming rather within the ambit of protection of patents. Computer programs, though a borderline case, passed these hurdles and qualified for copyright protection.[17]

As will be seen later,[18] adjustments had to be made. On the one hand, national legislation did not sit well with the new reality and had to be amended. On the other hand, the legislation of certain states, such as the Member States of the European Union, had to be streamlined, in order for a more efficient exploitation of computer programs to be achieved on the Single Market.

3.2.2 Compilations

Computer programs are only one example of depurification of the notion of copyright and its original aims.[19] Compilations are the other, earlier example of hybrid literary works that were included within the scope of copyright.

A genuine literary work was a work authored by one or more persons from the conception of the idea until its final expression. The number of persons authoring such a work was in most cases limited. The authored work as a whole constituted a new piece of literary expression. In contrast to inventions and patents, the work did not have to satisfy a novelty requirement. It was the expression that had to be new, not the idea. The idea could have been used in the past, since the idea as such was not protected by copyright. Anything else would unduly impinge on the freedom of intellectual creativity. The expression of the work at issue had to be

---

[17] In common law traditions the distinction between industrial property and copyright is not as marked as it is in the continental law traditions because the former place the emphasis of copyright law on the producer or exploiter of the work rather than on the author. This market-orientated philosophy is closer to the philosophy of patent law, which, although it places the emphasis on the work itself, is still a market-orientated philosophy. The gap between the producer and the work is one step closer to the gap between the author and the work, as continental traditions would put it. Interesting in this respect is the fact that both copyright and industrial property laws regulate equivalent aspects of human creativity. They each constitute part of the individual's personality and are derived from the same philosophical foundations and beliefs which led to the French Revolution. See Marinos, 'Nomiki prostassia vasseon dedomenon' at 134; G. Koumantos, *Pnevmatiki idioktissia*, 7th edn, Ant. N. Sakkoula, Athens, 2000, at 13.

[18] See chapter 7 below on computer programs.

[19] I.e. to protect genuine literary works and the personal bond they have with their authors.

original. Depending on the jurisdiction, the level of originality could vary from an expression which was not merely copied to an expression which had the personal intellectual imprint of the author. If no originality was to be found in the expression and content of the work, the work would not qualify for copyright protection. Originality of content is the principal factor for copyright protection.

This notion of originality of content of the work cannot realistically be present in any kind of compilation. Nevertheless, compilations as such come within the ambit of copyright protection for literary works, since they are referred to as collections in the Berne Convention,[20] but in reality they do not possess originality in the same sense as genuine literary works.[21] Originality in their case is tested on the grounds of the selection and arrangement of the material used to compile the final work. The persons compiling such works do not author them. They select and arrange the material already authored by third parties. Even so the same regime of protection as the one for literary works is granted to them.

Though compilations are a kind of derivative work, since they usually compile pre-existing original material, we have to distinguish them from the derivative works mentioned under article 2(3) of the Berne Convention. The latter, which are translations, adaptations and other alterations of a literary work, still possess the same kind of originality as the works from which they have been derived. Whether copyright of the original work is infringed or not does not play any role for the purposes of their independent qualification as literary works.[22] Thus, their inclusion within the scope of copyright does not really impinge on the original notion of a literary work, although one always has

---

[20] Art. 2(5) of the Berne Convention: 'Collections of literary works such as encyclopaedias and anthologies which, by reason of the selection and arrangement of their contents, constitute intellectual creations shall be protected as such, without prejudice to the copyright in each of the works forming part of such collections.'

[21] 'Compilations are not within the normal meaning of literary work.' See Lord Gorell's comments in the *Parliamentary debates*, 5th series, House of Lords, vol. X, HMSO, 1911, at 211. See also A. Monotti, 'The extent of copyright protection for compilations of artistic works' [1993] 5 *EIPR* 156, at 159: 'they are a special category of works which recognise the importance of selection, compilation and arrangement skills, even though they may have only slight literary content'. Not all compilations are thought to come under the scope of this provision (both in the UK and in Australian copyright law). Only compilations which can be described as 'written' (in the UK) or as 'expressed in words, figures or symbols' (in Australia, Copyright Amendment Act 1984, s. 3(f) which amended s. 10 of the Copyright Act 1968). *Ibid.*, at 161. According to Monotti, compilations of merely or essentially artistic works seem to be excluded by the *expressio unius est exclusio alterius* (an express reference to one matter indicates that other matters are excluded).

[22] The Berne Convention provides in art. 2(5) that the protection of these derivative works shall be 'without prejudice to the copyright in each of the works forming part of such collections'.

to take into consideration the different levels of protection and rights involved.

Taking into account the fact that compilations are to a greater extent hybrid works rather than adaptations, and adding to that the subsequent inclusion of computer programs in the category of literary works, it can be said that they have, in a sense, brought about the relaxation of the rules on copyright. The genuine literary work, which was a work of natural language, authored by a limited number of people responsible for its original content, now seems almost a distant and old-fashioned paradigm. The new reality has managed to set its own rules.

3.2.3 Databases

The inclusion of databases within the scope of copyright is another example of its depurification.[23] Databases are hybrid works in the same sense that compilations and computer programs are. Often elements of both a compilation and a computer program are involved in a database. Databases qualify for copyright protection subject to an originality test relating to the selection and/or arrangement of their materials. In the same sense as compilations, no new expression or idea occurs in a database. There is no newly created/authored work which carries weight in the assessment of the originality of the database. In fact it is data which is compiled together, information rather than works in the traditional sense of the word. In these circumstances the personal imprint of the author is extremely restricted, if there is any individual or personal imprint found in the first place.

This is particularly so if it is also taken into account that databases are rarely the work of an individual author. They are commissioned by companies and are built by teams of people, since the tasks involved in the construction of a database are far more complicated and numerous than the ones involved in a conventional compilation.[24] The process of making a database is very different from the process of authoring a traditional literary work. Many tasks require combined efforts, technical equipment and substantial investments. It is not creativity which is involved or which plays the only essential or decisive role. Any personal creative contribution

---

[23] Databases either were included in many national laws as protected material under copyright or were introduced in all EU Member States by the enactment of the EU Directive on the legal protection of databases, [1996] OJ L77/20.

[24] It is submitted that we are heading towards an 'impersonalisation' of copyright works. The old idea of every work having an individual author has been discarded. New technology products are the outcome of joint endeavours and an individual author can no longer be determined. On top of that are computer-generated works where there is no author in the traditional sense at all.

is always restricted by the project line, as this is usually designed by the company commissioning it and by the utilitarian, functional and comprehensive nature of the work. In this context any traditional personal bonds between the author and his work look rather weak or even absurd.

In addition, electronic databases contain a computer program in order to render access to them and the retrieval of their contents possible. Even in the case where a computer program is distinguished from the actual database (the compilation of the data), there are still parts closely related to it. These parts are the operating materials, indexation systems and thesaurus, which allow the user to browse through a database, and which are highly functional in nature. These are therefore incapable of being protected by copyright on their own merits. However, they form the object of copyright protection if seen in conjunction with a qualifying database. These systems accompanying the database strongly indicate that databases are functional and utilitarian works whose protection does not aim at the protection of a literary or artistic outcome (as would be the case with traditional literary works or other copyright works) but at the protection of the process of their creation, the investment put into that production and, in part at least, the idea.

Databases have stretched the scope of copyright in order to include the protection of technology in a process that had already been started by the inclusion of computer products within its ambit of protection. However, the protection of technology was left to patent law. Databases, along with computer programs, contributed substantially to the metamorphosis of literary and artistic copyright into an 'industrial copyright', or as the continental lawyers, who have a clear distinction between copyright or intellectual property on the one hand and industrial property on the other, would put it, into 'intellectual technology'.[25] These terms clearly point to an area of confusion between the boundaries of idea and expression, technology and art, machine and work. Modern copyright seems to come ever closer to the former (i.e. idea, technology, machine). However, by protecting the idea further, we in fact afford protection to the information (data) rather than the work. This might eventually have repercussions on competition law and on keeping the right balance between the commercial triangle of innovation/creation, production and consumption. Too many restrictions at innovation level might lead to the blocking of further development in the area and to the abolition of real competition in the field of information technology and communications.

---

[25] See M. Marinos, *Logismiko (software). Nomiki prostassia kai simvassis*, 2 vols. Kritiki, Athens, 1992, II, at 126.

3.2.4 An overall perspective

Taking into account the fact that compilations are to a greater extent hybrid works than adaptations, and adding to that the subsequent inclusion of computer programs and databases in the category of literary works,[26] it can be said that they have, in a sense, brought about the relaxation of the rules on copyright.[27] The genuine literary work, which was a work of natural language, authored by a limited number of people responsible for its original content, now seems almost a distant and old-fashioned paradigm. Copyright sets out to extend its protection to new technology products as well, even if their nature is incompatible with the nature of traditional works and traditional processes of creating a work with a literal and artistic content and putting it on the market.

3.2.5 Originality at common law as compared to its *droit d'auteur* counterpart

Common law jurisdictions have also played a significant role in the widening of the original notion of genuine literary works. Literary works as such are protected by any copyright regime in the world. However, not all of them are protected. Only original literary works are protected. But originality is a concept that is not defined in a uniform way. It can either widen or narrow the scope of protection for literary works according to the definition given to it.

So, although there is a unified regime of protection in relation to literary works, this regime unravels when it comes to the definition of originality. It basically splits into two systems of protection and two concepts of originality: the continental system (otherwise known as the *droit d'auteur* system) and the common law or Anglo-Saxon system (otherwise known as the 'copyright system').[28]

The question which seems to follow logically at this stage is that concerning the Berne Convention's position on this point. The drafters of the Berne Convention did not specify how original a work should be in order to qualify for copyright protection. The word 'original' is not even

---

[26] It is not certain that databases will be protected as literary works in all EU Member States. Even if that is not the case, they will still play an essential role in the reconceptualisation of copyright.
[27] The fact that copyright should be granted to works irrespective of their practical and functional utilities, and the fact that functional and utilitarian works should not be granted any copyright protection, has in the past created problems such as whether to include architectural works within the ambit of copyright protection. See Marinos, 'Nomiki prostassia vasseon dedomenon' at 128.
[28] Throughout this book the term 'copyright' is used as a general term, without having attached to it the special common law meaning.

referred to in the text of the Berne Convention. However, it is thought to be inherent in the very notion of a literary work.[29] According to the Brussels Conference in 1948, the notion of 'intellectual creation' was found to be implicit in the notion of a literary and artistic work. According to Ricketson, if a balance had to be struck between the two families of copyright law, the balance would turn towards the continental approach.[30]

The view that a work has to be the expression of a person's intellectual creation has taken over in almost all continental jurisdictions with only slight variations in the practical criteria for assessing the actual existence of originality.

The issue becomes even more problematic (at first sight) if one browses through some of the continental copyright laws. For example, no express mention of originality or of the degree of originality is provided in the French Copyright Act. Here this is derived from the very notion of a literary work and indirectly (by adopting a teleological/purposive approach) from the wording of various parts of the French Copyright Act (see, for example, article L113-7).[31] Also telling in this respect is the note of Saleilles under a French judgment delivered by the Court of Appeal in Paris, where he expressly states that 'the creative activity of the person is considered inherent to his personality, being an internal and thriving power'.[32]

The Belgian Copyright Act, which is one of the most recent in the area, does not expressly require a certain type of originality. Originality as in France is a notion based on case-law or scholarly opinion. The approach rests on the premise that the author of a work can only be a person. As long as a person creates the work, he also puts his personal imprint on it. In other words, the work is essentially the expression of the individual's personal intellectual effort.[33] The Belgian Supreme Court has ruled on two occasions that the law requires that the work has an individual character, in order for it to meet the requirement that an act

---

[29] The same reasoning is applied in the French and Belgian Copyright Acts.

[30] Berne Convention, Brussels Revision Conference, Documents 1948, 94–5 (Report by Plaisant). See also E. Ulmer 'Copyright protection of scientific works' (1972) 2 *IIC* 56; S. Ricketson, *The Berne Convention for the protection of literary and artistic works: 1886–1986*, Kluwer, Deventer, 1988, at 900. The various EU copyright Directives have attempted to harmonise the definition of originality, at least in respect to issues within their scope. The yardstick used is that the work should be 'the author's own intellectual creation'. This requirement is a bit stricter than the traditional common law concept and it seems to be a bit looser than the strictest continental views. Ricketson has argued that the continental views probably reflect better the intentions of the drafters of the Berne Convention. From this point of view the EU-initiated change in UK law must be a positive development. Ricketson, *Berne Convention*, at 900.

[31] The words 'intellectual creation' are used in art. L113-7.

[32] 1 February 1990, *Rec. Sirey*, 1900, vol. 2, 121.

[33] J. Corbet, *Auteursrecht*, Story – Scientia, Brussels, 1997, at 27.

of creation took place. The test for the individual character of the work was laid down as being that it had to be the expression of the intellectual effort of its creator.[34]

In contrast, German and Greek copyright laws are more explicit on this point. They state that 'personal intellectual creations alone shall constitute works',[35] and that 'the term "work" shall designate any original intellectual literary, artistic or scientific creation'[36] respectively.

The Anglo-Saxon system finds itself at the other end of the spectrum. In the UK Copyright Designs and Patents Act 1988 (CDPA 1988) a literary work has to be original to be protected by copyright.[37] Yet the express mention of the word 'original' in this context is not indicative of the British effort to meet the continental standards of originality. Some scholars would even argue that the Berne standards of protection are not met either.[38] It is more a consequence of the UK mentality to distinguish between various categories and the rules that apply to them, before subjecting the rules to the system of literal interpretation. In that sense the category of original works is distinguished from that of derivative works.

'Original' in a UK context implies a work which is not copied and which originates from the author.[39] The work is copyrightable as long as 'skill and labour' have been invested in it.[40] As Ricketson observes, common law jurisdictions have often lowered the level of intellectual creation required for copyright so as to accord deserving plaintiffs a protection that would be more appropriate under unfair competition law.[41] According to Cornish, the limited meaning of originality in UK law is justified on two grounds: 'First, it reduces to a minimum the element of subjective judgment (and attendant uncertainties) in deciding what qualifies for protection. Secondly, it allows investment of labour and capital that in some way produces a literary result: this is true equally of the compiler of mundane facts and of the deviser of a football pool form

---

[34] Cass., 27 April 1989, *Pas.*, 1989, I, 908; Cass., 2 March 1993, *Ing. Cons.*, 1993, 145.
[35] Art. 2(2) of the German Copyright Act.
[36] Art. 2(1) of the Greek Copyright Act.
[37] S. 1(1)a CDPA 1988.
[38] See Ricketson, *Berne Convention*, at 900.
[39] See Peterson J, *University of London Press* v. *University Tutorial Press* [1916] 2 Ch 601, at 608. See also Lord Pearce, *Ladbroke (Football) Ltd* v. *William Hill (Football) Ltd* [1964] 1 All ER 465, at 479, [1964] 1 WLR 273, at 291.
[40] Alternative expressions deriving from case-law are 'skill, judgment and labour', 'selection, judgment and experience' or 'labour, skill and capital'. See P. Torremans and J. Holyoak, *Holyoak and Torremans' intellectual property law*, 2nd edn, Butterworths, London, Dublin, Edinburgh, 1998, at 168.
[41] Ricketson, *Berne Convention*, at 901. See also S. Ricketson, 'Reaping without sowing' [1984] *UNSW Law Jo* (special issue) 1, 7–13.

whose real effort is in the market research determining the best bets to combine.'[42]

Examples of original works in the UK sense also include football fixture lists,[43] street directories,[44] trade catalogues,[45] timetable indexes,[46] sequences of numbers in a newspaper bingo game[47] and other kinds of works of very low or non-existent creativity. Copyright in the UK is often used as a sweeping legal provision for the protection of those works, for which no other legal protection, such as unfair competition law,[48] trade marks, patents, and so on, is available, if that protection is needed in situations where copying would result in an unfair competitive advantage for the party copying.[49] UK copyright law seems in this respect to close the gaps that are left by the absence of alternative legal solutions outside copyright law. As Cornish states,[50] the fact that the defendant who has been awarded copyright protection tends to be a direct business competitor in cases of this kind is not a mere coincidence.[51]

The US conduct in this area is also similar in this respect.[52] Copyright is approached as a legal protection for time and labour rather than as a means of protection for genuine literary works.[53] In this context it is not particularly difficult for someone to realise why for many years now moral rights have not (and in the USA still do not) fit in easily with common-law copyright systems.[54]

---

[42] W. Cornish, *Intellectual property*, 4th edn, Sweet & Maxwell, London, 1999, at 385.
[43] See *Ladbroke (Football) Ltd* v. *William Hill (Football) Ltd* [1964] 1 All ER 465, [1964] 1 WLR 273; *Football League* v. *Littlewoods* [1959] 2 All ER 546.
[44] *Kelly* v. *Morris* (1866) LR 1 Eq 697.
[45] *Collis* v. *Cater* (1898) 78 LT 613; *Purefoy* v. *Sykes Boxall* (1955) 72 RPC (89).
[46] *Blacklock* v. *Pearson* [1915] 2 Ch 376.
[47] *Mirror Newspapers Pty Ltd* v. *Queensland Newspapers Pty Ltd* [1982] Qd R 305 (Australia).
[48] Unfair competition law is non-existent in England.
[49] See, for example, *Exxon* v. *Exxon Insurance* [1982] Ch 119, [1981] 3 All ER 241, [1982] RPC 81, where no copyright was held to exist in the name Exxon. Trade mark law was clearly the more appropriate form of protection. In addition, copyright in the name Exxon would mean the same as copyright in the expression and the idea, which would be a breach of the most sacred rule of copyright: no protection for ideas. This is also an indication of the existence of a *de minimis* rule for UK copyright.
[50] Cornish, *Intellectual property*, at 385.
[51] The fact that UK law no longer distinguishes between copyright and neighbouring rights, although the substantive rules on copyright that apply to both categories are still different, could be seen as further circumstantial evidence of the ongoing depurification of copyright. If the right in a sound recording is now also called copyright, for example, it may be easier to bring further marginal works into the sphere of copyright.
[52] US Copyright Act, 17 USC § 102(a).
[53] Of course, this is now subject to the US Supreme Court's decision in the *Feist* case, which will be analysed in detail below.
[54] For a limited exception see the Visual Artists Rights Act 1990 (VARA); see further I. Stamatoudi, 'Moral rights of authors in England: the missing emphasis on the role of creators' [1997] 4 *IPQ* 478, at 483.

The inclusion of computer programs within the category of literary works, the provision of the same kind of protection for compilations, and also the fact that literary works in the UK system come very close to, and sometimes coincide with, factual and utilitarian works, has caused a bending of copyright rules in Europe. In many jurisdictions where the term 'literary works' was constructed in such a way as to include almost everything, the danger of granting a strong (or in the future even stronger) copyright to any new kind of work became apparent.[55] The danger is that the publishing and entertainment industries would be favoured in the short term but could eventually be blocked in the long term, especially if they were to create products comprising pre-existing original material. Copyright had, and perhaps still has, to undergo either a purification (and narrow its scope of protected works down to a core) or a loosening of its rules (and provide a looser protection for more and more works). In common law systems this protection should at least not be blocked by moral rights and uncertainty about the reactions of the authors involved. The interests of the industry are capable of destabilising or revitalising a national economy as a whole.

On the other hand, continental copyright was facing imminent difficulties in accommodating new technology products within its regime of protection. Software, databases, multimedia products and so on were obviously not presenting exactly the same problems as traditional literary works. For example, the utilitarian and functional nature of the product was a far more dominant factor in relation to software than in relation to literary works. The fact that often a certain result that is to be achieved imposes a particular means of expression contrasts with the view that an author of a particular work is free to choose his own way of expressing that idea. A computer program cannot be seen as an entirely free creation of the mind. Any digital result is assisted by a computer. In contrast with analogue works, the work deriving from such a process can only partially be the creation of its author, as the technical environment often imposes a single possible mode of expression.[56] Moreover, the exception allowing reverse engineering and the right of the user to tailor the product to his own needs impinged on copyright rules which were indispensable for the successful functioning of the market but which moved away from traditional copyright. Computer programs and the like were coming close to industrial products. Their protection was not aimed at favouring the author but the industry. In

---

[55] See also the article by H. Laddie, 'Copyright: over-strength, over-regulated, over-rated?' [1996] 5 *EIPR* 253.
[56] P. Deprez and V. Fauchoux, *Lois, contrats et usages du multimédia*, Dixit, Paris, 1997, at 43.

recent decades, of course, more and more people have been qualifying as authors.

3.2.6 Convergence of the two systems

The interesting point is that most systems have appeared to relax their rules on copyright. Moreover, they have also tended to narrow the gaps between each other. The pressure is twofold. First, intellectual property products have to survive in a market which is becoming increasingly international and borderless and which sets its own rules. Secondly, because of this new reality the need for uniform rules has become increasingly obvious and pressing. Particularly in the context of the Single Market, the need for the European Union to develop an all-embracing common commercial policy dictates uniform solutions, at least with regard to such commercially successful markets and industries as multimedia.

3.2.6.1 *Examples of convergence in common law jurisdictions*

3.2.6.1.1 USA

Recently, in the United States the *Feist* decision[57] has created a certain amount of turbulence. Until that time the 'sweat-of-the-brow' principle applied to copyright works. Skill and labour sufficed for a work to qualify as a literary work. In *Feist* the white pages of a telephone directory were not found capable of attracting any copyright protection, since not enough skill and labour were found to have been invested in them. Yet the qualification of these sorts of compilations in the United States was not unusual, leading many scholars to talk about the redefinition of certain aspects of copyright law. Whether this was a push towards a more intellectually orientated approach is not clear. Despite a huge literature in the area, we should not perhaps be very optimistic. The *Feist* decision was a decisive step towards the adoption of the EU database Directive, allowing databases in European Union Member States to be protected by copyright only when they constituted the author's own intellectual creation. For those databases which are valuable because of the investment of time and money in them, but which by reason of their factual nature would not attract copyright, a *sui generis* right has been introduced.[58]

---

[57] *Feist Publications* v. *Rural Telephone* 499 US 340 (1991).
[58] WIPO is currently also looking into the possibility of adopting an international legal instrument in the area of databases.

3.2.6.1.2 The UK

The UK seems to be moving in the same direction. Yet, the UK's attitude was not always the result of its free will. In the *Magill* case, Magill, an Irish publisher, came up with the idea of producing a weekly TV guide containing the programme listings of all channels broadcast in Ireland.[59] The British channels BBC and ITV and the Irish channel RTE successfully applied for an injunction, since they owned the copyright in their TV programme listings, for which they were not prepared to give out any licences.[60] Magill's argument was that the TV channels held a dominant position in the market, which they were abusing by denying licences.

The approach of the European Court of Justice until that time was that expressed in *Volvo* v. *Veng*.[61] The possession of an intellectual property right is very likely to make you commercially dominant, since it confers on you a monopoly, albeit a perfectly legitimate monopoly. The possession of a right as such can under no circumstances be an infringement of competition law rules. Yet, its exercise can. The refusal by Volvo to license a design right to a competitor in the spare parts market was not found to constitute an abuse of dominant position, but a normal exercise of its exclusive rights. The Court in *Magill*, however, did not regard the denial of licences by the TV channels as a legitimate exercise of their copyrights in the TV programme listings. According to the Court, this could not be the case in so far as 'exceptional circumstances' were found to have been present.

The Court's alternative competition-based approach, although referring impliedly to the copyright issues, focuses on the following exceptional circumstances. The first 'exceptional circumstance' to be found, which made this case and the legal solution adopted in it different from all previous cases, was the fact that the work examined constituted information rather than a work. Of course, it would have been out of the Court's jurisdiction to rule on the nature of the work, since this is an issue entirely left with the Member States.[62] The fact was that TV programme listings constituted information and that information was indispensable for

---

[59] Case T-69/89 [1991] 4 CMLR 586 and Case T-76/89 [1991] 4 CMLR 745, and see on appeal Joint Cases C-241/91P and C-242/91P, *Radio Telefis Eireann and Independent Television Publications Ltd* v. *Commission* [1995] ECR I-743, [1995] 4 CMLR 718.

[60] This case eventually came to appeal before the European Court of Justice. At the same time as it came before the Irish courts, the EC Commission took up Magill's case. The Commission's decision in favour of Magill was appealed unsuccessfully before the Court of First Instance. A further appeal to the Court of Justice followed. Joint Cases C-241/91P and C-242/91P, *Radio Telefis Eireann and Independent Television Publications Ltd* v. *Commission* [1995] ECR I-743, [1995] 4 CMLR 718.

[61] Case 238/87, *Volvo AB* v. *Erik Veng* [1988] ECR 6211, [1989] 4 CMLR 122.

[62] See in this respect the discussion in *Opinion 1/94* [1994] ECR I-5267.

the creation of the new product. Secondly, no alternative existed on the market for that product, though there was a constant and regular demand for it on the part of consumers. Thirdly, the TV channels were the only source of this information. They were not entitled to keep that information to themselves on the grounds of EU competition law, since their primary occupation was not publishing but broadcasting. On these grounds the broadcasting companies were finally obliged to grant licences.

This decision gave rise to a lot of comments and controversy as its wording seems to overstress the importance of competition law and question certain aspects of national intellectual property law. Many commentators felt it impinged on national competence and sovereignty and that it was in substance more a decision on whether TV programme listings merited copyright protection and less a decision on competition policy.[63] The fact that the UK and Ireland were granting copyright protection for functional and utilitarian works was bound to create problems in the context of a Single Market as this protection was reserved for a limited number of company monopolies. It was not justified on the grounds of particular creativity and personal expression, and many felt that functional and utilitarian works were not worthy of such a regime of protection and such a restriction on the level of innovation and production.

The BBC did not appeal to the Court of Justice as the UK had at that stage already amended its law in line with the decision of the Court of First Instance. The Broadcasting Act 1990 was introduced and it includes the compulsory licensing of TV programme listings.

Another upgrading of UK law took place with the incorporation of databases into the CDPA 1988 in the chapter on literary works. The novel thing about the incorporation of databases into the UK Act was not the incorporation as such, but the fact that the copyrightability of databases required an enhanced standard of originality compared to the standard the UK already provided for. Consequently the law provides that in order to attract copyright protection databases have to be 'the author's own intellectual creation'.[64] Apparently, the mere fact that they are not copied, or the observation that a sufficient amount of skill and labour has been invested in their construction, will not suffice. Yet, it is not clear to what extent this requirement alters the overall UK standard of originality.[65]

---

[63] See I. Stamatoudi, 'The hidden agenda in *Magill* and its impact on new technologies' (1998) 1 *Journal of World Intellectual Property* 153.
[64] Copyright and Rights in Databases Regulations 1977 (SI 1997/3032).
[65] I. Stamatoudi, 'The EU database Directive: reconceptualising copyright and tracing the future of the *sui generis* right' (1997) 50 *Revue Hellénique de Droit International* 436, at 453ff.

What is interesting to note at this point is that, although the originality requirement was found in the database Directive, the wording was in reality copied directly from the earlier software Directive. Computer programs, however, still fall under the 'normal' requirement of originality in the CDPA 1988, since no separate reference to 'the author's own intellectual creation' is made. Any idea that the general absence of a definition of originality would allow for the adoption of different criteria in relation to computer software must now be abandoned. Was that perhaps a conscious decision, which the UK followed in the case of databases where Community pressure was more substantial, or was it an erroneous placement of computer programs, which the courts will have to put right? Even if the latter is the case, it still fits uncomfortably with the UK tradition of concrete and specific legislation and literal interpretation of the law.

The introduction of the Broadcasting Act 1990 and the incorporation of the enhanced originality criterion for databases in the UK signify a turn, though under coercion, towards stricter originality criteria. Yet, this apparent change of heart should not be overestimated as both cases were the result of external pressure and not a conscientious national attempt at redefinition of certain issues of copyright. Street directories and trade catalogues have a fair chance of qualifying for copyright protection under the heading of literary works in the CDPA 1988.

3.2.6.2 *Examples of convergence in continental law jurisdictions*

3.2.6.2.1 The *droit d'auteur* tradition

The above is not simply a case of the Anglo-Saxon system heading towards, or accepting fragments of, an author-friendly approach. It is also a case of the continental system making some move towards the entrepreneurial approach, as a result of two types of pressure. The first one is brought about by the new reality emerging from new technology products and other works needing copyright protection. And the second one is the pressure deriving from the Communities' main commercial objectives.

First, the inclusion of computer programs and databases in copyright was altogether a bold step on the part of the continental system. The *droit d'auteur* system was always particularly orientated towards creations which were genuinely original and carried the personal imprint of the author. Computer programs and databases could only fit in badly with that model as the personal imprint of the author and the expression of his personality were far from evident in new technology products. Software and databases were considered to be more functional works, a utilitarian path towards achieving a technologically successful dialogue with computers, and in turn guaranteeing an equally successful entrance to the international market. Software and databases were more commodities than works.

This is also obvious from the fact that French copyright law with regard to the regulation of computer programs has more or less adopted the common law approach. Specifically in article L121-7 of the French copyright law, the author of a software program cannot prohibit its modification by the third party to whom he has assigned his economic rights, unless prejudice is caused to his honour and reputation. He cannot exercise his *droit de repentir*/right of withdrawal either. That has made many commentators wonder whether it is a sign that Anglo-Saxon copyright law is better equipped to deal with new technologies.[66] We should, however, bear in mind, as discussed earlier, that computer programs are theoretically at least not considered to be genuine literary works. This must surely be an aspect which creates problems in a system such as the French one with personality-orientated philosophical foundations.

The Belgian Copyright Act excluded computer programs altogether from its scope. However, a very similar Act,[67] issued the same day as the Copyright Act, affords computer programs protection along the same lines as copyright. Computer programs were deemed in this system not to sit easily with traditional literary works. Therefore they were given a tailor-made regime, which starts from a copyright basis. Such a *sui generis* regime also makes it easier to avoid any infringement of the EU software Directive.

Similar developments are expected to take place with the implementation of the database Directive in the national laws of many EU Member States, this time, perhaps, from the starting point that databases are valuable more for their collection of materials and less for the originality of their contents. In any event, with such widespread commercial value, computer programs and databases have been, or will in the near future be, incorporated into the copyright or copyright-like laws of the EU Member States. However, the same commercial value arguably makes them unlikely contestants for copyright protection.

The inclusion of copyright programs and databases in the laws of the EU Member States will not be without practical repercussions regarding

---

[66] Deprez and Fauchoux, *Lois, contrats et usages*, at 45.
[67] Law of 30 June 1994, 'Loi transposant en droit belge la directive européenne du 14 mai 1991 concernant la protection juridique des programmes d'ordinateur' [1994] *Moniteur Belge – Belgisch Staatsblad* (27 July 1994), 19315.

the traditional elements of continental copyright.[68] The originality criterion in relation to new technology products has clearly been lowered in many countries of the *droit d'auteur* tradition so as to make it possible for new technology products to qualify for copyright protection.[69] The 'new' originality criterion for both computer programs and databases is for the work to be 'the author's own intellectual creation'. In other words, the borderline is being drawn somewhere between the common law requirement and the continental one, perhaps with a slight tendency to favour the latter.

Also, the introduction in various continental systems of levies on the tapes or any other technical devices that can be used for copying purposes,[70] schemes of blanket licences for music and photocopying, and certain non-voluntary licences, has relaxed the rules on copyright which originally provided the author with total and absolute control over his work. The author's advance permission for the reproduction of his work is not always a necessary prerequisite (or, as the continental system would put it, the reproduction of certain parts of someone's work will not in all cases be found to be abusive). The interests of the exploiters of the publishing, recording and entertainment industry are taken into account to an even larger extent. In such cases the author is left with a simple entitlement to some remuneration but with no discretion. And this is increasingly going to be the case in the future because of the vast and ever growing number of collecting societies' schemes.

Lastly, the inclusion by continental law systems of sound recordings, broadcasts, cable programmes, and of rights of producers and performers in the scope of their intellectual property laws (even though only as neighbouring rights) undoubtedly signifies an essential departure from the concept of traditional copyright in the *droit d'auteur* countries.[71] Sound recordings, broadcasts and cable programmes are by their nature derivative works when they are compared to traditional literary works. Still, they should not be confused with the original derivative works, which are essentially the translations, adaptations and alterations of original pre-existing works. The former derivative works are more a sort of

---

[68] We have previously seen, of course, that in common law copyright the level of originality was raised in relation to new technology products.
[69] See especially the literature regarding the German originality criterion. Stamatoudi, 'EU database Directive', at 448. A. Raubenheimer, 'The new copyright provisions for the protection of computer programs in Germany' (1995) 4 *Law, Computers and Artificial Intelligence* 5, at 7ff.
[70] See, for example, art. 18(3) of the Greek Copyright Act 2121/1993.
[71] In common law countries, like the UK, the protection of all these works, plus the protection of some others as well, e.g. the protection of the typographical arrangement of a publication, is considered to be copyright.

incorporation of traditional original works into some kind of medium, either off-line (tapes, disks, video, CD-ROMs, etc.) or on-line (broadcasting, cable transmission, the Internet, etc.). With regard to the protection of producers and performers, this is based on the 'compiling' of the work they do, i.e. films and recordings,[72] rather than on their actual interpretation of it. Original works offer only the basis for the performance of such tasks.

Apart from the 'natural' convergence between the common law and continental systems, which is basically the outcome of mutual influencing and interaction, the European Union and the operation of the Single Market dictate solutions in the area of intellectual property for the sake of uniformity. When the European Economic Community was first set up, no one could possibly have foreseen the success of intellectual property products on the European market. Their importance was rather insignificant. At the end of the twentieth century the protection of the works and of the authors became a particular objective of the Community, though still not a first priority. Nowadays, legislation has been enacted in many areas of intellectual property rights. Their direct relevance to the Single Market and the Community's commercial policy is indisputable. The stability of the Common Market and its potential to compete in the area essentially depends on the ease with which intellectual property products are marketed. This is dependent on uniformity in the laws of the Member States. Uniformity, of course, always opts for one solution or the other. The provisions of both the copyright and the *droit d'auteur* systems can be used as starting points. The time when a common copyright law will be introduced and will be applicable in every Member State is arguably not too far away, although such an introduction will not be an easy task. The political interests of the various Member States will be taken into account, as well as the comments of those who allege that total uniformity can never exist,[73] since a lot will depend on the interpretation of the law and not only on its wording. However, a common text for everybody is a significant start. Even more apparent is that the national laws are heading in the direction of convergence. Yet, in this instance, any new copyright law is bound to start from the economic aspects of copyright whilst any change to the moral rights provisions will be left to the discretion of the Member States.

---

[72] We could also say that they contribute to the fixation of the work and to the finishing touches.
[73] It might even be undesirable since copyright reflects national cultures and it is generally accepted that these are different in the various parts of the Community. See in this respect art. 128 EC.

3.3 FIXATION OF LITERARY WORKS

Fixation in relation to literary works is not a necessary prerequisite in all jurisdictions.[74] However, even in those jurisdictions where this does not constitute an express prerequisite, the existence of a work in some kind of medium is either customary or appreciated on the grounds that it facilitates proof. In jurisdictions where this forms a prerequisite,[75] no precise material support is required. Yet whatever material support is used, its fixation on it needs to take some kind of permanent form.

The requirement of permanence may cause some inconvenience in these jurisdictions, if it is to be approached in its traditional sense. As technology progresses permanence is less straightforward, as the electronic format is used more and more. This is especially so from the point of view of on-line services. Of course, for those jurisdictions which have incorporated permanence on the grounds of its role in facilitating proof, 'less' permanence may still do the job, as long as it is enough to prove fixation. (Fixation and permanence seem to be notions that are inextricably linked.) Whether, for example, the RAM memory of a computer still complies with the requirement of permanence is not at all clear. The case-law in this area remains contradictory for the time being.[76] Dematerialisation seems inevitable in future for two reasons.

First, information will be valuable as such, irrespective of its carrier. Secondly, the lifespan of any fixation of the works may be reduced in any case to a fraction of a second as a result of the technical revolution. If the notion of fixation is to be shrunk to such an extent, this may make one wonder whether the concept of fixation still serves a useful purpose. Issues such as the above are indicative of the forthcoming problems in the area.

---

[74] Usually only common law countries require fixation for literary works. The relevant provision in the Berne Convention was inserted after pressure, especially from the UK delegation. The drafters were also afraid that if they did not include it the USA would not join Berne either. See Ricketson, *Berne Convention*, at 243. See also in this respect, Laddie, Prescott and Vitoria, *Modern law*, at 1: 'copyright springs into existence as soon as the work is written down or otherwise recorded in some reasonably persistent form'. See also the UK 1956 Act, s. 49(9), which states that the work has to be fixed because it is by nature a monopoly and 'there must be certainty in the subject matter of such monopoly in order to avoid injustice to the rest of the world'. The function of fixation as proof and hard evidence is apparent in common law countries.
[75] The USA and the UK are examples of jurisdictions which require fixation of the work.
[76] See the US cases such as *MAI Systems Corp. v. Peak Computer, Inc.*, 991 F 2d 511 (9th Cir. 1993) and *TriadSystems Corp. v. Southeastern Express Co.* (US District Court for the Northern District of California) 31 USPQ 2d 1239.

3.4 MULTIMEDIA PRODUCTS AND TRADITIONAL LITERARY WORKS

If we compare a multimedia work with a traditional literary work merely on a theoretical level, and not on the level of practical consequences, we observe the following differences.

By literary works, we essentially understand written or spoken text,[77] in other words a homogeneous original product, authored by one or more persons (in any case a limited number of persons), which is basically intended to be read or listened to. At this stage, fixation and personal imprint are not mandatory requirements according to the jurisdictions with which we are dealing.

If a work originates from a common law jurisdiction, fixation has to take place.

If we are to assume that traditional literary works originate from continental law jurisdictions and naturally come closer to a *droit d'auteur* definition of literary works, then we also have to admit that the work at issue has to have the personal imprint of the author, who in this case by definition can only be a natural person. That grants him, of course, both economic and moral rights.

It goes without saying that in every case the work has to be new, in so far as it expresses an idea in a novel way. This idea may have been expressed in the past, but not in the same way.

Taking the aforementioned points into account, we can observe the following in relation to multimedia products:

(1) *Multimedia products are not text.* Multimedia products by definition have to combine more than one form of expression. Thus, even if text predominates, which is only rarely going to be the case, it will still not be the only expression involved. Literary works hardly take into account the feature of combining different types of expression. They are always approached as being homogeneous works.
(2) *Multimedia products are not essentially meant to be read or listened to.* This follows on from the previous observation. Multimedia products are usually meant to be shown and browsed through, and this is also the reason why the use of a screen is vital in their case.[78]

---

[77] Words that are sung are generally also included, and singing is seen as a form of speech. See, for example, s 3(1) CDPA 1988.
[78] See also A. Latreille, 'The legal classification of multimedia creations in French law' in I. Stamatoudi and P. Torremans (eds.), *Copyright in the new digital environment*, Sweet & Maxwell, London, 2000, 43, at 71–3, where he argues that the regime of protection for literary works focuses too much on reproduction on paper of the work for it to be suitable for multimedia works. He also refers to specific provisions of the French Copyright Act to show the specific problems that the French regime of protection for

Traditional literary works 65

(3) *Multimedia products do not have any standardised permanent form.* Since manipulation of their contents is the rule, fixation and permanence, at least in the traditional sense, are impossible. There may be potential for a permanent form whenever the opportunity to manipulate the contents is used, but that potential may not be realised every time. It is important to realise though that in all cases the tools that allow for manipulation will take a permanent form, whilst in most cases very few, if any, of the results of such manipulations will take a permanent form.

(4) *Multimedia products are not works of language.* Multimedia works are not conceived and fixed in a linguistic form, through the use of language. Binary code is used for their construction. Binary code does not constitute a high-level computer language such as Cobol or Pascal, for example. The language of binary code is incomprehensible even to computer experts and is thought to remain outside the scope of artificial languages.[79]

(5) *Multimedia products are more similar to compilations than to genuine literary works.* Unless a multimedia product is commissioned, and its materials are written or created from scratch, it cannot form a literary work in the sense we described earlier. It can only be a collection of works, even though these works may be literary works. Since this is often the case, multimedia products are essentially compilations. However, all the other prerequisites of a conventional traditional written compilation are still lacking so far as the basic characteristics of a work of language are concerned, i.e. text, standardised form, etc.[80]

(6) *Originality of contents is scarcely present.* If there is any kind of originality to be found in a classic multimedia product, it will be only

---

literary works presents in relation to multimedia products: (1) it is simply not possible to quantify the number of copies that will be made of a first print (art. L132-10), (2) multimedia works are not exploited in the same way as other traditional copyright works (art. L132-12), (3) generally the publisher is given a very weak form of control over the creation of the work, whereas the creation of multimedia works requires much more room for manoeuvring on the part of the producer, (4) lastly, there is often reference to industry practices, which are often not applicable or suitable for multimedia products. Latreille also examines the possibility of multimedia works being protected under French law as printed publications (*oeuvre de presse*). A printed publication is defined as 'each written format that allows the distribution of thoughts amongst the general public or certain categories within the general public and which appears at regular intervals' (Law of 1 August 1886). However, he rejects this argument on the basis that this regime of protection provides for a silent and implicit assignment of rights to the employer which is limited in time. That means that it only suits publications that are distributed rapidly. Multimedia products are presented on a stable support, often in an expensive format, and they are there to last. Only a few multimedia works appear periodically in new versions. He also argues that this regime only applies to journalists who are employees and it does not extend to other contributors.

[79] See section 3.1.2 above.
[80] See chapter 4 below.

in relation to the presentation of its material. The originality of the materials themselves is not to be judged, since that forms the subject of separate rights.

(7) *Only rarely will the author be a natural person.* Multimedia products, because of the investment they require for their production in terms of time, money and human resources, will only rarely constitute a project undertaken by a single person. Large enterprises, which possess the capital and the equipment, are the only ones likely to produce multimedia products. That and that alone would suffice to demonstrate how difficult it is to show any personal imprint on the work. The work is not always derived solely from the author's mind, but is also the result of the influence of the tools provided by computers. It is not always expressed in the author's own way, but in the style which is required in order for the work to be able to operate when placed in its functional environment. Thus, the link between the person and the work is in certain cases non-existent. As a consequence, there is perhaps no longer any reason to grant the author anything other than economic rights (i.e. moral rights).

Apart from the theoretical problems multimedia products would present if they were to be included within the scope of traditional literary works, there are also a number of practical considerations that have to be taken into account. As will be seen, these considerations create even more obstacles for the inclusion of multimedia in the category of literary works.

First, in certain jurisdictions, for example in Germany, economic and moral rights are linked. They both form aspects of one and the same right, which is directly dependent on the author of the work. This is the expression of the monistic theory. In cases of commercial exploitation of his work the author has to license out only that part of these rights which is required by the specific nature of the exploitation, referred to in the German law as 'utilisation'. A party other than the author can never be the owner of the author's work.[81] He can only use it. The author is not supposed to assign the whole bundle of his economic rights to third parties, as he is allowed to do in jurisdictions governed by the dualistic theory.[82]

This German monistic approach has, of course, some parallel practical consequences. Every time an entrepreneur wants to proceed with

[81] The whole bundle of economic rights in a work can be fully transferred only on the death of, or by reason of the death of, the author.
[82] In essence the practical significance of such a differentiation is of limited interest nowadays, since licences in Germany can be drafted almost as broadly as an assignment of economic rights in a work is in other countries.

Traditional literary works

a new intellectual creation, or even digitise an existing one, he has always to ask the author's separate permission in cases where specific permission has not been provided in the contract.[83] Nothing seems to be implied unless it is expressly referred to in the exploitation contract. In cases of digital publishing, the publisher has to go back to the author and ask for a new licence. If all economic rights were transferred to the exploiter right from the start, the production of any new intellectual property works would be facilitated, by gaining time and money. In the new technology industries this is a vital point for efficiency and market success.

Moreover, this approach creates certainty for the exploiter with regard to how many rights he possesses and if these rights are sufficient to embark on a new project. Unless this approach is taken, the exploiter may have undergone lengthy negotiations and discussions in order to obtain licences, only to find at the end that 5 per cent of the authors, who are not willing to give out any more licences, are impeding the whole project. The problem as such might not look significant immediately. But it certainly is, if one takes into account that in a multimedia product, thousands of works can be involved, and some of them, especially those for scientific or educational use, have only one source of supply. Particularly in common law jurisdictions, where the work protected can be a work of low originality, the right of the author to deny access to his work can have social repercussions as well.[84]

In relation to the same problem, different standards will apply to different countries, even for works which are thought to have undergone substantial uniform regulation through international conventions. Small problems can quickly grow into big problems, capable of obstructing any normal function of the intellectual creations market.

Another significant difference between the various states is the provision for creators–employees. In the Anglo-Saxon system, copyright in a work created by an employee in the course of his employment, according to the CDPA 1988,[85] belongs automatically to the employer, unless an agreement to the contrary exists. These works are known in the USA as 'works made for hire'.[86]

---

[83] Older contracts that were concerned with the exploitation of the work through analogue technology present obvious problems in this respect, as electronic rights, as they are often called, are not necessarily included in the licence. Most *droit d'auteur* systems operate in addition a rule which stipulates that in case of doubt the advantage is given to the author (*in dubio pro auctore*).

[84] See the literature on the public access to information as a socio-economic need.

[85] '[W]here a literary work is made by an employee in the course of his employment, his employer is the first owner of any copyright in the work subject to any agreement to the contrary' (art. 11(2)).

[86] §2d(b) of the US Copyright Act.

Yet, the position as to the ownership of copyright for works created in the course of employment is different in the *droit d'auteur* system. *Droit d'auteur* systems start from the presumption that only a natural person can create a literary work. Consequently, the logical owner of any right created in the work must be the person–author who created it. This is so irrespective of the existence of a contract of employment or any other circumstances. It is only at a second stage that the author can transfer the economic rights to the work to someone else, such as his employer, or in the German model give the employer the right to utilise the work. This transfer of economic rights, though, can also take place through the contract of employment.

The presumption does not apply in all cases. In the case of computer programs, France provides that 'the economic rights in the software and its documentation created by one or more employees in the execution of their duties or following the instructions given by their employer shall be the property of the employer and he exclusively shall be entitled to exercise them'.[87] This does not necessarily imply that France has adopted the common law line or that it has bent its rules on copyright. As we explained earlier, computer programs are not considered to fall squarely within the definition of literary works. They are not seen as the personal expression of an idea by their individual creator. The looser link between a creator and the computer program justifies the different approach in relation to rights ownership.

The different regulation of the Anglo-Saxon and the continental systems with regard to employees' economic rights to their works calls for different practical solutions. It would seem logical that the former system favours a less time- and money-consuming attitude towards the clearance of rights as fewer rightholders may be involved in relation to each work. In reality, though, there are only a few cases, if any, where, in their employment contracts, employers have not foreseen the opportunity of having transferred to them the whole bundle of economic rights in a work created by their employees, in the course of their employment.

Moral rights can also constitute obstacles in the production and marketing of multimedia works. The position in each country differs. A product which might be perfectly legitimate in one state might infringe copyright when imported and marketed in another state. Such semi-infringing products cannot circulate freely and efficiently on the international market. Clear-cut solutions which lead to security in transactions are called for. This is an issue which will be discussed in further detail in chapter 10.

---

[87] Art. L113-9. See also art. 69b(1) of the German Copyright Act.

Differences in the exceptions to copyright infringement in the various legal systems create further impediments to the commercialisation of multimedia works. The main problem, however, in respect of our present discussion is the fact that many exceptions in the various legal systems have been drafted for special types of copyright works.[88] Certain exceptions have been drafted with the traditional literary works concept in mind. It is not a foregone conclusion that multimedia products, if they are to be put in the category of literary works, should also fall under these exceptions. For example, in the case of an exception for review and criticism or an exception on grounds of 'fair use' (common law system)[89] or citation from a work (France),[90] it is not immediately evident how much this exception is to allow. The same problem as the one relating to the estimation of what is a substantial part of a work arises. How small should an item of a work be so as to render its copying acceptable? In the case of literary works, that is not difficult to say. A small passage or two or three pages of a book, when referred to in another work, do not cause any problems, because they cannot stand independently. Yet, in the case of multimedia products, a tiny item of the whole work can still be a perfectly independent work on its own, e.g. extraction of a painting from a multimedia work reciting the life of Leonardo Da Vinci and the whole collection of his artistic works. In such cases, the exception provided in the national Copyright Acts can only find grounds of application in relation to literary works. In the case of multimedia, its interpretation is either problematic

---

[88] See the debate on the draft European Parliament and Council Directive on the harmonisation of certain aspects of copyright and related rights in the information society, Brussels, 10 December 1997 COM (97) 628 final concerning the point of exceptions (art. 5), as well as the changes in the Common Position, Brussels, 14 September 2000.

[89] This US concept should be distinguished from the narrower 'fair dealing' concept in the CDPA 1988.

[90] The right of citation raises another controversial issue. Any multimedia work almost necessarily contains a vast number of extracts from pre-existing works. The right of citation seems to permit the borrowing of these extracts in all freedom. A laxist application of this right would therefore necessarily mean that the multimedia producer will not even need to negotiate a licence with many rightholders. Questions need nevertheless to be asked, such as whether any exception should cover the commercial or competing use of these citations or whether systematic borrowing of small parts of works is not in reality an abuse of the right of citation because in practical terms it blocks the proper application of copyright. Even more questions would arise if one were to envisage the application of any exception to the borrowing of the entirety of a small existing work. See also G. Vercken, *Guide pratique du droit d'auteur pour les producteurs de multimédia*, commissioned by the European Communities, DG XIII (Translic) from AIDAA, 1994, at 71; Sirinelli Report on multimedia and new technologies, France, Ministère de la culture et de la Francophonie, Paris, 1994, at 70.

and insufficient or incapable of producing any effect.[91] New technology products have to be assessed on their own merits and according to their own needs.

Both from a theoretical and a practical point of view, it can be observed that multimedia products do not immediately qualify as original literary works. Taking first the theoretical problems, the notion of literary works would be unjustifiably stretched if it were to include multimedia products. It is vital to restrict each category to homogeneous groups of products. Any other solution would undermine the logic of any system of copyright that attempts to divide the mass of protected works into various categories with specific characteristics and specific legal provisions to match these characteristics.

---

[91] Perhaps a criterion other than the extraction of a substantial part of a work is called for. A part, though not substantial, which might economically harm the author of the new technology product by its reproduction by a third party seems to be more appropriate in this case.

4 Collections and compilations

4.1 TRADITIONAL APPROACHES TO COLLECTIONS AND COMPILATIONS

4.1.1 The Berne Convention

If multimedia products come close to literary works in any sense, it is in the category of collections. The leading text for the definition of collections is the Berne Convention.[1] Collections for the purposes of the Berne Convention are collections of literary or artistic works, such as encyclopaedias and anthologies, only. These works qualify as literary works, or else as intellectual creations, not by reason of the originality of their contents, as would be the case with any genuine literary work, but by reason of the selection or arrangement of their contents. If collections are thought to have any resemblance to literary works, it is mostly because they incorporate original literary and artistic works in a manner which is considered original, and because traditionally they also present themselves in written-book format. Their qualification as copyrightable material, however, is meant to be without prejudice to the copyright existing in each of the works forming part of such collections.[2]

The Berne Convention's provision on compilations has been incorporated into the national laws of the Member States in various ways. However, this does not cause too many problems since the Berne Convention provides only for *de minimis* rules. Member States can deviate from them as long as the protection they afford to works is stronger or wider

---

[1] Art. 2(5) of the Berne Convention. The TRIPs Agreement also refers to the definition in the Berne Convention. See art. 9 of TRIPs.
[2] Collections are also referred to in art. 2*bis*(3) of the Berne Convention, in the sense of collections of lectures, addresses and other similar works. If we are to stick to the letter of this provision only collections of works by one and the same author qualify for copyright protection. Such a solution, however, would unjustifiably restrict the scope of collections in art. 2(5). It is argued that to this end we have also to accept collections of works by different authors. See the Berlin Conference, Actes 1908, 232–4, and S. Ricketson, *The Berne Convention for the protection of literary and artistic works: 1886–1986*, Kluwer, Deventer, 1988, at 300.

in substance than the one provided for in the Berne Convention. Any extended protection with regard to compilations can take two forms: first, the exclusive rights afforded to collections can be wider in content than the ones provided in Berne, or second, the notion of collections can be drafted in such a way as to include a larger variety of works. Either of these forms can occur without the other, or alternatively both may apply.

Member States have incorporated collections in the regime of protection for literary works. Collections have been given the same form of protection as any other type of literary work. 'Collection', however, is not the only term used in the national legislations in order to comply with the Berne Convention's provisions on collections. The term 'compilation' is also used in various national laws. The French authoritative text of the Berne Convention refers to collections as *recueils d'oeuvres littéraires et artistiques*. This term has been translated into English as 'collections', though there was also the opinion that the term 'compilation' came closer to the exact meaning of *recueil*.[3] Any attempt at making a distinction between collections and compilations will not be easy. We could argue that a compilation involves more skill and labour. A collection can after all be the mere juxtaposition of whole works, one after the other, without the expenditure of any particular skill or effort.[4] 'Compilation', however, has inherent in it the concept of compiling. Compiling can be done in relation to whole works, but it is usually done in relation to parts or extracts of works. Therefore a more personal judgment is needed. This difference is, however, only of academic value, since the originality of a collection will be judged on the grounds of the selection and arrangement either of the parts or of the whole works incorporated in it. In this light, both terms can be used interchangeably.

Since the distinction between the term 'collection' and that of 'compilation' is only semantic, we will confine ourselves to the express differences deriving from the various national substantive provisions with regard to collections. All Member States have placed collections within the ambit of literary works, and therefore any rights granted to an author of a literary work are also granted to the person who has made the selection/arrangement or carried out the editing of the materials which he has compiled. However, the notion of a compilation is defined differently in some Member States when compared with that of the Berne Convention. Examples of jurisdictions extending the notion of collections are, amongst others, the Greek, German and US jurisdictions.

---

[3] See Ladas' opinion as referred to in Ricketson, *Berne Convention*, at 300.
[4] The definition given by the *Shorter Oxford Dictionary* suggests that to 'compile' means to construct a written or printed work out of materials collected from various sources.

4.1.2 Greece

According to article 2(1) of the Greek Copyright Act, what is protected are the collections of works, expressions of folklore or simple facts and data, such as encyclopaedias, anthologies and databases. These would be protected anyway by reason of the selection and arrangement of their contents, but under Greek copyright law, the notion of works from which a collection is compiled is not limited to literary or artistic works. It can comprise any work qualifying under the Greek Copyright Act.[5] Databases, for example, are included within the scope of compilations, and this inclusion took place even before the introduction of any legislation in the area of databases at Community level. Databases are essentially seen as collections of mere facts and data, where facts and data constitute the main contents of a collection, which might at the same time include a number of works (literary, artistic or other).

4.1.3 Germany

The German Copyright Act refers to collections in a general manner. As article 4 of the Copyright Act 1965 puts it: 'Collections of works or other contributions... shall enjoy protection as independent works.' Since 'other contributions' are distinguished from 'works', which are (or may form) one of the first possible components of a collection, an argument *a contrario* arises as to which 'other contributions' are not necessarily works. Information, data or mere facts are possible examples of what is likely to be meant by 'other contributions'.

4.1.4 USA

The Americans refer to compilations in more or less the same sense as the Greeks and the Germans. A compilation can contain practically anything from pre-existing materials (probably meaning works in the broad sense) to data.[6] What is interesting to note at this point is that compilations under the American Act are a notion of genus (genre), including 'collective works' which is a notion of species. The examples of collections given in the Berne Convention, such as encyclopaedias and anthologies, are here referred to as 'collective works' together with the example of periodical issues.

The fact that the Americans refer to collective works in almost the same sense as they refer to compilations, and the fact that within these notions they also include periodicals (and probably other similar works, such as

---

[5] See art. 2(1)–(3) of the Greek Copyright Act 2121/1993.
[6] §§ 101(5) and 103 of the US Copyright Act.

newspapers),[7] is perhaps a relic of two suggestions made by national delegations in the course of past reviews of the Berne Convention. One suggestion concerned the replacement of the term 'collections' with that of 'collective works'. This suggestion was rejected on the grounds that the introduction of this new term would cause confusion with the same term used in a completely different way in some national jurisdictions, for example the French.[8] The second suggestion, presented by the UK delegation at the Brussels Conference, was that magazines, newspapers and reviews should be included within the express wording of the definition of compilations. This was also partially rejected. Magazines, newspapers and reviews might eventually constitute examples of compilations, in so far as they satisfy the requirements of the relevant provisions and constitute intellectual creations. However, their express inclusion in the actual wording of compilations was not desirable, since they do not form characteristic paradigms of compilations. As was pointed out by Josef Kohler: 'The choice and organisation of articles in a newspaper [is] dictated by concern for the interest of readers, and not by any "preoccupation with giving the journal an intellectual unity expressed as a creative thought."'[9]

Greece, Germany and the United States have drafted the rubric of 'compilations' as widely as possible. Not only are compilations of literary and artistic works covered, but also compilations of any kind of works. In addition, not only do compilations of works qualify, but also collections of materials other than works, such as information, facts, data, figures and so on. This approach, quite unintentionally, came close to the European initiative which followed in the area of databases. Databases are arguably the successor of compilations in modern times.

4.1.5 France

France stays one step behind. Qualifying collections are 'collections of various works'.[10] The whole range of possible works is included within the ambit of collections. However, the term 'works' is defined in article L112-1 as 'works of the mind'. This wording immediately refers to

---

[7] § 101(5) of the US Copyright Act.
[8] 'Collections' should be distinguished from the notion of 'collective works' as this is referred to in some national laws, e.g. the French Copyright Act. The latter term is essentially used with reference to genuine literary works authored by more than one person, the individual contributions being hard to distinguish. A suggestion made at the Brussels Conference in 1948 for the term 'collections' to be replaced by that of 'collective works' was rejected on the grounds that it would be confusing (Documents 1948, 157).
[9] J. Kohler, *Gewerblicher Rechtsschutz und Urheberrecht* (1917), 1, referred to by the International Office in [1933] *DA* 72, 75, as referred to in Ricketson, *Berne Convention*, at 302.
[10] Art. L112-3 of the French Copyright Act.

Collections and compilations 75

creations by authors which reflect their personality. This slightly higher originality criterion provides the step backwards by limiting the number of literary, artistic, musical, dramatic or other works that qualify. As a result, facts and data do not qualify as forming collections which are able to be protected under the French law.

4.1.6 The UK

The UK's approach is even more restrictive, but that restriction originates from the inclusion of limited types of works rather than from the originality criterion used.[11] In the CDPA 1988, compilations are put under the heading of literary works,[12] which includes any work, other than a dramatic or musical work, which is written, spoken or sung. This wording, however, presents one express and one implied limitation. The express limitation is that dramatic and musical works are excluded from the scope of compilations. The implied limitation is that any work which is not capable of being expressed in a written format is also excluded. A written format of course, does not only imply words put on a piece of paper. 'Writing', according to the CDPA 1988,[13] is defined as including 'any form of notation or code, whether by hand or otherwise and regardless of the method by which or the medium in or on which it is recorded, and "written" shall be construed accordingly'.

Since compilations come within the category of literary works, they need to be expressed in writing.[14] However, this requirement has to be met by the compilation, and this necessarily means by the compilation as a whole. That includes both the contents of the compilation, which are taken from other works,[15] and the structure, linking paragraphs and so on of the compilation. It is, of course, understood that certain compilations may consist only of borrowed text without the compiler adding any text of his own. This does not prevent them from meeting the requirement that the work should be expressed in writing, since these borrowed texts form the whole of the work. In this sense the requirement that the work has to be expressed in writing is very similar, if not identical, to the fixation requirement.

---

[11] It has to be kept in mind that the CDPA originality criterion means that more works are seen as literary works. This destroys, at least in part, the restricting effect of the requirement that only literary works should be taken into account as forming the contents of a compilation.
[12] S. 3(1) CDPA 1988.
[13] S. 178 CDPA 1988.
[14] S. 3(1) CDPA 1988. See also Peterson J's reference to 'every work which is expressed in print or writing, irrespective of the question whether the quality or style is high'. *University of London Press Ltd* v. *University Tutorial Press* [1916] 2 Ch 601, at 608.
[15] Pre-existing works or works commissioned for that purpose.

Apart from having to be expressed in writing, the work also has to be original. This requirement logically applies at a second stage, though, once the work has passed the writing hurdle. In very practical terms a minimum investment of skill and labour in the compilation, or for that matter in any other literary work, needs to be shown. That minimum investment of skill and labour can be found in the selection, arrangement and use of existing elements on the basis of some kind of scientific and commercial judgment. This became clear in *Ladbroke* v. *William Hill*.[16] For a compilation this means that originality need not exist in relation to the copied text. It also means that the selection and arrangement need not necessarily be expressed in writing. All that is required is that the selection and arrangement are original. The originality can be implied by the structure of the compilation. Non-existent or minimalist linking phrases or paragraphs will not result in the whole work being *de minimis*.

If one brings together the definition of a compilation in the UK's Copyright Act and that of the concept of 'writing', one can draw the conclusion that compilations which cannot be put in writing eventually fall outside the scope of compilations in general. An obvious example of this would be, for instance, compilations containing only artistic works. Since artistic works can only be displayed, shown or presented, and cannot be written, in the sense required by the CDPA 1988, they fail to qualify as contents in a compilation that qualifies for copyright protection. As Monotti points out, 'there is no copyright protection for a compilation of artistic works only... under... UK copyright legislation, unless such artistic works can be described as "written"... it is also possible that there is no copyright protection when such compilations include an insubstantial quantity of written material'.[17]

With the introduction of databases this must now be wrong. But even without that, it is still unacceptable.

This conclusion is essentially a conclusion based on a literal interpretation of the UK Act.[18] Since artistic works are not considered to be works capable of being expressed in a written format, they remain outside the scope of protection of compilations. Yet, this conclusion is an undesirable one from two points of view. First, there is no justifiable reason for distinguishing between compilations of literary works and

---

[16] [1964] 1 All ER 465, [1964] 1 WLR 273.
[17] A. Monotti, 'The extent of copyright protection for compilations of artistic works' [1993] 5 *EIPR* 156, at 161.
[18] Monotti also draws the same conclusions with regard to Australian law. The Australian Copyright Act 1984, s. 3(f) requires compilations to be 'expressed in words, figures or symbols (whether or not in visible form)'.

compilations of artistic works. Both kinds of compilations require the same skill and labour for their creation. In common law jurisdictions, skill and labour suffice for a work to qualify for copyright protection, and in fact such jurisdictions take a liberal attitude towards the protection of works, favouring a wide range of products being capable of protection. Therefore the distinction between compilations of literary works and compilations of artistic works could not actually have been based on the grounds of more expenditure of effort on the part of the author.

The second point of view from which, perhaps, the failure to incorporate collections of artistic works within the definition of a compilation seems undesirable, is that it indicates that UK law is not in full compliance with the Berne Convention. Given the fact that the Berne Convention's rules with regard to literary works constitute minimal rules of protection, leaving those collections of artistic works only outside the scope of compilations is in fact a breach of the Convention. If the wording of the UK Act is seen against this background, coupled with the purpose the protection of collections is meant to serve, an extensive and teleological approach is called for. The exclusion of collections of artistic works unduly restricts the ambit of copyright protection, destabilising the equilibrium of protection with regard to collections, and favouring only parts of it, whilst excluding other parts without any logical or acceptable reason.

This situation has now been changed by the introduction of a regime of protection for databases. The new regime has changed the definition of a compilation. A compilation is now defined as any compilation which is not a database.[19] A database is basically any compilation in which the works that are included can be accessed individually. These works should remain independent of one another and there must be some method according to which the works have been organised. It must be kept in mind that the structure of the statute does not allow the originality criterion to interfere at this stage. The term 'database' is defined irrespective of any originality. Since originality only comes in at a second stage, it does not affect the definition of a compilation that is not a database. In practical terms a compilation must be a collection of works which are not independent and can no longer be retrieved independently. A compilation could, for example, be a collection of sentences from various documents, which have been put together to form a single new text. Although the materials included still form a collection of works, they have in a sense lost their independence. If they are retrieved independently they probably

---

[19] S. 3(1) CDPA 1988.

make no sense, or at least they do not serve the primary function of the collection.

Coming back to the problem created by a compilation of artistic works, one has to conclude that this has now been solved and that any incompatibility with the provisions of the Berne Convention arguably no longer exists. A collection of artistic works, in which these works remain independent of one another and can be accessed as such, as is, for example, the case with a catalogue for an exhibition, must now be a database, at least if it also meets the originality criterion at a second stage. A collection of artistic works, which are no longer independent from one another, but have, for example, been integrated to form a new work, must be a collage, and it is protected as such as an artistic work, once again subject to the originality criterion. A last point that can be added is that the Berne Convention leaves the definition of the originality criterion to the Member States. A natural consequence of this is that the use of a different originality criterion for databases cannot have any influence on the definition of a compilation. In practical terms a database that is not original cannot be picked up and put into the category of compilations. The two concepts, according to the recent amendments to the UK's Copyright Act, are mutually exclusive. On a few occasions one might be confronted with a database that is not original under the slightly higher EU criterion for originality, but that would meet the originality criterion for compilations. This database will not be protected, since a compilation has now been defined in such a way that it excludes databases. The originality criterion is not considered at all at this first stage. Although this is the UK approach, similar developments are bound to occur in other EU countries as a result of the introduction of a special regime of protection for databases.

4.1.7 Belgium

Almost the same restrictive approach as the British one is taken in the Belgian Copyright Act. By definition, literary works and the word 'compilation' do not appear in the Act. They are implied from the wording of 'writings of any kind'.[20] If the notion of 'writing' is approached in its strict sense, compilations of exclusively artistic works do not immediately fall within the 'writings of any kind'. Thus, it remains questionable whether or not compilations that consist exclusively of artistic works are protected under the Belgian Copyright Act.[21]

---

[20] Art. 8(1) of the Belgian Copyright Act. See also J. Corbet, *Auteursrecht*, Story – Scientia, Brussels, 1997, at 29.
[21] Their qualification, however, as artistic works should not be altogether excluded.

Collections and compilations 79

4.2 THE NOTION OF WORKS AS COMPONENTS OF A COMPILATION

Two further questions arise in the same context. First, does a collection qualify for copyright protection only when it includes copyrightable material or when it also includes some material which is non-copyrightable? Secondly, what if a collection includes works which are no longer under copyright protection, since their term of protection has expired? Do these works qualify as components of a copyrightable compilation?

These issues were considered in relation to the wording of the Berne Convention. By providing only for collections of literary or artistic works, the Berne Convention was clearly leaving out of the collections' scope of protection those collections of material which are not capable of attracting copyright.[22] This is only a minimum level of protection though, and Member States remain free to offer protection to other types of works as well as to raise the general level of protection. On top of their Berne commitments, they can also offer protection to compilations of non-copyrightable material. One could take the view that the words 'collections of literary and artistic works' refer back to the Copyright Acts of the Member States and that only works that qualify for copyright protection are included. This view was put forward in the original proposal for the text of article 2(5) of the Convention at the Brussels Conference. The actual wording that was suggested was '... without prejudice to any copyright which subsists in each of the works' or '... without prejudice to the rights of the author existing in each of the works'. That referred specifically to existing copyright in the literary works. That combination could no longer be met if copyright no longer subsisted in the works. The words 'subsists' and 'existing' have been deleted from that proposal even if the final text does not explicitly spell out that copyright in these works may have expired.[23] In spite of the remaining uncertainty in the text of the article, it must be presumed from this deletion that it is irrelevant whether copyright in the works still exists (or ever existed). The final conclusion must be that literary or artistic works should be seen as literary or artistic works that are in copyright or that have been in copyright for the purposes of article 2(5) of the Berne Convention.

Moreover, in the case where, in a compilation consisting of literary or artistic works, other non-copyrightable material, such as data, facts, etc.

---

[22] See in this respect the Greek (2121/1993), German (1965), Indian (1957) and Japanese (1970) copyright laws.
[23] Documents 1948, 94–5, 147, 152, 157.

is also found, the collection would still qualify for copyright protection, to the extent that this other material was ancillary and the literary or artistic works constituting the main content of the collection were selected or[24] had been arranged in such a way that the collection amounted to an intellectual creation.

4.3 THE BOND BETWEEN LITERARY WORKS, COMPILATIONS AND MULTIMEDIA WORKS

4.3.1 Differences between traditional literary works and compilations

Up to now we have seen that compilations and collections are generally dealt with as literary works, but that they do not fit in easily with the standard types of literary works. As we mentioned earlier, collections are one of the first examples of the depurification of traditional literary works. It is to those differences that we now return in more detail. The written format is still there but all other aspects are different. The first difference refers to originality. In a normal literary work the content of the work is the main area where originality is required and found. By definition the level of originality of a compilation is not determined with reference to its contents. Any originality refers strictly to the structure and the compiling of the contents. The works compiled retain their primary regime of protection. This is also the reason why many jurisdictions refer to them as derivative works, in other words works deriving from original ones. Their construction depends on the use of pre-existing original works. The task of compiling pre-existing materials is not always an original task. In order to be so it requires creativity. To make it clear that an original structure is required, the Berne Convention found it advisable to make a clear reference to the fact that compilations, in order to qualify for copyright protection, had to constitute 'intellectual creations'.

The same requirement does not appear with regard to traditional literary works. As Ricketson observes, 'this stipulation is necessary in the case of these kinds of borderline works, [but] it hardly needs to be stated in relation to the "mainline" works covered by article 2(1)'.[25]

---

[24] Although the provision of the Berne Convention referring to collections requires 'selection and arrangement' of their contents, the generally accepted interpretation is that selection and arrangement do not have to exist cumulatively. This interpretation is also supported by the authoritative French text of the Convention. This text does not provide for *et* but for *ou*. The two requirements should therefore be read as alternative requirements.

[25] Ricketson, *Berne Convention*, at 230.

This bond between literary works and collections became even looser when Member States decided to include collections of data within the scope of protection of collections. This was actually a clear indication that the market reality and the emergence of new intellectual property products was setting its own rules and that Member States had to catch up with the evolution. Copyright was stretched even more. What Ricketson describes as borderline works and all compilations of data, etc., are surely no longer standard examples of literary works that can be dealt with easily or satisfactorily within the standard literary works rules. If compilations are a case of bastard literary works, the fact that multimedia products are a case of bastard compilations[26] leads by implication to the conclusion that multimedia products have an even looser bond with literary works compared to the bond compilations have with them.

The contribution an author of a compilation is making is the selection, arrangement and editing of the works of others.[27] He does not create anything from scratch in the sense that a writer would, for example, author a novel. For that very reason what an author of a compilation really gains in the end is not the right to the contents of the collection but the rights in the creativity he has exercised in assembling the materials and arranging them. This is also the protection he is afforded in reality. Protection in this sense is a quasi-copyright protection, since the originality and creativity he exercises is quasi-creativity, by necessity limited in scope and one perhaps which resembles only vaguely the creativity exercised by an author of a traditional literary work.

The second difference between a compilation and a traditional literary work is that what is valuable and worth protecting about a compilation is not the content, as is the case with a standard literary work, but the structure, the arrangement and the selection of the content. Similar issues arise in relation to computer programs where the structure plays an important role in cases of non-literal copying. The difficulties that one is faced with when applying the substantial copying test for infringement were illustrated graphically by Jacob J in the *Ibcos* case.[28] In this case the judge pointed out that it is not only the 'literal similarities' between two computer programs that have to be taken into account, so as to find out if copying has taken place, but also 'program features' and 'design features'. This is especially so when literal copying on its own does not prove useful or adequate in cases where the computer program at issue was translated into another computer language. In such cases immediate literal

---

[26] See section 4.3.2 below.
[27] It can also be the compilation of his own works. See art. 2(3) of the Berne Convention.
[28] *Ibcos Computers Ltd and another v. Barclays Mercantile Highland Finance Ltd and others* [1994] FSR 275, at 302.

copying is not visible and therefore not adequate for establishing a case of infringement when comparing the original to the copied software.[29]

4.3.2 Multimedia products and compilations

4.3.2.1 *'Productions'*

One might wonder at this stage, if copyright were stretched to include compilations of materials other than works, whether multimedia products should merit a further deviation from traditional copyright law. Indeed the Berne Convention, in referring to literary and artistic works in article 2(1), uses the term 'productions'.[30] 'Productions' is considered to be a term that is charged with the values of a market economy and which carries commercial connotations. Probably the use of another less market-orientated term would indicate the inclusion of works only within the ambit of literary works. Yet, the word 'production' was not intended to play a central role in the definition of literary works. Creative elements are still required for the emergence of a new work. The definition of 'works' is to be found in the expression of literary and artistic works and not in that of 'production'. The latter is there to indicate that a work has to be first realised and come into existence before it is protected. The procedure of bringing a work into existence and realising it can well be called production. It is suggested here that one should consider its impact on any literary or artistic work to this extent only.

Multimedia products, though products in the same sense, can still be works in so far as they constitute independent creations of the mind and carry the author's personal imprint. The rule nowadays, however, is for multimedia products to be works serving particular commercialised functions. Their commercial function is the prevailing one, and their market success is decisive even for their structure. The form and structure in which they are marketed is dictated less by the judgment of their designer and producer and more by the market economy and the commercial needs. Multimedia products are successful only when they are comprehensive, affordable and easy to use.[31] In this sense multimedia works are conceived, planned and marketed as products in the narrow

---

[29] See, for example, *John Richardson Computers Ltd* v. *Flanders* [1993] FSR 497.
[30] 'The expression "literary and artistic works" shall include every production in the literary, scientific and artistic domain, whatever may be the mode or form of its expression...'.
[31] 'Retailers and distributors of CD-ROM titles recognise the inherent risk of selling titles into an emerging consumer market that wants products that combine the latest technology, design sophistication and ease of use.' J. Tamer, 'The returns of CD-ROM' in M. Radcliffe and W. Tannenbaum (eds.), *Multimedia and the law 1996. Protecting your clients' interests*, Practicing Law Institute, New York, 1996, at 23.

sense of the word.[32] Collections have been developed in a form that can be included in many national jurisdictions, and have lately been included in all European Union jurisdictions. There are also collections just of data and facts. As such, multimedia works might eventually sit well with the new legislative reality. The fact that multimedia products include pre-existing materials (copyrightable or non-copyrightable), compiled so as to create a new work, means they can occasionally come within the scope of compilations, in so far as the collection of materials is their prevailing characteristic. Certain issues, however, are bound to cause inconsistencies with the initial concept of a traditional compilation.

4.3.2.2 *Analogue and digital environments*

The traditional notion of collections was conceived and drafted in an analogue environment. That means that any works within the scope of protection of the collections (which is also the scope of protection of other literary works) have been designed in such a way as to protect the rights of authors of works fixed on hard copies, circulating as such and being copied in an environment which is more or less controllable. Multimedia products, though they may eventually appear in hard-copy format, i.e. CD-ROMs, CD-Is, etc., have long rejected any analogue environment in which to perform their functions. They are incorporated and operated in a digital environment. That means that their contents, which at first sight are illegible, can be manipulated, copied and transformed more easily.

4.3.2.3 *Manipulation of content in multimedia products*

Multimedia products do not even possess the characteristics of a compilation. Traditional compilations are found in hard-copy format and are accessed manually. No computer program is to be found in their actual corpus. The selection and arrangement of their contents is the initial and final work of their author–compiler. Their author chooses the material to be included in the compilation from potentially any material in the world. He arranges it and gives it its single, final and definitive format

---

[32] Intellectual property law should not in theory examine the end purpose of a producer of an intellectual property product. What is important for intellectual property law is whether the work at issue meets the requirements of a work, set out in the relevant provisions. Yet, at certain times it is in the market context that intellectual property works should be tested and the repercussions of the exclusive rights afforded to them on that market examined.

before marketing it. No possible alterations of his edition by third parties can take place, unless, of course, the author's permission is given. If such alterations occur, the rights of the author of the compilation are infringed.

In a multimedia product it is the user who makes the selection and arrangement of the contents of the work by ordering them on his screen. The alterations initiated by the user come within the scope of normal use. If any creativity is involved in the selection and arrangement, it lies with the user. The user is the real compiler of the end result and the one who re-arranges it as many times as he wishes. Of course, his selection and arrangement is somehow predestined and predefined by the prior selection of materials by the producer of the multimedia product and the number of entries available. It is predefined to a narrower extent than that of a compilation by reason of the materials being available in the public domain (materials which are accessible by reason of costs, difficulty of tracing them, confidentiality, etc.). The producer of the multimedia work supplies the contents and the tools for their manipulation. The user compiles the content and also interacts with them.

Does this mean that encyclopaedias and anthologies, as the characteristic examples of collections, cannot take the format of a multimedia product? On the contrary, they can take this format but it is not their traditional format. Digital interactive encyclopaedias and anthologies which are, for example, marketed as CD-ROMs or DVDs distributed or communicated on the Internet do not have much in common with traditional anthologies and encyclopaedias marketed as books.

4.3.2.4 *Integration of works in multimedia products*

Compilations traditionally incorporate one or two forms of expression. Usually the works incorporated are text, or text and images. Although these works are put in the form of a book in the pre-multimedia tradition, they still do not lose their original format. In other words, text remains text, and an image remains an image. A particular characteristic of multimedia products is that they incorporate a vast number of different kinds of works and expressions, which, because of their digitisation, are no longer found in their original format after their integration into the multimedia product. A photograph, a painting, a sculpture or a film are all images, which take the same format and which are made up of binary code from information inserted in the authoring computer program as 0s and 1s. When all this information is integrated,

Collections and compilations

it is one work only which is visible and comprehensive: the multimedia work as a whole. This work has taken a new single format, separate and distinguishable from the one its combining elements had. That format is digital.

4.3.2.5 Redefinition of the written format of a work

Since elements of a multimedia product are inserted into it as binary code, we may wonder whether they meet the requirements of being expressed in writing. Normally the requirement that the work be expressed in writing refers to the ordinary, standard way in which the work is expressed. This is how, for example, a written text is distinguished from an artistic work. It does not stop anyone though from describing the artistic work in writing in such a way that a reasonably clear image is conveyed to the reader and in such a way that the reader could eventually attempt to recreate the artistic work on the basis of the description, however difficult or nigh impossible such a recreation might be. The conclusion must therefore be that a sequence of binary code that is the expression of an artistic work should not be treated as the expression in writing of the work itself, making that work a literary work. It should rather be treated as analogous to a translation of a work. This means that the argument that a multimedia work, which includes various types of works, becomes a literary work because it is expressed in binary code cannot be accepted. Many of the works included will not originally have been expressed in writing. One could, of course, add the fact that in the near future more and more works, for example photographs and films, will be created in a digital format. This will happen through the use of digital cameras, for example. That could lead to the argument that these works should be treated as literary works because in their original format they were expressed in writing.

It is submitted that this argument cannot be accepted either. The primary aim of a photograph, irrespective of the way in which it is technically produced, is still to convey an image rather than a text. The impact of this becomes obvious if one takes a standard infringement case as an example. If it is alleged that a digitally produced photograph has been copied, it is highly unlikely that the court will first of all compare the two sets of binary codes to determine whether a substantial part of the original photograph has been copied. The court will rather look at the two photographs in the format in which they are presented to the general public to decide whether a substantial part has been copied. For those works that are perceptible in their conventional format, it would be counter-productive to argue that from a purely dogmatic legalistic point of view one should turn to the written format in binary code, simply because it now exists. This approach may be required for non-perceptible items, such as computer programs,[33] but it should be restricted to these cases. Binary code may be a form, but it is an incomprehensible form, which means that it cannot fulfil the clarifying role that was originally attributed to writing in copyright legislation. Originally, it was much easier to define the exact scope of the work if the work was expressed in writing. It was also easier to distinguish written works from other types of works, such as artistic or musical works. All this presupposes the use of the written version of a language that is comprehensible to at least part of the population. Binary code cannot fulfil that purpose and should therefore be distinguished even from the more sophisticated computer languages and from exotic languages.[34]

4.3.2.6 Functions of traditional compilations and multimedia works

A conventional compilation serves a role which is different from that of a multimedia product. The elements of a compilation are put together to provide some information in a particular area. The value of the compilation consists of bringing those elements together and editing them in that particular way. Although a multimedia product also brings some elements together (fewer works and more data), it does not aim at a particular selection and arrangement. It aims only at offering the opportunity to the eventual user for making various possible uses of them. A conventional compilation is valuable because of its definite format, and because of that format it is also afforded copyright protection, whereas a multimedia product is valuable because it has no definite format. The value of the former in descriptive terms could be compared to the value of the sum of its parts, whilst the value of a multimedia product consists of the value of the new works that can be initiated by the user using the sum of its parts.[35]

---

[33] A. Strowel and J. P. Triaille, *Le droit d'auteur, du logiciel au multimédia* (*Copyright, from software to multimedia*), Bruylant, Brussels, 1997, at 356. Computer programs are still not compared in a binary code format, but rather as their data are expressed in a high-level computer language, such as Cobol, Pascal, etc.

[34] *Ibid.*

[35] See B. Wittweiler, 'Produktion von Multimedia und Urheberrecht aus schweizerischer Sicht' (1995) 128 *UFITA* 5, at 9, where he argues that under Swiss law at least some multimedia products may be classified as compilations. See also, in the context of German law, F. Koch, 'Software – Urheberrechtsschutz für Multimedia – Anwendungen' [1995] *GRUR* 459, at 463.

4.3.2.7 The limits of interactivity

In conclusion, the main argument in favour of defining multimedia works as compilations for the purposes of copyright is the fact that interactivity, which is one of the main characteristics of multimedia works, can be seen as a further development of the assembling, cutting and pasting operation of a compilation. This argument, although it carries substantial weight, cannot be conclusive. A multimedia work takes this point much further, because not only are the works not independently accessible, but they are fragmented and reintegrated to such an extent that any result is necessarily composed of a vast number of these pieces the origin of which can no longer be established.[36]

The main argument against multimedia works being seen as compilations is that the definition of a compilation is closely associated with that of a literary work. In terms of components, a multimedia work should be composed of literary works to meet the criterion that it has to be in writing to qualify as a compilation. Whilst this may not cause problems for a limited number of rather primitive multimedia works, the opposite is true for the vast majority of more recent multimedia works that are wider in scope in that they necessarily include various other types of works on top of any literary work or works. The final outcome of this analysis must be that multimedia works cannot simply be considered as examples or a subcategory of compilations.

The disadvantage in relation to compilations can at first sight be seen as an advantage in relation to the classification of multimedia products as databases. Indeed, at first sight, databases form the next obvious candidate, since it could be said that most multimedia works include some form of database and a software tool to work with that database. It is to the relationship between multimedia products and databases that we now turn. This analysis will reveal that a superficial similarity may not render the database classification as viable as it may at first seem.

---

[36] The fact that the various components of a multimedia work can no longer be distinguished easily is due not only to their being digitised (for example, a photograph, a painting or an engraving are all images for the purposes of a multimedia product, and they can only be distinguished from sounds or text), but also to the fact that the volume of data they incorporate is far greater than that incorporated in a compilation. As we described in the first chapter of this book, such a quantitative differentiation necessarily has qualitative effects as well. A multimedia product cannot be approached as a mere collection of a limited number of works. In addition, integration plays a very important role.

5 Databases

5.1 THE DATABASE FRAMEWORK

When the EU database Directive was enacted in early 1996,[1] there was much discussion about it being at the same time a multimedia Directive. Multimedia products at that stage seemed to be blocked in many countries from coming under the protection of compilations on the basis that, although they were considered to form some sort of compilation, they did not contain only works (as originally required in the Berne Convention and consequently in the laws of many of its Member States), but other materials as well. In fact most of their contents were data, information which would not qualify under any regime as material capable of attracting copyright protection.[2] The second problem multimedia products were presenting was the fact that they were not coming anywhere near to the conventional book-format of manually accessible compilations. Multimedia products, if held to be compilations, could only be digital ones. It was not clear in the Berne Convention and the laws of many countries, which did not expressly provide for the protection of databases, that traditional compilations could be legitimately extended to cover digital or electronic compilations. Since, by the enactment of legislation concerning the protection of databases at Community level, these two hurdles disappeared, there were many commentators who stood by the opinion that any distinction between databases and multimedia products would be both unwise and impractical. This would be so especially in a period where the protection for both was seen to be at the heart of developments in the worldwide new technologies market.

The EU legislation was not the first legislation to provide copyright protection for databases. Apart from many national legislations, the TRIPs

---

[1] EU database Directive (96/9/EC) on the legal protection of databases, [1996] OJ L77/20.
[2] We should, of course, take into account the variations between the different jurisdictions. In the common law jurisdictions, as explained, it is more likely that functional and utilitarian material will attract copyright protection. See the TV programme listings in *Magill* (Joint Cases C-241/91P and C-242/91P, *Radio Telefis Eireann and Independent Television Publications Ltd* v. *Commission* [1995] ECR I-743, [1995] 4 CMLR 718).

Agreement did so in its article 10.2. The WIPO Copyright Treaty at a later stage provided for the same kind of protection: 'Compilations of data or other material, in any form, which by reason of the selection or arrangement of their contents constitute intellectual creations, are protected as such.'[3]

Both the WCT and the TRIPs Agreement provide copyright protection for databases by reason of the selection and arrangement of their contents. However, no precise definition of databases is given. The first complete definition found in a legal instrument is contained in the EU Directive. According to its article 1.2, a database is held to be 'a collection of independent works, data or other materials arranged in a systematic or methodical way and individually accessible by electronic or other means'.

A first issue which is clarified right from the start is that the computer programs used in the making or operation of databases are not to be included in the scope of protection of the databases. Any computer programs qualifying for copyright protection are to be dealt with under the software Directive.[4]

According to the EU Directive's wording, both manual and electronic compilations are covered. Electronic or digital compilations are those which are arranged, stored and accessed by electronic, electromagnetic, electro-optical or analogous processes. Not all stages of constructing a database have to undergo the aforementioned processes, though. It is submitted that it is the final one which is decisive. Thus, even if a database is manually arranged, stored electronically with the aid of a scanner and accessed electronically by means of a computer program, it is still considered to be an electronic database.

The contents of a database can be wide-ranging. Any literary work or text of any kind, any artistic or dramatic work as well as any kind of image, diagram, figure or number, any kind of musical work or equally any sound can qualify as contents of a database.[5] There is no limit to the number of works or materials included but there are some limits as to the type of content.[6] There is no requirement about the function these materials are meant to serve in the context of a database and no specific type of combination of the materials required. *In toto* the scope of the contents of a database is very wide. It is perhaps obvious to say that the materials included in a database do not have to be capable of

---

[3] WCT, signed in Geneva on 20 December 1996, art. 5.
[4] Council Directive (91/250/EEC) on the legal protection of computer programs, [1991] OJ L122/42.
[5] See Recital 17 to the EU database Directive.
[6] Three-dimensional objects and the mere storage of quantities of works or materials in electronic form are excluded. See the Explanatory Memorandum, COM (93) 464 final-SYN 393, at 41.

being put in a written format, as was previously required in the UK's Copyright Act in relation to compilations; firstly, because the Directive expressly provides for artistic works as well, and secondly, because the digitisation of the materials inevitably transforms any kind of information into one and the same digital format. Yet, three limitations exist. First of all the materials, which form the contents of a database, have to be independent. The two other requirements are that these materials have to be individually accessible and that the contents of the database have to be arranged in a systematic or methodical way. We will now turn to the detailed examination of each of these requirements.

5.1.1 'Independent' contents

That the contents of a database have to be independent seems to be a simple statement. What is meant by this requirement is not defined, though. If we combine this requirement with what we usually consider as being the classic example of a database, we could surmise that by 'independent' the drafters of the Directive meant materials which can stand on their own, whether they are extracts or whole works. It is reasonable to assume that by 'database' the average person understands a telephone or street directory, or some other kind of catalogue containing various related entries, each with a similar value in relation to the area covered. Independent materials from such projects as these can only be materials which are valuable on their own, because of the information they carry; information which is considered in some sense to be 'complete' information. For example, the information an address gives to its reader can be considered to be a complete and independent piece of information. Its value is enhanced in the context of a database because it brings various pieces of information together and combines them so as to give a global and comprehensive image in relation to a particular area or in relation to a particular subject.

5.1.2 'Individually accessible' contents

The requirement that the materials included in a database be independent forms only the first test for a project to qualify as a database. The second test, which seems to be linked to the first one, is that the materials have to be 'individually accessible'. The fact that these two tests are linked or closely related to each other derives from the fact that an element that is independent in a database can also perform a useful and complete function when it is retrieved on its own. In order for it to be capable of being retrieved on its own, it has to be individually accessible.

The requirement that the materials that are included in a database have to be capable of being accessed individually was put there to exclude any works which serve a different purpose and therefore do not present this option. For that reason any collective works which do not aim at the collection of data, but at a unified literary, artistic or dramatic result, clearly cannot qualify as databases. Films are a characteristic example of this. Although a film consists of separate frames carried on pellicle, these frames are meaningful only when seen as a series of moving images and not separate from one another. In the same sense any recording, or any other audiovisual or cinematographic work, would fall foul of the requirements of the database Directive.[7] Computer programs and video games are further examples.[8] The elements incorporated in them make sense and perform their actual intellectual and commercial functions only when seen in a sequence. They are clearly works which are not capable of being accessed individually. However, a collection of computer programs, of video games or of films is always possible and would fall within the definition of a database.

If the requirement for the elements of a database to be individually accessible did not exist, the wide-ranging definition with regard to the contents of a database would bring within its scope almost every possible kind of work. The result would be the creation of overlapping protection for certain works. Consequently, a second layer of copyright protection would exist, affording more exclusive rights to more people.[9] Apart from the fact that the general copyright system would become confusing, there would no longer be a reason for particular definitions of any specific types of intellectual property products. If, for example, a work could qualify for database protection, there would be no reason to check whether the same work came within the definition of a film as well. The provisions on databases could serve the database author well enough on their own without the need for recourse to any other intellectual property legislation.

This would destabilise the whole copyright system, especially in common law countries where every intellectual property product has to be put neatly into its correct category if it is to qualify for copyright protection. Any interchangeability between the various regimes of protection would lead to abuse of rights, circumvention of obligations and paralysis of certain provisions. What would be the purpose, for example, of offering a

---

[7] *Ibid.*
[8] L. Kaye, 'The proposed EU Directive for the legal protection of databases: a cornerstone of the information society?' [1995] 12 *EIPR* 583.
[9] It goes without saying that the presence of more layers of protection necessarily renders the commercial exploitation of the work more difficult, since more rights will need to be cleared.

database seventy-year copyright protection, if the same database could also qualify for protection as a film, and extend its seventy-year term of protection by starting to calculate it from the death of the last co-author of the film?

One possible solution could be to abandon the different categories of works altogether in the light of their transformation into a single digitised format[10] and provide for one kind of copyright protection only, applicable to all kinds of works.[11] That could theoretically facilitate the use of copyright and prevent possible abuses in the area. However, it would call for a radical reconstruction of the whole copyright system, which would at best disregard the differences in nature between the various intellectual property works. A level of detail would thus be lost in such a system, because these differences in nature lead to differences in the precise format of protection.

Instead of banning the various categories of works altogether, another idea, perhaps, would be to avoid attempts at defining the exact scope of these categories. The EU software Directive, for example, avoided any definition with regard to computer programs, out of fear that any definition was bound to be outdated sooner or later by reason of the rapid technological developments. Another example is the recent Belgian Copyright Act, which does not define the various categories of works, but nevertheless provides for different regimes of protection in relation to different categories of works by referring to them by their generic terms, e.g. literary works, databases, films, computer programs, etc. Such a regime of protection carries with it the danger in the future of losing track of the precise scope of the works it puts into the different categories. Although it is not difficult now to define with a great degree of certainty what a film is, and even easier to recognise one when you see it, this will not necessarily be the case in the future. Different products will be capable of falling into different categories, and there will be no precise definition to prevent them from doing so. That will result in undesirable overlaps between the different regimes of protection.

In conclusion, two feasible options remain. However, whether one opts for various categories of works, each linked to a specific bundle of rights and exceptions, or whether one opts for a single category of works, with a single bundle of rights and exceptions, problems remain. Neither system produces an ideal solution.

---

[10] This argument disregards the fact that a work exists in an analogue format before it is digitised. That analogue format can be very different depending on the type of work. Its subsequent digitisation cannot undo that original difference.
[11] See A. Christie, 'Reconceptualising copyright in the digital era' [1995] 11 *EIPR* 522, at 525.

5.1.3 Systematic and methodical arrangement of contents

The third and final test for a work to qualify as a database is whether its contents are arranged in a systematic or methodical way. The mere storage of quantities of works or materials in electronic form will fall foul of such a requirement.[12] Yet, it will only be rare or remote cases where the contents of a database will not be subject to some kind of method or arrangement.[13] In most cases this method or arrangement is also the one that enables the contents to be individually accessible with the help of a software tool. Yet, the kind of method or arrangement required is not specified in the text of the Directive. What is likely is that any arrangement of the contents of a database in most cases will not be the result of the individual judgment of its author. More and more databases are the result of planning on the part of their developers, who, in order to realise them, have to make them subject to certain technical rules, dictated by their making and operating software. Thus, part of the planning of a database is initiated or semi-initiated and realised by computers. Any arrangement would look even more absurd, if one applied it in relation to the storage of the contents in the memory of some computer in binary code.[14] This requirement, of course, is banned by Recital 21 to the Directive. What is not specified, however, is whether any method of arranging the materials will be judged before or after the materials have been inserted into the memory of the computer. If it is the latter, what is the role, if any, of the user of the database who initiates the various selections and arrangements of this material on his screen? Are these selections and arrangements to be taken into account? Is the user of such a product to be afforded any rights, at least to works that give him a wider scope of discretion and creativity, as is the case with interactive multimedia products?

Once these three requirements are met (independent materials methodically or systematically selected or arranged and capable of being accessed individually), a work can qualify as a database. No express, or even indicative, examples of such cases are given in the Directive. Yet, a number of works which do not meet the above tests are excluded.[15] Amongst these works one work, which does not immediately seem to fall foul of the aforementioned requirements, but which is however excluded from the scope of the Directive, is an ordinary audio CD. According to Recital 19 to the Directive, 'the compilation of several recordings of

---

[12] See the Explanatory Memorandum to the EU database Directive, at 41.
[13] Pure random arrangement of the contents of a database can eventually be held to be a kind of structure as well.
[14] Recital 21 to the Directive provides that it is not necessary for the contents of a database to have been physically stored in an organised manner.
[15] See the examples in section 5.1.2 above.

musical performances on a CD does not come within the scope of this Directive, both because as a compilation, it does not meet the conditions for copyright protection and because it does not present a substantial enough investment to be eligible under the *sui generis right*'.[16]

These requirements can refer to two points only: either to the originality requirement regarding the selection and arrangement of the contents of a database, or to the elements of the definition of a database. The former point has to be examined on a case-by-case basis and no theoretical conclusion is to be drawn in advance. In relation to the latter there is nothing to indicate that an ordinary CD does not include independent works, which have been arranged subject to a particular method or system, and which can be retrieved independently.[17] However, the inclusion of CDs in the scope of the Directive would unnecessarily extend a protection already afforded to sound recordings in the national copyright laws as neighbouring, related rights or copyright.[18] Yet, it is not clear whether the exclusion of CDs implies the exclusion of phonograms in general. This might eventually cause problems in case of databases seeking to provide information in the area of music. CD-ROMs and CD-Is, however, remain expressly within the Directive's scope of protection.[19]

5.2   BEYOND COPYRIGHT

The information which constitutes the contents of a database, whilst independent, is not separately or additionally protected by the copyright which is afforded to the database itself. This is so irrespective of whether the contents themselves are within copyright protection or not, or within any other kind of protection, e.g. trade marks, trade secrets, know-how, confidentiality, etc. Since databases are considered to be, in fact, an extension of traditional compilations, and since their value consists of the assemblage of the various materials, copyright protection can be afforded to them only in relation to the selection and arrangement of their materials.[20] This selection and arrangement has to be the author's own intellectual creation,[21] according to the wording of the database

---

[16] EU database Directive.
[17] Doubts remain in relation to the legally binding force of a Recital to a Directive or any other international, national or regional instrument. However, the interpreting impact of a Recital to the Directive seems to play a rather significant role.
[18] See CDPA 1988.
[19] See Recital 22 to the EU database Directive.
[20] The copyright protection afforded to the database has to be without prejudice to any rights subsisting in its contents. See art. 3.2 of the database Directive.
[21] Art. 3.1 of the database Directive.

Directive, which is the same in all EU Directives.[22] This is the yardstick against which databases are measured in order to pass the hurdle of originality, and to qualify as original databases within the requirements of article 3.1.

The originality criterion for a database to constitute its author's own intellectual creation, though lower than the continental one (which requires creativity and personal involvement to a greater degree), is still higher than the common law one (which requires skill and labour only). That means that many databases, which previously qualified for copyright protection under the common law system, will no longer be able to do so. There are, however, databases which remain outside the scope of copyright, even though a substantial amount of skill and labour has been invested in them, not to mention a substantial financial investment in most cases. These databases are in need of protection, albeit to a lesser degree, and that need for protection has been addressed.

It was essentially the aforementioned need which dictated the introduction of a *sui generis* regime of protection in relation to the contents of a database. That need is created irrespective of the fact that the contents of a database are themselves already protected by copyright or by some other right. The role of their initial copyright is to stop them from being copied without the authorisation of their rightholder. The role of the person who has incorporated those contents into a database, after having acquired the authorisation of their rightholder, is insignificant or non-existent in relation to their potential inclusion in a new database. That results in all the investment in time, money, effort and energy put into the construction of the database remaining unprotected, or partially protected through unfair competition law in those countries which provide such a law.

It is exactly the solution to this problem that the *sui generis* right, which was introduced by the database Directive, offers. The *sui generis* right is granted to the maker of the database, so as to allow him to prevent third parties from extracting[23] and/or re-utilising[24] the whole or substantial parts of his work without his authorisation. Yet, this right is subject to one prerequisite. The making of a database has to

---

[22] See the software Directive, and the Council Directive (93/98/EEC) harmonising the term of protection of copyright and certain related rights, [1993] OJ L290/9.

[23] Meaning, according to art. 2(a) of the database Directive, the 'permanent or temporary transfer of all or a substantial part of the contents of a database to another medium by any means or in any form'.

[24] Meaning, according to art. 2(b) of the Directive, 'any form of making available to the public all or a substantial part of the contents of a database by the distribution of copies, by renting, by on-line or other forms of transmission'.

involve a qualitatively and/or quantitatively substantial investment in the obtaining, verification or presentation of its contents.[25] This requirement constitutes the *raison d'être* of the *sui generis* right, which in fact is an unfair competition rule conceptualised and transformed into a positive intellectual property right.

It is essential to note three things so far. First, the *sui generis* right is a right afforded to the contents of a database and not to the database itself (meaning the selection, arrangement or other structure of its materials). Second, granting of a *sui generis* right instead of copyright to the maker of the database removes the potential danger of having two copyrights in the same material owned by different parties; one owned by the author of the original work or his successors in title, and the other owned by the maker of the database, in which the work is included. It could even be argued that the *sui generis* right itself has the potential to create ownership conflicts with the owner of the copyright in the database. Lastly, we have to bear in mind that the *sui generis* right is a *passe-par-tout* right, which is afforded to the contents of a database, irrespective of the fact that they themselves are protected by copyright or some other right, or irrespective of the fact that they form part of a database which is protected by copyright. The *sui generis* right is an additional layer of protection for any kind of independent materials of a database, which form the contents of a copyrightable or non-copyrightable database.

5.3   MULTIMEDIA PRODUCTS AS DATABASES

Many of the elements contained in the definition of a database are not easily transposed to a multimedia context.[26] We will consider these points in more detail in the next pages. Suffice it to say here that the requirement of systematic and methodical arrangement of materials does not create problems in relation to multimedia products. In the same way as a database, a multimedia product contains many materials and these materials are always arranged, one way or the other, in a systematic or methodical manner.

---

[25] Art. 7.1 of the database Directive.
[26] *Contra* U. Loewenheim, 'Urheberrechtliche Probleme bei Multimediaanwendungen' [1996] *GRUR* 830, at 832, who argues that in many cases a multimedia product can be classified as a database for copyright purposes. The Second Sirinelli Report (*Le régime juridique et la gestion des oeuvres multimédias*, CERDI, Paris, 1996) presents a more balanced view. It is argued there that many multimedia works will not meet the criteria of the EU database Directive and that it is not desirable to protect certain multimedia works in one way and others in another way. See also F. Genton, 'Multimedia im französischen Urheberrecht: der zweite Sirinelli Bericht' [1996] *GRUR Int* 693, at 695.

5.3.1 Interactivity versus 'individually accessible' contents

One could argue at this point that Recital 22 to the Directive, which expressly provides for the protection of CD-ROMs and CD-Is in relation to electronic databases, may actually refer to multimedia products as well, or at least refers to them in so far as interactive databases are held to be multimedia products. With regard to the definition that we gave of multimedia products in the first chapter of this book, we could argue that it is broad enough to include interactive databases as well. Still, more than one expression is combined on a single medium, either non-linear or linear, in a digitised form. Even if the database at issue contains only text accessed through hypertext links, the presence of a computer program, which allows for the retrieval of those texts and for the interactive dialogue between the user and the information included in the database, allows the database at issue to meet the requirement of combining more than one element of expression.

If we now look at the definition of a database, we will arrive at similar conclusions, though from the other end of the spectrum. The database definition allows for the simultaneous existence of more than one expression, and dictates the use of a computer program. However, there is no mention of interactivity. That does not seem to create any problems since it is not true of databases that by not expressly mentioning something, we imply that it must be excluded. Interactivity sits perfectly well with databases. It does not add to or transform any of their essential characteristics. On the contrary, it makes the requirement of 'individual accession' of their contents easier and more commercial. On top of that, some could also argue that interactivity is a feature attached to the computer program that runs the database, and that it is not to be judged under the definition of a database in the first place. Since interactivity substantially affects the image, nature and function of the whole multimedia product, we have to admit that, on this point at least, distinguishing databases from their operating software tool might make sense.[27]

Yet, not all multimedia products are databases in this sense. The modern multimedia applications do not aim to collect pieces of information, which the user can simply track down and access individually. Nowadays multimedia products are more than that. If we look into the components of a modern multimedia product and those of a database, we will probably see that both databases and multimedia products include a computer program to operate them. They both contain a large number of different kinds of works and expressions in some kind of systematic or methodical

---

[27] This issue will be discussed in chapter 7 below.

arrangement. In the case of a database, however, some things remain out of the scope of qualifying contents. For example, three-dimensional objects are not included. Some, of course, would regard this exception as insignificant compared to the bulk of works qualifying, but in the case of multimedia this is not so. If we admit that multimedia products will very soon move into the virtual reality world, where three-dimensional objects are more common, even if as will be seen later there is at least an issue as to whether all virtual works are really three-dimensional, excluding them is in fact putting a substantial obstacle in the way of their evolution. Of course, the exclusion of three-dimensional objects is not incorporated as such into the actual provisions of the database Directive. It is found only in the guidelines offered in its Explanatory Memorandum.[28] This Memorandum has by no means the same value as an express provision. It can only be interpreted with regard to the historical and social environment present at the stage of drafting the legislation to which it refers. That implies, of course, that it would not be illegal in the future if three-dimensional objects were found by a national judge to qualify as contents in a database. In reality, of course, most of the three-dimensional works that will be included in a multimedia work will be represented in a two-dimensional format that creates a three-dimensional impression. For these works the problem does not arise.

Apart from the computer program operating the work (both for databases and multimedia products), and the arrangement of almost the same scope of contents in a systematic or methodical way (as the law for databases requires), multimedia products seem to distinguish themselves when it comes to the requirement for their contents to be 'individually accessible'.[29] Two options are possible in relation to a multimedia product. The first is where the contents are both individually accessible and accessible in conjunction with one another, depending on the command the user of a database enters into the system. The second option is where the contents have been integrated into one another to such an extent that no individual access to them is possible. The question arising here is whether these multimedia products can still come under the protective umbrella of databases.

---

[28] Explanatory Memorandum, at 41.
[29] The exclusion of films from the scope of the database Directive also hints at the fact that the works in a database must be 'independent' from one another. This may not create problems in relation to encyclopaedia-style multimedia works, but many multimedia works unfold similarly to a film. The components of these latter works are surely not independent from each other. S. Beutler, 'The protection of multimedia products through the European Community's Directive on the legal protection of databases' [1996] *Ent LR* 317, at 323–4, argues therefore that this is another reason not to treat multimedia works as databases.

5.3.2 Multimedia products containing 'individually accessible' contents or contents which are both 'individually accessible' and capable of being retrieved conjunctively

We have to look separately at each of these two possible cases. In the case where the contents of a multimedia product are both individually accessible and accessible in conjunction with each other, part of it, relating to the entries which are individually accessible, can qualify as a database. The problem is, however, that it is not in practice feasible or advisable to protect only a part of a work, as would be the case here with the multimedia product. One of the possible protections has to take precedence. The question is which one? In a case where all (or most of) the contents of a multimedia product are individually accessible, undoubtedly that product qualifies as a database. The fact that the same contents can also be viewed in conjunction with each other should not normally create a problem. In this sense the multimedia product could qualify as a database.

In addition, the protection of a multimedia product as a database also presents the advantage that the contents of the former, by analogy with the latter, will also be protected when they are not selected or arranged in an original way. This protection will be afforded to them by reason of the *sui generis* right, if substantial investment in their collection, verification or presentation is made by the developer of the multimedia product. The mere storage, of course, of quantities of works or materials in electronic form will not qualify for copyright protection nor for *sui generis* protection.[30] Since the cases where such an investment will not exist will be rare, and since multimedia products do not necessarily always involve an original structure (selection and/or arrangement) in relation to their contents, the *sui generis* protection in relation to the latter is both desirable and commercially advantageous.[31]

Moreover, *sui generis* protection seems at first sight capable of closing gaps in the protection of multimedia products, analogous to those faced by databases some time ago. Although the existence of a *sui generis* protection for the contents of a multimedia product is good, it does not go far enough. This is because a multimedia product is more than the collection of its contents. The protection of the original structure of its contents by copyright and the protection of the assemblage of those contents by the *sui generis* right fails to encompass the whole of a multimedia product.

---

[30] See the Explanatory Memorandum to the Directive, at 41.
[31] See one of the first cases to be decided in Europe concerning databases under the new EU regime of protection, *Union nationale des mutualités socialistes* v. *SA Belpharma Communication*, Civ. Brussels (cess.), 16 March 1999, *JT* 1999, 305.

It encompasses only two-thirds of it, which in fact constitutes only the database that a multimedia product includes as part of its functions, together with the computer program. Yet, as we mentioned earlier, the multimedia product is more than just a database. It is a new creation,[32] the functions of which share few of the functions of a database. The protection of only parts of it disregards the nature of the multimedia product and disregards its arguably different needs as a totally new product.

In order to represent a multimedia product graphically, we could present it as a circle. One-third of the circle will be occupied by the computer program and the operating materials of the product. The second third will be occupied by the database contained in the multimedia product. The final third will be occupied by the new creation, which allows for the contents to be viewed in conjunction with each other. It is this final third which outstrips the concept of a database. Here we can refer only to a new creation which, though it encompasses a database, is the multimedia product.

Exceptionally, very simple, or should one say simplistic, multimedia products may present a different picture. If there is no real added value in terms of original work, and if the interactivity element is contained solely in the software, it might be argued that one is really confronted with a combination of a database and a computer program. In this exceptional scenario, where there is no full integration of the contents and where, in combination with the interactivity, this does not lead to the addition of another layer of added value, the resulting multimedia product could be protected as a database if one keeps in mind that the database model also includes separate protection for the computer software.[33]

5.3.3 Conjunctively retrieved contents in multimedia products

The second case is where a multimedia product does not contain a database at all, because its contents can only be accessed in conjunction with each other. The application of the protection of databases in a multimedia product is not possible, since the database Directive specifically requires works to be individually accessible. In such cases we have to look for a regime of protection, the purpose of which is not the mere collection of materials, their systematic editing and their individual access. What is

---

[32] The additional value of this creation was made possible by the software (tools) that forms part of the multimedia product.
[33] For a favourable view on the database qualification see A. Wiebe and D. Funkat, 'Multimedia-Anwendungen als Urheberrechtlicher Schutzgegenstand' (1998) 2 *Multimedia und Recht* 69.

required is protection which covers the collection of materials and their systematic editing, so as to produce a literary, artistic or other outcome, which shows its value only when accessed as a whole, or at least as a sequence of some of its contents. This is where the emphasis is shifting: away from the collection of existing materials and towards the creation of a new integrated work. The new work has a substantial added value superseding that of the sum of its parts and deserving protection for that reason,[34] rather than simply for the structured collection of materials. This is something which is rather different from the normal concept of a database.[35]

Alternatively 'individually accessible' could in relation to multimedia products also mean that the work or component as such appears or can be made to appear independently on screen. That requirement can be met even if at the same time some other item appears too. Examples could be background pictures that go with text, or sound that is combined with images. In this sense a vast number of multimedia works could be taken to meet the database criteria. This interpretation bends the rules on databases to a great extent, and is clearly motivated by an overriding desire to find an adequate regime of protection for multimedia. Those who advocate it see the investment in a multimedia work (that uses other original works as components) as the essential point.[36] The database model

---

[34] This added value is partly due to the interactivity of the multimedia work. As Feldman points out, 'there is really little new in the notion of interactivity in electronic media. From the earliest times, electronic databases have been accessed by means of search and retrieval software. The design of the software coupled with the internal structuring of the database define the interactions users can have with the database. In other words, interactivity is really just another word for the ways in which a user can search and browse through an electronic database, the process being more or less constrained by the control software... The real difference in designing interactivity for multimedia lies in multimedia's *added richness and complexity*. To design a means of navigating effectively amongst thousands of images, video sequences, sound, text and numerics, all seamlessly combined as a single information resource, is a challenging problem and one that lies at the heart of successful multimedia applications', T. Feldman, *Multimedia in the 1990s. BNB Research Fund Report*, British Library, 1991, at 8–9 (emphasis added).
[35] Perhaps this type of multimedia product has more in common with a film. See also A. Latreille, 'The legal classification of multimedia creations in French law' in I. Stamatoudi and P. Torremans (eds.), *Copyright in the new digital environment*, Sweet & Maxwell, London, 2000, 43, at 70–1, where he argues that 'a multimedia product distinguishes itself from a database by means of the creativity that is required for its creation. A multimedia work is a work based on a script or scenario, whereas the database corresponds simply to a rational logic. Evidence of this is found in the fact that the computer software can often be detached from a database, whereas it is an integral part of a multimedia work.' In relation to the point concerning creation the author further refers to the Report of the Sénat, *Les nouveaux services de communication audiovisuelle et l'industrie multimédia* (Document Sénat No. 245, Paris, 1995, at 24).
[36] Some have argued in this respect that the multimedia model is primarily suited to a collection of data and that it is less suited to a collection of original works. That objection must also play a part here since most multimedia works will be composed of original works rather than of data. See T. Desurmont, 'L'exercice des droits en ce qui concerne les

has that kind of protection as its essential feature and is therefore a suitable model. In reality this is not what 'individually accessible' is supposed to mean. The user should be able to lift a single item out of a compilation of data in isolation, otherwise almost anything could potentially be seen as a database.[37] A multimedia work does not make that possible. Rather it offers combinations and integrated versions of bits and pieces of elements that are contained in it. It tries to offer added value on top of that of the single components.[38]

5.3.4 The compilation alternative

If databases are to be abandoned (wholly or partly) as a possible or as the only possible regime of protection for multimedia products, the first obvious alternative which comes to mind is compilations. A compilation may in certain cases, where this is provided by the law of a state, contain materials other than works. These materials are not necessarily capable of being put into a written format and do not have to be individually accessible. This addresses the difficulty raised in the previous paragraph in respect of databases. In that sense at least, certain multimedia products might have more in common with the concept of a compilation. However, as we explained in the chapter on compilations, this is not entirely true since a compilation puts the emphasis of the protection it offers on the stable selection and arrangement of existing materials, whilst the multimedia work is in need of protection for the new work that is created and that corresponds better to the content rather than the structure.[39] A study by the Max-Planck-Institut demonstrated that both compilations and databases suffer from the same defect when they are drafted in to protect multimedia products. They focus on the selection and juxtaposition of individual elements. A multimedia product focuses on the integration

"productions multimédias"' in *WIPO international forum on the exercise and management of copyright and neighbouring rights in the face of the challenges of digital technology*, Seville, 14–16 May 1997, WIPO, 1998, 169, at 178; Sirinelli Report on multimedia and new technologies, France, Ministère de la culture et de la Francophonie, Paris, 1994, at 58–9.

[37] Such a wide application of the concept of a database was clearly not the intention of the drafters of the database Directive. They saw the 'individually accessible' requirement as an essential tool to block an unduly wide application of the Directive.

[38] M. Bullinger and E.-J. Mestmäcker, "Multimediadienste – Aufgabe und Zuständigkeit von Bund und Ländern – Rechtsgutachten," Opinion prepared for the Bundesministerium für Bildung, Wissenschaft, Forschung und Technologie, 1996, http://www.pitt.edu/~wwwes/teu.mspr-ge-b.html. See also J. Bizer, V. Hammer, U. Pordesch and A. Rossnagel, 'Entwurf gesetzlicher Regelungen zum Datenschutz und zur Rechtssicherheit in Online-Multimedia-Anwendungen', Opinion prepared for the Bundesministerium für Bildung, Wissenschaft, Forschung und Technologie, 1996, http://www.uni-muester.de/jura.itm.hoeren/materialen/njw.pdf.

[39] See chapter 4 above.

of these individual elements into something 'extra' that gives added value to the product. This means that the compilation model is as little suited to multimedia products as the database model.[40] In addition, compilations present all the problems that are associated with the requirement of a written format and with the exclusion of certain types of works from their scope, at least in certain jurisdictions. This means that compilations cannot be a universally accepted alternative. A last important point is the fact that multimedia products are associated with the concept of interactivity. This means that they take the integration of the materials contained in them one step further than traditional compilations. In compilations the integration of works is given a fixed format. Such a fixed format will in most cases still allow individual access to each of the materials. Interactivity is the antithesis of any fixed format and allows for the full integration of the contents in a flexible way.

The second obvious candidate for protection with regard to multimedia products is films. In a film, different pre-existing works are put together in a systematic and methodical combination, so as to produce the artistic and/or informative result that the film is aiming at. In relation to films, the requirement of 'individual access' to their contents is also missing as it is in the case of some multimedia products. In the chapter that follows, we will discuss whether films are obvious or realistic candidates for the type of works that will offer effective protection to multimedia products.

---

[40] G. Schricker (ed.), *Urheberrecht auf dem Weg zur Informationsgesellschaft*, Nomos, Baden-Baden, 1997, at 41.

6 Audiovisual works

Unless multimedia works are projected onto a screen, their contents cannot be read, accessed or manipulated by users. The experience of copyright lawyers and others to date shows that there is, arguably at least, a strong presumption that data including, or mainly composed of, sound and images, which are projected onto a screen, falls within the category of audiovisual works. Thus, if we were to judge multimedia works according to their appearance or looks alone, we could argue that the one category of protection which seems most capable of accommodating multimedia products is that of audiovisual works.

This chapter will examine whether this initial presumption corresponds to the actual characteristics and needs of multimedia works when the issue is considered in detail. It will also consider whether the inclusion of elements of image and sound in a multimedia work is enough to place it under the legal umbrella of audiovisual works or related categories such as cinematographic works, films or motion pictures.[1]

6.1 'AUDIOVISUAL WORKS' AS A GENERIC TERM

6.1.1 Audiovisual works

Not all national jurisdictions contain a definition of audiovisual works in their copyright laws.[2] However, the French Copyright Act, in article L112-6, defines audiovisual works as 'works consisting of sequences of moving images, with or without sound'. From this definition it can be seen that an audiovisual work cannot exist unless a 'sequence of moving images' is not only present but also prevalent. This is the criterion for the existence of an audiovisual work. Although the term 'audiovisual' also

---

[1] Art. 95 of the German Copyright Act refers to 'moving pictures' as a notion which adds to the concept of cinematographic works. The former seem to include any sequence of images or images and sounds, which are not cinematographic works, in the sense that there is no performance involved.

[2] By the term 'copyright laws' we also mean the laws on neighbouring rights.

Audiovisual works

implies the existence of a sound element, this element is not necessary. Silent pictures or documentaries which present only visual documents without the addition of any sound also qualify as audiovisual works.

The definition of audiovisual works in the US Copyright Act, though more precise and descriptive, seems to be broader and more relaxed in relation to the existence of an element of 'moving images'. According to 17 USC § 101 (1988), audiovisual works are those works which 'consist of series of related images which are intrinsically intended to be shown by the use of machines, or devices such as projectors, viewers, or electronic equipment, together with accompanying sounds, if any, regardless of the nature of the material objects, such as films or tapes, in which the works are embodied'. According to the wording of this article no requirement of 'moving images' exists. Images have only to be sewn together, linked and shown one after the other.

Works containing 'moving images', though a subcategory of audiovisual works, constitute a separate category of works under the US Copyright Act. 'Motion pictures', as these works are called under the US Act, are in fact audiovisual works which contain the particular characteristic that 'when shown in succession, [they] impart an impression of motion'.[3]

Both in the USA and in France, as well as in Belgium,[4] 'audiovisual works' is a generic term within which certain subcategories are contained as species, i.e. cinematographic works, films and so on. So far one difference is apparent. As far as motion is required, we should look at a more precise kind of work than a general audiovisual work. Under US law, for example, we should look for 'moving pictures'. The notion of motion is not the only point of differentiation under the wide umbrella of audiovisual works. A second one is put forward in the Berne Convention in relation to the definition of cinematographic works.

6.1.2 Cinematographic works

In article 2(1) of the Berne Convention only cinematographic works are mentioned.[5] The decisive feature in relation to them is not the image or the sound, the motion or the absence of motion, but the use of a cinematographic process. The presence of the elements of image and sound are simply implied, as is the aspect of movement or at least the potential for movement. The definition or the requirement of these features is left with the Member States or implied by the traditional notion of cinematography. However, the Berne Convention mentions that cinematographic

---

[3] 17 USC § 101 (1988).
[4] Article 14 of the Belgian Copyright Act 1994.
[5] See also art. 9 of TRIPs, which refers to the Berne Convention.

works are not only those which we traditionally know as such. Works which are expressed by a process analogous to cinematography are also included.

At this point a first observation should be made.[6] Audiovisual works which are not expressed by a process analogous to cinematography may exist. These works, however, are not to be assimilated into cinematographic works. In practice, it would be rather rare for a work to be fixed and for the fixation or subsequent expression not to be subject to a method analogous to cinematography. However, even if such a case did exist, we can safely say that since cinematographic works stipulate more prerequisites in their definition, audiovisual works are larger in scope. The former therefore form a subcategory of the latter.

Berne's requirement of a process which is either cinematography or something similar to it strongly suggests the need for some kind of fixation. If there is no fixation, it is difficult to find or to assess any kind of process. This in a sense, however, contradicts article 2(2) of the Berne Convention, which provides that it is for the Member States 'to prescribe that works in general or any specified categories of works shall not be protected unless they have been fixed in some material form'.

According to Ricketson: 'in the case of cinematographic works, properly speaking, the question of fixation does not seem relevant, as the very process of making such a work implies fixation in a material form, that is, the recording of the optical images and sounds of the work on some material support'.[7]

The issue of which processes are analogous to cinematography was left open in the text of the Berne Convention, since it would have been far too risky and, at the same time, restrictive to place limits on a rapidly developing film industry, which also promised processes incapable of being predicted or defined at that stage. The wording of article 2(2), though flexible, has been tested severely on at least two occasions since its inclusion in the Berne Convention at the Brussels Revision of the Convention.[8]

The first time was immediately after the Second World War, when there was a big explosion of television and televisual works and massive developments in the industry were taking place. Among the problems that arose were: (1) Could televisual works come within the scope of

---

[6] Cinematography is a notion derived from the ancient Greek word 'kinesis', which means movement. It can therefore be argued that any cinematographic work at least involves the potential for movement.

[7] S. Ricketson, *The Berne Convention for the protection of literary and artistic works: 1886–1986*, Kluwer, Deventer, 1988, at 562. Ricketson extends this argument to videographic works as well.

[8] Documents 1948, 156. However, its origins are found in art. 14(4) of the Berlin Act, Actes 1908, 266.

cinematographic works? And could that be the case even though the notion of fixation was not implied in their definition and was not essential to their existence, whilst by definition cinematographic works had to be fixed on some material support? (2) Could televisual works qualify for the same kind of protection as cinematographic works, even though the method of their production and communication to the public was not the same as, nor even similar to, that of cinematographic works?

In relation to the first issue, it was argued that article 2(1) of the Berne Convention was non-limitative, and, when coupled with article 2(2), it could lead to the conclusion that Member States were free to include unfixed works in the field of protection of cinematographic works. This was especially so since in many countries television and radio broadcasts were already protected by copyright or neighbouring rights and were also the object of protection of the Rome Convention, signed in 1961.[9] In relation to the second issue, weight was placed on the effects and the results produced by both works being very similar. Both cinematographic and televisual works produce analogous visual effects,[10] a combination of visual images and sounds projected onto a screen. At certain stages the processes used in cinematography, such as the operations of cutting and montage, are also common in the production of televisual works.[11] Yet, that was held to be a broad interpretation of the notion of cinematographic works. Cutting and pasting are procedures used in almost any work and do not represent a process of cinematography or a process that is similar to it *stricto sensu*. Cinematographic works are recorded optically, whilst televisual works might not be recorded at all in some cases, or they might be recorded on magnetic tape before they are broadcast. In the latter case televisual works come closer to the prerequisite of a process analogous to cinematography. The final outcome of the debate was that televisual works were held to come within the scope of protection of cinematographic works, whether they were fixed on some kind of material support or not. This was held to be so by reason of the pressing need for the protection of these kinds of works due to their widespread availability on the international market and to the strong growth in demand for them. At that stage these works were essentially unprotected. The protection of cinematographic works applied by analogy to the case of audiovisual works.

The second case which tested the limits of the concept of cinematographic works related to videographic works. It was easier in this instance,

---

[9] Rome Convention on the Protection of Performers, Producers of Phonograms and Broadcasting Organisations, 1961.
[10] Doc. S/1, Records 1967, vol. I, 85, and Ricketson, *Berne Convention*, at 558ff.
[11] Discussions of the Main Committee I, Records 1967, vol. II, 863–5, 881.

especially after the inclusion of televisual works in the same category, for it to be maintained that videographic works produced the same visual results as cinematographic and televisual works. Moreover, these works were normally fixed on some kind of material support. In fact it was pre-existing cinematographic works which were fixed on the new material supports, such as video discs, tapes or cartridges. For this reason the process of their production and their fixation was found to be analogous to cinematography, even though these works were put to a different use than the traditional one of being shown to a large audience or, in the case of a televisual work, being broadcast. The fact that the videographic works were used for separate viewing by each consumer–individual (private use instead of public use) did not affect their assimilation into the category of cinematographic works. In addition, videographic works provided a clearer case than televisual works since they quite evidently came closer to cinematographic works than the latter. That reason would suffice to preclude any debate.

6.1.3 Films

The CDPA 1988 (UK) refers neither to audiovisual works nor to cinematographic works. It refers to films. According to section 5B, a film is 'a recording on any medium from which a moving image may by any means be produced'. Films require the element of a 'moving image'. This element is either provided for expressly in the national laws of some countries in relation to audiovisual and cinematographic works or implied by these notions. A part of the literature supports the view that cinematographic works constitute the contents of a film, whilst the film itself is the recording of a cinematographic work, in other words its fixation on pellicle.[12] This, however, should not necessarily be seen to be so after examination of the Berne Convention on the point of cinematographic works. Films and cinematographic works are notions which should be used interchangeably: first, because they both require some kind of fixation, and secondly, because if this were not the case, the Berne Convention would have provided for their separate treatment or at least mentioned it, especially in a period when the film industry was flourishing.

The fact that section 5B of the CDPA 1988 does not provide for a 'series or sequence of images' as would be expected in any audiovisual, cinematographic work or the like, should not be a problem. A certain sequence of images is implied by the notion of 'moving images'. It would be rather difficult to imagine the existence of 'moving images' without

---

[12] G. Koumantos, *Pnevmatiki idioktissia*, 7th edn, Ant. N. Sakkoula, Athens, 2000, at 132.

these images being subject to a certain logic or scenario, however bizarre or accidental. If that is the case, in order for the scenario to be developed normally, an unfolding of frames is required. These frames must be related to each other, linked, or else exist in a sequence. In the notion of 'moving images' such a link is almost always a necessary prerequisite.

What is of interest in the British definition of films is the provision that a film is a recording on any medium from which a moving image may by any means be produced. Thus, the problem of testing, according to the requirements of the Berne Convention, whether the process by which a particular work has been produced is analogous to cinematography is overcome. The definition is wide enough to encompass any kind of possible recording on any medium, as long as such a recording exists of course. Unfixed works are not protected. On-line works are protected, however, on condition that there is a pre-existing recording from which the on-line transmission can be made.[13]

Having examined the various definitions of audiovisual works, cinematographic works and films, we could, perhaps, attempt a schematic classification. For such a purpose we will consider films and cinematographic works as essentially the same thing. 'Sequences of moving images' is a necessary prerequisite. If the images are not moving then we do not have an audiovisual work or film, but instead an artistic work, a painting, a literary work in another form, or a photograph. None of these categories necessarily require the existence of any sound.

'Audiovisual works' seems to be a generic term.[14] It possesses all the common characteristics of cinematographic works or related works, apart from that of fixation. Cinematographic works and films are found one

---

[13] S. 10(1) of the Australian Copyright Act 1968 defines 'cinematograph films' as 'the aggregate of the visual images embodied in an article or thing so as to be capable by the use of that article or thing (a) of being shown as a moving picture; or (b) of being embodied in another article or thing by the use of which it can be shown, and includes the aggregate of the sounds embodied in a sound-track associated with such visual images'. The Australian Copyright Law Review Committee (CLRC) in its *Final report on computer software protection* (Attorney-General's Department, Canberra, April 1995) concluded that multimedia works fell within the scope of protection offered to cinematograph films under the Act and that the interactive and composite nature of multimedia works did not require the introduction of a new category designed specifically to include these works. However, the CLRC thought that this category needed to be relabelled 'audiovisual work' because it was stretching the generally understood meaning of 'cinematograph film' to apply that term to a multimedia production. See A. Fitzgerald and C. Cifuentes, 'Copyright protection for digital multimedia works' [1999] *Ent LR* 23, at 25. In 1999 the CLRC expressed a revised view of the adequacy of protection for multimedia products (*Simplification of the Copyright Act 1968, Part 2: Categorisation of subject-matter and exclusive rights, and other issues*, AGPS, Canberra, 1999). See T. Aplin, 'Not in our galaxy: why "film" won't rescue multimedia' [1999] *EIPR* 633, note 3.

[14] Aplin, 'Not in our galaxy'.

level down.[15] Their fixation is required. The process for their fixation should be either cinematography or something similar, or any kind of fixation, as is stipulated by the UK's Copyright Act. In the light of this we could maintain that when an audiovisual work is fixed it falls either within the category of cinematographic works or within that of films. Yet, it still remains a broader notion than that of cinematographic works or films.[16] In Britain audiovisual works are considered to be the same as films.[17]

The definition of films which is enshrined in the European Directive on rental and lending rights[18] seems at first sight to put forward the opposite view. According to article 2.1 of the Directive, the term 'film' 'designate[s] a cinematographic or audio-visual work or moving images, whether or not accompanied by sound'. In fact what it has done is to reverse the order we just described and suggest that a film is a notion which contains both moving images which are fixed, and moving images which are not fixed. In other words, the notion of films is broader than that of audiovisual works. The latter is contained in the former. In article 2 of the EU term Directive[19] cinematographic works are referred to as if they were not a subcategory of audiovisual works.[20]

There is no definite way of distinguishing between audiovisual works, films and cinematographic works, and most national copyright laws use one of the terms to include the others[21] or use all or some of the terms interchangeably. It is thus considered advisable for the purposes of this book to use these notions interchangeably. In any case the problems they present are in most cases identical, or at least very similar.

---

[15] *Contra* A. Strowel and J.-P. Triaille, *Le droit d'auteur, du logiciel au multimédia (Copyright, from software to multimedia)*, Bruylant, Brussels, 1997 at 363.
[16] If we look at the origins of audiovisual works we could suggest that they form part of dramatic works, their predecessors in the national copyright laws of many countries. That, of course, does not preclude the fact that they were protected by various methods in the past before their own separate and distinctive protection was established, i.e. through the protection of photographs, and so on. See also H. Laddie, P. Prescott and M. Vitoria, *The modern law of copyright and designs*, 2nd edn, Butterworths, London, Dublin, Edinburgh, 1995, at 365ff.
[17] In art. 23 of the Greek Copyright Act (2121/1993) the term 'cinematographic film' is treated as having the same meaning (i.e. it is used interchangeably) as that of cinematographic works. Yet, the former is used to indicate the material support on which the cinematographic work is fixed. See Koumantos, *Pnevmatiki idioktassia*, at 132.
[18] Council Directive (92/100/EEC) on rental right and lending right and on certain rights related to copyright in the field of intellectual property, [1992] OJ L346/61.
[19] Council Directive, (93/98/EEC) harmonising the term of protection of copyright and certain related rights, [1993] OJ L290/9.
[20] Koumantos, *Pnevmatiki idioktassia*, at 286.
[21] 'The 1988 Act talks of "film", but defines it in a way which embraces audio-visual production in general', W. Cornish, *Intellectual property*, 4th edn, Sweet & Maxwell, London, 1999, at 394.

6.2 COMPOSITE CHARACTERISTICS OF AUDIOVISUAL WORKS

All the above-mentioned works have certain characteristics in common, which entitle them to the same protection. The nature of these characteristics indicates whether or not other works that are related to them fall within the same scope of protection. Because of this it is useful to examine these characteristics one by one.

6.2.1 The meaning of 'images'

All of these works combine a visual and a sound element, although the latter is not a necessary prerequisite.[22] These elements are not always the only elements to be found. Text, graphics or other elements can be included as well. It is vital, however, that images are the prevailing element.

At this point the notion of 'image' should be clarified. Does the law refer only to real images or to whatever can be projected or shown in the form of an image on a screen, such as text, graphics, speech, literary or artistic works?

This question arose in cases concerning Minitel, programs for games and teletext. It was unclear whether they should be considered as audiovisual works or not. Even if they were not strictly speaking audiovisual works, it might nevertheless be advisable to consider them as such. The views thereon diverged. In the US Court of Appeals for the 7th Circuit, in the case *WGN Continental Broadcasting Co. v. United Video, Inc.*,[23] it was held that a teletext, which accompanied an information program broadcast at the same time on the same television signal as the teletext, but on a different channel, constituted, together with the information program, an audiovisual work. Yet, this decision was not based on the existence of teletext only. It seems that the leading view in the literature on audiovisual works holds that teletext as such cannot qualify as an audiovisual work in view of the lack of any real images.[24] However, it could be protected by the European Arrangement for the Protection of Television Broadcasts, signed in Strasbourg on 20 June 1960, by those countries that have ratified it. Berenboom holds the view that even teletext qualifies as an

---

[22] Koumantos talks about an inaccuracy in the definition of audiovisual works (audio + visual works) which is justified by the historical origin of cinematographic works and the advisability of a unified regime of protection for both works containing only images and those containing images and sound together. This inaccuracy, however, is one-sided. It cannot work in favour of the sound element alone. For example, radio broadcasts, which contain only sound and no images at all, do not come within the scope of protection of audiovisual works. *Pnevmatiki idioktassia*, at 132.
[23] 693 F 2d 622 (7th Cir. 1982).
[24] Strowel and Triaille, *Le droit d'auteur*, at 360.

audiovisual work, since it meets the criteria of law, according to his view. However, further explanation as to how these criteria are met, and what they are, is not given.[25]

The qualification of teletext as an audiovisual work would confuse the boundaries between audiovisual works and literary works. When a book with illustrations is turned into a film, meaning that its illustrations unfold one after the other, it also qualifies as a film.[26] Yet, if the book as such is presented on a computer screen and read, though accompanied by illustrations, it still remains a book. Its fixation on a CD-ROM or on a video tape should not alter its primary nature as a literary work.[27] In the same way, an encyclopaedia which is carried by a linear or non-linear electronic medium should remain subject to the provisions of its publishing contract and its author should not lose his rights in favour of the publisher (director or producer). In this case the medium should be distinguished from the work it carries. In the same sense it should be considered that the (e.g. visual) result that is produced should not alter the nature and expression of the work, for example a written text (book or other literary work). A literary work can be fixed on new media which are analogous to those used in cinematography, television or in the computer industry, without at the same time altering the nature of the first work, provided that remains essentially unaltered.[28] The carrier or medium, however, is capable of creating a presumption in favour of certain classifications. The digitisation of works will simply be held at this stage to be an adaptation of the work, which does not constitute a significant alteration of its nature.

6.2.2 The requirement of '(sequences of) moving images'

The essential characteristic of all the works falling within the 'genus' of audiovisual works or films is the existence of 'a sequence of moving images'. Yet, not all national laws refer to this feature as such. The CDPA 1988 refers to 'moving image',[29] the German Copyright Act refers to 'sequences of images'[30], whilst the US Copyright Act refers to 'a series of related images' or, in the case of 'moving pictures', to pictures which

---

[25] A. Berenboom, *Le nouveau droit d'auteur et les droits voisins*, Larcier, Paris, 1995, at 193.
[26] Groupe Audiovisuel et Multimédia de l'Edition, *Questions juridiques relatives aux oeuvres multimédia* (Livre Blanc), Paris, 1994, at 20.
[27] Strowel and Triaille, *Le droit d'auteur*, at 81ff. and 361.
[28] There will always be minimal alterations, of course, in order for a work to be adapted to the chosen carrier.
[29] Section 5B(1).
[30] Art. 95 of the Copyright Act of 9 September 1965. This article is entitled 'moving pictures' and it refers to certain articles dealing with cinematographic works (i.e. 88, 90, 91, 93 and 94) without, however, defining the notion of cinematographic works. What is

are 'shown in succession and impart an impression of motion'.[31] If we attempt a literal interpretation of the above phrases, we will observe that the required existence of a link between the images or pictures does not always imply the existence of motion. A series of pictures may unfold onto a screen without imparting the impression of motion. The only motion involved may be one picture succeeding another. But that is not considered to be motion in its literal sense. It is only movement.[32]

Even in the case of the French Copyright Act, which expressly provides for 'sequences of moving images',[33] the notion of motion (animation) is approached broadly. However, the instances where fixed frames are stuck together, or where still images or photographs follow one another in the sense of an exhibition, are excluded from the notion of audiovisual works altogether.[34] Otherwise an overlap, or at least confusion, with the category of artistic works may be created. If images or frames are linked to each other and constitute a unit, their unfolding onto a screen allows them to qualify as an audiovisual work where this unfolding is subject to some kind of scenario.[35] In the same sense an encyclopaedia of artistic works should not fall within the notion of audiovisual works, although one image may follow the other, because these images have not been sewn together subject to a scenario.

A second issue which arises at this point is whether the required sequence of images has to be a standard and stable sequence of images or whether it can be altered without impinging on the notion of audiovisual works. The question was answered graphically in *Midway Mfg Co. v. Artic International, Inc.*[36] In this case the US Court of Appeals (7th Circuit) held that a video game was an audiovisual work in so far as it possessed a series of related images, referred to as 'any set of images displayed as some kind of unit'. The fact that the sequence of these images varied according to the use initiated each time by the user was not held to affect the qualification of the video game as an audiovisual work. This was

---

of interest at this point is that the German Copyright Act distinguishes cinematographic works from moving pictures. Yet, it is not clear whether the idea of motion is implied in the notion of moving images, although it is not specifically referred to. If that is the case it is not clear on which basis the German Act differentiates cinematographic works from moving images.

[31] § 101 of the US Copyright Act 1976.
[32] As we mentioned earlier, a 'sequence of images' might not imply motion, but motion implies a 'sequence of images'.
[33] Art. L112-6 of the French Copyright Act.
[34] See also Strowel and Triaille, *Le droit d'auteur*, at 360, and *contra*, Berenboom, *Le nouveau droit d'auteur*, at 193, footnote 13, where he argues that a succession of fixed frames can also qualify as an audiovisual work.
[35] Groupe Audiovisuel et Multimédia de l'Edition, *Questions juridiques*.
[36] 704 F 2d 1009 (7th Cir. 1983).

perhaps so because in video games the possible sequences of images are still very much predefined by the manufacturer. The user's influence on these sequences is still rather limited.

6.2.3 Fixation

In relation to audiovisual works there is no express requirement for some particular kind of fixation or for any kind of fixation at all.[37] In relation to films and to cinematographic works fixation is either implied by the 'process of cinematography or analogous to it', or it is expressly mentioned by the requirement of a 'recording'.[38] However, the form of fixation required in these instances is not standard, definite or precisely described. Particularly under the CDPA, any kind of recording would qualify. Requiring a particular recording would ignore the fast-developing new media industry and would lead to the provision being soon outdated. Thus, a wide range of supports can qualify as appropriate supports for the recording of audiovisual works as long as the work originally recorded can be reproduced from them unaltered. Pellicle, video tapes and CD-ROMs are just some examples. On-line transmissions as such do not qualify as recordings. However, technically speaking these transmissions normally involve a form of recording. Whether this transient recording meets the requirements of the CDPA for recordings must remain open to serious doubt.

What we can observe so far is that in the course of examining whether a work qualifies as an audiovisual work or not, the carrier of the work at issue should not play any role. The test of whether a work qualifies as a cinematographic work or not (decided according to whether the process used in the work is analogous to cinematography or not), the history of cinematographic works, and the incorporation of televisual and videographic works within their scope of protection, have shown that cases where the work possesses the essential characteristics of an audiovisual or cinematographic work, but does not qualify as such by reason of the support on which it is incorporated, will be rare or non-existent.

6.2.4 The intention to show audiovisual works to the public

In the preparatory works of the Legal Affairs Committee of the Chambers of Deputies in Belgium,[39] audiovisual works have been defined as a mixture of sounds and moving images which are intended to be shown in

---

[37] Common law countries require fixation for each kind of work.
[38] S. 5B CDPA 1988.
[39] Report of the Clerk, Lobbying and Disclosure Act 1995, at 181.

public. Although preparatory legislative work does not have the binding force of a legal provision, it nevertheless throws light on the interpretation of the law, by revealing nuances of meaning implied in the notions contained within it. The present wording puts forward one more prerequisite in relation to audiovisual works. They are intended to be projected in front of the public.[40]

The notion of 'public' is not clear though. Does it refer only to a projection in front of large groups of people or also to a use which, though private, is not restricted to a certain group of people but is open to everyone? The literal interpretation of the wording of the preparatory work would offer a presumption in favour of the classic example of the projection of a film in a cinema to people who would constitute the public in the eyes of the law. However, such an interpretation would unjustifiably restrict the notion of audiovisual works, especially in a society where entertainment has begun to be more private in nature rather than a collective activity. In the light of this, the medium on which it is carried should either not play any role at all, or its role should not be decisive. If that were not the case, a huge bundle of works would stay out of the scope of audiovisual works, running the risk of not finding any appropriate legal provisions for their accommodation at all.

In addition, taking into account the examples of televisual works and videographic works which have been included in the notion of cinematographic works, even if projection in front of the public had another meaning, this meaning has been redefined and allows private unrestricted use as well. In the era of new technologies, any particular provisions for a special kind of fixation would ignore the reality of the digitised world. All works are nowadays fixed in the same format and communicated by more or less common methods. These methods are increasingly moving away from collective activities (e.g. collective entertainment, collective education, etc.) as well as from the requirement of the presence of many persons at the end use of the product. Therefore the requirement of a large public would seem absurd. We have moved on from the era where the broadcaster/performer was one and the receivers many. Now broadcasters/performers and receivers may be many at the same time, or, what is even more common, the broadcasters/performers may be many and the receiver one. The receiver makes his choices privately, in his home, from the moment he chooses whether or not he will turn his computer

---

[40] In art. 4(3)(b) of the previous Copyright Act (no. 1597/86) a cinematographic film was defined as the copy of a completed cinematographic work which is the same as the original (or master copy) and is intended for public or private use. Thus, there is no absolute requirement in all national laws for an audiovisual work to be shown only in public.

or TV on. He chooses what he will bring onto his screen, download, etc. In the light of this, projection in front of the public should no longer be such a substantial and decisive factor in the legal provisions surrounding audiovisual works. It should have been used only to create presumptions and has been invalidated by the circumstances as explained earlier. It is not that the notion of the public has disappeared, rather it has been re-defined. If private users of audiovisual works, who either view their video tapes at home or receive on-line films onto the screen of their TVs or computers, were counted, they would doubtless form a 'large' public in the same traditional sense required by the drafters of the law who initially had in mind the projection of films in front of large audiences.

6.2.5 Concluding remarks

In conclusion we could say that in all audiovisual or related works, the only prevailing characteristic is the existence of a sequence of moving images. The idea of motion might vary from the unfolding of fixed images which are linked to each other by a scenario to the existence of real motion, which by itself precludes the existence of any fixed frames or still images. The end purpose and the form of fixation of these works do not constitute composite elements of their definition. Televisual works, videographic works and video games are also included within the ambit of these works.[41]

6.3 A COMPARISON BETWEEN AUDIOVISUAL WORKS AND LITERARY WORKS, COMPILATIONS, DATABASES AND COMPUTER PROGRAMS

It is interesting at this point to examine how the different kinds of works we have discussed up to now (with the exception of computer programs) compare to each other, in order to find out whether an overlap is apparent, and whether in such a case a work can qualify for protection in more than one category of works. It may also be possible to spot the reasons why one or other of these categories is excluded or why more than one category is applied.

Audiovisual works and literary works seem to be at opposite ends of the spectrum. Literary works are essentially works of language, which are meant to be written, spoken or read. They are not meant to be shown/displayed. Their dominant element therefore is text and not images.

---

[41] Documentaries, video clips and publicity slots are also included within the notion of audiovisual works.

Moving images in particular play no part. The law itself[42] precludes a work from qualifying as both an audiovisual work and a literary work. Article 3(1) of the CDPA 1988 provides that ' "literary work" is any work *other than* dramatic...',[43] whilst article 101 of the US Copyright Act provides that ' "literary works" are works, *other than* audiovisual works, expressed in words...'. The fact that the US Court of Appeals has recognised teletext as an audiovisual work rather than a literary work, though arguably not scientifically correct, is due to two reasons. First, it was not considered to exist in isolation but to be part of a television programme of information, broadcast at the same time, and secondly, it was the characteristics of the latter which counted in its qualification.[44]

Although audiovisual works are complex works and in most cases include combined visual and sound elements, their nature is different from that of a traditional compilation. The first obvious reason is that, although compilations combine more than one work, including images, graphics and other elements, their prevailing element is still text, and their purpose is the same as that of literary works. They are meant to be read. A compilation which forms part of a literary work cannot be displayed, though it contains elements which as such can be displayable. Arguably its prevailing element cannot be an image and it is not capable of incorporating any sound. Moreover, it is incapable of either giving the impression of motion or of containing any moving images which cannot take the form of a written format. In the light of this, if a work qualifies as a compilation, it is logically incapable of qualifying as an audiovisual work as well. The two notions are mutually exclusive.

What, however, are more difficult to distinguish from audiovisual works are databases. This is the case because databases offer the opportunity of visual and sound elements being combined in the same way as they are combined in a film. Yet, the very notion of a database, as this is defined in article 1.2 of the EU Directive on the legal protection of databases,[45] is incompatible with that of an audiovisual work.[46] Specifically, a database is defined as 'a collection of independent works, data or other materials arranged in a systematic or methodical way and individually accessible

---

[42] Anglo-Saxon law in particular provides for this expressly.
[43] We have explained that an audiovisual work is a dramatic work in the broad sense of the notion.
[44] *WGN Continental Broadcasting Co.* v. *United Video, Inc.*, 693 F 2d 622, 628 (7th Cir. 1982).
[45] EU database Directive (96/9/EC) on the legal protection of databases, [1996] OJ L77/20.
[46] See also Recital 17 to the Directive; I. Stamatoudi, 'The EU database Directive: reconceptualising copyright and tracing the future of the *sui generis* right' (1997) 50 *Revue Hellénique de Droit International* 436, at 442.

by electronic or other means'. Vital in this definition is the feature of individuality that every work contained in a database has to possess and the opportunity of accessing each work individually. A film does not possess these characteristics. The frames which go to make up a film are not independent from one another. Neither are they accessible on their own by electronic or other means.[47] Recital 17 to the database Directive is explicit: 'A recording or an audiovisual, cinematographic, literary or musical work as such does not fall within the scope of this Directive.' In other words, even if we take the loose meaning of the notion of moving images, which considers images as only being linked or related to each other and unfolding according to a scenario, this interpretation is still not wide enough to make a case where a database and an audiovisual work can co-exist.[48]

It is, perhaps, easier to argue that computer programs and audiovisual works have less in common with each other than with almost any other work. Although computer programs possess visual and sound elements, these elements are only minimal in nature. The language, structure, form of fixation and end-use of computer programs are completely different from those of audiovisual works. They are not meant to be projected as moving pictures which are to be viewed from beginning to end but are rather meant to perform particular tasks initiated by the choices and needs of their users. In addition, computer programs are functional only in a computer environment. Nothing can be accessed, read or downloaded without the aid of a computer. The characteristics of audiovisual works and computer programs, as well as the different purposes they serve, render them mutually exclusive notions.

Thus, if one decides that a multimedia work falls within one or other of the above-mentioned categories, certain other categories of works are automatically excluded, either explicitly by law or by reason of the mutually exclusive elements which comprise some of them. In the light of this, cumulative protection of multimedia works is not possible. Yet, that should not prevent us from arguing that in the cases where a multimedia product comes closer to one category than another it should be included in this category, or that parts of the work can come within the scope of

---

[47] Stamatoudi, 'EU database Directive'; L. Kaye, 'The proposed EU directive for the legal protection of databases: a cornerstone of the information society?' [1995] 12 *EIPR* 583.
[48] See *contra*, without any explanation, Strowel and Triaille, *Le droit d'auteur*, at 367. If databases came anywhere near to one of the aforementioned categories, it would be to audiovisual works, where the requirement of 'moving pictures' is looser, and not to the category of films, as held by Strowel and Triaille. The case of video games, which qualify in certain cases as audiovisual works (though the sequence of their images is not stable and unaltered), will be discussed in chapter 8.

different categories.[49] The category assigned to it might vary according to the particular case. A difficulty inherent in the phenomenon of multimedia works is that their looks, structure and nature are highly variable.[50] And the issue is aggravated by the rapid evolution of technology and of the choices it offers to both developers and users.

6.4 DISTINCTIVE FEATURES OF THE REGIME OF PROTECTION OF AUDIOVISUAL WORKS

In order for a multimedia work to qualify as an audiovisual work, not only do its components have to match those of an audiovisual work, but also the whole regime of protection of an audiovisual work must be capable of accommodating the needs of a multimedia product. The examination of the distinctive features of the regime of protection of audiovisual works can throw some light on this issue.

6.4.1 Originality

Under the CDPA 1988, films do not have to be original to come within the scope of section 5B of the Act. However, if they constitute a copy of a previous work, e.g. a mere lifting of the images and frames of a film without any transformation or modification,[51] they do not qualify for protection under the CDPA 1988. This can be held as a *de minimis* rule of originality which, however, does not mention any traditional common law requirement for skill and labour in the course of the creation of a film. In continental Europe, films or cinematographic works have to be original in the same sense as any other work which qualifies for copyright protection. Films form one more example of the general regime of protection.

6.4.2 Authorship

The authorship of a film has in certain countries, and particularly in common law countries, been drawn on a different basis than the one applied to other intellectual property works. It mirrors an entrepreneurial approach, which favours the investors and distributors rather than the real creators of the work. This clear favouring of entrepreneurs in relation to films[52] is due to the particular features and problems films present in

---

[49] Whether that is advisable or not will form the subject of a different section.
[50] Of course, we admit that there is always a common core in the multimedia phenomenon on which a common and unified regulation should be based.
[51] It is alleged that even adaptations of lifted images can allow a work to qualify as a film on its own merits.
[52] Entrepreneurs are favoured more in relation to films than in relation to any other intellectual property work.

comparison to other intellectual property products. The production of a film demands large investments in administrative and technical personnel, equipment, machinery, expensive processes of production, multiple creators, parallel production of the material carrier on which the work will be incorporated, e.g. the video tape, celluloid, etc. When other intellectual property works demand such large sums, it is the exception rather than the rule or it is at the stage of their distribution rather than their production.[53] The person or company which provides these investments is called a 'producer'. And it is this person or company that the CDPA 1988, as it was originally adopted, designated as the author of a film. The argument is that production budgets will not be provided unless an investor is secured. The most efficient way of securing the investor is to designate him as the author and first owner of the rights in the work. In section 9(2)(a) of the CDPA, the author of a film is held to be the person by whom the arrangements necessary for the making of the film are undertaken.[54] In the US Copyright Act, no specific regime is put in place but it can be readily accepted that the 'work for hire' rule will apply and that a similar outcome will therefore be achieved.[55]

Such a solution would not be admissible in the copyright laws of continental Europe. The author should always be the real and actual creator of the work[56] and this creator can only be a natural person. Thus, companies or other legal entities are excluded altogether from the category of authors, along with the producer, who can only obtain rights in a film by reason of a contract (licence or assignment) as a subsequent rightholder and never as a primary (original) one. Even in cases where the producer interferes with the final 'look' of the work, so as to make it more marketable or economically attractive for example, the character of his work is considered to be more technical and financial rather than anything else.

In continental copyright law either a number of persons who have contributed to the creation of a film are designated as authors, or the director alone is. The director is held to have a creative role since he coordinates and regulates the structure, content and appearance (image) of the whole film.[57] His role is highly creative although his contribution cannot be traced to a particular distinguishable part of the film, e.g. the script, the

---

[53] See Koumantos, *Pnevmatiki idioktassia*, at 324–5.
[54] It is understood that this is in fact the producer.
[55] See §§ 201(a) and (c) and 101 of the US Copyright Act.
[56] A personal bond between the person creating the work and the work itself should exist, as that is the rationale of the whole system of continental *droit d'auteur*.
[57] See the French Copyright Act, art. L113-7; Belgian Copyright Act, art. 14; German Copyright Act, art. 65(2) and Greek Copyright Act, art. 9. 'Film-making has today acquired an irreversible status as an art-form and the Directive acknowledges the clear case of directors being treated as authors.' Cornish, *Intellectual property*, at 393.

Audiovisual works

music, etc. For that reason many countries have introduced a legal presumption in favour of the director. In France, the author of the script, the author of the adaptation of the dialogue and the author of the musical compositions (with or without words) specially composed for the work are considered to be the joint authors of a film with the director.[58] In other countries, such as Greece, the designation of a single person as the author of a film, i.e. the director, was held to facilitate the regime of protection of films and their clearance of rights.[59] After the enactment of the Council Directive on rental and lending rights,[60] which followed the continental paradigm of protection with regard to films, all Member States were required to designate the principal director of a film as its author or one of its authors. The latter option was obviously open only to those Member States that also wanted to designate other persons as authors.[61] Under the current transformation of UK law, the principal director and the producer of the film are considered to be joint authors of the film.[62]

The author of the film is also the first owner of the rights in it. If this presumption is coupled with the one deriving from the fact that the name of the author/rightholder appears on copies of the work in a manner usually employed to indicate authorship,[63] the tracking of the person responsible, to whom one can apply for permission or licence in relation to an audiovisual work, becomes easier and more convenient. It creates security in law. In this sense clearance of rights is facilitated, and future users of the work in the new technological era are more inclined to include it in new productions.

6.4.3 Works of joint authorship, collective works, etc.

The fact that only a few contributors[64] are recognised by the laws of the various states as authors of an audiovisual work creates the presumption

---

[58] Art. L113-7 of the French Copyright Act.
[59] Art. 9 of the Greek Copyright Act.
[60] EC rental and lending rights Directive, [1992] OJ L346/61.
[61] Art. 2.2 of the Directive provides that 'for the purposes of this Directive the principal director of a cinematographic or audio-visual work shall be considered as its author or one of its authors'. The same article continues that 'Member States may provide for others to be considered as its co-authors'.
[62] Of course, nothing has changed from the fact that, according to the UK Act, the rights of works created by employees are automatically transferred to their employers. In the case of films, if the director is an employee his rights are automatically transferred by reason of the employment contract to the producer of the film, if he is his employer. See Cornish, *Intellectual property*, at 393–4.
[63] Art. L113-1 of the French Copyright Act, and s. 10(1) CDPA 1988.
[64] Or only two now in the UK, the producer and the director.

that an audiovisual work is a work of joint authorship. It is a work produced by the collaboration of two or more authors whose contribution towards the work cannot be distinguished from that of the other(s).[65] In the French Copyright Act, a film is a *de iure* collaborative work.[66] According to article L113-2 of the French Copyright Act, 'a "collaborative work" shall mean a work in the creation of which more than one natural person has participated'. In other words, whenever a creative elaboration or contribution by many natural persons has been made for the realisation of a project, which ends up being the collaborative or joint work of many persons, the work at issue is also by definition a collaborative work or a work of joint authorship. However, these two definitions are not the only definitions available in relation to an audiovisual work. The notions of collective and composite works are also available.[67] A 'composite work' under article L113-2 is a 'work in which a pre-existing work is incorporated without the collaboration of the author of the latter work', whilst a 'collective work' is 'a work created on the initiative of a natural or legal person who edits it, publishes it and discloses it under his direction and name and in which the personal contributions of the various authors who participated in its production are merged in the overall work for which they were conceived, without it being possible to attribute to each author a separate right in the work as created'. In the case of French law these latter definitions play a role which is only of secondary importance.[68] Yet, in other countries, such as Greece, an audiovisual work is held to be a collective work, since it is supposed to have been created under the initiative of one person, namely the director. The above-mentioned qualifications of audiovisual works, whether *de iure* statements or simply legal presumptions, can in some jurisdictions be rebutted according to the facts and particularities of each case.[69]

---

[65] S. 10(1) CDPA 1988. In the Greek law an audiovisual work is held to be a collective work rather than a collaborative work. See art. 9 of the Greek Copyright Act 2121/1993, and D. Kallinikou, *Pnevmatiki idioktissia kai syggenika dikaiomata*, P. N. Sakkoulas, Athens, 2000, at 80.

[66] See especially B. Edelman, 'L'oeuvre multimédia, un essai de qualification' [1995] 15 *Recueil Dalloz Sirey* 109, at 114. The distinction between collective, collaborative and composite works is not recognised in all countries. See, for example, the CDPA 1988 which provides for works of 'joint authorship' instead of collective works. The former are defined in s. 10 of the Act as works 'produced by the collaboration of two or more authors in which the contribution of each author is not distinct from that of the other author or authors'.

[67] How the notions of collective, collaborative and composite works relate to each other will be discussed in the next section.

[68] See Edelman, 'L'oeuvre multimédia', at 110.

[69] Under French law there is no presumption and the qualification cannot be rebutted. Audiovisual works can only be collaborative works. See the *Ramdam* case, Cour d'Appel de Paris, 16 May 1994, (1995) *JCP* GII 22375, annotated by X. Linant de Bellefonds

The role of the producer of an audiovisual work has been recognised and promoted in addition to the role of authors–creators in continental copyright systems. However, since his protection is essentially a hybrid of copyright and not a genuine right deriving from his actual creative role in relation to the work, it has been put under the rubric of neighbouring rights rather than copyright. The producer is deemed to be the rightholder of the rights in the work, the first fixation of which is made by him.

6.4.4 *Cessio legis* in favour of the producer

In order to assist the producer in his role of assembling and publishing the audiovisual work, the law has introduced the legal presumption that those rights of the contributors of a film which are necessary for its creation and commercialisation have been transferred to the producer even if this is not expressly mentioned in the contract for the production of the film.[70] This *cessio legis*, which is in fact a form of quasi-compulsory licensing, though it exceeds the limits and boundaries of the traditional copyright system and the freedom of the authors, has been considered necessary for the completion of the film. It prevents the creative participants from creating obstacles that are capable of impeding the production of a film.

6.4.5 A modified regime on moral rights

Under the same philosophy, restrictions on the moral rights of the contributors (co-authors or not) of an audiovisual work have also been imposed, until the work is completed. According to article 16 of the Belgian Copyright Act, 'The authors' moral rights may only be exercised by the authors with respect to a completed audiovisual work', such completion being 'when the final version [of the audiovisual work] has been fixed by

---

and A. Kérever in (1994) 164 *RIDA* 474; see also Cour de Cassation 1ère Chambre Civile, 26 January 1994, (1994) 164 *RIDA* 433 and A. Lucas, 'Multimédia et droit d'auteur' in AFTEL, *Le droit du multimédia: de la télématique à Internet*, Les Editions du Téléphone, Paris, 1996, 113, at 148. This approach has been criticised as completely inappropriate for multimedia works in Groupe Audiovisuel et Multimédia de l'Edition, *Questions juridiques*, at 22–3, where it is argued that only a rebuttable presumption would suit multimedia works if they were to be fitted into the category of audiovisual works.

[70] The rights held by music composers or songwriters are not subject to this automatic transfer of rights in the UK (s. 5B CDPA 1988) or in Greece (art. 34(2) of Copyright Act 2121/1993). In most national Copyright Acts the contributors of works in a film can also use them separately in other intellectual property products, always, of course, with the reservation of unfair competition law. See, for example, arts. L132-23–L132-30 of the French Copyright Act, art. 89 of the German Copyright Act and art. 34(2)(c) of the Greek Copyright Act. In the Anglo-Saxon tradition this depends on the contractual agreements between the parties.

common accord between the main director and the producer'.[71] Until the completion of the audiovisual work, no work in the sense of the law is deemed to exist to which the moral rights principles can be applied. No relevant provision is enshrined in the UK's Copyright Act. Moral rights would not be a problem in Britain in any case, since moral rights provisions are not *ius cogens*. They can be waived, and even the right of paternity needs to be asserted before it comes into being. They do not apply at all in the case of employees. In cases where they do apply they can be waived not only for existing but for future works as well.[72]

The provisions enshrined in the laws of most countries in relation to the implied transfer of certain rights in favour of the producer, and the restrictions on the moral rights of co-authors of an audiovisual work, facilitate the production of such a work by making certain procedures more efficient, secure and stable. This results in any future clearance of rights being more convenient, since one can easily find out to whom one should address the request, and the number of people to whom one should address it is limited. The main reason and philosophy behind these provisions is that importance is placed on the audiovisual work as a whole and not on its constituent parts. The parts as such might not have been created without the impetus of the creation of the whole audiovisual work and in most cases they do not have the economic and market value that the complete audiovisual work will have. According to this approach, concessions in relation to the contributors of the constituent parts of a film are allowed and do not contradict the free spirit or essence of the copyright law.[73] This logic might be desirable and welcomed in the case of multimedia products as well.

6.4.6 A full panoply of rights

In addition to all of the above, audiovisual works are granted a full panoply of economic and moral rights,[74] equivalent to those possessed by genuine copyright works. These rights comprise production and reproduction, diffusion, communication and distribution, lending and rental rights.

---

[71] See also art. L132-24 of the French Copyright Act, art. 34(1) of the Greek Copyright Act and art. 90 of the German Copyright Act. In the Anglo-Saxon tradition these matters are covered by the contractual relationship between the parties. This can involve a waiver of moral rights. The rights to a film are also traditionally vested in the employers in the Anglo-Saxon system. See s. 11(2) CDPA 1988.

[72] SS. 87(2) and (3) CDPA 1988; see also I. Stamatoudi, 'Moral rights of authors in England: the missing emphasis on the role of creators' [1997] 4 *IPQ* 478, at 494.

[73] The UK system clearly puts the emphasis on the work and the investors rather than the author. The author is only protected indirectly.

[74] Recently moral rights have been granted to performers as well by the introduction of the WPPT.

Also, special provisions are made in the event of new modes of exploitation of audiovisual works, provisions which are particularly important in the era of new technologies.[75] Moreover, in any case where a new right seems to be about to be added to the bundle of traditional copyright rights (either by genesis or by teleological interpretation of the law), audiovisual works are always going to be under discussion. This was, for example, the case with the 'right of destination', which seemed to derive from article L131-3 of the French Copyright Act. The Act provides that 'all assignments of copyright are made subject to the condition that each of the rights granted be delimited by reference to its extent and purpose [destination], its place and its duration'. This right was held to mean the author's right to restrain the loan, exchange or hire of books or audiovisual cassettes, or the broadcasting of records commercially purchased, since he could control the purpose for which his work would be used. This was held to imply the notion of destination as well.[76]

Another provision relating to the exploitation of audiovisual works is the one referring to the remuneration of authors. Article L131-4 of the French Copyright Act provides that 'the author's remuneration may be calculated as a lump sum'. In the *droit d'auteur* system, this provision is exceptional since initially it was held to impinge on the economic and fair remuneration of the authors which is usually calculated in percentages each time the work is exploited. However, the specific requirements of audiovisual works and the reality of their production have dictated less liberal solutions in this area.

6.4.7 Term of protection

Special provisions also exist with regard to the term of protection of audiovisual works. Member States of the European Union have incorporated the provisions of the term Directive into their laws.[77] Article 2.2 of the Directive designates a number of contributors to an audiovisual work, which the Member States may or may not have considered as co-authors of an audiovisual work, and it also provides that the term of protection of cinematographic or audiovisual works shall expire seventy years after the death of the last of those persons to survive.[78] *De facto* the list

---

[75] See, for example, art. 19 of the Belgian Copyright Act which provides that 'save for audiovisual works belonging to the non-cultural field or to advertising, authors shall be entitled to separate remuneration for each mode of exploitation'.
[76] See M. Gotzen, *Het bestemmingsrecht van de auteur*, Larcier , Brussels, 1975, at 376; and A. Lucas, 'Copyright and the new technologies in French law' [1987] 2 *EIPR* 42, at 43. This theory was however never adopted in practice.
[77] EC term Directive, [1993] OJ L290/9.
[78] US law provides for 75 years from first publication or 100 years from creation, whichever expires first. See § 302(c) of the US Copyright Act. The EC term Directive presents a

of contributors, and thus potentially also the duration of the copyright in the audiovisual work, varies between the Member States. A separate term of protection is provided in article 3.3 of the Directive for the rights of producers. This term, which is a neighbouring right in continental copyright,[79] starts to run from the first fixation of the film and expires fifty years after the fixation is made. However, if the film is lawfully published or lawfully communicated to the public during this period, the rights expire fifty years from the date of the first such publication or the first such communication to the public, whichever is earlier. The date of first fixation of a film is easy to prove, avoiding tests of originality and difficulties in relation to titularity, but if the work has been released, the date of release is even easier to ascertain for anyone involved. The latter is an act in the public domain whilst the former may not be.

6.5 MULTIMEDIA WORKS AS AUDIOVISUAL WORKS

6.5.1 Multimedia works as *de iure* audiovisual works

6.5.1.1 *Complex works*

Having analysed the definition of audiovisual works and of categories related to them (cinematographic works and films), we will now examine whether multimedia products fit neatly within this category of works, or whether they can at least fit in it by analogy (purposive interpretation). For the needs of this section, we will refer to audiovisual works and films interchangeably, as if there were no differences between them. This was thought to be advisable, firstly, because their actual differences are almost non-existent and *de facto* assimilated in the intellectual property literature of the various states, and secondly, because many countries, for example the UK, do not have separate provisions for audiovisual works and films.

---

contradiction between para. 2 and para. 1 of art. 2. Although para. 1 provides that the principal director of a cinematographic or audiovisual work shall be considered as the author or one of the authors of these works, para. 2 provides that the term of protection for an audiovisual or cinematographic work shall expire seventy years after the death of the last of the following persons to survive, whether or not these persons are designated as co-authors: the principal director, the author of the screenplay, the author of the dialogue and the composer of the music specifically created for use in the cinematographic or audiovisual work. The fact that for the first time a term of protection might run from the death of a person who is not held to be the author of a work is a novelty which depurifies the notion of copyright. See also Koumantos, *Pnevmatiki idioktissia*, at 286.

[79] Cornish mentions that even after the EU rental and lending rights Directive, Britain still gives the copyright in a film to the principal director and the producer jointly. This must count as the ultimate hybrid among intellectual property rights and demonstrates a thoroughly British determination not to subscribe to the authors' rights/neighbouring rights dichotomy: *Intellectual property*, at 393.

Thus, the problems multimedia products face in terms of assimilation with audiovisual works are in most cases identical to the ones they face in terms of assimilation with films, cinematographic works, etc.

Audiovisual works are, like multimedia products, 'complex' works, which in most cases combine *de facto* more than one type of work, i.e. image and sound. The latter is not however a necessary element of their nature. The complexity of audiovisual works, wherever this complexity exists, is not a vital and essential component of their definition. The national copyright laws of the various states do not expressly refer to it. On the contrary, the existence of more than two different types of works is an essential element in the definition of multimedia products. In addition, it is not only the case that different kinds of works are combined to form a multimedia product, but that the number of the combined works is well above that found in any traditional film or audiovisual work, even in those cases where the latter works combine both sound and image. Thus, the difference in quantity unavoidably becomes a difference in quality as well (a limited number of works compared to a vast number of works). Also, in the case of films the constituent works have been combined so as to form an amalgamation of sound and image where these two co-exist and are independent at the same time. In the case of multimedia products the works contributed are assimilated, and nothing of their independence is retained.[80]

One could argue that national laws on audiovisual works, as they were presented in the first section of this chapter, have been worded and construed in such a way as to read that creations bringing together data of any nature, other than images or where images are not prevalent, and also data which, though prevalent, does not form a sequence of animated or moving images, are excluded from the scope of protection of audiovisual works.[81]

On the basis of the above observation, the following should be pointed out. By definition certain data does not fall within the category of moving images. This is the case where the law of a country requires pre-existing moving images to be recorded as a film, and the data recorded does not meet that requirement. Another case is where certain data, though not moving images by nature, can still be recorded in such a way as to form a moving image. The question here is whether it suffices for the law of a country that the motion of images derives from the recording of the data and not from the nature of the data itself as moving images. In the

---

[80] G. Koumantos, 'Les aspects de droit international privé en matière d'infrastructure mondiale d'information' [1996] *Koinodikion* 2.B, 241, at 243.
[81] Groupe Audiovisuel et Multimédia de l'Edition, *Questions juridiques*; see also P. Deprez and V. Fauchoux, *Lois, contrats et usages du multimédia*, Dixit, Paris, 1997, at 48.

CDPA 1988, there is no requirement for the data actually to be a moving image, even before it is recorded. Yet, in the Copyright Act 1956, which the CDPA 1988 replaced, it was implied that the image had to be moving in nature before it was recorded.[82] If this were still the case the scope of audiovisual works would be substantially restricted, and it would *de facto* present severe difficulties to any attempt to fit multimedia works into the category of audiovisual works. Data, which is not a moving image and which cannot form a moving image even if one tries to record it as such, is any kind of still images, e.g. photographs, artistic works, diagrams, text or other.

In contrast to audiovisual works, multimedia products combine various types of works. This feature is a key element of their nature. Multimedia works are by definition complex creations,[83] composed of contributions of different types of works.[84] These contributions consist of works that are not restricted to a mode of adaptation and transformation in order to fit into the format of an audiovisual work, as is the case with audiovisual works and films. The wide and diverse range of individual creative contributions that a film incorporates consists not only of the labour of adapting the story and setting the scene of the film. Items such as the script, acting, directing, filming, sound recording, responsibility for the make-up, clothing, lighting, music, properties and so on are also included in this.[85] These contributions do not necessarily consist of works, in the sense of intellectual property law. In other words, they are not works which fall within one of the categories of intellectual property and are protected as such. They consist of technicalities, which do not possess any originality or creative character in the traditional sense. Indicative of this point is the fact that, although many people contribute to the production of a film or an audiovisual work, it is only to a few that the law grants the status of authors. It grants author status to those who have contributed actual works to the production of the film (e.g. the director, the author of the script or adaptation, etc.). Thus, the complexity of audiovisual works, when compared with that of multimedia works, is qualitatively different. It is only the combination of image and sound in an audiovisual work which is comparable to a multimedia work. But, even here, it is apparent

---

[82] See M. Turner, 'Do the old legal categories fit the new multimedia products? A multimedia CD-ROM as a film' [1995] 3 *EIPR* 107, at 108. The wording of the Copyright Act 1956 was that cinematographic works were 'any sequence of visual images recorded on material of any description (whether translucent or not) so as to be capable, by the use of that material, (a) of being shown as a moving picture, or (b) of being recorded on other material (whether translucent or not), by the use of which it can be shown'.
[83] P.-Y. Gautier, 'Les oeuvres "multimédia" en droit français' (1994) 160 *RIDA* 91.
[84] Edelman, 'L'oeuvre multimédia', at 110.
[85] See Laddie, Prescott and Vitoria, *Modern law*, at 365.

that legislation on audiovisual works has been designed to accommodate works combining only image and sound, whilst text or other data is either of secondary importance or is left out entirely.[86]

Even in those cases where something more than images is included in an audiovisual work, the number of works incorporated is always limited. Perhaps because of the technology available at the time of the drafting of the various national laws, films were never thought of as capable of including more than two kinds of works, i.e. image and sound, together with some minimal amount of text (e.g. opening and closing titles). They were probably not thought capable of incorporating more than one kind of image, sound or text. Even when such a three-element combination was made, no one would refer to vast numbers of works or amounts of data. The mere inclusion of works other than the aforementioned, or the inclusion of data, for example numbers, where image was not a prevailing element (or which could not be presented as data), automatically made any lawyer exclude them from the definition of audiovisual works. The additional layer of content as such came within the definition of literary works or other categories of works, hence the difference between the contents of an audiovisual work and those of a multimedia product.

6.5.1.2 *'Image' as a prevailing element*

One of the essential characteristics of audiovisual works that is contained in every single national definition is the presence of images. As we explained earlier, there is no express exclusion of other elements from the definition of audiovisual works. On the contrary, sound is also referred to as being potentially included. However, the prevailing element is always the image.[87] The requirement of the image as the dominant element in an audiovisual work predefines also the purpose of an audiovisual work.

---

[86] I.e. in cases where text is included in the film it usually comprises only the opening and closing titles.

[87] Indeed Lucas argues that even though the law does not specifically stipulate that an audiovisual work should consist exclusively of sequences of moving images, one would no doubt be stretching the meaning of the words unduly if one regarded a work that includes only a limited number of sequences of moving images as an audiovisual work. In most cases the components of a multimedia work will be of a diverse nature and the work will lack the coherence of a normal audiovisual work. Nevertheless putting such a work in the inappropriate straitjacket of the category of audiovisual works does not seem suitable. Lucas, 'Multimédia et droit d'auteur', at 145–6. See also A. Lucas, 'Les oeuvres multimédias en droit belge et en droit français' in C. Doutrelepont, P. Van Binst and C. Wilkin (eds.), *Libertés, droits et réseaux dans la société de l'information*, Bruyland and LGDJ, Brussels and Paris, 1996, 55, at 67; H. Bitan, 'Les rapports de force entre la technologie du multimédia et le droit' [1996] *Gaz Pal* (26 January 1996) 12; H. Pasgrimaud, 'La qualification juridique de la création multimédia: termes et arrière-pensées d'un vrai-faux débat' [1995] *Gaz Pal* (11 October 1995); and Edelman, 'L'oeuvre multimédia'.

Audiovisual works are meant to be shown, either in public or privately. They are not meant to be read, as would be the case with literary works.

'Image' is a notion that is somehow larger than the notion of a 'picture'. The term 'picture' was found in the Copyright Act 1956, which was replaced by the CDPA 1988. It seems more difficult for the term 'picture' to include images which are not derived from pictures as such but from computer-generated devices, which can transform data into image, as would be the case, for example, with a computer-programmed automatic puppet show[88] or a figure generated by a computer by putting bits and pieces of the images of well-known artists together and programming their moves. Thus, images do not have to stay unchanged from the traditional format in which they are found in conventional films. Apart from two-dimensional images, three-dimensional images, holograms and virtual reality shows are also covered. Images can also be produced by digitised pre-existing information and computer-generated displays, such as the 'attract' mode of an arcade game (video game in which a moving picture is generated by computer).[89] The fact that the new technologies make these images far more diverse and complicated than the ones found in conventional films, as well as the fact that these kinds of pictures are not usually found in films as we traditionally know them, should not affect the notion of the image as this notion is enshrined in the national definitions of audiovisual works.[90]

It follows logically from the above that the medium from which an image is produced or generated, and the support, linear or non-linear, on which it is reproduced and communicated, should not affect the notion of the image. For that very reason no special support or medium is required by the law. Images can either be produced by filming, putting drawings ('cells') together (as in cartoons), or be computer-generated (as with the special effects in films such as *The Day After*, *Independence Day* and *Jurassic Park*).

In the light of the above, any multimedia product in which (moving) images form the main element should qualify as an audiovisual work. However, in multimedia products, though they are expressed in an audiovisual way[91] and though they look like an audiovisual work, images are rarely the most important element.[92] This is especially so in cases where a multimedia work is the adaptation to an electronic format of an

---

[88] See Laddie, Prescott and Vitoria, *Modern law*, at 377.
[89] *Ibid.*
[90] See the thoughts of Turner, 'Old legal categories', at 108.
[91] See X. Linant de Bellefonds, Note under CA Paris, 16 May 1994, (1995) *JCP*, GII 22375.
[92] The need to know which is the prevailing element in a work (or contents of a work) is dictated by the definition of the separate kinds of works themselves and is also the

encyclopaedia or other work which was primarily fixed, or could be fixed on paper. In such a case one might wonder whether the transfer of a work from a paper support to a CD-ROM is a new mode of exploitation, where separate contracts, transfer of rights by the author and additional remuneration is required, or whether it is another use covered by the rights conferred by the initial contract. If it is the latter no separate transfer of rights and supplementary remuneration are required.[93] The view which seems to be closer to the reality and needs of authors is that digitisation is indeed a separate mode of exploitation, giving rise to what are usually known as electronic rights. This is also implied by the fact that 'electronic rights' of authors are not automatically transferred to publishers and producers unless they are precisely defined in the licensing contract. If they are not, any legal presumption works against their transfer and in favour of the authors.[94] An example of a multimedia product is an encyclopaedia which is put on CD-ROM. Although the encyclopaedia is shown on the screen, the user simply reads it. Images are accessory, whilst text is the main element. Its transfer from paper onto CD-ROM should not alter the nature of the work, even if adaptations to match the new mode of exploitation are made, e.g. interactive retrieval and browsing of the information. Of course, separate licensing of rights is required as well as additional remuneration. In the Anglo-Saxon tradition this area is predominantly left to the contractual relationship between the parties. Very few, if any, statutory provisions regulate these issues.

However, does the existence of text, or of text as a prevailing element, exclude these works from the notion of audiovisual works altogether? The attempt of various lawyers to include teletext and Minitel within the ambit of audiovisual works has shown only that in certain cases this should not be so. According to them, text shown on a screen performs the same task as an image. In this sense teletext is an audiovisual work.[95] Yet, this would confuse, if not discredit, the boundaries between audiovisual and literary

---

essential/accessory test run by the courts in many countries in order to find the nature (essence) of a work. See Edelman, 'L'oeuvre multimédia', at 114 and note 44.

[93] See Edelman, 'L'oeuvre multimédia', at 115.

[94] Most continental systems seem to have a theory *in dubio pro auctore* which means that the terms of any licence or assignment have to be interpreted restrictively and that in case of doubt the author is assumed only to have assigned the absolute minimum of rights that are necessary for the specific exploitation that was envisaged in the contract. This theory is also known in Germany as the *Zweckübertragungstheorie*. (On its applicability in a multimedia context see R. Kreile and D. Westphal, 'Multimedia und das Filmbearbeitungsrecht' [1996] *GRUR* 254, at 254.) However, in the UK there is no such theory. On the contrary, it is fair to say that the presumption works the other way round. See G. Vercken, *Guide pratique du droit d'auteur pour les producteurs de multimédia*, commissioned by the European Communities, DG XIII (Translic) from AIDAA, 1994, at 114.

[95] See also Berenboom, *Le nouveau droit d'auteur*, at 193.

works, and would unjustifiably place too much emphasis on the medium of communication, culminating in the medium defining the nature of the work, rather than the work itself. In addition, the qualification of works as audiovisual would no longer be possible, since in practice such a solution would lead to all kinds of works being placed indistinguishably in one copyright basket. If copyright is to be redefined this is definitely not the most appropriate way to go about it.[96]

6.5.1.3 *'Sequence of moving images' and interactivity*

6.5.1.3.1 A *de minimis* rule

The inclusion of images as such does not suffice for a work to qualify as an audiovisual work. Most national laws require, expressly or impliedly, the existence of 'moving images'.[97] Yet, what each national law refers to or implies by 'moving images' is not immediately obvious. The notion of 'moving image' can be construed either narrowly or broadly. In either case a *de minimis* rule should be applied. A moving image is not just a changing image.[98] Nevertheless, despite the variety of definitions, there is at least a

---

[96] Even if in the future the various categories of copyright works are abolished, the regime of protection will have to be adapted to cover all needs. This is clearly not the case now.

[97] The requirement of a 'moving image' is found in the national copyright Acts in relation to films (UK), motion pictures (USA) and cinematographic works (France and Germany), and not in the definition of audiovisual works as such (it exists in the preparatory works of the Belgian Commission of the Chambers of Justice in relation to audiovisual works, Report De Clerck, LDA, at 181). (In fact, the lack of this requirement in the definition of audiovisual works seems to be the distinctive line between audiovisual works and films.) Yet, since most countries provide only a single definition (e.g. only for films or only for audiovisual works), they mean or use the aforementioned definitions interchangeably or by analogy (see, for example, the Greek Copyright Act which refers to films before their fixation as audiovisual works and after their first fixation as films). The fact that this analogy is very common in reality derives also from the Berne Convention which assimilates all works using the process of cinematography or something analogous to it. Since, as we explained in the first section of this chapter, the category of audiovisual works is held to be the broader category which contains the rest, and since the most common sort of audiovisual works are cinematographic films, we will use the terms audiovisual works and films interchangeably for the needs of this chapter. Moreover, we hold that the notion of moving images, wherever it is not expressly mentioned (as it is, for example, in the UK, US and French Copyright Acts in relation to films and cinematographic works), is implied by the strong relationship of audiovisual works to the rest of the aforementioned categories. We also hold that the European definition of films, as enshrined in the rental and lending rights Directive (OJ L346/61) and which refers to films as cinematographic or audiovisual works or moving images, does not imply any essential or actual difference between the three. It tries to encompass these cases only where national laws might want to, or do, differentiate in relation to the scientific definitions they use for the aforementioned categories of works. However, this does not admit or legitimise such differentiations.

[98] Turner, 'Old legal categories', at 108.

Audiovisual works

common link with the notion of motion. Is motion a recording of apparently identical images, which have, however, been recorded at different moments, or do the images themselves have to communicate or create the impression of some kind of movement? If the second option is taken then even when images are filmed with a traditional filming technique, if the average person cannot see with his bare eye that movement exists, the moving images, though moving in reality, are not held to be 'moving' for the purposes of the law. However, such a solution would disregard the essential criterion that is contained in the Berne Convention, namely the use of cinematography or a technique analogous to cinematography. If the first option is taken then we could argue that the recording process is sufficient to qualify a work as an audiovisual work. It may not communicate movement in all instances but at least the potential for movement is there. A straightforward example is that of a plant which grows extremely slowly. Even if a single picture is taken every hour over a period of three months, once projected as a film at a speed of twenty-four pictures per second little or no movement may be visible. Nevertheless this is an audiovisual work due to the technique used and, scientifically speaking, there is constant movement even if this is not readily perceived. An even more extreme example is found in a shot of a desert landscape which is used to create a certain atmosphere. A one-minute shot may continue to offer the viewer exactly the same view of the landscape. Nevertheless, due to the use of the cinematographic technique and its potential for movement, this is also an audiovisual work.[99]

Fixed frames or still images alone are excluded altogether.[100] A sequence of fixed frames sewn together (sequence of images *inanimé*) should also be excluded.[101] Berenboom asserts that the latter should not be the case as long as these fixed frames have undergone a montage

---

[99] As will be seen later, the particular technique that is used to reproduce images is not of primary importance. What is, however, of importance is the content of the product and the fact that a certain type of recording has been made. For example, the shooting of pixels onto a television screen does not define the type of work. A photograph can be reproduced in that way onto a screen, and so can a text. What counts here is the process of recording, as well as the content of the recording.

[100] A series of archive photographs should not fall within the category of audiovisual works: Strowel and Triaille, *Le droit d'auteur*, at 360.

[101] See also Edelman, 'L'oeuvre multimédia', at 114. See *contra* Strowel and Triaille, in relation to a series of slides, which, according to their view, qualify as an audiovisual work, *Le droit d'auteur*, at 360. We hold the opposite view, similar to the one shared by J. Corbet, *Auteursrecht*, Story – Scientia, Brussels, 1997, at 38 and the Belgian Association of Copyright, oral process of 2 April 1992 on audiovisual works. D. Nimmer (*Nimmer on Copyright*, Mathew Bender, New York, 1995) holds that although a show of slides qualifies as an audiovisual work under the US Copyright Act, it does not qualify as a film because it fails to confer the impression of movement to the viewer, vol. I, § 2.09 [C].

which allows them to unfold in such a way as to create the impression of motion.[102] In his view, a succession of fixed frames should qualify as an audiovisual work, and he refers as an example to the film of Chris Marker, *La jetée*. His view comes very close to confusing the boundaries between artistic works and audiovisual works. If the notion of moving images is so broadly construed and approached, then there is nothing essentially different between the viewing of an artistic work and the viewing of a series of moving images on a screen. In this case the unfolding (the technical French term is *déroulement*) of these images can no longer be distinguished from one's tour of an exhibition or even from turning over the pages of a book if these images or pictures are found in a conventional book.[103] In this sense a multimedia work containing fixed frames, which can be retrieved and browsed through according to the needs and commands of the user, and which do not impart an impression of motion or a continuous impression of motion occupying the greater part of their contents, cannot qualify as an audiovisual work. It comes closer to literary works, databases or artistic works.

6.5.1.3.2 Two ways of construing the notion of 'moving images'

If the *de minimis* rule is applied so as to rule out fixed frames altogether, then a broader view is the French one. According to this view, the images have to be related to and linked to each other in such a way that they can unfold, subject, for example, to a scenario.[104] By 'related to' and 'linked to each other' it is not meant that the images have to be relevant only to each other, or that they just follow one another in a logical sequence. They have to be sewn together in such a way that even if they are not 'moving images' right from the start (e.g. filmed as moving images or computer generated as such) they can at least impart the impression of motion to their viewer when they are communicated.[105] Thus, it is submitted that it is the sequence of images that should be recorded and not just the visual images.[106] The sequence of images, when combined with the other ingredients of a film, should be capable of producing a moving picture in a 'fluent movement'. Yet, the degree of that fluency is a question of fact, subject to the judgment and discretion of the judge. It is alleged, though, that this 'fluent movement' can derive even from

---

[102] Berenboom, *Le nouveau droit d'auteur*, at 193.
[103] Especially in the case of an encyclopaedia; see also Edelman, 'L'oeuvre multimédia'.
[104] Groupe Audiovisuel et Multimédia de L'Edition, *Questions juridiques*, at 20.
[105] This is also the American view. See § 101 of the US Copyright Act, under the entry 'moving pictures'. From a UK perspective it could be argued that s. 5B(1) CDPA 1988 is wide enough in scope to include this possibility.
[106] Laddie, Prescott and Vitoria, *Modern law*, at 385–6.

pictures taken in a rapid sequence (e.g. by still cameras in motor races capturing almost every second of action) if the gaps between them are small enough.[107] In this case 'the resulting spool might satisfy the definition of "cinematograph film" even though the photographer was using neither a cine camera as commonly understood nor had any intention of making a moving picture'.[108]

If the notion of 'moving images' is construed narrowly, one could argue that what the law is really looking for are actual moving images and, in certain cases perhaps, images that are moving before they are recorded as films. Under UK law this has been particularly so after the replacement of the definition of films in the Copyright Act 1956 by that of the CDPA 1988. Under the former, one could perhaps have assumed that the moving image had to exist before it was recorded,[109] but the CDPA 1988 no longer requires the pre-existence of the 'moving image'. An actual moving image can be an image taken by a cine camera, generated by a computer so as to be in motion. Yet, this narrow legal approach would leave out of the scope of the law the individual drawings (cells) included in cartoon films, which worldwide are held to qualify as films.[110] It is true, however, that these are held to qualify as films after they are collected, put in sequence and recorded on any medium (not only on pellicle) in such a way that motion can arise.[111]

If the first view is adopted, it may be easier to fit multimedia works into the category of audiovisual works and films. These are clearly not images that already move before they are recorded but one could assume that most multimedia works introduce some kind of impression of movement. This becomes clear when one looks at an even more radical approach which requires an audiovisual work to be just a series of related images which are intrinsically intended to be shown by the use of machines.[112] Most multimedia works could indeed be said to contain a

---

[107] Even if the gaps are not small enough, in the way they have been described in the text, a reasonably fluent picture might still be produced if the subject was moving slowly enough, e.g. the filming of a germinating seed with a slow cine camera which is then speeded up for display. *Ibid.*, at 386.

[108] *Ibid.*, at 385–6. Under German copyright law a 'sequence of moving images' is interpreted as a series of images and sounds that create the impression of moving images. See G. Schricker, *Urheberrecht. Kommentar*, C. H. Beck, Munich, 1987, at 1002; 2nd edn, 1999, at 1371; and W. Nordemann, K. Vinck and P. Hertin, *Urheberrecht*, Kohlhammer, Munich, 1994, at 523.

[109] Turner, 'Old legal categories', at 108.

[110] See Koumantos, *Pnevmatiki idioktissia*, at 132.

[111] Laddie, Prescott and Vitoria, *Modern law*, at 378.

[112] See, for example, § 101 of the US Copyright Act. A similar approach is adopted under Spanish and Dutch copyright law. See also A. Estève, 'Das Multimediawerk in der spanischen Gesetzgebung' [1998] *GRUR Int* 1.

series of related images and the issue of movement is more or less sidestepped. It is submitted though that whichever approach is adopted, multimedia works do not fit in well with the category of audiovisual works, and that each link remains artificial.[113]

6.5.1.3.3 'Sequence of moving images' and interactivity

We should examine at this stage what exactly the requirement of 'sequence' adds[114] to that of 'moving images'. It is clear that 'moving images' might be present in a work without necessarily forming a sequence or else a unity. Fragments of films, cartoons, documentaries and frames in motion in relation to motor races or sprinting do not alone allow a work to qualify as an audiovisual work or a film. Take as an example a collection of fragments of films shown in the 1980s and 1990s. This encyclopaedia of films does not present a unity in the sense that the notion of a film requires.[115] Rather it comes within the ambit of a database, as this is defined in the EU Directive.[116] The moving pictures included in a film have to be coherent and united in serving one particular project, plot, scenario or otherwise. Simple audiovisual 'touches' or 'spreads' of fragments of moving images are not covered.[117] According to Edelman,[118] if we have a collection of fragments of audiovisual works, without these works co-existing in a legal sequence or coherence

---

[113] T. Desurmont, 'L'exercice des droits en ce qui concerne les "productions multimédias"' in *WIPO international forum on the exercise and management of copyright and neighbouring rights in the face of the challenges of digital technology*, Seville, 14–16 May 1997, WIPO, 1998, 169, at 176.

[114] The CDPA 1988 does not contain this element *expressis verbis*. Later in the text we will analyse whether it nevertheless forms part of the concept that is contained in the Act.

[115] According to Cornish a digital encyclopaedia, which does not produce moving images, does not fit within the definition of films, *Intellectual property*, at 533.

[116] There is, of course, a part of the literature that would consider such a collection of works as being an audiovisual work. Yet, if this kind of collection qualifies as an audiovisual work, it cannot qualify as a database at the same time, because, as Laddie has pointed out (and it seems logical), different categories of works are intended to accommodate different (and mutually exclusive) kinds of works. In addition, in those national laws where the notions of databases have been placed under the wider umbrella of literary works, there is one more argument against the parallel protection of a work as an audiovisual work and as a literary work. These two categories of works are not only logically exclusive, but also expressly mutually exclusive from a legal point of view.

[117] According to Turner, 'Old legal categories', at 108, the requirement of 'moving images' in the British definition of films 'obviously covers some of the displays that may be produced on screen by a multimedia product'. Yet, he finds it doubtful whether it covers animation, the different levels of compression below full motion video, screen scrolling and all other movements that are generated on screen.

[118] 'An audiovisual work can only be protected if it exists as a work. This means that it needs to have a certain degree of coherence in the sense that the sequences of images need to form a certain unit': Edelman, 'L'oeuvre multimédia', at 114.

(*sans queue ni tête*), it is not an audiovisual work we are dealing with but a collection of citations. The regime of protection for audiovisual works should not apply. In this case the resemblance comes closer to literary works, databases or the reading of a book than to the performance/showing of a film.

What is not clear at this point is whether or not the sequence of moving images which is required should be uninterrupted. In some national laws, interactivity in relation to conventional films was an unknown concept. Films were traditionally designed and produced subject to a linear form, inextricably linked with and dependent on the unfolding of images that were sewn together, so as to produce the effect of continuous motion. In other words, the viewer who was seeing the film was a passive receiver, whose task was no more than to watch the 'story' from the beginning to the end. The notion of interactivity, which is embedded in multimedia works, is by definition contradictory to any uninterrupted linear unfolding of a sequence of images, favouring a dialogue between the user and the system and the interference by the former with the latter according to his needs and choices.[119]

Nevertheless, this conclusion or observation is not watertight. There is also a part of the literature which contends that interactivity is not a notion completely alien to the area of audiovisual works and films. Early films did not possess any interactivity. But later, slow or quick motion commands became available, as well as freeze frame, scanning, time shifting[120] and other options. The choose-your-own-end films which appeared on the market offered a better example of a primitive form of interactivity. The viewer does not have only a passive role (i.e. viewing the film only in the way it is presented). He intervenes and predetermines the end of the film by selecting from the choices available. Yet, the aforementioned commands which were available to viewers of films were not commands inherent in the notion of films. They were essentially commands made available by machines, such as video cassette players, which could manipulate the image to a certain extent. (Films are not structured to serve such purposes. They are not structured in fragments so that their contents can be accessed independently.) These commands are referred to by Choe[121] as the first sperm of interactivity, or manual interactivity, and should be distinguished from the film itself, which presents no

---

[119] Deprez and Fauchoux refer to interactivity as 'la négation du déroulement linéaire, au profit d'accès commandés par l'utilisateur', *Lois, contrats et usages*, at 48.
[120] Recording of a film so that it can be viewed at a later, more convenient, time by the viewer.
[121] J. Choe, 'Interactive multimedia: a new technology tests the limits of copyright law' (1994) 46 *Rutgers Law Review* 929, at 935.

interactive options whatsoever. In addition, manual interactivity was not only a primitive form of the actual interactivity that modern multimedia products present, but it was also so basic and limited that it was qualitatively different from the interactivity possessed by multimedia products today. It did not allow for any substantial dialogue between the viewer and the film, only for the exercise of certain primitive commands. These commands in no way turned the passive viewer into an active user and manipulator. Although they presented certain options, impinging on the development (stopping and starting) of the picture, in no way did they offer the ability to manipulate and reconstruct the image itself.

In the case of choose-your-own-end films, the viewer is not afforded any substantial degree of action. He is not allowed to 'enter' the image itself and transform it. What he is allowed to do though is to interfere with the sequence of images presented to him. This has only a little to do with interactivity, since changing the sequence of images is only one of the interactive possibilities, and a very basic one at that. Choose-your-own-end films can be compared with video games. The latter, which allow for the intervention of the player and thus for a degree of interactivity, were found in many jurisdictions to qualify as audiovisual works.[122] Specifically, in *Midway Mfg Co. v. Artic International, Inc.*, the US Court held that even if the sequence of images varies after any new use of the game by the player, the notion of 'a series of related images', as this is referred to in § 101 of the US Copyright Act, is still not affected. The work still possesses a certain unity, which is enough to allow the work to qualify as an audiovisual work.

The element of interactivity which video games possess is more advanced than the one possessed by the choose-your-own-end films. But it is more limited in degree. It allows for no more than just a variation in the presentation of the sequence of the set of images which are included in these works. The user is restricted to choosing options A, B or C. In

---

[122] Cass. Ass. Plén., 7 March 1986, [1986] D. 405, concl. Cabannes, note B. Edelman; *Atari* c. *Valadon*, TGI Paris, 8 December 1982, *Expertises* 1983 no. 48, 31 (France). *Atari Games Corp. v. Oman* 888 F 2d 878 (D.C. Cir. 1989) and 979 F 2d 242 (D.C. Cir. 1992); 964 F 2d 965 (9th Cir. 1992), 115 S Ct 85 (1994); *Computer Associates International, Inc. v. Altai, Inc.* 982 F 2d 693, 703 (2nd Cir. 1992); *Stern Electronics, Inc. v. Kaufman* 669 F 2d 852, 855–6 (2d Cir. 1982); *Williams Electronics, Inc. v. Artic International, Inc.* 685 F 2d 870, 874 (3d Cir. 1982); *Midway Mfg Co. v. Strohon* 564 F Supp 741, 746 (N.D. Ill. 1983); *Midway Mfg Co. v. Artic International Inc.* 704 F 2d 1009, 1011 (7th Cir. 1983) (USA). *Pac Man* decision, as referred to in [1984] *EIPR*, at D-226 (Japan). *Nintendo* c. *Horelec*, Court of First Instance, Brussels, 12 December 1995, [1996] *IRDI* 89 (Belgium). *Amiga Club* decision, Oberlandesgericht Köln, 18 October 1991, [1992] *GRUR* 312 (Germany). *Galaxy Electronics Pty Ltd v. Sega Enterprises Ltd* (1997) 37 *IPR* 462 (Australia). *Nintendo v. Golden China TV-Game* (1993) 28 *IPR* 313 (South Africa). The case of video games is considered in chapter 8 below.

fact A, B or C follow automatically after a first choice of action is made by the user/player. Nevertheless, this kind of interactivity has not reached those levels which are usually possessed by multimedia works, where the user has even more active and creative roles.[123] One such example is a palette where colours and designs are offered to the user with which he can reconstruct or create images from scratch. Another is where various possibilities are offered for musical composition by adding melodies, changing keys or missing out instruments in an orchestra, and so on. This kind of result is often reached through the use of techniques such as morphing and blurring. In these cases the intervention of the user exceeds the level of options and reaches the level of reconstruction or simply new unpredicted creation.[124] In this context, it is difficult to understand how any sequence of moving images can be maintained.[125]

There is a serious argument that, with regard to the definition of moving images for example, UK law has been construed widely enough to encompass any notion of interactivity, especially in view of the lack of any precise prerequisite of a 'sequence of moving images'. However, this argument looks weak in view of the practical reality as presented above. It seems that these moving pictures should exist in a sequence, or at least in some sort of coherent unit. Even if that requirement is not mentioned expressly in the law, it must purposively be derived from it, especially if it is referred to in relation to the notion of a film, which represents a certain form in our minds. This, of course, does not mean that this form is not subject to evolution. Yet, we all know that the excessive stretching of certain notions and categories, as well as the departure from the historical interpretation of certain provisions, creates problems and presents gaps in the laws of the states. Most laws have been designed to accommodate certain forms of works and rarely others which could not have been foreseen at the time. In this case interactivity, and especially 'reconstructive' creative interactivity, cannot easily co-exist with this idea of unified moving pictures.[126] Nevertheless we should not ignore the tendencies derived

---

[123] The Green Paper also requires a minimum degree of interactivity: Green Paper on copyright and related rights in the information society, COM (95) 382 final, at 19.
[124] Always in the context of the choices offered, which can however be great enough to render the outcome unpredictable.
[125] Yet, it always remains open to discussion whether video games are a separate category of works, or whether they are multimedia products. In the latter case they can still be considered to require a separate protection from that afforded to other multimedia products.
[126] Schack argues that the advanced form of interactivity that is found in modern multimedia works means that a multimedia work can no longer be considered to be similar to a film. H. Schack, *Urheber- und Urhebervertragsrecht*, Mohr Siebeck, Munich, 1997, at 101. See also M. Marinos, *Pnevmatiki idioktissia*, Ant. N. Sakkoula, Athens, 2000, at 96–7. *Contra* Desurmont, 'L'exercice des droits', at 176.

from the example of video games, especially if these are held to be a kind of multimedia work. In the judgments referring to them it was not perhaps the actual nature of video games that gave rise to these decisions as much as their expression, appearance and need for protection.[127] This must have seemed appealing and must have come as a relief to the national judges who found themselves facing a gap in the law. Video games, of course, are a case which we will consider separately.

6.5.1.3.4 Concluding remarks

It is submitted that, despite all the apparent similarities, the concept of moving images creates serious problems concerning the classification of multimedia products as films or audiovisual works. The apparent similarities are over-emphasised by the common use of the technique of projecting images onto a television screen in the form of pixels and by the fact that in both cases some form of movement or activity seems to be involved. As section 5B of the CDPA 1988 makes clear, the particular technique used to reproduce the moving images is not important. The essential element is found in the substance of the work, in the images that are projected onto the screen. It is submitted that these images are different, rather than similar in nature.

Let us return to section 5B of the CDPA 1988 with regard to films. The essence of a film is that moving images are reproduced. The moving nature of the images is the crucial element. Sound can be an interesting addition, but it is not even necessary, let alone required. The essential element of moving images involves in some way the concept of a predefined sequence of images. The sequence of images creates the movement and is defined in advance by the makers of the film. The user gives one command and is then presented with a sequence of many images. This sequence may be the whole film or a rather limited section of it. In the latter case the viewer is invited to introduce a new command to release a new sequence of images. The content of the latter sequence may be influenced by the specific command given by the viewer. A limited and primitive form of interactivity is possible, but that interactivity leads only to the release of predefined sequences of moving images.

---

[127] See in this respect A. Bertrand, *Le droit d'auteur et les droits voisins*, Masson, Paris, 1991, at 509. A. Bertrand, 'La protection des jeux video', *Expertises* 1983, no. 56, at 230; and Edelman, 'L'oeuvre multimédia', at 110, where he alleges that a 'multimedia work is characterised on the one hand by the intervention of a computer program that allows for interactivity and on the other hand by an audiovisual expression'. This audiovisual expression seems to have prevailed in the judgments of the courts before whom the video games cases came.

Multimedia presents a different picture. A variety of images are projected onto a television or computer screen. Still images, such as photographs and text, are combined with moving images.[128] The images as such, and especially the moving images, are not the essence of a multimedia product. Not only are non-moving images involved, but the sound element is also of equal importance to the final product. The essential aspect of a multimedia product is found in the combination and in the integration of the various expressions. That integration leads to an advanced form of interactivity which allows the user to create his own version of the work while using it. The user picks and chooses from a wide variety of elements, expressed in different media, to make, for example, his own tour of the ancient Greek cultural heritage, as it is found in the various museums in Greece. Often the use of the multimedia product will involve a certain form of movement and, at the very least, movement from one screen to another will create an impression of movement. However, that movement is often based not on recorded 'moving' images that are reproduced from the recording, but on the interaction of the user with the various materials that are made available to him. Looked at in this way, the similarity is rather with a set of (un-)related photographs that can always be stitched together and shown at a rate of twenty-four photographs per second to create an impression of movement. We are trying to define the nature of the product that allows for interactivity. In this context we must return in our example to the individual photographs. They remain photographs in nature. Any subsequent use cannot change that, even if such use can lead to the creation of an additional work. It is therefore submitted that a multimedia product should not be classified as a film simply because its use would allow the user to create a sequence of moving images that could qualify as a film. The essence of the multimedia work lies in the element of interactivity. It does not have to be a recording that is made in such a technical way the first time round that moving images necessarily result from its normal intended use. It could rather be seen as a set of elements and data, a database in its non-legal sense, which is combined with software that allows for a sophisticated form of interactivity.

6.5.1.4 *Fixation/recording*

Fixation or recording, as this is provided for in the national laws on audiovisual works and films, would not be a hurdle if multimedia products

---

[128] According to J. Cameron, multimedia works are not films since they essentially contain text rather than images: 'Approaches to the problems of multimedia' [1996] 3 *EIPR* 115, at 116.

were to qualify as audiovisual works. Under section 5B of the CDPA 1988, the notion of films has been drafted very widely in relation to the medium on which a work can be fixed. Almost any recording falls within this definition. Some examples are films carried on celluloid, filmstock, print, negative, magnetic tape, videotape films, recordings on laser discs, CD-ROMs, DVDs and films stored in computer memories. Thus, copyright in relation to films is not tied to any particular technology.[129] In the light of this, although multimedia products are always put in a digitised format, whilst films are communicated or transmitted in an analogue format, this differentiation is one made *de facto* and not derived from the wording or the spirit of the law and thus it does not affect the law. Whether or not digitisation is included within the definition of films in relation to their recording is not a contested issue. According to the record of the discussions at the time of the introduction of this law, it was stated in the House of Lords[130] that the definition of films was intended to include recording on magnetic tape, but that since it was impossible to foresee what new technologies for recording and presenting moving pictures might arise in the future, the object of the definition was to avoid being tied to any particular sort of fixation.[131] No specific method of recording is required. Thus, according to Turner, 'digitisation is clearly a reproductive process analogous to older processes such as Braille and Morse code in reducing creative work into a binary form'.[132] In relation to the medium required, he mentions that 'neither the medium from which the moving image is produced, nor the means of producing the image, are of relevance [to a film] and can therefore clearly include a CD or other formats of multimedia products just as much as it does celluloid or video tape'.[133]

In addition, one can contend that the medium on which a work has been recorded (either originally or derivatively) should also not affect the nature of the work, if, of course, the work has been fixed or transferred onto the new medium without any substantial modifications, adaptations or alterations to it.[134]

Thus, if multimedia products were to qualify as audiovisual works, the fact that they are in a digitised format, capable of being manipulated by the user with the aid of a computer, and the fact that they are

---

[129] Laddie, Prescott and Vitoria, *Modern law*, at 377.
[130] *Hansard*, 16 February 1956, cols. 1085–6.
[131] Laddie, Prescott and Vitoria, *Modern law*, at 374, 383.
[132] Turner, 'Old legal categories', at 108.
[133] *Ibid.*
[134] Gautier, 'Les oeuvres "multimédia"', 99; Edelman, 'L'oeuvre multimédia', at 114, and at 110, where he contends that the concept of the 'document', or that of the 'support', should not be decisive in the characterisation of a work.

communicated to third parties through both material and non-material media, does not contradict the notion of fixed audiovisual works as found in the CDPA 1988 or other national Copyright Acts, and consequently does not create any definitional problems.[135]

6.5.2 The possibility of cumulative protection

A decision by Laddie J regarding a company memo dealt with the dilemma of whether this memo, which contained both text and graphics, could qualify at the same time both as a literary and as an artistic work.[136] It would be hard to imagine that a single work could qualify for more than one category of work at the same time, when it is supposed that the classification of categories of works is made in the first place because each category represents different and distinguishable kinds of works.[137] This is also the very reason why each separate category of work is governed by different rules. If the nature of the work were to overlap with another category, any differentiation in protection would be meaningless. In the decision at issue Laddie J held the same view. In fact he contended that the particular work could be either a literary or an artistic work. Since elements of both were included, the author had the right to separate the memo into a literary and an artistic work and pursue separate protection for each of them. Alternatively he could be afforded the protection of the category of work, the element of which was most prevalent in the memo, e.g. if it were text, the work should qualify as a literary work, or if designs, as an artistic work, etc.

This solution is more persuasive when the law expressly excludes cumulative qualifications of works. For example, in section 3(1) of the CDPA

---

[135] See also Cornish, *Intellectual property*, at 532–4.
[136] *Electronic Techniques (Anglia) Ltd* v. *Critchley Components Ltd* [1997] FSR 401: 'However although different copyright can protect simultaneously a particular product and an author can produce more than one copyright work during the course of a single episode of creative effort, for example a competent musician may write the words and the music for a song at the same time, it is quite another thing to say that a single piece of work by an author gives rise to two or more copyrights in respect of the same creative effort. In some cases the borderline between one category of copyright and another may be difficult to define, but that does not justify giving the author protection in both categories. The categories of copyright work are, to some extent, arbitrarily defined. In the case of a borderline work, I think there are compelling arguments that the author must be confined to one or other of the possible categories. The proper category is that which most nearly suits the characteristics of the work in issue.' See also *Anacon Corporation Ltd* v. *Environmental Research Technology Ltd* [1994] FSR 659, per Jacob J.
[137] See the Sirinelli Report on multimedia and new technologies, France, Ministère de la culture et de la Francophonie, Paris, 1994, at 58, where it is argued that protection for a single multimedia work both as an audiovisual work and as a database would lead to incompatible solutions because of the different rules that apply to each of these categories.

1988 a literary work is held to mean any work, *other than* a dramatic or musical work, which is written, spoken or sung. Yet, in the case of video games this line of thought has not been followed, since we have had cases where video games qualified as both audiovisual works and computer programs. These two qualifications probably co-existed for different parts of the same work, i.e. the part where moving images were included qualified as an audiovisual work and the structure of the system operating these moving images qualified as a computer program. This situation seems to arise when one category of work is not broad enough to cover the whole scope of a new work adequately, as was the case, for example, with video games and as might well be the case with multimedia works. Is it advisable in such cases to look for a cumulative definition, or simply to recognise the inefficiency of the particular categories to cover the needs of the new products?

In some countries the problem of overlaps between the various categories of copyright works does not arise. In general terms, those countries that have a general category of copyright works do not find it necessary to put a work in one single category. There is no urgent need that a work should go in one of the specialist categories in order to attract protection, and that seems to bring with it an attitude which also relaxes the requirement that a work can only go in one category.

Returning to the CDPA 1988 system, it would, perhaps, be more politically and theoretically correct, if we want to keep the distinctions between the different types of works and the boundaries which serve for the maintenance of these distinctions in place, to introduce new legislation, directly and exclusively applicable to the new category of works, in the same way that the database legislation has been introduced by the EU.[138] The repercussions of the failure to introduce legislation appropriate to the new technology will be felt in the market and in the intellectual property and cultural industries of the various countries by complicating legal issues and confusing the question of what is the appropriate regime of protection. Different solutions in the various states can only cause bewilderment in the international market.

It should in this respect be noted that the strict separation between the various categories of copyright works, which is accepted under English law, does not necessarily apply in continental legal systems or in the USA.[139]

---

[138] Distinguishable parts which form works on their own merits, e.g. a database and its operating computer program, should still be distinguished and treated as separate works for the purpose of copyright.

[139] J. Ginsburg alleges that in the USA multimedia works may be considered as audiovisual works or compilations or both. It is interesting to note that the USA does not seem to

6.5.3 Summing up

Multimedia products are not *de iure* audiovisual works.[140] First, moving images are rarely the prevailing element in a multimedia work. Multimedia works combine different types of works, and it is usually either text or still images[141] which are their major element. Moreover, it is not their purpose to be shown in public, and consequently to be watched by viewers. They are meant to be communicated to private individuals and are not intended to be viewed by a larger public. This is so since the general task of a multimedia work is to allow a dialogue between the system and the user. This dialogue, of course, presupposes the element of interactivity, which as such is a negation of any continuous sequence of images, linked together and constituting a unity.[142] Fragments of sequences of moving images alone do not allow a work to qualify as a film or as an audiovisual work. This becomes more apparent if one looks into the terminology used in the area of multimedia and that used in audiovisual works. A multimedia work is supposed to be read, watched and heard, and also to be used at the same time, while a film is simply to be watched. The person receiving the information in the first case is a user, with an active role, and even on occasions a creative one, whilst in the second he is a passive viewer. The notion of interactivity is altogether absent in audiovisual works or films, whilst it is a vital component in multimedia. All the above, of course, do not preclude the case where a film can be designed and fixed as a multimedia work. If that occurs, of course, all the components of a film are present and the work should qualify as an audiovisual work. The existence or not of the interactivity element should then be assessed on its own merits. If the work has been designed in order to produce moving images, then this lets it stand out from the normal multimedia case in which the essence is not moving images, but interactivity.

---

draw strict borderlines between the various categories of copyright works. 'Domestic and international copyright issues implicated in the compilation of a multimedia product' (1995) 25 *Seton Hall Law Review* 1397, at 1399. See also Strowel and Triaille, *Le droit d'auteur*, at 366.

[140] See also the doubts expressed by Kreile and Westphal, 'Multimedia', at 255; Edelman, 'L'oeuvre multimédia', at 114; and Turner, 'Old legal categories', at 109, who contends that, perhaps, multimedia products will be squeezed into the films definition on a case-by-case basis. This approach also receives support from B. Wittweiler, 'Produktion von Multimedia und Urheberrecht aus schweizerischer Sicht' (1995) 128 *UFITA* 5, at 9; and see also F. Koch, 'Software – Urheberrechtsschutz für Multimedia – Anwendungen' [1995] *GRUR* 459, at 463. With regard to difficult cases, there is always the risk that these cases might make bad multimedia law.

[141] See also Aplin, 'Not in our galaxy', at 637.

[142] *Ibid.*; G. Wei, 'Multimedia and intellectual and industrial property rights in Singapore' (1995) 3 *IJLIT* 214, at 248; Turner, 'Old legal categories', at 108.

6.6 MULTIMEDIA PRODUCTS AND THE REGIME OF PROTECTION OF AUDIOVISUAL WORKS

Since we came to the conclusion that multimedia works are not *stricto sensu* audiovisual works, we should examine whether they might come within the scope of protection of audiovisual works by reason of analogy. Often the real question is not simply what a new product, such as multimedia, is, but also what we need to protect and how we want to protect it. There would of course be no reason for analogous application of the regime of protection to multimedia works (which has then to apply as it is (*in toto*)) if we did not first examine whether this regime of protection is capable of accommodating the needs of these products. This section sets out to do exactly that.

The first obvious point of dispute is whether a multimedia work can fit in with the specific legal requirement that an audiovisual work necessarily involves contributions by many persons. For example, in French law an audiovisual work is *de iure* a collaborative work.[143]

If we take into account the way a multimedia work is produced and distributed we can easily come to the conclusion that the classification as a collaborative work will not be convenient in most cases. Although in the production of a multimedia work many persons are required to collaborate and join forces and expertise in a concerted effort, it will very often be the case that there will not be a new creation developed for the production of a multimedia work. We will rather be confronted with the incorporation of pre-existing materials without the collaboration of their authors, as is the case with composite works. Moreover, in many cases the whole initiative for the production of a multimedia work will be taken by one person (the entrepreneur) or a legal entity which possesses the means to manufacture works requiring large investments. In this case the persons participating in the production of a multimedia work will be either other companies or employees of these companies.

According to Edelman,[144] multimedia products will in most cases be collective works, if they do not qualify as audiovisual works, whilst the qualification as collaborative or composite works will only be residual.[145] This approach favours the entrepreneurs, since it puts the emphasis on the way the multimedia work has been constructed and on the financing and control of the whole project.[146] One should also take into account

---

[143] Art. L113-7 of the French Copyright Act.
[144] Edelman, 'L'oeuvre multimédia', at 114.
[145] See also D. de Werra, 'Les multimédias en droit d'auteur' [1995] *Revue Suisse de la Propriété Intellectuelle* 237, at 243–4.
[146] A. Lucas, 'Droit d'auteur et multimédia' in *Propriétés intellectuelles, mélanges en l'honneur de André Françon*, Dalloz, Paris, 1995, 325.

the means by which these products are distributed. This is done mainly through third companies, rather than through the initiator of the project. Often these third companies are computer manufacturing companies, which put their brand name on the product so that they can push the sales up and distribute them in computer shops and bookshops in the same way software and books are distributed. This form of marketing and distribution is very different from the one used for films and audiovisual works, bringing it closer to the system used for books and literary works rather than to the one used for audiovisual works.

What is characteristic in the definition of collective works is that it is one person, either a natural person or a legal entity, who directs the whole project.[147] This description seems to be a convenient one in relation to financially big projects involving many works. Legal entities will in most cases be the ones to undertake large investments by reason of their ability to match the financial needs of such projects to the needs of specialised and qualified personnel and the need for technological equipment. They are better placed to risk commercial failure. For this reason legal presumptions of transfer of rights in favour of these persons have been put in place.

In addition, most special national regimes for audiovisual works or films give the status of authors to certain contributors. In most legal regimes one can add to that list, and the status of author should not necessarily be given to all of them. For example, in the French and Belgian jurisdictions, the author of the screenplay, the author of the adaptation, the author of the words, the graphical author in the case of animated works and the author of musical compositions with or without words specifically composed for the work have all been designated as the presumed authors of the audiovisual work together with the principal director.[148] Proof to the contrary can be adduced.

First of all, the existing list of presumptive authors does not suit most multimedia works.[149] There may not necessarily be an author of an adaptation or of the words, but there may be other significant contributors such as the photographer in the case of a multimedia work that is based on an encyclopaedia of modern photography, and the designer of the operating software of the multimedia product.[150] Secondly, it is undesirable

---

[147] In contrast to collaborative and composite works.
[148] Art. L113-7 of the French Copyright Act and art. 14 of the Belgian Copyright Act.
[149] See also Groupe Audiovisuel et Multimédia de l'Edition, *Questions juridiques*, at 21 where it is argued that most provisions that relate specifically to audiovisual works are not easily transposed to multimedia works.
[150] Lucas questions whether the list of co-operators in a film, especially the more extensive list used in French law rather than the restrictive one used in English law, is suitable for multimedia works since it is not obvious that all the authors are necessarily linked to the creative process. Lucas, 'Multimédia et droit d'auteur', at 149.

that in most multimedia cases the standard presumption needs to be overturned, and that specific proof of that needs to be adduced. The overturning of the presumption should not be an easy task and should be reserved for exceptional cases.[151] If multimedia works are put in this category the overturning of the presumption will become the rule rather than the exception.[152] Thirdly, even in those systems where authorship of a film is given to the producer and the principal director, problems might arise as to which contributor needs to be identified as the principal director of a multimedia product. Multimedia works are produced in a different way. There may not be an obvious equivalent to the producer and the director of a film.[153] Fourthly, the aim of the presumptive list of contributors of audiovisual works is to arrive at a manageable number of authors for each work. Whilst this may well work for audiovisual works in the sense that the main contributors are identified and they are few in number, this is not necessarily the case for a multimedia work where the role of each contributor on the list may be fulfilled by many persons. This could result in a vast number of persons being presumed authors. In that way the workable nature of the rule is destroyed. Sirinelli suggests an alternative approach. In his view one might conclude that in a large number of cases the producer will *de facto* be the author of a multimedia product. He then finds it bizarre that in those countries where the producer also gets a neighbouring right in the first fixation/recording of the film, these two rights which were in origin supposed to be separate rights for separate people will now be given to the same person. One has to examine whether such a situation would be desirable or whether it would result in the producer getting an unduly high level of overall protection. It is submitted that the latter will occur only when non-original parts are

---

[151] In most cases it may not even be legally possible to overturn these presumptions. See Desurmont, 'L'exercice des droits' at 179; C. Colombet, *Grands principes du droit d'auteur et les droits voisins dans le monde, approche de droit comparé*, 2nd edn, Litec, Paris, 1992, at 31; A. Bercovitz, 'La titularité des droits de propriété intellectuelle relatifs aux oeuvres audiovisuelles: le plan législatif' in Congrès de l'ALAI, *Audiovisual works and literary and artistic property*, ALAI, Paris, 1995, at 204–5.

[152] 'Some authors have proposed legislative changes to remedy the uncertainty that results from all of this. The aim of these changes would be the establishment of a list of participants who would be considered authors of the multimedia work. It is submitted that this temptation should be resisted. The multimedia industry is subject to rapid change and any new rule could become obsolete fairly quickly. It is preferable to let the professional custom develop itself.' A. Latreille, 'The legal classification of multimedia creations in French law' in I. Stamatoudi and P. Torremans (eds.), *Copyright in the new digital environment*, Sweet & Maxwell, London, 2000, 43, at 63. He refers to A. Vincent as the proposer of this change: 'Droit d'auteur; droit des auteurs et multimédia', interview conducted by F. Dooghe, *La Vie Judiciaire*, 22–6 May 1995, at 4.

[153] See section 2.3 above on project participants in the creation of a multimedia product. See also Berenboom, *Le nouveau droit d'auteur*, at 218.

included in the recording, otherwise any copyright will already cover *de facto* whatever could be offered in terms of protection by the neighbouring right.[154]

The fact that many authors are involved in the creation of a multimedia product necessarily has repercussions on the issue of moral rights and duration as well. The authors' works which have been included in such a product are more easily subject to alterations and therefore to infringement of the integrity right. The regime of audiovisual works has already put in place a structure for protecting moral rights, in the same way that they are protected in relation to any other copyright work. However, in certain continental systems this is accompanied by the particularity that they are protected only after the work has been finalised (after the final cut). The existence of many authors makes it virtually impossible to calculate the duration of the right in an accurate way.[155] At the very least the system becomes impractical because too many people have to be traced. This multiplicity of authors was not envisaged when the system of calculating the duration of copyright in audiovisual works was set up.

If parallels are to be drawn between the contributors to a film and those to a multimedia product, at first sight it could be argued that the obvious comparison would put the director of a film and the editor of a multimedia work on the same level.[156] The same could be said about the producer of a film and the producer of a multimedia work.[157] The editor of a multimedia work undertakes to select, acquire, bring together and edit the various works which are to be included in the product. The tasks of the director of a film are apparently not the same, as he undertakes primarily to direct the performance of the actors and to turn the script into a film. The producer of a multimedia work occasionally shares creative tasks with the editor of the work. On these occasions this can turn him into an author. If the roles of the four participants are compared, they appear not to have much in common. This is so because the contributors to a multimedia work do not have stable and well-defined roles. Even if their roles are well defined, it could be alleged that the editor of a multimedia work compares well to an editor of a literary work rather than to the director of a film, whilst the producer of a multimedia work compares more easily to the producer of a film if he has not undertaken any creative tasks but has restricted his role to the provision of investment.

The definition of collective works provides for various contributions which are merged together in such a way that they are no longer

---

[154] Sirinelli Report, at 58.
[155] See art. 2.2 of the EU term Directive, [1993] OJ L290/9.
[156] For the terms used in this chapter see section 2.3 above.
[157] Compare Lucas, 'Multimédia et droit d'auteur', at 149.

distinguishable. Since these contributions are no longer distinguishable, they obtain value only if they are seen in conjunction with each other and thus their whole (entity) should be retained and promoted. For this reason a quasi-compulsory transfer of rights is provided for in favour of the producer, and there is a restriction on the moral rights of the authors involved in the creation of the audiovisual work. In the case of various contributors agreeing to contribute their works to the making of a film, and the contract not having precisely defined all the rights that have been transferred to the producer, because reliance is placed upon the promise of the contributors, or the contract generally being incomplete, 'the contract shall be deemed to transfer to the producer all the economic rights which are necessary for the exploitation of the audiovisual work, pursuant to the purpose of the contract'.[158] This system of quasi-compulsory licensing was considered necessary by many countries for the finalisation of such a project. Since the financial risk remains with the producer, the one person who has undertaken the necessary investments for the production of the work, it would be very unfair to him if the production were to be impeded by reason of bad will or unclear clauses in the contract of production. In the Anglo-Saxon tradition no statutory provisions to this effect exist. The whole issue is regulated by the contractual relations between the parties.

Another obvious advantage for multimedia products is the existence in most jurisdictions of a separate right in the recording for the producer if the work is classified as an audiovisual work. In this context there is no originality requirement and the separate right offers an easy and additional protection to the producer. This may be of particular value in those jurisdictions with a higher originality requirement for the pure copyright protection.[159]

---

[158] Art. 34(1) of the Greek Copyright Act. See also art. L132-24 of the French Copyright Act, art. 18 of the Belgian Copyright Act and art. 88 of the German Copyright Act.

[159] In France, for example, art. L215-1 of the Copyright Act 1994 provides for a specific regime of protection for *vidéogrammes*. It has been argued that this special regime of protection suits multimedia works extremely well. The *vidéogramme* is essentially the material support on which a sequence of images has been fixed. As such it can be distinguished from the work or content (e.g. an audiovisual work) that is being fixed. Such a classification that is independent of the content of the work but rather depends on the support would fit in very well with the concept of a multimedia work which is essentially a CD-ROM containing a collection of pre-existing works in an integrated format. Groupe Audiovisuel et Multimédia de l'Edition, *Questions juridiques*, at 25. German copyright law has a concept that is similar to that of the *vidéogramme*, i.e. *Laufbildern*. For further details see Schack, *Urheber- und Urhebervertragsrecht*, at 280–2. Schricker argues, however, that under German law multimedia works, whilst they can contain *Laufbildern*, are clearly not to be classified as simple *Laufbildern*: *Urheberrecht. Kommentar*, 2nd edn, at 1479.

It has to be concluded from the above analysis that the category of audiovisual works has certain attractions when the classification of multimedia works is undertaken. It is equally clear though that multimedia products do not fit in well and that their classification as audiovisual works is problematic and has serious drawbacks. They are certainly not the most obvious and straightforward examples of audiovisual works.[160]

[160] It is also interesting to note that both in the UK and in Australia, it is the literal reproduction of a film that is prohibited and not the copying of the audiovisual work embodied in the recording. This means that if a multimedia work qualifies as a film it will only be afforded 'thin' protection since infringement will only occur if the actual recording, and not substantial parts of the underlying work, is copied. See, for example, *Norowzian* v. *Arks Ltd*, *The Times*, 14 November 1999 and 143 *Solicitors' Journal Lawbrief* 279 (United Kingdom); *Telmak Teleproducts Australia Pty* v. *Bond International Pty Ltd* [1985] 5 *IPR* 203 and [1986] 6 *IPR* 97 (Australia); and, in relation to sound recordings, *CBS Records Australia Ltd* v. *Telmak Teleproducts (Aust.) Pty Ltd*, [1987] 9 *IPR* 440 (Australia). See also I. Stamatoudi, ' "Joy" for the claimant: can a film also be protected as a dramatic work?' [2000] *IPQ* 117. As Aplin, 'Not in our galaxy', mentions at 638, 'where multimedia is concerned, this recording or embodiment will be either the program code or digital code (data) or both. Provided the code or the actual images produced from the code are not copied, there is nothing to prevent a competitor from imitating the user interface (both visual and non-visual) of a multimedia product, in terms of any "film" copyright. If this is the case, then it is questionable how effective and worthwhile this solution is for better protecting multimedia, especially given how crucial the user interface is to interactivity.'

7 Computer programs

7.1 A MULTIMEDIA WORK AS A COMPUTER PROGRAM

A multimedia product cannot perform its tasks unless it is assisted by a computer program.[1] It is the computer program which produces the interactive effects and allows the user to retrieve and arrange the contents of the multimedia work on his screen. The multimedia work and the computer program are marketed as one product.[2] Both are developed in a digital environment and distributed on a digitised medium or as a digitised service. The facts that both multimedia works and computer programs operate in a digitised environment, that the presence of the computer program is indispensable to the functioning of a multimedia work and that the architecture of a multimedia work relies on the design of its computer program[3] have urged many to think that we should investigate the possibility of whether a multimedia work can be protected as a computer program.[4]

Any attempt to protect a multimedia product as a computer program can only be based on certain grounds. It can be based either on the fact that in essence a multimedia work is nothing more than a computer program, or alternatively on the fact that if a multimedia work is more than just a computer program, this 'more' is only subordinate to a computer program and not substantial enough to warrant differential treatment. What is involved in the first case could simply be called

---

[1] More than one computer program can be contained in a multimedia product.
[2] In the case of a multimedia service it is not always certain that all of the software which operates the work is transmitted along with the multimedia work on-line. Usually the user is given the installation/operation tools before any data is sent to him.
[3] See A. Strowel and J.-P. Triaille, *Le droit d'auteur, du logiciel au multimédia (Copyright, from software to multimedia)*, Bruylant, Brussels, 1997, at 357. The materials of a multimedia work have to be put in such a form and order as to fit their operating software tool. In this sense part of their structure and arrangement is dictated by the software used for their manipulation. Of course, we should not disregard the fact that the scenario that the computer program brings into action is predestined and predefined by the manufacturer of the multimedia work according to its needs.
[4] For a clear example, see F. Koch, 'Software – Urheberrechtsschutz für Multimedia – Anwendungen' [1995] *GRUR* 459.

a sophisticated computer program. In the second case protection of the computer program can also cover the protection of those parts of the multimedia work that come in addition to the software it includes, but only when these parts do not form a work on their own, distinguishable and capable of attracting protection on their own merits.[5] In order to examine whether either of these two cases are applicable, we have to look first at the definition of a computer program and that of a multimedia work.

Many national and international legal instruments which refer to computer programs avoid defining them. This is mainly due to the fear that any definition runs the risk of becoming outdated very soon by the rapid developments in the area of information technology and therefore rendering any legal instrument in the area inflexible and incapable of coping with the new technological reality.[6] The EU software Directive,[7] which sought to harmonise the software protection throughout the Community, is also an example of a legal instrument that avoids defining the notion of computer programs.[8] It only provides in one of its Recitals that 'the term "computer program" shall include programs in any form, including those which are incorporated into hardware ... [it] also includes preparatory design work leading to the development of a computer program provided that the nature of the preparatory work is such that a computer program can result from it at a later stage'. However, computer programs are defined in the European Commission Green Paper on copyright and the challenge of technology as 'a set of instructions the purpose of which is to cause an information processing device, a computer, to perform its

---

[5] Sirinelli points out that it is clear both in the law and in the case-law that the special regime of protection is applicable to that part of a multimedia product which is a computer program and the common law is applicable to the rest. Sirinelli Report on multimedia and new technologies, France, Ministère de la culture et de la Francophonie, Paris, 1994, at 58. See also A. Lucas, 'Multimédia et droit d'auteur' in AFTEL, *Le droit du multimédia: de la télématique à Internet*, Les Editions du Téléphone, Paris, 1996, 113, at 144; *contra* H. Pasgrimaud, who argues that the real issue is the way in which the work is fixed and therefore a digital fixation makes a multimedia work a computer program: 'La qualification juridique de la création multimédia: termes et arrière-pensées d'un vrai-faux débat' [1995] *Gaz Pal* (11 October 1995) 13. It is submitted though that the medium on which the work is fixed is only of major relevance in relation to neighbouring rights such as sound recordings. Original copyright works are not primarily categorised on the basis of the medium of fixation. Multimedia works are in this respect first of all original copyright works.

[6] International protection for computer programs is provided for in the Berne Convention, TRIPs and the WCT.

[7] Council Directive (91/250/EEC) on the legal protection of computer programs, [1991] OJ L122/42.

[8] At a stage where the notion of a computer program is more or less certain and recognisable, that seems to be a wise solution. But no one is in a position to foretell what tasks computer programs will perform in the future and whether we will be able to define these new products as computer programs. At that stage, security in law might become a more apparent and prevalent need.

functions.... The program together with the supporting and preparatory design materials constitute the software.'[9]

Central to the definition of a computer program is the fact that a series of coded instructions is put together in order to perform some particular functions or to produce some particular results. These functions may vary according to the design and the needs of the users, but they all come down to a common core. They are technical and utilitarian functions, which characterise the computer program more as a functional tool than as a work.[10] This tool is usually the intermediary for the execution of a task which leads to the creation or operation of another work. This is also the case with the tasks a computer program performs in relation to a multimedia product. It is the functional tool which allows for the manipulation of the contents of the multimedia work and which makes it interactive.[11] Any intention or aim of combining different types of works so as to produce a 'multi-expression' result, a creative entity in the sense of integrated amounts of various data and works, is absent in the definition of a computer program. A computer program does not involve a variety of expressions. Even if text, images or sound are somehow combined or involved in the operation of software, they are by no means central to its function or operation. They form only minimal parts of it and in most

---

[9] Green Paper COM (88) 172 final, at 170. Another definition of a computer program is that it is 'a set of statements or instructions to be used directly or indirectly in a computer in order to bring about a certain result', § 101 of the US Copyright Act; I. Lloyd, *Information technology law*, 3rd edn, Butterworths, London, 2000, at 250.

[10] 'Contrary to the situation of a computer program, the multimedia product requires an artistic input. This work is not only created by the intellect, but also by the imagination. The utilisation of a computer program does not put the emphasis on the work, but on the result that is produced. The opposite is true for multimedia products. The format of a multimedia work produces results that can directly be seen by the user. Despite its interactive character it cannot simply be reduced to a tool. It can be used without external input. One uses a computer program, but one communicates with the other creations. Whereas the computer program makes the machine work, the multimedia work is reassembled and reproduced by the machine. A multimedia product is not overall a linguistic work, contrary to the situation of a computer program. It is impossible to write the entire multimedia work in source code. The works that are incorporated in it are put in digital code by a computer, but they cannot be assimilated to a literary work. The similarity between the procedures by which both works are created cannot eclipse the different conditions under which they are created. A multimedia work may well be a digital creation, but it is not the work of computer technicians', A. Latreille, 'The legal classification of multimedia creations in French law' in I. Stamatoudi and P. Torremans (eds.), *Copyright in the new digital environment*, Sweet & Maxwell, London, 2000, at 66–7. In relation to his last point he refers to Lemarchand, 'Aspects juridiques du multimédia' (part two), *Expertises* 1994, no. 175, at 307.

[11] Sirinelli argues that it is clear that a multimedia creation consists of one or more computer programs and 'something else'. Legal protection will necessarily be composite. What remains to be decided is the status (nature) of this 'something else'. In the case of video games and certain other programs that extra element is called 'audiovisual effects'. Lamy audiovisuel no. 638 *in fine*, at 517.

cases their role is auxiliary, decorative or residual. From this point of view a computer program comes closer to a tool (albeit a creative one) whilst a multimedia work comes closer to a collection of works or a film.

On the other hand, the combination of different types of expression (text, images, sound, etc.) in a seamless fashion on a single medium[12] is a vital and essential feature of a multimedia work.[13] The inclusion of these expressions in a multimedia work is not done in a cursory manner, or simply as an auxiliary support or for market or instructive purposes only. It is the object of the work itself, the central feature which characterises it and which is also implied in its terminology (multi-media). If this feature is isolated from its technical base, it still forms a work on its own (in certain cases even a highly creative one), and it is essentially that part of the multimedia product which gives it its real value. The computer program included in a multimedia work, known as the driver,[14] is nothing more than the key to operation (retrieval and projection onto a screen) and to interactivity.[15] In this sense the added value of a multimedia product derives from its contents (timeliness, comprehensibility, rarity, quality, etc.) rather than from the software incorporated in it.[16] The latter only makes the product market-attractive by rendering it interactive. In that sense Microsoft's *Encarta* encyclopaedia is more appealing to users than a conventional encyclopaedia on hard copy.

This conclusion is not a difficult one to reach, especially if one looks into the EU database Directive.[17] A database may, in the same sense as a multimedia work, be accompanied on the market by a computer program which allows for the retrieval of its data. The database is valuable for the data it carries and the way in which this data is presented on screen,

---

[12] See the definition of a multimedia work in chapter 2 above.

[13] The fact that both the multimedia work and the computer program are digitised is unimportant. Lucas, 'Multimédia et droit d'auteur', at 144 and Sirinelli, Lamy no. 638.

[14] The driver, along with a number of other parts, forms the technical base of a multimedia product, i.e. the platform on which a multimedia product runs, the manufacturing program of a multimedia work, its command procedure and the media (on-line or off-line) on which a multimedia work is distributed. The command procedure can also be considered a part of the multimedia work and not part of its technical base along the lines of the database Directive. See Recital 20 to the EU database Directive (96/9/EC) on the legal protection of databases, [1996] OJ L77/20.

[15] The software tool used for the operation of the multimedia work does not necessarily render the work itself operational. It might render only the support on which the work is carried operational. P. Deprez and V. Fauchoux, *Lois, contrats et usages du multimédia*, Dixit, Paris, 1997, at 49.

[16] Strowel and Triaille argue that the software which allows the manipulation of the multimedia work is only a marginal element of the work, the essential value of which remains the importance and the quality (*l'actualité*, etc.) of the assembled information in a literary, photographic, musical or other form: *Le droit d'auteur*, at 357.

[17] [1996] OJ L77/22.

and not for the computer program which reads the data. The computer program is an important part of the database only in so far as it is a necessary tool for the electronic retrieval of the information. The computer program which accompanies the database is afforded protection on its own merits under the provisions of the EU software Directive.[18] This train of thought has also been followed in the case of video games. Many video games qualify both as computer programs for the part of them which is a computer program (their technical base) and as audiovisual works for the additional part that creates the audiovisual effects.[19] In the cases where video games were found to be computer programs as a whole, this was justified on the grounds that the work as a whole did not present the variety and features of a genuine multimedia work. The essential element of it was interactivity rather than anything else.[20]

It is clear that a computer program is only one part of the multimedia product, namely the technical part.[21] In addition to that part, there is the visual effect of the compilation of the materials which is produced by the computer program and which is not created by materials contained or generated from it. These materials can be an amalgamation of sets of images, text, sound or other expressions which are projected onto a screen. Thus the similarities between a multimedia work and a computer program are due to the fact that the latter is part of the former's development and marketing and not because a multimedia work is a computer program. If the computer program contained in a multimedia work is taken out, the 'remaining part' is a valuable work in its own right that is capable of attracting copyright protection on its own merits. If in this case we were to protect this 'remaining part' by the regime of protection for computer programs, we would disregard its particularities and separate nature. The protection of the multimedia work would fall short of what would be required to encompass every aspect of the multimedia work and would be inadequate.[22]

---

[18] See Recital 23 to the database Directive which provides that 'the term "database" should not be taken to extend to computer programs used in the making or operation of a database, which are protected by Council Directive 91/250/EEC of 14 May 1991 on the legal protection of computer programs'.
[19] See Lucas, 'Multimédia et droit d'auteur', at 144.
[20] See Strowel and Triaille, *Le droit d'auteur*, at 350 and 356. See also chapter 8 below on video games.
[21] See also the EC Green Paper on copyright and related rights in the information society, COM (95) 382 Final, at 19 and the US White Paper, B. Lehman and R. Brown, 'Intellectual property and the national information infrastructure', Report of the Working Group on Intellectual Property Rights, US Patent and Trademark Office, Washington D.C., September 1995, at 44.
[22] See also G. Vercken, 'Les contrats des oeuvres multimédia' in *Guide de la nouvelle loi sur le droit d'auteur*, SACD–SGDL, Brussels, 1995, 45.

7.2 MULTIMEDIA WORKS AND THE REGIME OF PROTECTION FOR COMPUTER PROGRAMS

If nominalism is left aside, the regime of protection for computer programs might be regarded as a possible candidate for accommodating the needs of multimedia products. We will now turn to that regime of protection and examine whether it can adequately cover multimedia products.

Although computer programs are protected under the EU software Directive as a particular type of literary works, adaptations had to be made to that regime in order to be able to accommodate computer programs. As we explained in chapter 3,[23] the inclusion of computer programs within the ambit of protection of literary works was a strongly debated and highly disputed issue. Computer programs are works that are functional and utilitarian in nature and therefore their inclusion within the scope of literary works, which are works of high creativity and personal expression, would upset and alter the traditional equilibrium of copyright. Software was considered to be a borderline case between copyright and patent protection with the balance shifting slightly towards the former. A *sui generis* regime for computer programs was not an option at a stage when the pressing need for protection required an internationally accepted regime of protection for products already widespread on the market. The choice in favour of copyright protection was above all a policy decision.

7.2.1 The 'reverse engineering' exception

The general regime of protection for literary works could not remain unchanged in relation to computer programs. The most essential change to it was probably the introduction of 'reverse engineering'. In general, reverse engineering involves starting from an existing program in order to see how it works and how it is made and then producing a new work which is based on these findings. In the area of computer software, reverse engineering is a process in which the object code version of a program is converted into a more readily understandable version, such as the source code.[24] This conversion allows the user to understand how the program works. It allows him to isolate the idea behind its construction which he might use later for the creation of a new but not similar or identical program or to make the decompiled program compatible with another existing program. The copyright regimes that are based on the EU software Directive allow decompilation and reverse engineering only for

---

[23] See section 3.2.1 above on computer programs.
[24] See P. Torremans and J. Holyoak, *Holyoak and Torremans' intellectual property law*, 2nd edn, Butterworths, London, Dublin, Edinburgh, 1998, at 504.

the purposes of achieving interoperability. Although the concept of decompilation fits well with computer programs, it does not suit multimedia products very well. In cases where a multimedia product is not compatible with a PC or other hardware that is used, this is a problem relating to the software incorporated into the multimedia product rather than to the work itself. There is nothing that can be decompiled in relation to the visual effect/compilation of sound, images, text, etc. The interoperability of the multimedia product is solely regulated by its technical base. Even if one seeks to explore the idea behind the compilation of the works presented on the screen, this idea becomes evident only by browsing through the product itself. What needs decompiling is the idea behind the software that operates that compilation.

If one nevertheless tries to imagine what would be the impact of the application of the software protection regime on the whole of the multimedia product, one is bound to find that decompilation would create havoc in relation to the collection of works that is contained in the multimedia product. Any attempt to unravel the digital code would necessarily give the decompiler access to the digital version of the works that are contained in the multimedia product. The digital code of these works could then easily be extracted and used in another multimedia product, one eventually operated with a different software tool. It is submitted that this form of decompilation really amounts to what the database Directive calls extraction/re-utilisation under the *sui generis* regime for databases. It is hard to see why what is specifically outlawed in relation to a certain type of collection of materials should specifically be allowed in relation to another type of collection of materials. The fact that decompilation is only allowed to achieve interoperability is not a good criterion to judge whether such a decompilation is *de facto* legal or illegal. The use of the same digital material would no doubt bring the two multimedia products closer together, but there is no real interoperability, since there is no reason why two multimedia products should work together. It is submitted that the whole concept of interoperability, especially as a tool to mark the borders of what is allowed, makes no sense whatsoever in relation to multimedia works. Clearly the whole special reverse engineering/decompilation provision simply cannot work in relation to multimedia works.

7.2.2 The right to make back-up copies and slight adaptations and to correct errors

Another series of issues which are equally problematic in relation to multimedia products relate to the right granted to the user of a computer program to make back-up copies, to adapt (slightly) the program if the standard version fails to meet his needs fully and to correct possible errors that are found in the program. Back-up copies of a computer program are justified on the grounds of the ease with which something can go wrong or become lost in the memory of a computer. In this case the user should not be obliged to purchase the whole software package since only a part of it is not available.[25] In addition, any damage or loss can cause great inconvenience to his work if we take into account that software is a tool for technical functions such as calculating, setting up the cashflow of a company or simply keeping its books, etc. A multimedia program does not necessarily or immediately serve technical and utilitarian functions. In the same way that one is not entitled to a second copy of a book if that book gets lost or is burnt, neither is one entitled to a second copy of a multimedia work. That would unjustifiably restrict the rights of the authors of the work at issue. The same applies in relation to the rights to adapt or correct errors in the multimedia work. Adaptation of a computer program is regarded as a necessary act in order to make it interoperable with another program or to adapt it to the specific needs of the user in the same sense as decompilation is permitted. Yet decompilation might not be enough. Upgrading and debugging might also be required. Since a multimedia work is not a tool in the sense that a computer program is, adaptation or correction cannot be justified. These actions can only be held to be impermissible actions, and therefore infringements of the rights of the rightowners in a multimedia work.

7.2.3 The status of the employee

Another issue which differentiates the regime of protection for computer programs from that of other literary works is the status of employees. There have been no changes in countries such as the UK, which already provided that the economic rights in works created in the course of employment are by definition transferred to the employer who becomes their first owner through the operation of law.[26] The EU software

---

[25] Computer programs are primarily functional tools. Therefore it is quite readily accepted that if a functional tool breaks down its owner is allowed to repair it. Practically speaking this means that the owner of the program needs to have a back-up copy of the damaged files so that he can reload them onto the hard disk of the computer. This operation is only possible if the owner has kept a copy of the whole product. In the same way, a library has a right to photocopy some pages of a journal in order to replace them if those pages have been ripped out of the journal. An obligation to purchase the whole journal again would be rather unfair.

[26] S. 11(2) CDPA 1988: 'where a literary, dramatic, musical or artistic work is made by an employee in the course of his employment, his employer is the first owner of any copyright in the work subject to any agreement to the contrary'.

Directive has followed the British paradigm in relation to the manufacturing of computer programs in the course of employment and it has introduced it as a general provision in the national laws of all Member States.[27] Any rights in a computer program which an employee produces in the course of his employment are automatically transferred to his employer, unless a contractual clause to the contrary is found. Even in cases where an employee's contract does not provide such an express and specific clause for the transfer of the economic rights in the work to the employer, such a clause is implied by law. Clearly the emphasis here has been put on the facilitation of the development and marketing of the work. The entrepreneur is invested with all those rights that are necessary for the efficient exploitation of the computer program. The character of a computer product is commoditised to such an extent that any special provisions which were traditionally based on the nature of a genuine literary work are no longer justified.[28] This, however, is not a provision which is necessarily ill-fitted for multimedia works if we consider that these works are also the work of a team which demands large investments and whose creation and exploitation must be secured in favour of the person or company which is prepared to invest in it.[29] Of course, another way of doing it would be to designate the producer of the multimedia product immediately as the author of this work. However, this solution impinges on the spirit and purpose of copyright that grants authorship only to the actual creators of a work. Any other solution would add to a further depurification of copyright.

7.2.4 A modified regime of moral rights

The area of moral rights is one which has been adapted by many national laws in order to fit the needs of the commercialisation and use of computer programs. Also, the general impression shared in those countries with a traditionally strong moral rights tradition is that moral rights fit badly with

---

[27] Art. 2.3 of the software Directive: 'Where a computer program is created by an employee in the execution of his duties or following the instructions given by his employer, the employer exclusively shall be entitled to exercise all economic rights in the program so created, unless otherwise provided by contract.'

[28] The software Directive aims at the protection of the producer and of the work rather than the protection of the author as is the case with other copyright works. See A. Dietz, [1990] *ZUM* 54, at 57 and M. Marinos, *Logismiko (software). Nomiki prostassia kai simvassis* 2 vols., Kritiki, Athens, 1992, II, at 141ff.

[29] It is interesting to note at this point that the EU Directive on databases does not provide for the automatic transfer of economic rights of works created in the course of employment to the employer of the creator. In that sense it was judged to be more sensible to apply the classic provisions on copyright to databases. (Databases do not necessarily need to be protected as literary works.)

computer programs.[30] Moral rights are essentially justified by the strong bond between a creator and his work. The more industrial/utilitarian the good is, the more the bond between an author and a work loosens. In addition, software is often the work of a team and the subject of continuous adaptations. The author or authors cannot easily be identified. The development of a computer program requires large investments and has commercial purposes only. That is another aspect that has made drafters of national and international legislation on computer programs place more weight on the ease and security of the investor, the work and the user rather than on the author.

The EU software Directive does not expressly refer to moral rights protection. It provides only that computer programs come under the provisions of the Berne Convention, and thus article 6*bis* on moral rights must also apply.[31] Yet, whether this provision refers to the application of the traditional duo of moral rights (the right of paternity and the right to integrity, but the latter only in cases where the honour and reputation of the author are prejudiced) or to the full national moral rights provisions which apply to any literary work, is not clear.[32] Some national copyright laws have saved themselves from this dilemma by providing for specific moral rights protection relating to computer programs. However, even in these cases the problem remains if these provisions are not exhaustive. In most EU Member States restrictions have been placed on moral rights protection for software either by express provisions in the copyright laws or by restrictive teleological interpretation of the law.[33] Indeed, if we leave aside the UK where moral rights have been abolished altogether in relation to computer software and computer-generated works,[34] most Member States limit moral rights protection to the rights of paternity and integrity. On most occasions the latter is limited to situations where actions prejudice the honour or reputation of the author.

At this stage the issue of employer ownership of rights must also be taken into account. In the UK system no problems arise because moral rights do not apply to computer programs. In the systems that grant moral

---

[30] Marinos, *Logismiko*, at 49ff.
[31] Art. 1.1 of the EC software Directive.
[32] See the De Clerck Report commissioned by the Belgian Ministry of Justice, Chambers of the Representatives, 17 March 1994, Doc. Parl., no. 1071 (SO 1993–4), 11–14 where it is alleged that computer programs, according to the EC software Directive, should only be afforded 'a minimal moral right' corresponding to the scope of art. 6*bis* of the Berne Convention. See also the Edelman Report commissioned by the Justice of the Sénat, 6 June 1994, Sénat, Doc. Parl., no. 1054-2 (SO 1993–4), 6.
[33] Also by applying the provisions on abuse of rights.
[34] See ss. 79 and 81 CDPA 1988.

rights for computer programs, these rights are granted to the author, i.e. the employee. Economic rights, however, may belong to the employer through the operation of law, or in most other cases there will be a contractual transfer or a transfer by way of legal presumption of these rights to the employer. Moral rights, on the other hand, cannot be transferred to the employer. This could give rise to a situation in which the employee, being left with the moral rights in the computer program, attempts to interfere with the commercial exploitation of the work by the employer. More specifically, the integrity right could be invoked to object to the exploitation of the work if the latter has been subject to substantial amendments, as is quite often the case in the software industry. In practical terms, the employee would be given an opportunity to use his moral rights for economic purposes in such a case. Particularly for highly utilitarian and functional works, this is undesirable. However, moral rights do not exist in isolation and there must be a balance between moral rights and other legitimate rights (e.g. rights of free speech or privacy) of other parties. In this particular area the contractual transfer of rights to the employer, taken in combination with the highly functional nature of the work, must mean that the employee cannot be allowed to (ab-)use his integrity right if that in effect means that he is changing the terms or effects of the original contract. In a case where such a clash occurs preference should be given to the right of the employer, and the employee should be able to rely on the integrity right only to stop an exploitation which clearly goes beyond the terms of the contract, i.e. because his honour and reputation are prejudiced. Where honour and reputation are prejudiced, the employee's integrity right becomes more important in the balancing act than the economic right of the employer. Apart from this exceptional situation, the contract on economic rights has a *de facto* implication that there is an implied waiver, or reduction in scope, of the moral rights of the author[35] (or at least the author must be taken to have consented to not

---

[35] In France the leading view is that since art. L121-7 provides specifically that the author of a computer program should restrict his right of integrity only to modifications which are prejudicial to his honour and reputation, whilst he has no right of reconsideration or withdrawal, all other moral rights apply. Yet, the exercise of some rights is much disputed by reason of the nature of computer programs. See A. and H.-J. Lucas, *Traité de la propriété littéraire et artistique*, Litec, Paris, 1994, at 319; M. Vivant in Logiciel 94: 'Tout un programme?' Law no. 94-361 of 10 May 1994, (1994) *JCP* G, at 434. In Belgium it is submitted that only the moral rights provided in art. 6*bis* of the Berne Convention are applicable. This is derived from art. 4 of the Law of 30 June 1994 implementing the European Directive of 14 May 1991 concerning the protection of computer programs in Belgium. See also J. Corbet who summarises them as a right of paternity, a weaker right of integrity and no right of divulgation: *Auteursrecht*, Story–Scientia, Brussels, 1997,

invoking his moral rights in cases where the exploitation of the work and of the rights that he had transferred complies with normal industry standards).[36]

It is interesting to note at this point that the highly commercial and utilitarian nature of computer programs has led many countries to reconsider moral rights protection in relation to computer programs. The clear conclusion was that a hybrid copyright product requires a hybrid moral rights protection. However, it is a highly dubious contention that multimedia products share the same nature as software and therefore require a similar treatment. As was explained in earlier sections of this book, multimedia works are more than just a tool or simply a utilitarian work. Although their commercial side is undoubtedly the prevailing one, a highly creative side is also involved. This is the side relating to the part of the multimedia product which comes on top of the software, i.e. the collection of the different expressions or visual effects of the multimedia work. For that part no restrictions on moral rights are immediately justified in the same way that they are not justified in relation to films, databases, compilations, etc. Thus, computer programs might resemble multimedia products with regard to their commercial nature but not with regard to their final aims and objectives. These final aims and objectives do not necessarily require concessions in the area of moral rights.

Yet, what we should bear in mind is that the differentiation of the regime of protection for computer programs in the area of moral rights and rights of employees makes sense only in a continental law tradition. These 'exceptions' to traditional copyright were already present in common law traditions in relation to all literary works. In that sense it might be argued that the issue is not whether we should afford to multimedia works a

---

at 39 (no. 100) and 57 (no. 147); J. Keustermans, 'Software, chips en databanken' in F. Gotzen (ed.), *Le renouveau du droit d'auteur en Belgique*, Bruylant, Brussels, 1996, 447, at 462. In Greece there is no special restriction on the moral rights of authors of computer programs, but this does not mean that the courts will not impose restrictions if a case comes before them. They will probably do so on the basis of a teleological interpretation of the law. That means that they will take into account the specific nature and function of computer programs which as such will dictate restrictions. See Marinos, *Logismiko*, at 68 and G. Koumantos, *Pnevmatiki idioktissia*, 7th edn, Ant. N. Sakkoula, 2000, at 246–7. It is also argued that in all these countries, even though waivability and absolute transferability of moral rights is not allowed in principle, in relation to computer programs this can take place by interpretation of the purpose and the scope of a licence or assignment given to the entrepreneur. For the position in other EU Member States see C. Doutrelepont, *Le droit moral de l'auteur et le droit communautaire*, Bruylant, Brussels, 1997.

[36] In the same sense it is readily accepted that a newspaper journalist consents to or waives his moral right in respect of the normal editing of his piece by the editor of the newspaper.

'different' status of protection along the lines of that afforded to computer programs but whether the whole copyright structure for new technology products, such as computer programs, databases, multimedia works, etc., should undergo a general revision in order to meet the needs of the new reality of the market and the needs of the users.

7.3 SUMMING UP

Having looked into the definition of a computer program and that of a multimedia work we can observe what Sirinelli had already observed some years ago. 'The fact that multimedia works are carried by digital supports should not lead us to the application of the special regime of computer programs. Even if computer programs constitute an important part of the multimedia product, they should not be allowed to assimilate the nature of the other elements.... The special regime of protection is applicable to the computer program and the provisions of common copyright are applicable to the rest.'[37] Any attempt to qualify a multimedia work as a computer program would miss out substantial parts of it and would prove to be too limited and inadequate a provision to cover the whole scope of a multimedia work.[38] Computer programs in relation to multimedia works are functional tools aiming at the operation and the manipulation of the materials of the latter.[39] As such they come on their own under the protective umbrella of the EU software Directive as this has been implemented in the copyright laws of the Member States.

As could be expected when two works are of a different nature, the application of one of the regimes of protection to the other can only be a difficult and unsuccessful exercise. The concepts of reverse engineering, back-up exceptions, adaptations and correction of errors show graphically how difficult it is for the software regime to accommodate any multimedia works. Multimedia works have to be assessed on their own merits and after taking into account both their technical base and their multi-expression visual effect, in other words both their utilitarian and their

---

[37] Sirinelli Report, at 58 (author's translation). See also G. Schricker, *Urheberrecht. Kommentar*, 2nd edn, C. H. Beck, Munich, 1999, at 1083.
[38] Vercken, 'Les contrats', at 45.
[39] B. Wittweiler, 'Produktion von Multimedia und Urheberrecht aus Schweizerischer Sicht' (1995) 128 *UFITA* 5, at 10, clearly makes the distinction between the classification of the multimedia work and the software that is used to operate it. The classification of the latter cannot, in his view, simply be transposed to the whole multimedia work. See also in this respect U. Loewenheim, 'Urheberrechtliche Probleme bei: Multimediaanwendungen' [1996] *GRUR* 830, at 832.

creative aspects. This combination of ends favours a composite regime of protection as well.[40] Whether this regime of protection tailored to the needs of multimedia products will have to borrow solutions enshrined in the software Directive is another issue. However, that does not advocate to any extent the application of the software regime of protection *per se* to multimedia products.

[40] See P. Sirinelli, Lamy audiovisuel no. 638 *in fine*, at 517.

8 Video games as a test case

8.1 VIDEO GAMES AS MULTIMEDIA WORKS

The only 'multimedia cases' that have come before the various national courts up to now are cases on video games. Indeed, video games were the first forms of multimedia products that appeared on the market. 'Multimedia works' is a generic term and as such it is capable of encompassing a great variety of products. Some of them are already on the market whilst others have yet to appear. These products can be considered to come under the umbrella of multimedia works provided that they contain the essential elements or the common core of a multimedia work.

Video games possess the general/basic characteristics of a multimedia work. They combine on one medium (either off-line or on-line[1]) different forms of expression in a digitised format. Images and sound are the most frequently combined expressions, though text can also be included, usually in the form of commands, pathways or score results. All these elements make up the visual effect (sights and sounds) of the video game. The visual element is an audiovisual expression as long as images and sound, or images alone, or images as the main element are projected onto a screen.[2] If that is not the case then, although the visual element necessarily remains, since the video game can only be displayed on screen, the audiovisual expression is replaced by a literary (if it is primarily text that is included) or other expression and it is on these grounds that the product qualifies as a work.[3]

---

[1] On-line distribution of video games has increasingly become the rule, especially in relation to distribution over the Internet.

[2] This screen might be a television screen, a computer screen or a screen forming part of the whole package structure of the video game. This would be the case with coin-operated games found in public places, such as pubs, casinos, etc. In this case the video game is distributed as a service. With regard to 'domestic video games', which can be purchased in computer or multimedia outlets, the video game is distributed as a good (a reproduction of the original copy). Of course, if this video game is rented in a video shop, it will be provided as a service.

[3] See the *Minitel* case where text was the main element, TGI Paris, 16 September 1986, *Expertises* 1987, no. 93, 107.

Video games are also interactive. In fact, interactivity is a core element of these games. Without it no game is possible. Interactivity in video games allows the user to participate in and control the progress of the game. The user has the choice of selecting between the various options available. These will in their turn give rise to one of the pre-destined scenarios or predefined sequences of images. A certain number of scenarios are available in each video game and the choices of the player activate a particular scenario corresponding to each of these choices.[4] Although the user selects these scenarios, he cannot intervene and change their content. In this sense his role is functional rather than creative.

The similarities between video games and other multimedia products have prompted many commentators to think that what applies to video games should necessarily apply to other multimedia works as well.[5] Yet that can only be the case if video games are in all aspects (composite elements, appearance, method of manufacturing, degree of interactivity, etc.) the same as any other multimedia work. If that is not the case, multimedia works in general can be afforded the same legal protection as video games if the differences they present are not substantial enough to justify a differential legal treatment. After we have considered the legal solutions afforded to video games by various national jurisdictions, we will examine whether these solutions would be suitable for any other multimedia product. To this end we will also look into the nature of video games and compare it to that of other multimedia works.

8.2 THE CASE-LAW ON VIDEO GAMES

Judgments on video games are found in many jurisdictions. Perhaps this is so because video games have enjoyed great commercial success which, from an early stage onwards, has prompted others in the area to invest minimal effort and money into producing similar or identical results or games and to infringe or allegedly infringe copyright in existing products.

---

[4] Another aspect in which video games resemble other multimedia products is that they are usually distributed in the same outlets, i.e. in computer or multimedia shops, along with other information technology products. Yet there are places where video games alone are distributed, such as video shops. Any other multimedia product would only be rented in such places if its sole purpose was entertainment. In the same sense there are multimedia products which are also sold in bookshops. Thus, distribution is not always a sound point of similarity between video games and other multimedia works.
[5] See, for example, B. Edelman, 'L'oeuvre multimédia, un essai de qualification' [1995] 15 *Recueil Dalloz Sirey* 109, at 112.

Such cases are mostly found in the USA, France, Belgium and Germany.[6] It is interesting to note that, early on at least, the judgments in these countries were not uniform. This was partly due to the fact that video games were new on the market. Their commercial value was not immediately evident and neither was their need for protection. It was also partly due to the fact that traditionally there were difficulties in fitting new technological products within the scope of conventional intellectual property works. Three phases can be identified in the history of qualification of video games. In the first one video games were denied copyright protection altogether. In the two following phases video games qualified, according to the case at issue, either as computer programs or as computer programs and audiovisual works simultaneously (for different parts of the same product). The leading view today is that video games are in part computer programs and in part audiovisual works.

8.2.1 Lack of protection for video games

Video games were initially denied copyright protection altogether. This denial was largely based on two grounds: a lack of fixation of the work and a lack of originality and aesthetic value.[7] The non-fixation argument of the courts in relation to video games arose on the basis that, on the one hand, video games were not fixed on a tangible medium that was human-readable (at least for those countries where fixation on such a medium is a necessary requirement for copyright protection) and, on the other hand, fixation on such a medium was not sufficiently stable and permanent since it allowed the intervention of players.

8.2.1.1 *Absence of fixation*

Under the US Copyright Act

protection subsists... in original works of authorship fixed in any tangible medium of expression, now known or later developed, from which they can be

---

[6] The UK has no case-law on video games at the time of writing. The English literature on video games is almost non-existent.

[7] 'The [French] judges' attitude in refusing video games legal protection under the Statute of 11 March 1957 seems to be based on two considerations. Firstly, they believed they were dealing with a technical creation in the meaning of the law of industrial property. Secondly, they decided, in accordance with the most classical principles, that graphics of a purely technical nature, which in addition showed no original conception or presentation, cannot be classed either as belonging to the five arts system – as the civil parties had attempted to claim – or, in a more general sense, as an intellectual creation in the meaning of the copyright statute.' X. Desjeux, 'From design to software: software, video games and copyright, the analytical method in the test of technology' (1986) 2 *Journal of Law and Information Science* 18, at 42–3.

perceived, reproduced, or otherwise communicated, either directly or with the aid of a machine or device.[8]

A work is 'fixed' in a tangible medium of expression when its embodiment in a copy or phonorecord, by or under the authority of the author, is sufficiently permanent or stable to permit it to be perceived, reproduced or otherwise communicated for a period of more than transitory duration. A work consisting of sounds, images, or both, that are being transmitted, is 'fixed' for the purposes of this title if a fixation of the work is being made simultaneously with its transmission.[9]

The form, manner or medium of fixation in which an author chooses to present his work is of no legal significance to the US Copyright Act as long as the work is fixed on a tangible medium from which it can be communicated. On-line media are also covered by the Act if the work can be perceived for a period of time that is more than transitory. It is also of no interest under the US Copyright Act whether the medium on which the work is fixed was known or unknown at the time of its drafting or whether communication from this medium can be achieved directly by humans or indirectly through the aid of technical devices. Protection is also afforded irrespective of the number of copies that are made of the work.[10]

However, the medium on which a work is fixed and the work itself should not be confused for the purposes of the classification of copyrightable subject matter. The fact that a medium of fixation is not a tangible medium of expression, qualifying as such under a Copyright Act, does not necessarily mean that the work it carries is not copyrightable material. In *Midway Mfg Co. v. Dirschneider* the District Court for Nebraska pointed out that '[f]irst, the Court must determine whether the plaintiff's works fall within one of the copyrightable subject matters enumerated in the Act 17 USC § 120(a). Second, the court must determine whether the work is fixed in a tangible medium of expression.'[11] The video game at issue was found to be an audiovisual work[12] (therefore copyrightable subject matter) and to be fixed in the printed circuit boards which directed the video sequences. The printed circuit boards were found to be tangible objects from which the audiovisual works might be perceived for a

---

[8] § 102(a) of the US Copyright Act 1976. See also the US Constitutional Limitation and the previous US Copyright Act 1909 where copyright can only be granted to the 'writings' of an author. Under the previous US Copyright Acts a work was not copyrightable if it could only be seen or read with the aid of a machine or device. Under the 1909 Act only media existing at the time of its drafting, which were also media explicitly listed in it, qualified. This problem has been solved by the Copyright Act 1976. See also M. Nimmer, *Nimmer on Copyright*, Matthew Bender, New York, 1982, at § 1.08.
[9] § 101 of the US Copyright Act.
[10] See HR Rep No. 1476, 94th Cong., 2d Sess. 52.
[11] 543 F Supp 466, 479 (D. Neb. 1981).
[12] See also Nimmer, *Nimmer on Copyright*, at § 2.18(H)(3)(b).

period of time that was more than transitory or of more than momentary duration. Of course, for a work to be granted copyright protection it has to be both copyrightable and fixed on a tangible medium of expression.

The US Copyright Act 1976, contrary to its predecessor the US Copyright Act 1909, makes it clear that non-human-readable media also qualify as capable of carrying copyrightable material.[13] This is the view taken in most other countries through the interpretation of the notion of fixation. Now, the stability and permanence of fixation is an issue common to any national copyright law. Transitory fixation is the counterpart of permanent and stable fixation. Transitory fixation either is a fixation which exists only for a fraction of a second or, we could also argue, it is also that fixation which does not have the prerequisites of being permanent, stable or capable of being read or seen again and again if required. '"Purely evanescent or transient reproductions" referred to by [the US] Congress are those arising from live telecasts or performances that are nowhere separately recorded. Clearly the lack of any recording of such events would preclude their ever again being identically reproduced.'[14]

It was also alleged that the lack of fixation was in part due to the fact that in video games there was no stable and permanent display of the work. In fact the participation of players made the display of the game appear different every time the game was played. It looked as if it were a different work each time and one that was expressed only in evanescent images.[15] Evanescent or transitory images as such do not qualify as images fixed on a tangible medium. This argument was promptly rejected by both the US and the French courts.[16] '[T]he sequence of images for each configuration produced by the player is fixed and predetermined in the game's circuits. In a sense the player could be viewed as part of the "machine or device" with the aid of which the work is "perceived, reproduced, or otherwise communicated".'[17] The sequences of images which are displayed each time according to the choices of the user are already permanently fixed on the microcircuits and memory boards (ROMs)

---

[13] Under the US Copyright Act 1909 computer games could not qualify for copyright protection on grounds of fixation.

[14] *Midway Mfg Co. v. Artic International, Inc.* 547 F Supp, at 1008.

[15] *Midway Mfg Co. v. Artic International, Inc.* 704 F 2d 1009, 1011 (7th Cir. 1983); *Williams Elecs., Inc. v. Artic International, Inc.* 685 F 2d 870, 874 (3d Cir. 1982); *Stern Elecs., Inc. v. Kaufman* 669 F 2d 852, 856 (2d Cir. 1982).

[16] *Midway Mfg Co. v. Artic International, Inc.* 704 F 2d, at 1011, and see also the note of J. Bonneau, [1985] *Gaz Pal* (28 May 1985), at 345, Paris, 20 February 1985.

[17] M.-P. Culler, 'Copyright protection for video games: the courts in the *Pac-Man* maze' (1983–4) 32 *Cleveland State Law Review* 531, at 559–60.

of the game. If they were not there they could not be invoked by the player.

Despite the variance of sights and sounds resulting from the player's actions, much of the game's appearance and sequence of play remains constant no matter who is at the controls. The characters on the screen look the same, and the sounds heard whenever a player moves or causes a particular action to occur are always the same, even though an unskilled player may never see every possible display. As the court noted, the images and sounds remain fixed, and although the player can vary the movement of the images, he can never produce a display which was not initially fixed in the memory devices.[18]

The fact that interactivity is not provided for expressly in the copyright laws of the various countries is because it was a phenomenon that could not have been foreseen at this stage.[19] Yet many national laws set out to cover new technologies by expressly saying so in their national copyright laws and by making their legal definitions technology neutral.[20]

8.2.1.2 *Absence of originality*

The second reason for which video games were denied copyright protection was their alleged lack of originality. It is true that video games contain many non-copyrightable elements, such as facts, figures, settings, characters, themes and expressions of issues that on most occasions are not readily capable of forming a work within the notion of copyright.[21] In addition, video games seemed at the beginning to follow the general trend that games are (in general) 'works of utility'. At least that part of them which was highly functional was incapable of attracting copyright protection.[22] The design and structure of video games seemed to come

---

[18] As K. Maicher refers to the *Midway Mfg* decision of the US Court (paras. 855–6) in her article 'Copyrightability of video games: *Stern* and *Atari*' (1983) 14 *Loyola University Law Journal* 391, at 405.
[19] The economic philosophy behind permanent fixation is that there is little sense in granting a monopoly to an ephemeral fixation which will not be able to be reproduced. In such a monopoly there would be almost nothing to exploit.
[20] 17 USC § 102.
[21] The US courts refer to those as 'fact-intensive works' and 'scènes à faire'. 'Scènes à faire are "incidents, characters or settings which are as a practical matter indispensable... in the treatment of a given topic." Scènes à faire are afforded no protection because the subject matter represented can be expressed in no other way than through the particular scène à faire. Therefore, granting a copyright "would give the first author a monopoly on the commonplace ideas behind the scènes à faire".' *Whelan Associates Inc.* v. *Jaslow Dental Laboratory Inc. and Others*, US Court of Appeals (3d Cir.) [1987] FSR 1. See also *Atari Inc.* v. *North American Philips Consumer Elecs. Corp.* 672 F 2d 607, 616 (7th Cir.), 459 US 880 (1982) and *Landsberg* v. *Scrabble Crossword Game Players Inc.* 736 F 2d 485, 489 (9th Cir.), 105 S Ct 513 (1984).
[22] See S. Bennet, 'Copyright and intellectual property – portions of video games may constitute protected property' (1983) 66 *Marquette Law Review* 817, at 818. See the

closer to an idea (which some will argue also includes the only possible way to express or construct such a product) than to an expression of the author (the individual way of constructing such a product, which was a choice among other options available) and therefore to fall foul of any copyright protection, at least for those parts which were utilitarian, functional and did not present any originality.[23]

Although the presence of non-copyrightable elements in video games was apparent in most national jurisdictions, the extent of these elements varied according to the level of originality required in each country and, even if in all countries the axiom that the idea is not protected is respected, the delineation between the idea and the expression is a matter of interpretation subject to the various copyright traditions. As could be expected, common law countries traditionally held a more lax attitude towards the qualification of video games as protectable subject matter.[24] In continental law countries with strong copyright protection and strong convictions about works being the expression of the personality of the author, it was held that video games did not present any aesthetic value[25] which could justify their inclusion within the ambit of copyright, and that in any case there could be no way in which 'technological patchworks' of this kind could be included within the same regime of protection as works of the mind.[26] The prerequisite of aesthetic value was soon abandoned by the courts as being irrelevant in relation to copyright. Statements such as 'legal protection extends to each work that constitutes an original intellectual creation independent of all aesthetic or artistic consideration' are indicative on this point.[27]

'abstractions test' that the US courts use to distinguish the idea from the expression: P. McKenna, 'Copyrightability of video games: *Stern* and *Atari*' (1983) 14 *Loyola University Law Journal* 391, at 400–1. See also Nimmer, *Nimmer on Copyright*, at § 2.18.

[23] See *Whist Club* v. *Foster* 42 F 2d 782 (SDNY 1929) where it was argued by the court that '[i]n the conventional laws or rules of a game, as distinguished from the forms or modes of expression in which they may be stated, there can be no literary property susceptible of copyright'; *Chamberlin* v. *Uris Sales Corp.* 150 F 2d 512 (2d Cir. 1945); *Morrissey* v. *Proctor & Gamble Co.* 262 F Supp 737 (D. Mass. 1967) where no creative authorship was found in a sweepstakes entry-form rule which elicited information which was to be expected from a would-be contestant; and *Durham Industries* v. *Tomy Corp.* 630 F 2d 905 (2d Cir. 1980).

[24] In the USA it is argued that for a work to be original it suffices that there is a little more than actual copying. Works which are no more than trivial variations of pre-existing creations will not be protected. It is also interesting to note that the closer a work comes to an idea the less one is allowed to copy.

[25] See the note of J. Bonneau, [1984] *Gaz Pal* (13 October 1984), at 345, Paris, 4 June 1984.

[26] See A. Strowel and J.-P. Triaille, *Le droit d'auteur, du logiciel au multimédia (Copyright, from software to multimedia)*, Bruylant, Brussels, 1997, at 350–1.

[27] Translation by the author from the French judgment. *Atari c. Valadon et Williams Electronics c. Mme Tel*, Cass. Fr., 7 March 1986, [1986] D. 405, concl. Cabannes and the

A series of video games were denied copyright protection both in the USA and in France, but particularly in France since they were found to come very close to an idea rather than an original expression. In 1975 Atari tried to register a video game with the US Copyright Office as an audiovisual work. It was denied protection on grounds that the game at issue was not substantially original and that it was consequently incapable of attracting copyright protection. The case was heard on appeal on two occasions.[28] On both occasions the court found that, although there was no copyright in relation to the colours and the generic forms of the game, the combination of these elements together with sounds and movements was adequately original so as to allow the registration of the game as an audiovisual work. Although in this instance, especially after the decision in *Feist*, a more stringent approach was expected in relation to copyrightability of a work, still the court admitted that the video game at issue satisfied the minimum level of originality as this was set out in *Feist*.[29]

The Court of Appeal in Paris in two cases of alleged infringement and copying of video games also dealt with the issue of originality. It found that the similarities between the two video games alone did not suffice to make out a case of infringement since in fact they revealed only the common idea behind them. Any exclusivity granted to the idea would lead to an unjustifiable monopoly in non-protectable material.[30] In the second case the Court found that 'these facts in our times do not originate in a particularly original imagination or a very original intellectual effort'.[31] In both cases the video games were not protected by copyright by reason of their lack of originality.

The French decisions on video games went perhaps one step further than those in the USA. That was due to the fact that an idea in the USA was held to be whatever could not be expressed by a video game developer in another way, whilst in France an idea was held to be whatever was not creative enough to qualify as original (or rather what was commonplace). The French decisions were criticised by a part of the literature as being

---

note of B. Edelman. See also (1986) 129 *RIDA* 136 (July), note A. Lucas and [1986] *JCP* II 20631, note J. Mousseron, B. Teyssie and M. Vivant, as referred to by Strowel and Triaille, *Le droit d'auteur*, at 351, footnote 56.

[28] *Atari Games Corp.* v. *Oman* 888 F 2d 878 (D.C. Cir. 1989) and 979 F 2d 242 (D.C. Cir. 1992).

[29] For discussion on the *Feist* decision see section 3.2.6.1.1 above.

[30] '[T]he only similarity between the two video games is found in the theme adopted but Atari cannot claim a monopoly in the genre at issue which can be summarised in a fight between a marksman and moving objects' (translated by the author). Paris, 4 June 1984. See also *Atari* c. *Valadon et Williams* c. *Mme Tel*, Cass. Fr., 7 March 1986, [1986] D. 405.

[31] *Midway Mfg Co.* v. *Artic International, Inc.*, Paris, 20 February 1985. See also *Minitel*, TGI Paris, 16 September 1986, *Expertises* 1987, no. 93, 107.

too strict, perhaps in view of the danger that many video games will go onto the market unprotected and will become easy prey to potential trespassers or marketers in the same area. In this way investments could be blocked in the video game industry.[32] On the other hand, of course, protecting too much could equally be a hurdle to new creations. Strowel argues that it is possible to wonder why French copyright law affords protection to expressions less creative than the traditional ones, like, for example, photographs and objects of applied arts, and not to video games. However, the functional character of these works is highly apparent in so far as they are designed in a way which is comprehensible and which makes it easy for the user to operate the video game.[33] This latter element must be an argument against copyright protection in any *droit d'auteur* tradition, since such functionality clearly devalues any claim to originality as an expression of the personality of the author.[34]

8.2.2 Protection as computer programs

Video games can qualify as various types of works. Predominantly, however, they qualify as computer programs and audiovisual works.[35] In the early video game cases certain national courts expressed a strong preference for video games to qualify as computer programs.[36] This preference was essentially based on two grounds. First, it was based on the finding that the screen outputs of the video games were not original enough to

---

[32] This was also the case with the strict originality requirements in Germany in relation to computer programs until the introduction of the EC software Directive.

[33] Strowel and Triaille, *Le droit d'auteur*, at 351. The same authors also argue correctly at p. 352 that the choice of a title for marketing–functional reasons or the choice of appealing colours for a screen display or the functional order in which a game is presented do not take away the potential copyright protection for these items. Functional considerations do not alter the copyrightable character of the material.

[34] Other French judgments where video games were not granted copyright protection are Criminal Court of Nanterre, 29 June 1984, *Expertises* 1984, no. 67, 301 and Criminal Tribunal of Paris, 8 December 1982, *Expertises* 1983, no. 48, 31.

[35] The definition given to video games by the US Court in *Stern Elecs., Inc. v. Kaufman* 669 F 2d 852, at 853 (2d Cir. 1982) also points to this. Video games are 'computers programmed to create on a television screen cartoons in which some of the action is controlled by the player'. Strowel and Triaille argue that video games may also qualify as databases. Yet, we fail to see how this can be the case under the present definition of databases in the EU database Directive which requires the contents of a work to be individually accessible. Unless there is a special type of video game which meets this criterion the database qualification for video games will not be met. See Strowel and Triaille, *Le droit d'auteur*, at 347. However, there have been cases where video games contained mainly text rather than anything else. See the *Minitel* case, TGI Paris, 16 September 1986, *Expertises* 1987, no. 93, 107.

[36] See, for example, A. Bertrand, *Le droit d'auteur et les droits voisins*, Masson, Paris, 1991, at 508.

qualify as audiovisual works (in those countries, of course, where originality is a prerequisite for films) since the images and their sequences were essentially generated by the computer program contained in the video game. Secondly, it was based on the fact that the essential characteristic of films, i.e. a predefined or uninterrupted sequence of moving images, was not met by reason of the intervention of the players and their interaction with the video game. In *Pengo*[37] the German Court of Appeal in Frankfurt ruled that, although it is possible for video games to qualify as both computer programs and audiovisual works, not enough originality was found in the video game at issue to qualify as an audiovisual work. It was found to have been conceived by its developer in such a way as 'to create a simple play activity which requires no more than attention and reflex actions'. In fact it was submitted that it is the software which creates, determines and operates the images that appear on the screen. Apart from that there is not enough originality put in the audiovisual displays to turn them into a film. The fact that everything was computer-generated did not allow the German Court to opt for the film qualification of the work.[38] In *Donkey Kong Junior*[39] the same Court denied protection to a video game as an audiovisual work because of its nature. The fact that players were allowed to interact with the video game, undertake different steps each time and achieve different things, necessarily led to different images. It was exactly this plurality of possible outcomes in terms of sequences of images that was thought by the Court to make it impossible for the game to qualify as a film. The absence of predefined sequences of images was found to be contradictory to the notion of a film.[40]

It is interesting to note that the difficulty of identifying a video game as both a computer program and an audiovisual work was usually encountered by countries with a strong copyright tradition and strict requirements on the issue of originality. These decisions, however, were also in part due to the fact that at that stage courts were not familiar with the idea that elements of a work can qualify as a computer program whilst other elements of the same work can qualify as an audiovisual work. In other words, it is irrelevant for films whether their images are generated by computer software or not. As Schack observes, the medium on which a work is fixed and the technology used to operate this work are irrelevant

[37] OLG Frankfurt, 13 June 1983 [1983] *GRUR* 753.
[38] *Ibid.*, at 756.
[39] OLG Frankfurt [1983] *GRUR* 757.
[40] *Ibid.*, at 758. See also in this respect [1985] *ZUM* 26, at 30; W. Nordemann [1981] *GRUR* 891; von Gravenreuth [1986] *DB* 1005, at 1006; Seisler [1983] *DB* 129, at 21293. See also in France Bertrand, *Le droit d'auteur*, at 508. For a different view see OLG Frankfurt [1983] *GRUR* 753, at 756.

for films.[41] 'The copyright is not defeated because the audiovisual work and the computer program are both embodied in the same components of the game.'[42] What counts is how much creativity, if any, has been invested in the sights and sounds of the video game. If no creativity is found, then the provisions for a film cannot apply. The equivalent in an Anglo-Saxon system is the absence of even a minimum investment of skill and labour.

8.2.3 Protection as computer programs and audiovisual works

Nowadays the literature on video games seems to accept that theoretically video games, which are original works, are capable of attracting three forms of protection. They can qualify as computer programs, as audiovisual works, as a combination of the two or, where not enough originality is found to classify them as such, they can perhaps attract copyright protection as drawings for their characters, figures or other designs.[43]

If the originality criterion is left aside, what it is perhaps important to examine is whether video games possess the basic characteristics of an audiovisual work, in other words whether their interactivity and the intervention of players are enough to preclude any real sequence of images, at least for those countries which understand 'sequences of images' as an uninterrupted and predefined set of moving images.[44] In *Midway Mfg Co. v. Artic Int'l, Inc.*, the US Court of Appeals held that the US Copyright Act, by referring to a 'series of related images',[45] refers 'to any set of

---

[41] H. Schack, *Urheber- und Urhebervertragsrecht*, Mohr Siebeck, Munich, 1997, at 101 § 217.
[42] *Stern Elecs.* v. *Kaufman* 669 F 2d, at 856.
[43] See especially G. Schricker, *Urheberrecht. Kommentar*, C. H. Beck, Munich, 1987, at 1010 § 44; and 2nd edn, 1999, at 1380. See also Nimmer, *Nimmer on Copyright*, at § 2.18, who argues that the 'pattern or design of game boards' are copyrightable as pictorial or graphic works or as maps. Under German law there is also the option of a qualification as *Laufbildern*. These are in fact moving images which possess no originality and form a neighbouring right. A. Lucas, 'Multimédia et droit d'auteur' in AFTEL, *Le droit du multimédia: de la télématique à Internet*, Les Editions du Téléphone, Paris, 1996, 324, at 146, suggests a similar possibility under French law when he argues that the qualification of a video game as a *vidéogramme* gives rise to fewer problems in respect of originality and presence of a scenario than the qualification as an audiovisual work. For the qualification of video games as computer programs and audiovisual works, see Schack, *Urheber- und Urhebervertragsrecht*, at 101 § 215. For the position in France see A. Lucas, *Le droit informatique*, PUF, Paris, 1987, no. 276. For the position in Belgium see P. Peters, 'La protection des jeux-vidéo électroniques' [1984] 2 *Dr. Inform.* 11. For the position in the USA see Nimmer, *Nimmer on Copyright*, § 2.18. C. Millard suggests also that video games are audiovisual works: 'Copyright' in C. Reed and J. Angel (eds.), *Computer law*, 4th edn, Blackstone Press Ltd, London, 2000, 177, at 184.
[44] See in this respect section 6.2 above on audiovisual works and sequences of moving images.
[45] '...which are intrinsically intended to be shown by the use of machines or devices such as... electronic equipment...' 17 USC § 101.

images displayed as some kind of unit' and not an entirely fixed sequence of sights and sounds which reappear every time the game is activated. In addition, the US Act provides that an audiovisual work is performed when its images are shown to the public in any sequence.[46] This is also in compliance with the legislative history of the Act which suggests that it should be interpreted flexibly so as to encompass new technologies.[47]

In Germany a series of judgments on video games covered almost exhaustively the issue of whether video games meet the necessary prerequisites for film protection. The Bavarian Supreme Court stated that the fact that there is no predefined sequence of images in video games is irrelevant, as is the medium on which fixation took place.[48] Although the players are given the opportunity to interact with the video game, they can still steer it only within the boundaries set up by the designer of the software which as such does not alienate the nature of a video game from that of an audiovisual work.[49] Lastly, the fact that images in a video game are generated by a computer program should by no means impinge on the qualification of a video game as an audiovisual work.[50]

The role of the player was not found to be creative or in any aspect capable of transforming the form and nature of the work. '[Any] movements [in the video game] do not originate in the actual creativity of the player, but in the fact that the player, by using his arm, gives rise in a pre-established program to one or other situation, the number of which is by definition limited.'[51] The player was in fact viewed as a part of the 'machine' or 'device' with the aid of which the work is perceived, reproduced or otherwise communicated,[52] whilst the playing of the game was compared to changing channels on a television since '[t]he player... [has no]

---

[46] According to 17 USC § 101, to 'perform' a work means 'to recite, render, play, dance, or act it, either directly or by means of any device or process or, in the case of a motion picture or other audiovisual work, to show its images in any sequence or to make the sounds accompanying it audible'.

[47] *Midway Mfg Co. v. Artic International Inc.* 704 F 2d, at 1011 (7th Cir. 1983).

[48] 12 May 1992, [1992] *ZUM* 545, at 546.

[49] Puckman, OLG Hamburg, [1983] *GRUR* 436, at 437.

[50] OLG Karlsruhe, 14 September 1986, [1986] *CR* 723. *Galaxy Electronics Pty Ltd v. Sega Enterprises Ltd*, (1997) 37 *IPR* 462. Other German cases where video games qualified as both computer programs and films are *Super Mario III*, OLG Hamburg, 12 October 1989, [1990] *GRUR* 127, and *Amiga Club*, OLG Cologne, 18 October 1991, [1992] *GRUR* 312. In Belgium a similar conclusion was reached in *Nintendo v. Horelec*, judgment of the President of the Court of First Instance in Brussels, 12 December 1995 [1996] *IRDI* 89. In France there is the judgment of the Cour de Cassation (Ass. plén. 7 March 1986) *Atari v. Williams Electronics* (1986) 126 *RIDA* 136 (July) (annotated by A. Lucas).

[51] *Atari v. Valadon*, TGI Paris, 8 December 1982, *Expertises* 1983, no. 48, 31 (overruled by the Court of Appeal, but only for the judgment of the Court of Appeal to be annulled by the Cour de Cassation).

[52] Culler, 'Copyright protection for video games', at 559.

control over the sequence of images that appears on the... screen', but rather selects from the sequences stored in the circuits.[53] In the same judgment the playing of the video game was also viewed as 'a little like arranging words in a dictionary into sentences or paints on a palette into a painting. The question is whether the creative effort in playing a video game is enough like writing or painting to make each performance of a video game the work of the player and not the game's [author].'[54] This conclusion is based on the German and US case-law in this area. As we pointed out earlier, other jurisdictions have adopted a different view and have denied copyright protection as an audiovisual work to those works whose images can appear in a random or player-designed order.[55]

8.2.4 The current position

It is apparent so far that any obstacles relating to whether video games qualify as computer programs and/or as audiovisual works have been solved by the national courts. Video games are held to be fixed on media that are both stable and permanent irrespective of their form and technology and irrespective of whether they are human-readable or not. They are found to possess the sequences or series of images required for their qualification as audiovisual works, and it is also stated in all jurisdictions that the intervention of players through the option of interactivity is not capable of transforming the form and nature of the work by impinging either on its fixation on a tangible medium or its sequence of images.

The German cases where video games seemed to fulfil the requirements only in so far as their computer program component was concerned mirror the early stage of the judicial history of video games. Today it seems to be accepted in most countries that video games consist of two main components. They consist of a computer program, which produces the effects and operates the game, and an audiovisual work, which is presented as the screen displays that communicate to the player the image, the movements of the characters and the sounds of the game. Both these works should be assessed separately and on their own merits. If they meet all the requirements which a computer program classification and an audiovisual work classification require and at the same time possess the level of originality that is required, then the protection for both these types of works should be afforded to a video game. If a video game fails to qualify for one form of protection, only the corresponding part will be

---

[53] *Ibid.*, at 560 as she refers to *Midway Mfg. Co. v. Artic International, Inc.* 704 F 2d 1009, at 1012.
[54] *Midway Mfg Co. v. Artic Internationl, Inc.* 704 F 2d 1009, at 1011.
[55] See chapter 6 above on audiovisual works.

able to be copied by third parties, and not the whole video game.[56] Of course, those elements which are linked to the nature of the work that is protected, i.e. the computer program or the audiovisual work, will still be under copyright protection and should not be copied by unauthorised third parties.[57]

8.3 VIDEO GAMES AS A MODEL FOR OTHER MULTIMEDIA WORKS

8.3.1 Combination of different types of elements

8.3.1.1 *'Image' as a prevailing element*

Up to now the courts have dealt with cases of traditional video games. In other words, all video games possessed a computer program, which generated images and sounds and allowed the players to interact. They also possessed an audiovisual element: screen outputs displaying the generated images and sounds to the users. So far, one thing is clear: video games are capable of combining many different kinds of works, e.g. text, computer programs, still images along with moving images, musical compositions, etc. However, the reality is that the majority of video games today are composed of images only. Although sound and text might also be present, the sounds are only basic sounds, which on most occasions do not attract copyright on their own merits as separate works, and the presence of text is only minimal, and it is used only in so far as this is required to set out the rules of the game, the scores or the pathways a player should follow for the achievement of his target.

Although moving images are in fact the essential component of the screen displays of video games, still images, pictures, graphics, figures and drawings might also be present. A video game by its very nature is more heavily dependent on the images than anything else because it

---

[56] The protection of video games as films is preferred by most people on the grounds that cases of infringement are more straightforward to prove in relation to films than in relation to computer programs.

[57] Although the US definition of audiovisual works (§ 101 of the US Copyright Act) is more flexible than the UK and Australian definitions and therefore more capable of protecting multimedia works since infringement is assessed on whether substantial elements of the work have been copied instead of the actual recording, difficulties have still arisen in applying the notion of non-literal copying to video games and courts have tended to focus only on visual videographic similarities and differences between video games in their substantial similarity analyses and not on game play. S. McKnight, 'Substantial similarity between video games: an old copyright problem in a new medium' (1983) 36 *Vand LR* 1277, at 1312, as referred to in T. Aplin, 'Not in our galaxy: why "film" won't rescue multimedia' [1999] *EIPR* 633, at 639.

has to be comprehended quickly and easily and allow for the fast and efficient reactions of its players. It also aims to promote the game rather than provide information or initiate creation or full interaction with most of its components. Sound is only there to complement this effect, for reasons of marketing. The role of the text resembles that of the opening and closing titles of a film.

8.3.1.2 *Combination of different types of elements rather than different kinds of works*

From this point of view, it is apparent that the visual displays of video games are very similar to films. What, however, has to be noted is that the variety of elements a video game presents is really a variety of types of works rather than different kinds of expressions of works. A video game comprises various types of images and pictures and not a variety of expressions, i.e. balanced amounts of images with sounds, text and other data.[58] That becomes even more apparent if one compares the merits of the various elements incorporated into a video game. The potential outcome will be that, although images might be capable of attracting copyright protection on their own merits, i.e. as films, drawings, designs, artistic works, etc., the sounds, text or other elements remain rough data, incapable of attracting copyright protection or coming within the notion of a 'work'. On top of that, the elements other than images are fewer in number than the images in any one work. In this sense video games essentially contain images and they are primarily moving images which are presented on the screen during the game, and which are capable of transmitting the passion and rhythm of the game to the player as well as the necessary visual tools for it.

8.3.2 The degree of interactivity

The fact that all video games possess a certain degree of interactivity is uncontested, since the notion of interactivity is central and necessary for the operation of the game. That fact has also prompted many to think that perhaps the qualification of a video game as a computer program might be justified solely on grounds that it is its interactivity which is its central element and the main motivator for its purchase by the users.[59]

---

[58] Video games differ from other multimedia products in so far as they are homogeneous works. T. Desurmont, 'L'exercice des droits en ce qui concerne les "productions multimédias"' in *WIPO international forum on the exercise and management of copyright and neighbouring rights in the face of the challenges of digital technology*, Seville, 14–16 May 1997, WIPO, 1998, 169, at 178.
[59] Strowel and Triaille, *Le droit d'auteur*, at 356.

All the other elements seem to be somehow accessory, assembled to make up the external decor, the marketing package which allows the game to look more marketable and commercially attractive.[60]

The question, though, should be how much space for intervention and manipulation the interactivity found in video games gives its users and how radically new is interactivity in video games when compared to the traditional forms of manual interactivity in television and video films, and especially in choose-your-own-end films, video-on-demand, pay-per-view, pay-per-read, etc. It is interesting to note in this respect that when the national courts ruled on the issue of whether the intervention of players impinged on the nature of a video game as a film or precluded it altogether from qualifying as a film on grounds of lack of fixation and originality, they contended that this was not the case. The intervention of users and their interaction with the game was not found to affect fixation since the sequences of images and other elements were permanently fixed on the microcircuit chips (ROMs) of the video game from which they were invoked by the player in their initial form. Neither was the originality requirement of the work affected. The work always remained the same even after being played. In fact the players could not alter the work. They could only temporarily arrange the sequence of the images they received and the order in which they received them. The initial work fixed on the ROMs always remained the same. The sequences of images which were stored on the ROMs of a video game were predetermined and predefined and they were also limited in number. In this context the player could not exercise any creativity and his role was restricted by both the limited selection of images and the option of selecting images only according to the steps he took rather than by morphing, blurring, etc. The US courts compared playing a video game to changing the channels on a television, and to arranging words in a dictionary into sentences or paints on a palette into a painting.[61] The courts, however, made clear that selecting words from a dictionary or paint from a palette is not like writing or painting where creative effort is required.[62] In the interactivity available in a video game, creative effort is not required and therefore it cannot be exercised. In this sense a video

---

[60] It is worth noting here that this remark is also reinforced by the fact that many elements of a video game remain unprotected by reason of lack of originality and their strong link to the idea which underlies the game rather than its expression. Indicative of this is the case-law in the various countries as referred to in the previous sections of this chapter.
[61] *Midway Mfg Co. v. Artic International, Inc.* 704 F 2d, at 1011–12. The player has no control over the sequence of images appearing on the screen. He can select only from the few sequences stored in the circuits.
[62] *Ibid.*

game is indeed like a choose-your-own-end film where the user can select only from the moving images stored in the memory of a machine. These images or their sequences cannot be altered or changed. In the light of this, the interactivity offered by both choose-your-own-end films and video games is not a re-creative, full interactivity. It is a limited interactivity, which does not leave the user any space for personal creation and authoring.[63] Nevertheless, the above considerations do not exclude the case where sophisticated and modern video games will allow for further intervention of the users. At this stage, however, it might be legally more advisable to talk about manipulation rather than about a mere ability to intervene.

8.3.3 A comparison between video games and other multimedia works

If we were to compare video games with most other multimedia works of the same period, we could perhaps easily reach the conclusion that there are no real differences. Yet, the purpose of this section is not to compare video games with any early multimedia works but to compare them with the new reality of modern and sophisticated multimedia works as these currently appear on the market.

Although video games come within the genre of multimedia works in general, the progress of technology prompts us to argue that differences in quantity that were introduced into modern multimedia products (i.e. many more different kinds of works combined on one medium, vast numbers of data, an advanced degree of interactivity, etc.) necessarily result in differences in quality as well. From this point of view, judicial solutions which were entirely based on one primitive form of multimedia products might no longer be appropriate to serve the needs of the most modern versions of these products.

First, as we explained earlier, image is the only element absolutely necessary to and dominant in a video game. Sound, text or other elements either are non-existent or they play only a residual role. If variation is encountered in a video game this is a variation in different types of images (such as moving images, still images, graphics, figures, etc.) rather than a variation in different kinds of works (i.e. musical works, literary works, computer programs, etc.). In contrast, in modern multimedia works the combination of various kinds of expressions is found at the heart of these products and constitutes their essential feature and one of the main reasons for their purchase.

[63] See section 2.1.4 above.

The other main reason for their purchase is that modern multimedia works contain huge numbers of works. These works have been seamlessly integrated in a digitised format which allows them to co-exist in vast numbers on one medium that is both comprehensive and handy for the user. This aim is almost absent from the construction purpose of a video game. A video game is not set up in the first place to offer vast amounts of information and neither does it combine a great variety of expressions. Essentially the only work which is contained in video games is a combination of sets of moving images. The combination of these sets allows the work to qualify as an audiovisual work, provided it is original. Yet, if we take these sets of images apart, they might not always qualify as separate works. Any other elements contained in a video game will be even less likely to qualify as separate works. Thus, video games contain combinations of images rather than anything else, plus other non-copyrightable material. It follows therefore that no problems will be encountered in the clearing of rights, assemblage of components,[64] etc. In contrast, in a modern multimedia work one of the main difficulties is that in order for the work to come into existence it has to combine various works, most of them being under copyright protection.[65] Here, the authors involved and the rights to be cleared are numerous and require different strategies of assemblage, construction and marketing when compared to video games, especially if issues such as moral rights are to be taken into account.

Last but not least, there is the difference in the degree of interactivity in video games when compared to that of modern multimedia works. Interactivity in video games, as was explained earlier, is limited in nature. The role of the player is restricted by the choices available. In reality the player has only the choice to select between the various sets of images available. His choices cannot extend further than that selection.[66] In this respect his role is not creative or imaginative and his moves form part of the machine or device which operates the game. However, interactivity still forms an indispensable element of video games. In modern multimedia works interactivity goes further than just a selection of the elements available. A versatile, full interactivity actually allows the user to have a creative role, to use his imagination to reconstruct existing

---

[64] Most of the elements contained in a video game are created by its manufacturer. There is almost no inclusion of pre-existing works.
[65] Either pre-existing works or newly authored works.
[66] '[T]he multimedia user has a greater ability to affect the display of a work than a video game player does... Multimedia works (other than video games) do not work on the premise that some sort of overall sequence or narrative will emerge if the player or user enters all the correct inputs... [they] aim for as much random access as possible for the user, so that the user can gain the most flexible and individualised access to information within', Aplin, 'Not in our galaxy', at 639.

works or construct entirely new works from the contents of the product. Sampling, blurring and morphing are some examples of the possibilities offered. Multimedia products are popular just because of the variety of the options they offer. They not only allow one to choose the paints from a palette or the words from a dictionary but they also allow one to paint and write.

One could argue that although that is possible, the selection of items contained in a multimedia work is still limited by the selections made by the developer of the multimedia product and that the initial works, even after their manipulation, still remain as they were initially stored in the memory of the product. That, however, does not place a modern multimedia work on the same level as a video game, firstly because the selection available is usually significantly broader than the one offered in video games, and secondly because of the fact that the use of the data allows for a far higher level of interactivity and creativity. There is almost no limit to the choices and the degree of manipulation by the user. The user is given the opportunity to manipulate the contents of the multimedia work fully, to be creative and imaginative. He can transform the works contained in the multimedia product to such an extent that they are unrecognisable, in effect qualifying as new works, capable, perhaps, of attracting copyright on their own merits. Modern multimedia works will be increasingly used simultaneously as sources of information, creation and entertainment.

8.4 CONCLUSIONS

Video games are only primitive forms of multimedia products. Interactivity is their central element and the one that allows the game. The features of combining vast amounts of data and various types of expressions are present in only a limited way. In this respect, and as far as their main elements are 'moving images' juxtaposed in an original way, they qualify as audiovisual works. They obviously also contain a computer program for their operation.

Modern multimedia works, or multimedia products as the notion is understood today, possess a greater degree of interactivity which allows the user not only to select elements but also to combine and create. In other words, a full manipulation option is available. Multimedia works contain more than just moving images and they contain these other elements at least to the same degree as moving images. Interactivity is not central in the definition of a modern multimedia product, though it is the feature that makes it possible to market it successfully. What is of central importance is the comprehensibility and combination of the various kinds of works. The feature of combining different kinds of works in one medium is more apparent and essential in a modern multimedia work than it is in relation to video games. In addition, the elements of modern multimedia works are on most occasions works rather than data, and in particular there are vast numbers of works. In this sense, their marketing as well as their development requires other forms of expertise if one focuses on their sights and sounds rather than on their computer program component. Usually multimedia works are authored and distributed by publishers rather than computer companies or outlets, although this is a situation which might vary in the future according to the conditions of the market.

In the light of the above, video games can serve as a model for multimedia products only in so far as they indicate that both products contain two components: a computer program which operates the work and the 'sights and sounds' of the work. In relation to the first component, virtually all problems have been solved. In relation to the second, there is no clear indication from the above discussion that the desirable solution is the inclusion of a modern multimedia work within the ambit of audiovisual works along the lines of video games. The similarities which audiovisual works present in relation to modern multimedia works are far fewer and looser than those they present in relation to video games. Modern multimedia works will have to be assessed on a different basis and on their own merits. This is perhaps an assessment that ought to take place in relation to more sophisticated video games as well.

9 Multimedia products and existing categories of copyright works

9.1 ORIGINALITY AND QUALIFICATION FOR COPYRIGHT PROTECTION

Having examined the existing categories of copyright works that might eventually be capable of accommodating multimedia products, and having identified the difficulties they would present if they were to serve the needs of these products, one might wonder whether it would be a wiser solution to afford copyright protection to a multimedia work irrespective of whether or not it comes within one of the existing categories of copyright works. In other words, one should examine whether the classification of a new work is a necessary prerequisite for the work to attract copyright protection. The essential question therefore is whether a multimedia work can qualify for copyright protection by reason of its originality alone if, of course, it is taken for granted that a multimedia work is by nature a 'work' that is adequately fixed to meet the criterion of fixation in those countries where such a criterion is indispensable for the qualification of a work as a copyright work.[1]

The answer to this question necessarily involves two aspects or considerations. One aspect is whether in all national copyright laws, classification of a work is a necessary prerequisite for it to attract copyright protection. The second is, where such a requirement is not present, whether the option of the protection of a multimedia product outside the special regime of a particular class of works, i.e. as a traditional literary work, a film, a computer program, etc., suffices for its protection and satisfies its needs fully.

9.1.1 Guidance in the Berne Convention

A first element of guidance in this area can be found in the Berne Convention which provides for a minimum standard of protection that needs

---

[1] In certain countries the notion of a 'work' presupposes originality.

to be met by all Member States. We will analyse how the Member States have implemented and built upon this minimum standard.

The Berne Convention defines as copyrightable material literary and artistic works, meaning every production in the literary, scientific and artistic domain, whatever its form or mode of expression. Article 2(1) of the Convention gives some illustrative examples of what the concept of literary and artistic works includes: books, pamphlets and other writings, lectures, addresses and so on.[2] Thus, any work which meets this description and which is at the same time original and consistent with what is implied by the notion of 'production' in the same article[3] qualifies for copyright protection. It is clear from the above description and wording that the notions of 'literary works' and 'artistic works' represent generic terms rather than special categories of works in the narrow sense of the term (i.e. traditional literary works). Thus, any work which possesses the essential characteristics contained therein,[4] together with the required creativity that is implied by the nature of these works, qualifies for copyright protection without any further requirement or consideration. Prior classification of a work is not required.

Yet, Berne requires only that all works that come within its scope are protected. How this is achieved is left to the Member States. Two approaches have appeared over the years. A first approach sticks rather closely to the text of the Berne Convention and prior classification does not take place. This approach has mainly been adopted by countries of continental Europe and those that follow their lead.

9.1.2 A first approach

Belgian copyright law keeps the broad generic category of literary and artistic works as the first and only test for qualification of a work as a copyright work. The notion of 'literary and artistic works' is not defined. Article 2 of the Belgian Copyright Act simply refers to literary works as 'writings of any kind' and gives a limited number of examples.[5]

---

[2] See S. Ricketson, *The Berne Convention for the protection of literary and artistic works: 1886–1986*, Kluwer, Deventer, 1988, at 228.

[3] Originality is a concept that is implied by the nature of literary and artistic works (especially by the term 'production' in art. 2 of the Convention) and which, in the Berne Convention, comes closer to the continental standard of originality that requires the personal imprint of the author, rather than the common law one that requires only that the work not have been copied (otherwise known as the 'skill and labour' doctrine). See also Ricketson, *Berne Convention*, at 230ff.

[4] Since no particular characteristics are provided for, it can also be any work which resembles them.

[5] See A. Strowel and J.-P. Triaille, *Le droit d'auteur, du logiciel au multimédia (Copyright, from software to multimedia)*, Bruylant, Brussels, 1997, at 8–9.

Definitions or examples of artistic works or of sub-categories to the broad literary and artistic works genre are not given. In the German Copyright Act, the generic category of works is the category of 'literary, artistic and scientific works'. The list of works in article 2 of the Act which come within its ambit of protection is only illustrative.[6] The French and the Greek Copyright Acts opt for a category of qualifying subject matter which is linguistically even wider. The French Act refers to any 'work of the mind',[7] whilst the Greek Copyright Act refers to 'works' in general. 'The term "work" ... designate[s] any original intellectual literary, artistic or scientific creation, expressed in any form, notably written or oral texts....'[8] In all these cases any list of examples is not exhaustive. Thus, in these countries virtually everything qualifies as a copyright work. The criterion that is used to ensure that the quality standard that Berne adopts through the introduction of the terms 'literary and artistic works' is respected is the originality criterion. Only original works will be seen as copyright works and the high originality criterion is there to make the selection.

The 'no prior qualification' approach has also been adopted by the United States. It opts for a general term and definition which, in the first instance, does not immediately refer to literary and artistic works, works of the mind or works generally. Section 102(a) of the US Copyright Act provides that '[c]opyright protection subsists ... in original works of authorship fixed in any tangible medium of expression, now known or later developed, from which they can be perceived, reproduced or otherwise communicated, either directly or with the aid of a machine or device'. Similarly in Greek law, the concept of a 'work' is the starting point. However, the American version immediately adds further requirements. In practice there are three necessary prerequisites for a work to qualify for copyright protection. First, it has to be a work, second it has to be original and third it has to be fixed in a tangible medium of expression.[9] Although the US Act later enumerates eight categories of works, these categories play an indicative role only. Works that do not belong in one of these categories may also qualify for copyright protection if they possess the features mentioned above.[10]

---

[6] See also H. Schack, *Urheber- und Urhebervertragsrecht*, Mohr Siebeck, Munich, 1997, at 77.
[7] Art. L111-1 in part 1 which is entitled 'Literary and artistic property'. That indicates that all works of the mind are essentially literary and artistic property.
[8] Art. 2(1) of the Greek Copyright Act 2121/1993.
[9] US White Paper, B. Lehman and R. Brown, 'Intellectual property and the national information infrastructure', Report of the Working Group on Intellectual Property Rights, US Patent and Trademark Office, Washington D.C., September 1995, at 24.
[10] 'The list in Section 102 is intended to be illustrative rather than inclusive.' US White

At first sight the US three-condition test of qualification seems to be more restrictive[11] than the requirement found in most continental law systems that a work should simply come within the notion of a literary or artistic work in order to qualify for copyright protection.[12] Nevertheless, if one takes into account the loose criterion of originality in the USA, one soon realises that the number of works qualifying for copyright protection in the USA is substantially larger than that on the continent.[13] The broad generic category of literary and artistic works, which is provided for in the continental copyright laws, is substantially restricted by the requirement that a work carry its author's personal imprint. Such a restriction goes a good deal further than the US three-condition test for works.

9.1.3 A second approach

The countries we have just mentioned adhere to the first approach in implementing the Berne provisions. A second and rather different approach has been taken by the UK. The CDPA 1988 follows a different route of qualification. Here classification is a necessary requirement. In order for a work to qualify for copyright protection, it has first to come within one of the specifically designated categories of copyright works. According to section 1 of the Act, a work should fall within the description[14] of original literary, dramatic, musical or artistic works, sound recordings, films, broadcasts or cable programmes, or the typographical arrangement of published editions. If that is not the case the work at issue does not qualify as a 'copyright work' for the purposes of this Act.[15] From section 3

Paper, at 42. See also footnote 123 on the same page which refers to House Report at 53, reprinted in 1976 US CAN 5666. The Report mentions that the list of categories of copyright works 'sets out the general area of copyrightable subject matter, but with sufficient flexibility to free the courts from rigid or outmoded concepts of the scope of particular categories'.

[11] Especially if we take into account that a work has also to be fixed, which is on some occasions in addition to the originality criterion that in turn constitutes the only passport of qualification for works in many continental copyright laws.

[12] Even if the notion of literary or artistic works in the Berne Convention is construed as broadly as possible, direct reference to it is always subject to certain implied limitations.

[13] See the analysis of the fixation requirement in section 8.2.1.1 above (video games).

[14] As this description is set out in other parts of the CDPA 1988.

[15] See section 1(2). See also P. Torremans and J. Holyoak, *Holyoak and Torremans' intellectual property law*, 2nd edn, Butterworths, London, Dublin, Edinburgh, 1998, at 167; H. Laddie, P. Prescott and M. Vitoria, *The modern law of copyright and designs*, 2nd edn, Butterworths, London, Dublin, Edinburgh, 1995, at 27–8; and W. Cornish, *Intellectual property: patents, copyright, trade marks and allied rights*, 4th edn, Sweet & Maxwell, London, 1999, at 378, where he argues that the criteria to enable a work to qualify for copyright protection are principally of two kinds: the nature of the material and the intellectual or entrepreneurial activity that produced it on the one hand, and the qualifying factor, which brings into account international considerations stemming from the

onwards the description of these particular categories of works is set out, whilst fixation is there as an additional requirement for qualification. Originality is required only in those cases where it is specifically mentioned. In other words, only literary, dramatic, musical and artistic works have to be original. The originality criterion, as we mentioned earlier, is confined to the issue of whether there is enough skill and labour involved in the creation of the work. It is interesting to note that although the *numerus clausus* of the copyright categories available in the UK Copyright Act seems to restrict the scope of protection of works, the low originality criterion or the absence of any originality requirement at all in certain cases,[16] coupled with the broad definition and description of these limited categories of works, allows for an extensive number of works to qualify.[17] In this sense, copyright in the UK is much broader than copyright in continental law countries.[18]

The fact that in the UK a work has first to be designated as a particular type of work, for example a literary work, a film, a sound recording, etc., in order to attract copyright protection is not necessarily restrictive to the number of works qualifying. The description of each category of works is usually wide enough to encompass many variations of the same expression. If at the same time the originality and the fixation requirement are respected, this is actually how a work comes within the scope of the CDPA 1988.[19] After this classification the work necessarily qualifies for the regime of protection which corresponds to the class of works at issue, e.g. the audiovisual works regime of protection if the work qualifies as film, the phonograms regime of protection if the work qualifies as a musical work, and so on. However, the risk with broadly defined classes of works is that if a work could qualify for copyright protection under more than one category of works, it might not fit well with the regime of protection of one single category of works. Theoretically, one work

copyright conventions and similar arrangements, on the other hand. He also alleges that the qualifying factor depends upon what constitutes publication.

[16] Even works without an author, i.e. computer-generated works, qualify for copyright protection, a situation which would be unacceptable to continental law systems.

[17] See, for example, the definition of a literary work in s. 3(1) CDPA 1988.

[18] The US Copyright Act is as broad as the UK Copyright Act in defining the different classes of works. In addition both Acts favour a low originality criterion.

[19] In fact it is easier for a work to qualify as a copyright work in the UK than it is on the continent by reason of the broad definition of the various classes of works and the low originality criterion. The originality requirement either comes in addition to (as is the case in the UK) or on most occasions is part of the nature of literary and artistic works (as is the case in the Berne Convention). There is also the requirement of fixation in the UK and the USA. Nevertheless, even in the case where fixation is not an explicit requirement in other copyright systems, it is often implied either by the nature of the work (there is no phonogram, for example, if there is no recording) or by its definition (e.g. literary works as 'writings of any kind').

should qualify for no more than a single category of works otherwise the general copyright system malfunctions. This view was also confirmed in the case-law. Laddie J ruled in *Electronic Techniques (Anglia) Ltd* v. *Critchley Components Ltd* that

> [i]n some cases the borderline between one category of copyright and another may be difficult to define, but that does not justify giving the author protection in both categories. The categories of copyright works are, to some extent, arbitrarily defined. In the case of a borderline work, I think there are compelling arguments to say that the author must be confined to one or another of the possible categories. The proper category is that which most nearly suits the characteristics of the work in issue.[20]

Thus, if a newly qualified work comes under the classification of films but is not a film *stricto sensu* and presents a different range of particularities, it is very likely that the regime of protection for films will not serve it well, at least in respect of those characteristics which come on top of the traditional characteristics of the film.[21] The same, of course, applies to any regime corresponding to particular classes of works.

9.1.4 Problems arising from these approaches

Up to now we have discussed the system of qualification of works as copyright works in relation to both approaches found in the area. Yet both approaches present inherent problems when they have to accommodate multimedia products. We will first deal with the problems deriving from the approach which does not involve prior classification of works.

In the copyright laws where the procedure is usually independent of any prior classification of the work, a work has to possess the general characteristics of the genre of literary and artistic works in order for it to qualify for copyright protection. If that is the case and the work at issue is also original enough, it qualifies for copyright protection without any further requirement. Only in a second phase does classification take place and this happens only when the work possesses the particular characteristics of one of the categories of literary and artistic works for which

---

[20] [1997] FSR 401. See also *Anacon Corporation Ltd* v. *Environmental Research Technology Ltd* [1994] FSR 659, per Jacob J; Sirinelli Report on multimedia and new technologies, France, Ministère de la culture et de la Francophonie, Paris, 1994, at 58, where it is argued that the assertion of commentators that a multimedia work is somewhere between a database and a film disregards the risk that two special regimes of protection will be applicable at the same time and the dangers this simultaneous application may create, especially if these regimes are not compatible between themselves.

[21] The problem becomes more apparent if one realises the problem the *ius cogens* provisions relating to one category of works present in relation to products which do not really fit well with that particular category of works.

special rules were deemed to be required. In this case the relevant regime of protection applies. In case classification is not possible by reason of the particularities of the work and the absence of a specific category for multimedia products, then the work is afforded the general copyright regime of protection which coincides with that of traditional literary works. In that case, although the work does not remain unprotected, it can be protected only partially since the general regime of protection covers in essence those parts of a work which come close to a traditional literary work. The issue of how far multimedia products resemble traditional literary works has been discussed earlier in this book, and it is apparent that these two works do not necessarily have much in common.[22] Therefore, if multimedia products were to be protected as traditional literary works it is clear that their protection would not be wide enough to cover their entire scope.

Although the UK approach takes another starting point, it still gives rise to a number of problems. In this case multimedia products cannot be afforded copyright protection unless they are first classified in one of the existing categories. Yet classification is not an easy task here either. The different classes of works have been designed to accommodate specific products, although it is obvious that most of them are worded in very broad terms. Three conclusions can therefore be drawn. First, a work might not qualify for copyright protection at all if none of the categories available is found capable of protecting the work at issue because the work does not come within the definition of any of the categories. Second, fitting the new product into one of the given categories of works, e.g. protecting a multimedia product as a computer program, would inevitably result in protecting the whole product as a computer program and thus attributing features as well as rights and obligations to it which are not relevant or functional in its context. Consequently, the accommodation of multimedia products in any category will inevitably offer copyright protection for those parts of the work that coincide with the characteristics of the works meant to be included in that category of works but not for those characteristics which differ or are additional to it.

The third conclusion that can be drawn is that a work (the multimedia product in the case at issue) might be divided into different parts and each part might be protected on its own merits. However, this is not a

---

[22] See especially Groupe Audiovisuel et Multimédia de l'Edition, *Questions juridiques relatives aux oeuvres multimédia* (Livre Blanc), Paris, 1994, at 13ff. And the Sirinelli Report, at 70 where it is argued that the Cour de Cassation has never allowed the right to citation to be applied outside the category of literary works. The same problems might also arise in the exception for the purposes of research and private study in relation to digitised works.

viable solution from a market, as well as a practical, point of view.[23] This is because most parts of a multimedia product can be seen only in conjunction with each other and evaluated as a whole. If one misses the value of the interaction of the different components of a new work one also misses the added value which is put on the work exactly by reason of the interaction of these elements. That will inevitably lead us to situations where inseparable and indistinguishable parts (in the sense that they cannot be distinguished or, if distinguished, they give another result) will inevitably stay unprotected.[24] In that sense both approaches present equally grave problems in relation to the protection of multimedia products. Replacing one with the other does not seem to solve the problem. Both approaches are incapable of offering full protection by reason of the difficulty which they will face at some stage in the procedure for qualification of new products. Thus, rejection of one for the sake of the other does not take us very far.

Classification is not an undesirable process, and it is not necessarily that which creates the problems in relation to the protection of a new work as a copyright work. It reflects the need for the appropriate protection for each work. Without classification at either a first or a later stage, a work runs the risk of being misplaced or left partly unprotected. This is also demonstrated in the US White Paper where it is argued that 'however absent the addition of a new category, a work that does not fit into one of the enumerated categories is, in a sense, in a copyright no-man's land'.[25] In addition, the categorisation of a work allows creators and third parties to pursue their rights and fulfil their obligations relating to the particular work. In other words, it is not clear whether an act is permitted under the exceptions to economic acts until one knows whether the work at issue is, for example, a literary work. In the same sense, development of works is neither secure nor even possible if an entrepreneur does not

---

[23] Sirinelli argues that a possible solution is to divide a work into parts and protect each part on its own merits. P. Sirinelli, 'Le multimédia' in P. Gavalda and N. Piakowski (eds.), *Droit de l'audiovisuel*, Lamy, Paris, 1995, 511, at 522. See also *Electronic Techniques (Anglia) Ltd* v. *Critchley Components Ltd* [1997] FSR 401, per Laddie J.

[24] This was also the case with databases where legislative action was required by reason of the added value of the combination of these elements and the investment put into their combination. In any case it would be highly impractical to deal with one product if each of its components were protected under entirely different regimes of protection. Rights and obligations in relation to the product would become obscure.

[25] US White Paper, at 43. See also T. Desurmont, 'L'exercice des droits en ce qui concerne les "productions multimédias"' in *WIPO international forum on the exercise and management of copyright and neighbouring rights in the face of the challenges of digital technology*, Seville, 14–16 May 1997, WIPO, 1998, 169, at 174, where it is argued that the determination of the classification of a work is an extremely delicate exercise but it is important in so far as it determines the choice of a particular regime of protection which is appropriate to the needs of the work.

know to what he is entitled. Contract law cannot always close the gaps that are there because of the special nature of intellectual property rights and the existence of *ius cogens* provisions. Classification is necessary in so far as it determines the applicable regime of protection, and this regime offers the framework within which parties participate in the development, marketing and use of an intellectual property product.

9.1.5 Possible solutions

From a legal point of view there is much discussion relating to the abandonment of the different categories of copyright works in view of the creation and production of more and more hybrid works which cannot easily be classified. Under the current regime of protection the only possible solution for these works to be protected is their submission under the regime of protection for literary works (literary works in the sense of the Berne Convention rather than in the sense of the CDPA 1988). That, however, is as unsatisfactory as it is for a work to qualify for any other inappropriate regime of protection. Consequently, only three solutions are possible. First, a new classification must be introduced for the group of new technological productions (which will probably in the future take us down the route of a case-by-case study of copyright works and perhaps necessitate the introduction of new categories of works). Alternatively, there must be an annulment of any specific categories of works and a flexible copyright system, which can be adapted according to the will of the parties and the works at issue, must be designed.[26] A third solution would be the restriction of the scope of copyright only to works which are strictly literary and artistic works (restricting the copyright regime to a core of highly original and creative works as was initially intended), and the design of *sui generis* rights for the accommodation of the rest. In any event, multimedia products, in view of the difficulties they present when compared with any of the existing categories of works, require special treatment along the lines of either the introduction of a new category of copyright works or the design of a *sui generis* category of works which will combine copyright and other 'non-copyright' provisions. In addition, they may also call for a combined regime of protection, i.e. copyright protection together with *sui generis* protection along the lines of databases. This will form the subject of the following sections.

From a purely economic point of view, one could argue that there might not be a need for any legislative action in the area of multimedia.

---

[26] See in this respect A. Christie, 'Reconceptualising copyright in the digital era' [1995] 11 *EIPR* 522, at 525.

If under the current copyright regimes of protection a class of works is found which can even partly accommodate multimedia products, then the remaining elements of these products, which are not protected under this class of works, could arguably still be satisfactorily protected by the operation of the market. There may indeed be circumstances where the normal operation of the market takes care of the problem and offers adequate protection to multimedia products in the sense that they get the protection they deserve and that that protection goes to the persons who deserve it. On the other hand, it could be argued that multimedia products do not always appear in such circumstances. In the same sense that databases needed a *sui generis* right to correct a market failure because copyright was not capable of protecting the most valuable aspect of the average database, it can be argued that most multimedia products are not adequately protected by any of the existing copyright regimes. If their real value is found in the combination of various and numerous bits of information, interactivity and integration, no single category of copyright works can offer adequate protection. The aspect of integration is particularly valuable but it is unknown in the current copyright regimes. This means that multimedia products will lose out in terms of protection under any of the existing regimes. The additional value they present remains unprotected and, in a climate of digital ease of copying at a fraction of the original investment costs, the market is unable to correct this failure through its own mechanisms. The result of this is an absence of an optimum level of protection and therefore an absence of an incentive for the creation of new high-quality multimedia products since the creators cannot recoup their efforts nor the entrepreneurs their investment.[27]

In addition, there is no function of the market which can compensate for those parts of a work which are not protected under current law apart from the fact that the first competitor on the market benefits from some lead time, i.e. the time necessary for competitors to prepare and release a competing product. However, in many cases this is a minimal form of protection. The market characteristically favours trading parties which are somehow bound by an agreement or contract. It is therefore not possible for the owner of copyright in a work to bind by contract every third party which has access to his work and which can easily copy and reproduce it.[28] In these circumstances one can reach the conclusion that there exists a market failure requiring correction by the introduction of a new

---

[27] M. Marinos, *Pnevmatiki idioktissia*, Ant. N. Sakkoula, Athens, 2000, at 10.
[28] This depends on Privity 4 (P4) exceptions. See J. Adams, R. Brownsword and D. Beyleveld, 'Privity of contract – the benefits and burdens of law reform' [1997] *MLR* 238.

class of works or the creation of a new right.[29] In relation to multimedia products two options are open. Either an adequate classification can be found for a particular type of work or a new type of work or a new (*sui generis*) right needs to be created.[30]

9.1.6 Summing up

In conclusion, one can say that under some national regimes of protection a multimedia product can attract copyright protection irrespective of any classification. This is not so in the UK though. Yet under both approaches described above multimedia products are protected either under the general regime of protection for literary and artistic works or under the regime of protection for specific categories of works. In both cases certain aspects of multimedia products remain unprotected. The argument that these aspects can be dealt with satisfactorily by the operation of the market is not convincing. The only feasible solution seems to be the introduction of special rules for multimedia products. The method and content of these rules is a matter to which we will return later.

9.2 QUALIFICATION OF MULTIMEDIA WORKS ACCORDING TO THE TYPE OF CO-OPERATION OF THE CONTRIBUTORS (THE FRENCH PARADIGM)

9.2.1 Introduction

The way in which the various contributors to a work co-operate can arguably be used as a criterion to distinguish between various categories of works. This is done to a fair extent, for example, in French copyright law. But even there the only real issue for discussion is that of authorship and ownership of copyright. It is worth examining whether such an approach makes it easier to fit multimedia products into copyright.

Article L113-2 of the French Copyright Act provides for three types of works according to the type of co-operation between their various contributors (collaborative, composite and collective works). 'Collaborative works' are works in the creation of which more than one natural person

---

[29] On the socio-economic analysis of copyright see W. Landes and R. Posner, 'An economic analysis of copyright law' (1989) 18 *Journal of Legal Studies* 325; Z. Chafee, 'Reflections on the law of copyright' (1945) 45 *Col LR* 503; S. Sterk, "Rhetoric and reality in copyright law" (1996) 94 *Michigan Law Review* 1197. Market failure can be defined as the inability of the market to provide an optimum level of competition.

[30] See E. Mackaay, 'Economisch-filosofische aspecten van de intellectuele rechten' in M. van Hoecke (ed.), *The socio-economic role of intellectual property rights*, Story – Scientia, Brussels, 1991, at 1.

has participated. These works are the joint property of their authors and any rights in them are exercised by common accord. 'Composite works' are new works in which a pre-existing work is incorporated without the collaboration of the author of that work, and are the property of the author who has produced them. 'Collective works' are works created on the initiative of a natural or legal person who edits them, publishes them and discloses them under his direction and name and in which the personal contributions of the various authors who participated in their production are merged in the overall work for which they were conceived, without it being possible to attribute to each author a separate right in the work as created. There is a legal presumption that these works are the property of the natural or legal person under whose name they have been disclosed.[31]

9.2.2 Multimedia products and collaborative works

The notion of collaborative works presents certain limited attractions in relation to multimedia products. Multimedia products are indeed the outcome of the contributions of many participants who, according to the traditional copyright axiom, have to be compensated for their work. It is therefore fair enough to bestow on them the quality of author, together with the full panoply of exclusive rights. However, in the context of a multimedia product this presents certain inherent difficulties. First, the number of contributors involved in such a work is substantially larger than the number of persons involved in a traditional collaborative work, often becoming so great as to render any co-authorship and co-ownership of rights impractical to operate in the market. Clearing rights and reaching a common accord in these circumstances are highly difficult and risky tasks since the whole project or any future project depending thereon can be put in jeopardy if one of the authors involved does not co-operate in the end or does not agree to the further exploitation of the work. Second, not all the contributors involved in a multimedia product deserve the status of author. That, of course, is true in relation to other collaborative works, such as films, too. The technicians or people having undertaken non-creative tasks are never given authorship. Yet, in a multimedia context this distinction is not always an easy one to make. Some of the contributions involved, though technical, might also involve creative tasks because of the nature of the multimedia work. Examples are the contributions made by phototypesetters, info-designers, ergonomicists, page and screen designers, index drafters, documentalists, sound

[31] Arts. L113-2–5 of the French Copyright Act 1992.

engineers, designers of hypertext links,[32] etc. In a collaborative works regime such considerations are more problematic and have to be solved and considered at every stage when the work is used or exploited and not only at the stage of the production of the work. Even if successful financial arrangements are made, there is always the risk that one of the authors might exercise his moral rights in bad faith or want to create problems in the further exploitation of the work.

In addition, a multimedia product is not in essence a collaborative work. There is no common inspiration of the persons involved in its production.[33] There is also no common work or collaboration in the same way as in a collaborative work. Even if in the beginning different kinds of individual works are meant to be put together, their individuality soon disappears by reason of the commercial function and appearance of the multimedia product. The multimedia product presents an image of merged works and contributions which can no longer be distinguished or separated.[34] These contributions are put together by one natural or legal person. This is the person who conducts the whole project, edits the various contributions and puts them in the format of the multimedia product. It is occasionally the same person who decides the image and the marketing of the work and makes the funds available. The other scenario is where in the main there are companies that undertake all these tasks (producers) and commission other companies for the physical development, technical organisation, form, packaging and marketing of the final product (makers or developers).[35] It is usually under the second company's trade mark that this product reaches the market. In the regime

---

[32] A. Lucas does not hesitate in considering this a creative job which is clearly within the scope of the authorship provisions of copyright. This is not necessarily an obvious conclusion though. 'Multimédia et droit d'auteur' in AFTEL, *Le droit du multimédia: de la télématique à Internet*, Les Editions du Téléphone, Paris, 1996, 113, at 148.

[33] *Contra* Lucas who seems to suggest that there could be a collaborative work as long as there is a common project. But even he feels it is necessary to exclude certain contributors whose work does not contribute in a creative sense to the common project. *Ibid.*, at 149–50.

[34] Art. L113-3 para. 4 of the French Copyright Act 1992 stipulates that each contributor (who is also a co-author) can exploit his/her own contribution separately in so far as this contribution is of a different type to any of the other contributions and in so far as the separate exploitation does not cause any harm to the joint exploitation of the work. In fact the courts have authorised the separate exploitation of individual frames of comic strips (Court of Appeal of Poitiers, 6 September 1989, [1991] D. Somm. comm. 93, annotated by Colombet). 'However, when extended to multimedia works this kind of concept could become dangerous. Any graphic contribution may seem to be independent but its actual format is often defined by other contributions such as that of a scenario writer': A. Latreille, 'The legal classification of multimedia creations in French law' in I. Stamatoudi and P. Torremans (eds.), *Copyright in the new digital environment*, Sweet & Maxwell, London, 2000, 43, at 49.

[35] See section 2.3 above on project participants.

of collaborative works these practices are not taken into account and therefore there is no legal presumption in favour of legal persons.

Another interesting point to note is the fact that in France audiovisual works are *de iure* collaborative works. If multimedia products were to qualify as audiovisual works they would necessarily qualify as collaborative works as well. Whilst the combination may be attractive from certain points of view, this section as well as chapter 6 on audiovisual works has clearly demonstrated that this is by no means the most suitable solution.

9.2.3 Multimedia products and composite works

Composite works[36] are another potential category for multimedia products. Indeed, multimedia products contain a bulk of pre-existing works and materials in the same way as composite works. It would be unrealistic for the producer of a multimedia product to include only newly commissioned works in such a project.[37] It would be costly, time-consuming and, on most occasions, it would also be commercially unattractive. Although this is usually the case, it would be equally unrealistic for one to suppose that only pre-existing works are contained in a multimedia product. New works can also be included, especially in cases where the persons commissioned to produce such works are needed to offer their services until the last minute in the form of putting the finishing touches to their works once they have been incorporated into the multimedia product and merged with other contributions. However, the participation of authors other than the collector in a work prevents the work from being a composite work. It is apparent that the category of composite works was included to accommodate mainly collections of works and anthologies or derivative works such as translations, adaptations, etc.[38] However, this type of work seems to have little in common with multimedia products.

Although composite works also have the advantage of conferring the rights of an author on the person who has realised the collection of the works, i.e., on one person, they are still inflexible on the issue of conferring authorship on any legal person.

---

[36] Also known as derivative works.
[37] A newly commissioned work which is included in a multimedia product after its completion is theoretically not rendered a pre-existing work.
[38] Latreille argues that although a multimedia work may in many cases be a composite work it is rarely a purely derivative work because there is usually a main contribution and a large number of secondary contributions. In that sense he asserts that a multimedia work can be described as a collaborative work which is in part composite. He also argues that the author and the party exploiting the work have to respect the rights of the authors of the pre-existing works and, in the case of a multimedia product, the high number of owners of pre-existing rights makes the exploitation of the work very difficult. 'Legal classification' at 50–1.

9.2.4 Multimedia products and collective works

Collective works seem to come closer to multimedia products than any of the previous types of works.[39] The advantage of this classification is that, irrespective of the nature of the works that are brought together and the nature of the work that results, one can establish a single rule which deals with the fact that there are multiple contributors. For the final work, however, there should ideally be one rightholder. To a certain extent what is achieved by this approach is that a work that results from the collaboration of various authors is given copyright protection and the ownership of that protection can be attributed to one person. Furthermore, given the fact that multimedia products are projects that are essentially undertaken by companies, the law provides in such situations that the company under the name of which the work is disclosed can also become the rightholder of the work. This is particularly helpful if one takes into account that it is mainly companies that invest money, know-how and personnel expertise in the creation of a multimedia product. And given the fact that multimedia products are essentially functional information-based works, the fact that companies can automatically hold the exclusive rights in them substantially facilitates the trade of these works on the international market.

In addition, collective works stipulate that their contents are merged in the overall work without it being possible to distinguish between them. This seems to sit well with the nature of multimedia products, the value of which consists not only in the contributions they contain but in the added value of the overall work in which these contributions have been brought together and put in a particular format. Indeed, on most occasions this format does not allow one to distinguish between the various contributions.

Perhaps the only problem in relation to collective works and multimedia products is that the author of a collective work is the person who edits, publishes and discloses the work under his direction and name. Yet the rights in the work are conferred on the person under whose name the work is disclosed, without any reference to his direction. However, this is bound to cause problems in the context of a multimedia product. As was explained earlier, the practice with multimedia products is that the person or company that edits and publishes the work is not always

---

[39] The French courts ruled that the input of a video sequence which had been commissioned for an interactive game was a contribution to a collective work. However, that was very much a case based on the facts. TGI Nanterre, 26 November 1997 [1998] *Gaz Pal* (25 March) 25; [1997] *RDPI* No. 80 (October 1997) 51; *contra* TGI Paris, 8 September 1998, unreported, as referred to in Latreille, 'Legal classification' at 55, note 68.

the person under whose name the work is disclosed. Disclosure and marketing of a multimedia work are usually undertaken by the company that develops its technical base and which happens to have a trade mark that is capable of contributing to its market success. These particularities have not been taken into account by the drafters of the notion of collective works.

The notion of collective works is alien to most national jurisdictions.[40] In Belgium and in the UK, for example, there are provisions only on collaborative works and works of joint authorship[41] respectively.[42] Works that involve contributions of more than one person confer authorship on all the persons involved, either individually or jointly.[43] Only at a second stage and through the operation of a contract can a natural or legal person become the owner of the work. However, moral rights remain with the author unless they have been waived in jurisdictions, such as the UK, where waivability is an option.

---

[40] Similar distinctions to the ones just mentioned are also found in Greece (art. 7 of the Copyright Act 2121/1993), though with varying content. In Greece the notion of the French collaborative works is reflected in works of joint authorship and composite works. In both works of joint authorship and composite works there are contributions of more than one author. Composite works are composed of parts created separately by different authors, each of whom has separate rights and the right of their separate exploitation (with certain reservations). In both works of joint authorship and composite works there is co-authorship of all the persons involved. In the Greek Copyright Act collective works have one author, the person under the intellectual direction and co-ordination of whom independent contributions of several authors are put together. Also in this case the authors involved keep their rights in relation to their personal contributions (if these contributions are distinguishable). In other jurisdictions, such as Germany (art. 8 of the Copyright Act 1965), Belgium (art. 5 of the Belgian Copyright Act 1994), the UK (s. 10 CDPA 1988) and the USA (17 USC § 101(a) (1988)), essentially there is only one category of works, called works of joint authorship (or collaborative works in Belgium), which comes very close to the French notion of collaborative works. In all these cases we have contributions of many authors which, after having been put together, are no longer distinguishable. In each case there is joint authorship or co-authorship. In Germany there is also the category of compound works which is nothing more than the combination of works of several authors (art. 9 of the Copyright Act 1965). This is another case of co-authorship.

[41] In s. 10(1) CDPA 1988 a 'work of joint authorship' is defined as a work 'produced by the collaboration of two or more authors in which the contribution of each author is not distinct from that of the other author or authors'. In the US Copyright Act (17 USC § 101(a) (1988)) a 'joint work' is 'a work prepared by two or more authors with the intention that their contributions be merged into inseparable or interdependent parts of a unitary whole'.

[42] See art. 5 of the Belgian Copyright Act and s. 10 CDPA 1988.

[43] See ALAI, *Audiovisual works and literary and artistic property*, ALAI, Paris, 1996 (report on a Unesco conference), at 734. Although 'collective works' in France do not confer authorship on all the persons involved, they still result in favouring even the authors of most insignificant pre-existing works more than those directly involved in the project who add the 'added value'. A. Latreille, 'La création multimédia comme oeuvre audiovisuelle' [1998] *JCP* (édition générale) I, 156 (nos. 31–5, 29 July 1998).

9.2.5 Conclusions

The above discussion leads us to the conclusion that the most suitable category for multimedia products is collective works.[44] But even here certain transformations have to be made regarding the tasks of the author and the contents of these works, which clearly come closer to the description of composite works in so far as they contain pre-existing materials. In this sense multimedia works are hybrid works (a mixture of composite and collective works) with prevailing features from the category of collective works. In this light, if one stretches the notion of collective works one might well argue that multimedia products can be considered as collective works. In a French copyright system that means that a multimedia work cannot by definition be an audiovisual work, because then the legal presumption would automatically make it a collaborative rather than a collective work. Therefore, in this case one has either to go down the path of collections, databases, etc., or simply to allow multimedia works (in jurisdictions where that is possible) to qualify as collective works and be given the protection of the general category of works (literary and artistic works). In such a case, of course, the inconsistencies of multimedia products with the various aspects of this regime (other than authorship/ownership) have to be considered separately.

Although this is a valuable conclusion in relation to French multimedia products, it can only be of limited value for those countries that do not provide for the category of collective works in their copyright laws. Even in France though, this conclusion is not particularly helpful for identifying the regime of protection of multimedia products. Identifying a copyright work as a collective work solves only the issue of authorship and ownership. It is not capable of offering a complete regime of protection for multimedia products. In this sense, even if the conclusion that multimedia products are collective works is a conclusion which one can arrive at with a substantial degree of certainty, it is still not a solution capable of solving the problems of the protection of multimedia products. In any copyright system one still has to assess multimedia products on the grounds of their nature rather than the type of co-operation between their various contributors.[45] In conclusion, the approach that starts by categorising a work as collective or collaborative provides only a stopgap

---

[44] See also B. Edelman, 'L'oeuvre multimédia, un essai de qualification' [1995] 15 *Recueil Dalloz Sirey* 109, at 114.
[45] Even if this conclusion is helpful for French lawyers in relation to multimedia products whose marketing is territorially restricted within France, it is not helpful in relation to internationally marketed products. Disparities in the protection of the same products in the various states can only cause confusion and bewilderment on the international market.

solution in practice in those countries where a detailed categorisation by the nature of the work is not required. If a work deserves some form of copyright, then the approach provides workable answers in terms of ownership. The fundamental questions of the nature of a multimedia work and its broader regime of protection are not resolved at all though.

9.3 QUALIFICATION OF MULTIMEDIA WORKS ACCORDING TO THEIR NATURE

In the previous chapters we have had ample opportunity to discuss the distinctive features of a multimedia work which can be summarised as follows: *a combination of several different kinds of works into an integrated digitised entity allowing users to interact substantially with its contents.*[46] We also discussed the various classifications provided in the national copyright laws which relate in some way to multimedia products, i.e. traditional literary works, compilations, databases, audiovisual works and computer programs. Thus, we have reached a stage at which we have to draw some conclusions as to the nature of multimedia products and how this nature relates to existing copyright categories of works.

Before we enter any discussion relating to the categorisation of multimedia products, one point should be clarified. Not all multimedia products are the same. This book clearly focuses on the second generation of multimedia products which possess versatile or creative interactivity. Even multimedia products that are found in that category can differ from one another. However, there are common characteristics found in all advanced multimedia works which render them distinctive.[47] To what extent these characteristics will remain unchanged by future technological developments in the area is an issue upon which we can only speculate.

Amongst the five categories of copyright works that we examined, three categories can immediately be excluded as candidates for accommodating multimedia products. These are the categories of traditional literary works, conventional compilations and computer programs. We demonstrated that works found in the first two categories, mainly comprising text, or text and images in the case of compilations, are found in a

---

[46] As Sirinelli points out, if the nature of a multimedia product is not defined then there is little sense in introducing new legislation which would create further demarcation problems and would bring about a solution in the light of the changing nature of multimedia products. However, one should add that this approach presupposes the existence of a general fallback category of copyright works. In France, for example, this category always offers some level of protection, but in the UK (to take the other extreme example) no such category exists, which means that the advantage of the solution disappears. Sirinelli Report, at 70.

[47] These characteristics were pointed out in section 2.1 above.

standard hard-copy format and cannot be altered. Interactivity is a notion which is alien to them. In relation to computer programs, it has been demonstrated that the only similarity they possess to multimedia products is that they constitute a part of them: their technical base. Classifying a multimedia product as a computer program would therefore disregard all the visual aspects of the work which make it valuable and which appear in addition to its technical base. The nature of all three of the above categories of works is far removed from the nature of any multimedia product.[48]

The remaining categories of works which come closer to a multimedia product are those of audiovisual works and databases. However, although audiovisual works capture some of the visual effects of multimedia products, they fail to accommodate the variety and changing nature of their contents; interactivity precludes any set 'sequences of images'. In addition, audiovisual works mainly comprise images, whereas multimedia products contain images but only as a part of their contents. In reality they contain all kinds of works and data which on most occasions translate into text.

Databases seem to overcome this hurdle. Any kind of work (e.g. text, images, music, etc.) can be contained in a database. On top of that, no 'sequences of images' are required. In fact, the notion of databases is antithetic to any sequences of images altogether. However, the problem here is that it goes even further than that and requires the elements included in databases to be individually accessible. The presence of interactivity in a multimedia product prevents access to elements in the same way as a database. The contents of most multimedia works are merged in such a way that what is accessed and retrieved contains bits and pieces of various elements that have been entered in the work in a first phase. Entries that have been independently inserted in a multimedia work and which are then as such independently retrieved by users of the work are rarely found in a multimedia product.[49]

---

[48] It must always be remembered that the various categories of copyright works were traditionally designed to accommodate conventional forms of creations which have little to do with new technology products. The argument that the form of creation is of no relevance for the protection of this creation as a copyright work in most continental systems carries little weight when affording a work the appropriate regime of protection. (See Lucas' argument that 'there are no creations which are protected by their nature', 'Multimédia et droit d'auteur', at 141.) Although this declaration is true in relation to the French copyright system (whilst definitely not true in relation to UK copyright law), it is perhaps of little value when one tries in practice to fit a work into a particular regime of copyright protection if there are specific provisions relating to the nature of the works coming under this regime of protection.

[49] Yet, it is more likely that a multimedia work qualifies as a database than as an audiovisual work.

In the light of the above, the following conclusions can be drawn. There is nothing to exclude the possibility of multimedia products qualifying as either films or databases as long as they possess the necessary characteristics of one of these categories of works.[50] Yet, parallel qualification of a multimedia product as both an audiovisual work and a database is not possible, not only doctrinally,[51] but also according to the EU database Directive which prevents films from qualifying as databases.[52] Splitting a multimedia work into various parts and protecting them on their own merits is also not a viable solution. It causes confusion on the market as to the identity of the authors/rightholders and the rights owned by them, and loses sight of the multimedia work as a whole (meaning the collection and arrangement of its elements in a way that is both comprehensible and interactive) and its added value.

Although advanced multimedia products might in rare cases qualify as audiovisual works or databases, this might often be the case with multimedia products of the first generation.[53] That is explained on the basis that advanced multimedia products are more complex works when compared to multimedia products of the first generation, with a qualitatively higher degree of interactivity allowing users to manipulate and intervene in the contents of the work through sampling, blurring, etc. They are essentially hybrid works that cut across many categories of works and are not capable of being fitted into any of the existing categories of copyright works.[54] Even if the regime of protection of these categories might

---

[50] The literature on multimedia works initially favoured the qualification of multimedia works as audiovisual works, this being consistent also with the decisions delivered in many countries with regard to video games. See Edelman, 'L'oeuvre multimédia', at 115. Recently the tendency in the literature seems to have been towards their qualification as databases. The introduction of the EU Directive on the legal protection of databases, the broad definition of the notion of databases (many relate it to the electronic version of a conventional compilation) and the fact that a *sui generis* (unfair competition law) regime has been put in place for investments with regard to databases has made this regime of protection look even more attractive. Yet, as discussed in chapter 5 above, reservations remain as to the requirement that database entries be 'individually accessible'.

[51] See section 6.5.2 above on the possibility of cumulative protection of works.

[52] Recital 17 to the database Directive, [1996] OJ L77/20.

[53] Examinations of the nature and needs of early multimedia works prompted many commentators to think that any legislative action on these grounds would be premature. Yet, they all seem to have their reservations as to whether this will also be the case in relation to future developments in the area. See in this respect the Sirinelli Report, at 78ff. See also the national reports in ALAI, *Audiovisual works*, at 722ff. (in relation to the third question of the questionnaire concerning multimedia products and the need to transform current national copyright laws).

[54] An example would be a multimedia product on Beethoven's life which contains pictures of his life as well as a database of all the musical works he composed. It might also contain clips with electronically re-enacted scenes, which can be manipulated by the user. The user would be able to interfere substantially with the contents of the multimedia product by including or excluding instruments, changing bits of the orchestration

theoretically serve the needs of multimedia products well (which as we proved can only rarely be the case), it is not possible to afford them the regime of protection of a category of works with whose nature they have little or nothing in common. Expansion alone of the existing categories of copyright works in order to accommodate multimedia products within their regime of protection would still need separate legislative action[55] in the same way the introduction of a *sui generis* regime within or outside the scope of copyright would.

9.4   A HYBRID PRODUCT IN NEED OF A *SUI GENERIS* COPYRIGHT CLASSIFICATION

We have come to the conclusion that although multimedia products cut across many categories of works, still there is no perfect match with any of them. We are presented with a *vide juridique* (i.e. a complete absence of directly applicable legal rules). It therefore follows that if we are to protect multimedia products effectively, new legislation is required as a means of either introducing a separate category of protection within copyright or abandoning copyright protection altogether and heading towards an unfair competition law right. The first solution presupposes that multimedia products are creations which are original and therefore

---

and the melody, blurring the pictures and so on. Another example is *Moorditj*, which is a multimedia CD-ROM concerning Australian indigenous cultural expression (Australian Department of Communication of the Arts, *Moorditj - Australian indigenous cultural expression (1998)*). 'When the CD-Rom begins, there is an introductory moving sequence of an indigenous dancer and the user is then introduced to the product through a video clip of a narrator. There is a "main menu" interface, which allows the user to move to the following levels: introduction; making of Moorditj; themes; challenge; explore by region; explore by type; and how to use. The "introduction" interface has a series of sections: cultural expression; sharing the culture; protocol and custodianship; cultural diversity; making choices; and traditional and contemporary. When the user clicks on one of these icons, he is taken to a video clip of a narrator and some images. Returning to the "main menu", the primary way of viewing the material is through the "themes" or "explore" sections. In the "themes" level, there is an introductory video blurb by the narrator combined with a display or montage of images. The user then moves to a screen where a selection of cultural expressions reflecting that theme is collected together. There are thumbnail images representing those cultural expressions, from which the user may call up a larger version by clicking on that thumbnail, as well as a biography of that work or, where appropriate, an extract from that work, whether it be a sound or video extract. In addition the user may click on the thumbnail photograph of the artist to see an enlarged photograph of the artist, as well as clicking an icon which displays a biography of the artist. The "explore" sections, either by type or region, demonstrate a similar sort of method of access to information: thumbnail images of cultural expressions and icons that reproduce either biographies, extracts from artworks or short video interviews with the artists or persons who know (or knew) the artists.' T. Aplin, 'Not in our galaxy: why "film" won't rescue multimedia' [1999] *EIPR* 633, at 636.

[55] Purposive or teleological interpretation of the existing copyright laws cannot take us far.

still merit copyright protection. The second one acknowledges that in reality it is the contents and the investment in money, time and effort that make the multimedia product valuable and not the presence of any originality. A third solution would envisage a combination of the two along the lines of the EU database Directive.

Before discussing any of the three potential options, one should address the problems deriving from an attitude towards new technology products that the role of copyright is not to protect works (products) and is definitely not to facilitate creation. Copyright law protects authors.[56] Any transformation of the law would only adjust it to this emerging new reality which is not necessarily compatible with the primary objectives of intellectual property, at least from a continental law perspective. Since authors are protected according to the existing copyright regimes, the issues of creation/production can be solved through the operation of the market, unfair competition law, contract and, lastly, technology. The latter are only side issues when compared to the protection of the author or authors of the multimedia work.

The fact is that, no matter how one defines copyright protection (e.g. protection of the author rather than the creation), one still touches on the relationship between the author and his work. In section 9.2 we demonstrated that a regime of protection which is not well placed to accommodate multimedia products can only afford protection to the wrong authors.[57] That, however, cannot be remedied by either the operation of the market or that of the contract. We explained that the market and the contract bind people who are parties to the same deal or transaction. They do not bind third parties who have access to the work and to whose financial benefit it is to copy as much as possible in order to avoid additional costs in the creation of identical or similar products. Such a situation jeopardises the rights of authors by putting at risk their efforts and investments. Without securing their intellectual labour and the investment that is needed to put it in the format of a product *erga omnes*, the system hits a blockage which cannot easily be overcome, if at all. It is true that the author of new technology works does not have much in common with a traditional author and that increasingly the creation has become a production, the value of which does not depend so much on the personal authoring of the work as it does on teamwork and market needs. This, however, is not a good reason to leave

---

[56] This is the French approach. The UK approach, however, is different from the continental one. It clearly protects works. The provisions for authors are weaker than those on the continent (diminished moral rights, employers' rights, film producers' rights, etc.). In this sense UK copyright seems to be better placed to protect new technology products.
[57] See section 9.2 above.

authors of the new era unprotected. Protecting the creation is like protecting the author, and facilitating his work is in fact giving him an incentive to continue to produce. The fact that his productions are dictated by the market and the new reality does not signify that the author is a second-class author, it rather signifies that the needs of present societies have changed and it is on this basis that the authors and their works should be assessed. Unfair competition protection in its turn falls short of taking into account principles of creation, intellectual effort and originality since it is based on a market-orientated approach. It therefore presents problems analogous to those we discussed in relation to the market. In addition, technology constitutes an essential argument but, as we will discuss later in this book, technology and technological devices alone, without the legal basis that legitimises them, are still not a solution.

There is little doubt that multimedia works can be original creations of the mind. This is also the reason that justifies their protection under copyright law. The fact that they do not currently fit in any of the existing categories of copyright works is clearly not an indication that they do not deserve copyright protection.[58] It is rather an indication that there is a need for the introduction of a separate category for multimedia works in copyright law which will take into account digitisation, the inclusion of several different kinds of works in one product and above all interactivity.

In this category of works there should not be such a thing as prevailing elements. All kinds of works can possibly be included, irrespective of their nature and initial format. Digitisation will indicate the large factual capacity of multimedia works and their form of expression which clearly departs from any conventional form of expression or carrier without, however, affecting the nature of the works included.[59] The works that are included do not lose their original status once they are digitised. They co-exist as parts of a larger entity. The fact that the elements included in a multimedia work are merged should also be mentioned. As such it does not preclude the instance where some works might not be merged (or entirely merged with others), but it facilitates any potential regime of protection with regard to the rights of the authors of the works included

---

[58] In the same way films and sound recordings deserved protection well before their introduction into the national copyright Acts.

[59] Providing for a separate category of 'digitised works' is not an option since works do not lose their primary nature after being digitised, e.g. a musical work remains a musical work, etc. A. Lucas with reference to M. Ficsor, 'New technologies and copyright: need for change, need for continuity' in *WIPO worldwide symposium on the future of copyright and neighbouring rights*, Louvre, Paris, 1–3 June 1994, 209, at 227. *Contra* A. Dixon and L. Self, 'Copyright protection for the information superhighway' [1994] 11 *EIPR* 465, at 467.

as well as to the rights of users.[60] Interactivity is important from two points of view: first, because no standard sequence or format of contents is required, and second, because the lack of standard format (or the intention of lack of standard format) offers users the freedom to elaborate or intervene in the work without infringing potential rights of authors. The combination of various kinds of works irrespective of their conventional earlier format, digitisation and interactivity will undoubtedly be the essential common characteristics of any new technology products. From that point of view, many future developments in the area can well be accommodated by this new category of works.

Dropping copyright protection in relation to multimedia products altogether is not a viable option. First, copyright has an internationally well-established regime of protection which allows a substantial degree of co-operation and reciprocity between the various states. Over and above that it has proved itself all along to be the most effective means of protection, perfectly capable of protecting new technology products. The common currency of intellectual creations has not been overtaken in any respect and therefore there is no reason to abandon the only protection that is going in this direction. However, this argument is not there to exclude the introduction of any *sui generis* or unfair competition rights in relation to intellectual property products which come close enough to a practice of industrial production and involve also issues of investment which cannot be successfully dealt with by copyright, especially in relation to creations which are not original. This was the case with databases. Here an unfair extraction/re-utilisation right has been introduced in relation to the contents of a database in the obtaining, verification or presentation of which a qualitatively or quantitatively substantial investment was made.[61] If a database is original, the unfair extraction right comes on top of its copyright protection to prevent third parties from extracting almost the same contents for use in a different structure or arrangement. If the database is not original, the maker of the database would still not jeopardise his investment in bringing these elements together should third parties be ready to copy them. That may also be the case for multimedia products. The investment put in in relation to their elements might be so substantial that it has to be afforded separate protection. This is especially true for multimedia products which are not original and therefore do not attract copyright protection. In addition, the way these elements interact with each other can also form the subject of an unfair competition law right (cf. the *sui generis* right for databases) if it is commonplace in terms

---

[60] E.g. rights to disclosure, moral rights, etc.
[61] Arts. 7ff. of the EU database Directive.

of originality but hard enough in terms of, for example, investment to bring it to realisation. Although interactivity derives from the computer program that operates the multimedia work, the way this operation is projected on screen can still form the subject of a separate right.

In conclusion, the best possible solution seems to be the introduction of a new category of copyright works, i.e. multimedia works, plus the introduction of a *sui generis* right relating to the investment put into the contents of the multimedia work and perhaps to the way its interactivity is presented on screen. This can set the foundations for special provisions on the protection of multimedia products, which, although they will closely relate to the existing provisions, will still be adjusted to their specific needs. This will form the subject of the following chapter.

10 A regime of protection for multimedia products

10.1 A COPYRIGHT REGIME FOR MULTIMEDIA PRODUCTS

No existing copyright regime can perfectly accommodate multimedia products.[1] Yet there is no doubt that most multimedia products constitute creations which are original and therefore merit copyright protection. In this chapter we will discuss the configurations of a specially tailored copyright protection for multimedia works, which, as will be shown, should be an amalgamation of the regime of protection for audiovisual works and that for databases.

In order for a work to qualify for copyright protection under UK copyright law, it has first to come within a category of protected works. For that purpose, and given the fact that no current category of copyrightable material is capable of accommodating all forms of multimedia products, a separate category for multimedia works should be introduced.[2] In this category multimedia works should be defined as *works which combine (on a single medium) more than one different kind of expression in an integrated digital format, and which allow their users to manipulate their contents with a substantial degree of interactivity.*[3] The essential features of the second

---

[1] G. Schricker, *Urheberrecht. Kommentar*, 2nd edn, C. H. Beck, Munich, 1999, at 1381 and at 84. J. Sterling, *World copyright law*, Sweet & Maxwell, London, 1999, at 201. According to Sterling, a multimedia work can be described as a 'mediagraphic work' with a particular emphasis on interactivity. See also S. Jones, 'Multimedia and the superhighway: exploring the rights minefield' (1996) 1 *Communications Law* 28, at 32.

[2] As we have demonstrated in earlier chapters, the need to introduce a separate category of multimedia products is equally relevant to civil law systems as the general category of literary and artistic works does not meet the needs of these products.

[3] The fact that these works are found on a single medium should be implied by the definition. In the same way the fact that the format of these works is digitised is implied by the fact that this is the only way of integrating works which are at the same time interactive. Interactivity as such implies the use of a computer program. To what extent, of course, these two will remain distinguishable in the future is an issue which can only be answered by future technological evolution in the area. Issues which are implied can well be left out of the definition of multimedia products, or put in Recitals or introductory points to the legislation. It is always better for legislation to remain short and general.

generation of multimedia products are the combination of various kinds of expressions on a single medium to a larger extent than ever before, the predominantly integrated and merged format of the works once they have been incorporated in the multimedia product, as well as the fact that the degree of interactivity that they offer to users is well above any primitive form of interactivity. Indeed it almost goes as far as to offer 'creative' roles to the users of the multimedia product.[4]

The issue of how many of the various expressions are required to qualify, as well as the degree of integration of these expressions, should be left open. The means of producing, delivering, presenting and manipulating these works, either as products or services, should also remain open. Technology in recent decades has progressed on a fast track and for that very reason any new legislation has to achieve the challenging and particularly difficult task of combining precision and flexibility. Inflexible legislation will not meet the needs of future developments and will fail to meet its task as technology-proof legislation. Moreover, multimedia technology, though substantially developed, is still at the first stages of a greater evolution that is to follow.

Before we enter the discussion relating to the substantive provisions of such a regime of protection for multimedia products, we should first answer the question of whether all multimedia applications should come within this definition and therefore be protected by the regime of protection we are to describe. It may after all be expedient to offer protection under this regime only to those multimedia products which are clearly hybrid works and therefore incapable of attracting protection under one of the existing categories of copyright works. As we mentioned earlier, the medium on which a work is carried and the digitisation of the works are not features capable of changing its nature. In other words, a musical work remains a musical work even after its digitisation or its incorporation into a multimedia product, an interactive encyclopaedia remains a literary work, etc. What, however, is likely to bring alterations to the initial nature of the work is its integration with other expressions and the presence of a substantial degree of interactivity. If, for example, a musical work has been integrated as a sound background in a multimedia product, the work does not lose its value if it is to be exploited separately, but the whole multimedia work will of course not be considered a musical work, even if the predominant element in it is sound. What, however, makes things more problematic is what happens in cases where an audiovisual work has

---

[4] Even from the definition one can appreciate that there must be an amalgamation of audiovisual works and databases. The feature of combining more than one expression in an integrated manner is clearly an audiovisual feature, whilst digitisation and manipulation with the aid of a software tool is a feature relating closely to databases.

taken the format of a multimedia product. In the author's view, interactivity is capable of transforming the nature of the work. If the frames and pictures of the audiovisual work at issue can be transformed, manipulated and tampered with, the audiovisual work is no longer, for example, a film but a multimedia product. On the other hand, if the manipulation of the contents is only minimal and is not capable of affecting the 'sequence of images' of the audiovisual work, then its nature remains unaffected. In the latter case, of course, we do not have a multimedia work in the first place, since the prerequisite of the 'substantial degree of interactivity' is lacking. Thus, it is highly unlikely that we will have cases where categories of works will clash, although we cannot surely exclude cases where the facts might themselves put a work on the borderline between two or more categories of works. This, however, is not unusual for copyright law.[5]

10.1.1 Originality in relation to the contents of the multimedia work rather than the selection and arrangement of its contents

If a multimedia work qualifies for copyright protection, it goes without saying that it also has to be original. That, of course, is not necessarily so for the CDPA 1988. If a multimedia work is to be compared to a film or a sound recording, then originality is not a necessary attribute. Section 5B(4) of the CDPA 1988 provides that a film qualifies for copyright protection to the extent that it is not copied. One could argue at this point that the CDPA 1988 aims to exclude the possibility of the same film attracting copyright protection on more than one occasion when multiple copies are made for its exploitation. This, of course, could equally imply that if a film is not copied it should involve at least some minimal effort on the part of its author. In other words, a minimum degree of skill and labour has been invested, though perhaps not to the same degree as that required for literary or other works. On the continent, films and audiovisual works in general are subject to the same originality criterion as any other copyright work: that is, in general, for a work to be an expression of its author's personality.

When one seeks to introduce new legislation in the area of copyright, one has also to decide on the level of originality required since originality is one of the yardsticks used to define which works merit copyright protection and which do not. With regard to computer programs and databases, the European Union came to the conclusion that the best

---

[5] For example, a digital encyclopaedia can equally well be defined as a literary work, a compilation or a database. Under the current copyright regime, of course, it is more likely that it will qualify as a database. See s. 3(1)(a) CDPA 1988.

possible originality criterion is for these works to be their 'author's own intellectual creation'.[6] However, computer programs and databases are both works of low creativity, with primarily a functional character. For low creativity works usually a low originality criterion is operated if copyright protection is desirable. Otherwise most works will remain unprotected. The above-mentioned criterion seems to satisfy this test. Arguably, this criterion lowered some continental law criteria which required a high degree of creativity and originality and which linked the creation of these works to the personality of the author. It is also arguable that the EU originality criterion comes very close to, or is a slightly more demanding version of, the UK 'skill and labour' requirement.[7]

If in relation to computer programs and databases such a criterion is found to be suitable, the argument should be that, since multimedia works are in the main more creative works, at least the same or a higher originality criterion should be sought. If even for purely functional works one requires a minimum level of creativity and originality before granting copyright protection, then surely one should not grant copyright protection to multimedia works that do not reach this minimum level. After all, in relation to multimedia works creativity is more important and is part of the value represented by the work. That value makes copyright desirable in order to stimulate the creation of more products.

Ideally the operation of a high originality criterion for more creative works (in the case at issue, multimedia products) is more likely to leave out those works which do not present a substantial enough reason to be granted exclusive rights and therefore restrict competition on the market. Such conduct would afford rights to authors that could not be compensated by increased activity at the level of innovation and creation. In other words, these rights would constitute unjustifiable monopolies. Yet a decision to go above this standard would, politically speaking, be impractical. First, there is the need for a uniform criterion of originality. Disparities between Member States can cause only inconvenience and uncertainty on the international market. Second, a compromise has already been struck at Community level between the EU Member States. Aiming at a different standard of copyright protection would be a very time-consuming and difficult task, and on most occasions would be bound to fail. Sticking to the present approach is a step that facilitates harmonisation and uniformity in the area.

---

[6] Art. 1.3 of the software Directive, [1991] OJ L122/42, and art. 3.1 of the database Directive, [1996] OJ L77/20.
[7] See I. Stamatoudi, 'The EU database Directive: reconceptualising copyright and tracing the future of the *sui generis* right' (1997) 50 *Revue Hellénique de Droit International* 436, at 448.

When one asserts that a multimedia work is original, it is not clear what one necessarily means. One can refer either to the contents of the work as a merged entity, as is the case with literary and artistic works, or to the selection and arrangement of the various contributions put in it along the lines of databases.

It is not uncommon for one to find multimedia works which closely resemble databases in the sense that their contents retain their individuality after they have been inserted into the multimedia work and, though interactive, they are still individually accessible. That undoubtedly leads us to the conclusion that in this case the multimedia product at issue is nothing more than a database. And it follows that it qualifies as a database without presenting any further problems of qualification and protection. Yet most multimedia works, because of their nature, are presented on screen in a merged way. Interactivity and hypertext links allow items to be viewed in isolation but these items, though individually projected, are not independent. Although they might have been inserted in the multimedia work independently, bits and pieces of these works come on one's screen as separate retrievable items. Each of these items contains elements of many works merged in the multimedia product, and although the operational system of the multimedia product allows the user to browse through them, it does not allow him access to the individual materials initially inserted in the multimedia work.

From the above it becomes clear that originality should be assessed in relation to the contents of the multimedia work rather than the selection and arrangement of its contents. The selection and arrangement of the contents of a multimedia work are important only at a pre-production stage, when the work is conceived and the ingredients are assembled in order to make up the final image. Nothing of this selection and arrangement is retained in the final production stage of the multimedia work. Everything appears as one coherent entity which is capable of being viewed in parts (in a format other than that in which the various works have been initially entered) through the operation of interactivity. Any originality in relation to the initial selection and/or arrangement of the materials of the multimedia product would disregard their subsequent transformation through a sewing and a merging process. The birth of a totally new and separable work which constitutes the added value of the multimedia product would be disregarded. Apart from that, the existence of creative interactivity alone, enabling morphing, blurring and transformation (though not permanent) of the original contents of the multimedia work, discredits any notion of selection and arrangement. Even if contents, after their use, return to their original status, they still represent no more than a selection and arrangement along the lines of words in a literary work or melodies in a musical work.

10.1.2 Exclusive economic rights of authors and their exceptions

10.1.2.1 Economic rights

Since we came to the conclusion that multimedia products deserve copyright protection, that means that we fully accept that they are also entitled to the full panoply of exclusive rights which are attached to that copyright protection.[8] In section 16(1) of the CDPA 1988 these rights are referred to as 'acts restricted by copyright'[9] and they are expressed in the following words:

> The owner of the copyright in the work has ... the exclusive rights ... (a) to copy the work (b) to issue copies of the work to the public (ba) to rent or lend the work to the public (c) to perform, show or play the work in public (d) to broadcast the work or include it in a cable programme service [and] (e) to make an adaptation of the work or do any of the above in relation to an adaptation.

In the copyright laws of most states these rights are summed up as two essential rights: the right of reproduction (in the broad sense) and the right to communicate the work to the public.[10]

In relation to the aforementioned rights, multimedia works do not seem to present any problems. They are works reproduced and communicated to the public in the same way as any other copyright work and it is in respect of these acts that the owner of the copyright in the work requires protection and exclusivity. However, it is likely that in the era of new technologies and on-line services the rights relating to these means of reproduction, communication and distribution will become more relevant. In this context reproduction will have to be redefined. The definition of reproduction should be refocused in such a way that it includes reproduction by any means, whether in material form or not, and whether in a permanent or a temporary form.[11]

---

[8] In many countries exclusive rights are held to include both pecuniary and moral rights of authors. However, the latter will be discussed later in a separate section.

[9] This follows from the fact that copyright in the common law tradition is essentially approached as a right to prevent copying.

[10] In French law pecuniary rights include the right of reproduction, performance (or representation) and the *droit de suite* (arts. L122-1ff. of the French Copyright Act 1995). The *droit de suite*, however, does not apply to multimedia products since it is unlikely that their production will be of only a very small number of copies. Exceptionally, artists make unique single-copy multimedia installations which can be classified as artistic works for copyright. In these cases the *droit de suite* applies. See in this respect M. Salokannel, *Ownership of rights in audiovisual productions. A comparative study*, Kluwer Law International, London, The Hague, 1997, at 320ff. However, the list of these rights is not exhaustive.

[11] Most copyright laws were designed in an era when reproduction was closely related to hard copies and to the notion of permanence. Digitisation and computer technology have redefined the notion of reproduction.

A regime of protection for multimedia products 217

As the US White Paper[12] puts it, reproduction is held to take place in all the following cases:

- When a work is placed into a computer, whether on a disk, diskette, ROM, or other storage device or in RAM for more than a very brief period...[13]
- When a printed work is 'scanned' into a digital file...
- When other works – including photographs, motion pictures, or sound recordings – are digitised...
- Whenever a digitised file is 'uploaded' from a user's computer to a bulletin board system (BBS) or other server...
- Whenever a digitised file is 'downloaded' from a BBS or other server...
- When one file is transferred from one computer network to another...[14]
- Under current technology, when an end user's computer is employed as a 'dumb' terminal to access a file resident on another computer such as a BBS or Internet host, a copy of at least the portion viewed is made in the user's computer. Without such copy in the RAM or buffer of the user's computer, no screen display would be possible.

This seems to be in line with the recent legislative initiative of WIPO[15] and the EU draft Directive.[16] The WPPT tried to clarify and harmonise the reproduction right in all those countries where it was not clear that this right included also temporary or incidental reproductions in the

---

[12] US White Paper, B. Lehman and R. Brown, 'Intellectual property and the national information infrastructure', *Report of the Working Group on Intellectual Property Rights*, US Patent and Trademark Office, Washington D.C., September 1995, at 65ff.

[13] *MAI Systems Corp. v. Peak Computer, Inc.* 991 F 2d 511, 519 (9th Cir. 1993).

[14] According to the US White Paper, multiple copies are made in such a case. 'For example, if an author transfers a file (such as a manuscript) to a publisher with an Internet account, copies will typically, at a minimum, be made (a) in the author's Internet server, (b) in the publisher's Internet server, (c) in the publisher's local area network server, and (d) in the editor's microcomputer. It has been suggested that such "copying" of files in intermediate servers is only of transitory duration and consequently not covered by the reproduction right. However, it is clear that if the "copy" exists for more than a period of transitory duration, the reproduction right is implicated. Whether such a reproduction is an infringement is a separate determination.' US White Paper, at 66, note 205.

[15] Art. 11 of the WIPO Performances and Phonograms Treaty, 20 December 1996 (hereinafter WPPT). The right of reproduction has been defined in the WPPT and not in the WCT because it was judged that this was where the problem lay. In relation to copyright the situation seemed to be abundantly clear in the Berne Convention. However, an Agreed Statement concerning art. 1(4) WCT was introduced. It reads as follows: 'The reproduction right, as set out in Article 9 of the Berne Convention, and the exceptions permitted thereunder, fully apply in the digital environment, in particular to the use of works in digital form. It is understood that the storage of a protected work in digital form in an electronic medium constitutes a reproduction within the meaning of Article 9 of the Berne Convention.' A similar Agreed Statement is also included in the WPPT concerning Arts. 7, 11 and 16 WPPT.

[16] Art. 2 of the EU draft Directive on the harmonisation of certain aspects of copyright and related rights in the information society, Brussels, 14 September 2000 '...the exclusive right to authorise or prohibit, direct or indirect, temporary or permanent reproduction by any means and in any form, in whole or in part...'.

electronic/digital environment.[17] However, it is only the reproduction right relating to computer programs and databases that is fully harmonised within the EU. In the EU software and database Directives the acts of reproduction and the legitimate exceptions to them are defined. Temporary reproductions are included in the right of reproduction and the list of exceptions is exhaustive.[18]

The fact that more and more multimedia products will be distributed on-line does not seem to create any special or exceptional problems in so far as multimedia services present the same problems as any other work distributed on-line. The problems raised by the increasing number of cases where reproduction of the work in material copies is replaced by on-line distribution,[19] rendering the exclusive reproduction right less valuable and ever vulnerable, have been addressed by the inclusion in international copyright law of a new exclusive distribution right. This is found in the WCT[20] and in the EU draft Directive,[21] and it makes it clear that on-line distribution of a work is a restricted act for which the copyright owner is entitled to remuneration.

Although reproductions which take place whilst a work is transmitted are covered by the reproduction right, the right of transmission as such is not covered. In fact the distribution right applies only to the distribution of physical copies. New forms of use and exploitation of intellectual property rights have given rise to the need for more rights or extended rights. Interactive on-demand transmission is such a new form of exploitation. These forms of exploitation have presented two difficulties in relation to the existing copyright laws. First, it was not clear that interactive on-demand transmission was covered by the right of distribution (since it applied only to physical copies)[22] and, second, it was not clear that it was

[17] However, this was considered to be a clarification rather than an extension of the existing right, since art. 9(1) of the Berne Convention covers all these situations as it provides that 'authors of literary and artistic works protected by this Convention shall have the exclusive right of authorising the reproduction of these works in any manner or form'.
[18] Art. 4 of the software Directive and art. 5 of the database Directive.
[19] On-line distribution of copyright works does not exhaust the rights in them within the EU.
[20] Art. 6 WCT: 'Authors of literary and artistic works shall enjoy the exclusive right of authorising the making available to the public of the original and copies of their works through sale or other transfer of ownership.' This right already existed in most copyright laws either as a separate right or as part of the communication to the public right.
[21] Art. 4 of the draft European Parliament and Council Directive on the harmonisation of certain aspects of copyright and related rights in the information society, Brussels, 10 December 1997 COM (97) 628 final: 'Member States shall provide authors, in respect of the original of their works or of copies thereof, the exclusive right to authorise or prohibit any form of distribution to the public by sale or otherwise.'
[22] Contracting parties to the WCT and WPPT are free to extend it to include immaterial copies as well. See, for example, §106(3) of the US Digital Millennium Copyright Act 1998.

covered by the right of communication to the public since communication to the public presupposed someone delivering a work to users rather than users picking up the works themselves irrespective of time and place. In addition, in some countries on-demand transmissions were considered to be non-public communications and were therefore left unprotected. This situation has been amended by the definition of the communication to the public right in the WCT and the EU draft Directive. They both extend this right specifically to include communication by wire or wireless means, even if the public decides when and from where it will access the work.[23]

10.1.2.2 Exceptions to economic rights

The issues explained above do not lead us anywhere in particular in relation to multimedia products and services since these issues are common to any intellectual product or service. Yet the aforementioned rights come with some exceptions which legitimise actions that would normally constitute infringements. In relation to multimedia works, no specific aspects of such exceptions are to be found. Overall the exceptions apply to multimedia works in much the same way as they apply to any other copyright work.

In relation to the reproduction right, private copying is usually allowed in some civil law countries as such or as fair dealing in the UK and similar systems for the purposes of research and private study, with the exception at present of computer programs and electronic databases. In the case of computer programs, private copying is allowed only when the person having the right to use the computer program is making a back-up copy.[24] This exception was largely dictated by the nature of computer programs. Being functional tools, data corruption and failure of the program could cause severe difficulties to the persons already possessing a licence to use them. In relation to electronic databases,[25] the philosophy behind this exception is not tied to the nature of the work as such but is one underlying all digital works. In the digital era, the ease of copying, the fact that cloned copies are produced in an infinite number without any loss in quality and

---

[23] Art. 8 WCT: '... authors of literary and artistic works shall enjoy the exclusive right of authorising any communication to the public of their works, by wire or wireless means, including the making available to the public of their works in such a way that members of the public may access these works from a place and at a time individually chosen by them'. See also art. 3 of the EU draft Directive: 'Member States shall provide authors with the exclusive right to authorise or prohibit any communication to the public of their works, by wire or wireless means, including the making available to the public of their works in such a way that members of the public may access them from a place and at a time individually chosen by them.'

[24] Art. 5.2 of the software Directive.

[25] Art. 6.2(a) of the database Directive.

the difficulty of tracing illegitimate acts to that end seemed to advocate the outlawing of the exception of private copying altogether. In addition, a harmonised regime of exceptions in all Member States would facilitate trade and integration in the Single Market. The possibility of extending this legal choice generally to all digital and analogue works, albeit for different reasons in relation to the latter,[26] is under severe scrutiny and debate in the context of the adoption of the EU draft Directive.[27] The WCT and WPPT do not offer any guidance on this point.

The introduction of this exception in relation to multimedia products is not dictated by any features relating to their nature since, on most occasions, multimedia works should not be considered as functional tools. If such an exception is adopted, it will be done only on the basis of their digital nature; and it will probably be consistent with any decision taken in relation to all digital works at an EU level. At an international level the option is left with the states in the absence of any compelling provision in the Berne Convention, the WCT and the WPPT.

With the aim of harmonisation in the digital era in mind, there is much discussion in the context of the EU draft Directive concerning the reduction in length of the list of exceptions. Fewer exceptions, applied almost in a uniform manner in all Member States, would, it is thought, create a level playing field in the European Union which would promote further integration in the Single Market.

However, what might eventually need redefinition are factual concepts such as what constitutes a substantial part of a work which one is allowed to use legitimately in an English context, and what is considered fair dealing in relation to research and private study, criticism, review and news reporting. The same would also apply to fair use in a US context. In view of the composite nature of multimedia products and the fact that they are capable of including an indefinite or extremely large number of works, the notion of a substantial part must be a decision on qualitative rather than quantitative grounds. Extraction of even a tiny part of a multimedia work might constitute extraction of a whole work attracting copyright on its own merits and whose place in the multimedia product might be of significant value. Such extractions might need to be outlawed explicitly.[28]

---

[26] See p. 31 of the Proposal for the EU draft Directive, Brussels, 10 December 1997 COM (97) 628 final, where it is alleged that analogue copying is increasingly disappearing.

[27] COM (97) 628 final. See also E. Tucker, 'Copyright plans win backing', *Financial Times* 11 February 1999.

[28] Sirinelli, in his Report on multimedia products, mentions the fact that the right of citation, as it is found in French law, might not be applicable in a multimedia context. Sirinelli Report on multimedia and new technologies, France, Ministère de la culture et de la Francophonie, Paris, 1994, at 70. That is especially so in relation to all works that constitute compilations or anthologies and whose contents comprise whole works.

In toto, one could argue that all the above suggestions relate to the general issue of how digital works should be treated in the information society rather than to the particular nature of multimedia products. In this respect, multimedia products seem to present the same problems as any other copyright work. The potential redefinitions of certain concepts, such as fair dealing or fair use, do not demand separate legal treatment but they can be based on a purposive interpretation of the law, subject to the new reality and the needs emerging therefrom.

10.1.3 Authorship/ownership

The questions of authorship and ownership of multimedia works have been answered more or less in the section in chapter 9 relating to the qualification of multimedia works according to the type of co-operation between their contributors.[29] In this section we will try to draw together the ideas found throughout this book.

Several contributions are necessary in order to create a multimedia work. These contributions take the form of protected works (irrespective of the fact that they are in copyright or their copyright has expired), data (factual information which does not attract copyright, though it might attract some other kind of protection, e.g. know-how, trade secrets, contractual protection) or technical assistance. Technical assistance can vary in nature. It may vary from the design of the technical base of the multimedia work (i.e. the computer program, indexes and other operational material) to the integration of the various materials in the multimedia work. It may also relate to the marketing and distribution of the product. The technical contributions just mentioned may or may not involve creative aspects and consequently may or may not confer the quality of author on their contributors.

Another feature relating to these contributions is that the persons providing them might or might not be involved in the project of the multimedia work in the sense of co-operation or co-authorship.[30] In other words, the works included in a multimedia product might have been commissioned works or they might simply have been pre-existing works. In both cases the role of the authors delivering these works cannot be predetermined. The authors of the pre-existing works might have put the finishing touches to their works in order to adjust them to the image of

---

[29] Section 9.2 above.
[30] Co-authorship requires some kind of direct or indirect participation. Distant relationships as such should not qualify, i.e. when someone creates a work which is commissioned for a project without knowing or having taken into account any details or particularities of the project.

the multimedia product or they might not have done so. Alternatively, the authors of newly commissioned works, whilst producing the works, might not have taken into account any specifications relating to the multimedia project and might simply have delivered the works by reason of a contract without any special provision for the incorporation or adjustment of their work into that multimedia product. On the other hand, they might have followed a particular plan they had been told to follow or which they needed to follow. In other words, there is no standard practice which neatly fits one or other category of definitions.[31]

10.1.3.1 *Alternative approaches*

According to the above scenario, three solutions are possible. One is to grant authorship to all the persons involved in the production of a multimedia work whose task is somehow creative. Although the various contributions in a multimedia product may be creative on their own merits, this creativity is not necessarily reflected in the final image of the product. The editor is the person who gives the final form and creates the product. He puts the various elements together, in the same sense as the compiler of a collection of works or the director of a film. The difference with these authors though is that the editor of the multimedia product goes one step further. He integrates the various materials to such a degree that on most occasions the final outcome does not resemble in any sense the individual contributions that have been incorporated in it. The multimedia work is a new work and the integration[32] of its materials represents the 'added value'.

In addition, if one considers the number of persons involved in the creation of a multimedia product and the number of the various tasks undertaken by reason of the specialisation that exists today in the entertainment industry, one also realises that any notion of co-authorship has either to be construed extremely broadly or to be abandoned altogether in relation to multimedia works. In any case the infinite number of contributors precludes any notion of collaboration and co-authorship, at least in the traditional sense of the word. The solution of co-authorship is viable only for works with a limited number of contributors, e.g. films and other audiovisual works. Most multimedia products today have an extremely large number of contributors. From a practical point of view there is the

---

[31] In that sense multimedia products cannot be considered to be collective, collaborative or composite works with any degree of certainty. In a UK context it is difficult to define whether a work is a work of joint authorship or not.
[32] This aspect of multimedia works is also emphasised by F. Koch, 'Software – Urheberrechtsschutz für Multimedia – Anwendungen' [1995] *GRUR* 459, at 463.

A regime of protection for multimedia products 223

difficulty of defining which tasks undertaken by the various persons are creative and which are not, especially in an environment where original creations are mainly commissioned on a predefined basis and can therefore be compensated by the provision of a fee. Creativity in this instance is not the pure creativity attached to traditional copyright works. Granting authorship to these persons, and thus full economic and moral rights, on most occasions clearly goes beyond the remit of their task.

A second solution granting authorship to only a number of the persons involved in the creation of a multimedia product is still not a viable solution. First, the tasks in the creation of a multimedia product are not clearly defined and we might end up with situations where we will have persons who have not participated in the project as co-authors whilst others who have participated will be left out. Secondly, if one wants to be fair one has to grant authorship to all potential creative contributors. That, however, still brings us back to the problems of the first solution. The more authors there are the more cumbersome is the creation, marketing and further exploitation of a work. Even if there were a legal presumption[33] in favour of transferring the economic rights to the publisher/producer or the editor of the multimedia work, the initial authors would still be in possession of moral rights. The possession of moral rights by more than one person in relation to a work is bound to cause more problems than the situation where one only person is the possessor of the moral rights in the work. Thirdly, and most importantly, only the editor's role is prominently creative in relation to the multimedia work. Contributors offer only the tools for that creative task.

The solution we are left with is that of single authorship. In contrast to UK copyright law, in most continental law systems only natural persons are entitled to authorship. Legal entities and companies can never become *ab initio* authors but acquire ownership only at a second stage by the operation of a contract or by *cessio legis*. As we explained above, the solution of having one author seems to sit very well with the process of creating a multimedia product. In that sense the editor of the project should be granted the status of author and with it a full panoply of economic and moral rights.

A possible model of authorship which could fit multimedia products in a UK context is the UK model on films. Authors of a film are both the director and the producer,[34] the first on grounds of his creative role (which

---

[33] This solution receives support from U. Loewenheim, 'Urheberrechtliche Probleme bei Multimediaanwendungen' [1996] *GRUR* 830, at 832.
[34] S. 9(2)(a) and (b) CDPA 1988. Initially the producer was the only author of a film. The director was added because of the introduction of the EU term Directive.

also constitutes the reason for granting him moral rights protection)[35] and the second on grounds of his investment. The task of a director in a film can well be compared to that of the editor of a multimedia product in the sense that he conceives the idea and realises it through the selection and arrangement of the various contributions. However, the editor of the multimedia work, by bringing these contributions together and integrating them in the product as a whole, creates the added value of the product. In that sense he creates a new work which is distinguishable in relation to the initial contributions and which goes further than any compilation or film. The task of the producer of a film can also be compared to that of a multimedia work in the sense that the investments of both are valuable for the production and marketing of the work. Granting authorship to the producer is in fact the means of securing the investment he has put into the project.

Moral rights are not granted to producers, however. In the case of employment, this model changes slightly in the sense that the employer has by law all the economic rights vested in the work, whilst the employee is left only with moral rights protection.[36] In relation both to films and to multimedia works, such a scenario can be a regular one. In conclusion, we should say that if we are to follow the UK model on films, then both the editor and the producer should be the joint authors of a multimedia work.

In the French copyright law system the solution of single authorship can be achieved through the definitions of collective or composite works.[37] In fact we could say that multimedia products are a mixture of collective and composite works.[38] The author of the work should be presumed to be the person bringing together and merging the various contributions, i.e. the editor of the work. To this person both moral and economic rights must be afforded, since authorship and first ownership of the works are concepts which are inextricably linked on the continent. However, in the case of employment a *cessio legis* should vest the economic rights in the work in the producer of the multimedia product along the lines of the French model on computer programs.[39] The producer is usually the natural or legal person under whose name the work has been disclosed[40] if that is not simply the name of the company responsible for the technical base, the trade dress and the marketing of the product. In the latter scenario

[35] Ss. 77, 80 and 84 CDPA 1988.
[36] S. 11(2) CDPA 1988.
[37] Art. L113-2 of the French Copyright Act 1992.
[38] Neither of them fits exactly, but according to French copyright law one has to make a choice and select one of them.
[39] Art. L113-9 of the French Copyright Act 1992.
[40] Art. L113-5 of the French Copyright Act 1992.

the presumption should be rebutted and the economic rights should be vested in the person who initiated and funded the production of the work. Investment should be the decisive point.[41]

The solution of single authorship (even if it is awarded jointly to two persons) seems to be ideal from two points of view. First, it reflects the reality of the creation of a multimedia work, and secondly, it overcomes the hurdles of multi-co-authorship at an early stage. In an era when use, clearance of rights and further exploitation of a work have to take place easily, quickly and with a great degree of certainty, the option of one author can only offer greater efficiency without at the same time taking any well-deserved rights from other contributors. These contributors still have rights in their separate contributions and can use them as long as they do not compete with, or cause harm to, the initial multimedia project.

10.1.3.2 A harmonised approach for the new category of multimedia works

Up to now we have been concerned primarily with the existing national approaches and solutions that could be devised according to these approaches. However, we feel that there is a need to create a special category of copyright works for multimedia products in which special rules apply. Earlier on we indicated how this category should be defined and which rules should apply in terms of originality. We have now come to the conclusion that multimedia works cannot simply use the system designed originally for compilations and films. In a multimedia work there is normally a full integration of the components and this leads to a high added value. That integration and added value are provided by the editor of the multimedia product who can therefore be seen as the creator of the work. Thus, it seems logical to suggest that a harmonised European model should designate the editor of a multimedia work as its author. As the author of the work the editor would also have the moral rights in the work and become the first owner of the copyright in the work.

Two additions need to be made to this system. The first one deals with the reality that on most occasions multimedia works are created in the course of employment. If the editor is an employee and he creates the work in the course of employment, the harmonised model should provide that the employer rather than the employee becomes the first owner of the copyright in the work through the operation of law. This idea can be copied from the existing provision in the CDPA 1988, and

---

[41] In such cases it would perhaps be helpful if on the package of any multimedia product and on the licence that is delivered with it the name of the owner of the economic rights in the work and a note as to who holds the moral rights in the work were to be found.

it is interesting to note that in similar circumstances where most works are created in the course of employment and at the instigation of the employer, both the French and the Belgian Acts operate a similar rule in favour of the employer of the creator of a computer program. The second addition proposes a slight change to the rule on authorship to take account of the important *ab initio* contribution of the producer of the multimedia work. In the same way that the UK approach to films recognises that contribution by awarding authorship of the film both to the director and to the producer, it could be envisaged that the editor and the producer of a multimedia product would both be considered to be the authors of the product. They would then also both get the first ownership of the work. In our opinion, this is a second-best solution. The producer's interest is primarily of an economic nature and in most cases that interest will be taken care of by the automatic transfer of ownership to the employer. In the cases that fall outside the employment context, the producer will normally be able to arrange a transfer of ownership through contract. A departure from the logical rules on authorship according to our model is therefore not warranted.[42]

10.1.4 Moral rights protection

Moral rights protection in relation to multimedia products has been a highly disputed issue. The problems which immediately arise from it are the following. How wide should the scope of moral rights protection for authors of multimedia products be? Should this protection be concentrated in the hands of one principal author alone, and, if that is the case, in whose hands and to what degree? Where do producers and users of multimedia products stand with regard to the problem of authenticity of multimedia works? Are authors' moral rights capable of impeding the production and marketing of multimedia works? To what extent are multimedia works by their nature (and method of distribution) a threat to their authors' moral rights? Should we reinforce or restrict the scope of moral rights?

The section which follows will attempt to provide some answers to these questions. The discussion will be divided into two main parts. First, the existing UK and French regimes of moral rights protection as applicable to the author or authors of multimedia products will be examined both in their present format and in the format they could possibly take if new legislation were to be introduced at national level. Secondly, the possibility of a harmonised regime on moral rights will be explored.

---

[42] This is also the approach advocated by Loewenheim, 'Urheberrechtliche Probleme', at 832.

10.1.4.1 Existing regimes of moral rights protection

10.1.4.1.1   The UK approach

The starting point for our discussion will be the CDPA 1988. According to this Act, authors are entitled to four moral rights: the right of paternity, the right of integrity, the right to object to false attribution and the right of privacy. If we take into account that the right to object to false attribution is theoretically included in the right of paternity (since one should not only have the right to see one's work attributed to oneself but also the right not to see a work that is not one's own being so attributed), and the fact that the right of privacy refers only to photographs and films, we are left with only two genuine moral rights which make sense in a multimedia context, the right of paternity and that of integrity.

According to the UK right of paternity, the author of a work and the director of a film have the right to be identified as such in relation to their work.[43] This right does not apply in relation to computer programs, designs of typefaces and computer-generated works. Neither does it apply in relation to employee–authors and to a number of other cases referred to in the law as exceptions to the rights of attribution.[44] Lastly, in order for the right to apply it has to be asserted.[45]

The UK right of integrity provides that the author of a work or the director of a film have the right not to have their work subjected to derogatory treatment, meaning any distortion or mutilation of a work which is prejudicial to their honour or reputation.[46] This right does not apply in relation to computer programs, computer-generated works and in a number of other exceptional cases.[47] No special provisions for employee–authors or directors are found and no assertion is required.

In the UK system all moral rights can be waived at any time in relation to a specific work or generally to any work or works, either existing or future.[48] Moral rights are non-assignable[49] and they expire together with the economic rights in the work.[50]

As can be seen, the scope of moral rights in the CDPA 1988 is very restricted and industry-orientated. This is not only derived from the limited number and scope of moral rights in comparison to other copyright

---

[43] S. 77 CDPA 1988.
[44] S. 79 CDPA 1988.
[45] S. 78 CDPA 1988.
[46] S. 80 CDPA 1988.
[47] S. 81 CDPA 1988.
[48] S. 87 CDPA 1988.
[49] S. 94 CDPA 1988.
[50] S. 86 CDPA 1988.

systems but also from the fact that the CDPA 1988 allows a global general waiver in relation to moral rights. In this system entrepreneurs are clearly put in a favourable position (by reason of their bargaining power), whilst authors are granted limited protection only.

If the UK provisions on moral rights are applied to multimedia products, the following can be observed. The author of a multimedia work will not be entitled to the right of paternity if he has not asserted it, if he has waived it or if he is an employee of the producer of the work. This last situation will occur often. Apart from the secondary exceptions that the CDPA 1988 provides for with regard to the right, this right applies. The author will be able to invoke his integrity right only in situations where he can prove that the producer or a third party have tampered with his work to such an extent that his honour or reputation have been prejudiced. It goes without saying that alterations to the work dictated by the needs of production, commercialisation and marketing of the product will almost never qualify as infringements. If the author has waived his moral right of integrity he will not be able to invoke it even in situations where damage to his honour or reputation is the ultimate result.[51]

Moral rights are afforded to the creator/author of the work. According to the analysis in the section on authorship, we have reached the conclusion that the author of a multimedia product is the editor or the editor and the producer, if one follows the UK model on films. That would mean that, depending on the model that applies, either the editor or the editor and the producer could receive moral rights. It needs to be clarified though that the existing UK model for films denies moral rights protection to the producer. The producer is only given the economic rights in the work by reason of his investment and not by reason of exercising any creativity in it. If the editor of the multimedia work creates the work in the course of his employment then the issue of moral rights becomes irrelevant because there is no recipient for them.

10.1.4.1.2 The French approach

On the continent things are quite different. If we take the example of the other extreme of moral rights protection within the EU, that of France, we will note that in this country, as in most civil law countries, authors are afforded full moral rights protection. First, the list of moral rights of authors is longer. The rights of divulgation, withdrawal and access

---

[51] This is only the case for a global waiver. In other cases it depends on the rights he has waived. For the position in England see I. Stamatoudi, 'Moral rights of authors in England: the missing emphasis on the role of creators' [1997] 4 *IPQ* 478. See also C. Doutrelepont, *Le droit moral de l'auteur et le droit communautaire*, Bruylant, Brussels, 1997.

to the work once the material support on which it is incorporated has been transferred, are added to the rights of paternity and integrity.[52] In addition, there is no requirement of prejudice to the honour or reputation of the author in relation to the right of integrity. Any change in the work is sufficient. Moral rights in France are also inalienable, perpetual and non-transferable.[53] Waivability is not allowed under any circumstances, although certain actions that might potentially infringe an author's moral rights might be permitted, subject to the particular facts and needs of each case. This, of course, is derived from a teleological and purposive interpretation of the law. Lastly, there are no special provisions for employee–creators apart from the case of computer programs.[54]

Such a broad moral rights protection seems to present problems in relation to multimedia products, particularly if there is a rigid application of the provisions of such a regime. Yet French law restricts the scope of moral rights in relation to certain works either by reason of their functional character or by reason of the needs for their production. Computer programs come within the first category. With regard to computer programs, the right of integrity applies only to modifications of the work that are prejudicial to the honour or reputation of the author.[55] The right of withdrawal does not apply at all in relation to computer programs.[56] Audiovisual works come within the second category. With regard to audiovisual works, the moral rights of the authors are restricted until the work is completed (i.e. only at the production level), and that is when a final version is established by common accord between the director (and possibly the other authors) and the producer.[57] After completion of the audiovisual work, the moral rights of the authors are restored but a slight preference is given to the director. When an audiovisual work is transferred to another kind of medium with a view to a different mode of exploitation, it is the director's prior consent that is required.[58]

---

[52] Arts. L121-1–L121-9 of the French Copyright Act 1992.
[53] Art. L121-1 of the French Copyright Act 1992.
[54] Art. L121-7 of the French Copyright Act 1992.
[55] *Ibid.*
[56] *Ibid.*
[57] Art. L121-5 of the French Copyright Act 1992.
[58] *Ibid.* According to Salokannel, 'the reason why the obligation of consultation is rendered only with respect to the film director is that the transfer of the film to another kind of medium affects only the framing of the film and the general filmic representation, which is ultimately composed by the director. Consequently the changing of format may affect only the moral rights of the director, since the dialogue or the music, for example, do not suffer from this. The practical significance of this provision has been questioned in the literature, since by choosing not to complement the consultation obligation with any sanctions, the provision has little practical bearing,' *Ownership*, at 273. See also footnotes 572 and 573, where he refers to B. Edelman, *Droits d'auteur, droits voisins: droit d'auteur et marché*, Dalloz, Paris, 1993, at 21 and 55.

Unless multimedia products in France come within the scope of the regime of protection of computer programs or of audiovisual works, they are granted a full panoply of moral rights. Any potential introduction of new legislation for multimedia products in French law will seek only to introduce restrictions in the area of moral rights if multimedia products are proven to be an exceptional case either on grounds of their functional character or because of the needs for their production. Indeed, multimedia products seem to fall squarely within the second category, perhaps to an even greater degree than audiovisual works. Both in audiovisual works and in multimedia products, the investments for their production are important. On top of that comes the fact that in a multimedia work there are many more contributors than in a film and therefore the risk of hurdles and obstacles to their creation and release becomes more apparent. In the light of this a restriction of moral rights at the production level might be worth considering.

Multimedia products are also an exceptional case with regard to their use. For that reason they might require a restriction of moral rights not only at the production level (as is the case with audiovisual works) but also after their commercialisation. Interactivity inevitably leads to the conclusion that the contents of a multimedia product are intended to be altered, adapted, modified, etc. Any such change can go well beyond any normal changes that a work traditionally undergoes, such as morphing, blurring, etc. Of course, on most occasions these changes will last as long as the use of the work,[59] whilst in other cases they will be saved for further use and they may even be circulated to other users.

10.1.4.2 *Towards a harmonised approach to moral rights*

Before we enter the discussion on the ideal harmonised regime of moral rights protection in Europe in relation to multimedia products, it should be noted that it is not certain that such a harmonisation will necessarily be needed in the event of the introduction of new legislation in the area of multimedia products. Such a regime will be envisaged only if it can be demonstrated that the disparities in moral rights between the various national copyright laws are capable of creating hurdles in the trade between the EU Member States. If that is not the case, the various countries will be able to keep their existing moral rights provisions, perhaps with slight alterations along the lines of those that we are to describe, in order to fit the new reality. However, given the highly commercial character of multimedia products and the fact that their marketing takes place mainly on

---

[59] Usually the contents of a multimedia product are altered during the use of the work. They return to their original format once the use is ended (cf. video games).

the international market, as well as the apparent economic repercussions which moral rights have in the digital era, a harmonised regime on moral rights would introduce further safety and certainty in transactions.[60]

The particularities of multimedia products in comparison to other copyright works are the following. First, multimedia products involve many contributions in their creation, large investments in their production and the materials included in them are usually subject to adaptations and modifications for technical, financial or other equivalent reasons. Second, multimedia products by reason of their interactive nature are intended to be modified, transformed or adapted in the course of their use. Third, multimedia products are delivered and used in an environment that facilitates transformation and change to an infinite degree and allows users to feed back to the system inauthentic and altered material. This is especially so in relation to on-line distributed material where the hurdles of the analogue format of the hard copies have disappeared completely. The issue of moral rights should be considered at two stages: first at the stage of production and secondly at the stage of commercialisation and communication of the work to the public. The second stage encompasses considerations both on the part of the authors and producers and on the part of the users.

10.1.4.2.1 Moral rights at the production stage of multimedia works

The first issue we should look into is the moral rights issue at the stage of the production of a multimedia product. As we mentioned above, the large number of contributors to a multimedia work is also likely to create problems in its realisation. However, such delays cannot be afforded because of the tight dates within which a multimedia product has to be produced in order to catch the market as well as with regard to the substantial investments its creation requires. Films present similar problems. Therefore a possible solution could be that the moral rights of contributors at the production level of a multimedia product should be designed along the lines of the French model on audiovisual works. That might be considered necessary in order for the required adaptations and transformations to take place and the completion of the work to be achieved.

---

[60] 'Digitisation and interactivity, by its very nature, will lead to a substantial increase in alterations of works and other protected matter, which will also affect moral rights. As these works will, as a general rule, be destined for Community wide exploitation, differences between Member States' legislation in the field of moral rights may lead to significant barriers to their exploitation, notably in the field of multimedia products and services.' Communication from the Commission, Follow-up to the Green Paper on copyright and related rights in the information society, COM (96) 568 final, Brussels, 20 November 1996, at 28.

However, although such a model provides for a stopgap solution at the production level of a multimedia work, it provides no solution whatsoever for the stage after completion.

After completion the authors of the contributions can once again exercise their moral rights. Yet in the case of multimedia products the final version is bound to include a modified version of the original contributions by reason of the nature of the product. This is so to a much larger extent than in relation to films. In practice the effect of this rule is simply that a discussion on whether or not the integrity right has been infringed is postponed until the completion of the work. In the light of the above, a partial waiver, restricted to certain acts only, might be a more desirable and effective solution to this end since it provides certainty for the stage after the completion of the multimedia work.

10.1.4.2.2 Moral rights after the completion of the multimedia work

10.1.4.2.2.1 The rights of divulgation, withdrawal and access to the work

The second stage we should look into is the stage after the completion of the work. At that stage one should examine all moral rights one by one and their operation in a multimedia context. As we pointed out in the section on authorship/ownership, the author is also the holder of moral rights in the work. The editor of the multimedia product should be considered as the author of the work. The full list of moral rights that authors are afforded in a continental context are the rights of divulgation, withdrawal of the work, paternity and integrity. In a common law system the first two rights are missing. The right of divulgation gives the author the right to decide whether he releases his work and what form his work takes once it is released on the market. In a digital environment where control of disseminated material is not always easy, it is useful both for the author to protect creations that he does not consider as being complete and for the public not to receive works and information that are not backed by the author under whose name they appear. Yet the right of withdrawal seems to be of diminished value for two reasons. First, once a work has been distributed to the public, its withdrawal might impinge on the rights and works of third parties that have relied on the initial work. In a digital and on-line environment the author has to think through the works he releases very carefully before these works enter the public domain. Any withdrawal afterwards will be difficult and nonsensical in an environment that disseminates information in bulk. Second, even if the right of withdrawal is afforded to authors of multimedia works, its practical value will be limited since its exercise on the part of the author may result in a large amount of damages being payable by the author for breach of contract, a situation which may restrict its exercise.[61] The right of withdrawal has very little practical significance because of the various conditions that are attached to it. In practice it is hardly ever used and it will become even harder in a multimedia context.[62] The right of access to the work also seems meaningless. It can only retain its value in relation to multimedia works which are artistic, unique and limited in number. In those cases the multimedia works will qualify as artistic works anyway and will therefore enjoy full moral rights protection.

10.1.4.2.2.2 The right of paternity

The fact that the author of a multimedia work should have the right to have his work attributed to him (or not attributed to him if it is not his work) has a twofold importance in a digital context. First, it represents one of the essential human rights-based rights that should be granted to any author of a copyright work as part of his personality. Secondly, in a digital environment where pirated material is difficult to distinguish from original material, the right of paternity helps to assure the public that what it receives on its screen is the original work and not copies that have been tampered with. Such a right should be absolute. It should not be subject to additional requirements or formalities such as assertion. It should also not be waivable. And it should be granted to authors irrespective of whether they are independent creators or employees. Assertion, waivability and special provisions for employee–authors contradict the provisions of the Berne Convention and undermine the public's interest in obtaining original material.

10.1.4.2.2.3 The right of integrity

The right of integrity seems to be the right that has been subject to most scrutiny in the digital era. That is essentially because, as the cornerstone of moral rights protection, it finds itself lying between two seemingly conflicting views. One view advocates the restriction of the author's right of integrity in view of the intended use of multimedia products. Interactivity necessarily means that the contents of the work will be changed. That can also be considered as the normal use of a multimedia product. On the

---

[61] Countries which do not expressly provide for such a right in their moral rights provisions nevertheless offer some protection in similar situations via the economic rights of authors.

[62] It will be difficult for the author, if he wants to withdraw a multimedia work, to compensate the producer of the work by reason of the large investments that are usually sunk into multimedia products.

other hand, technically there is no obvious limit to how much the contents of a multimedia work should be changed. That means that there is the opportunity of going well above what is allowed. And that fear in a multimedia context has become more serious than ever before. Thus, the second view advocates a reinforcement of the right of integrity.[63]

Reconciliation of these two views is not an easy task. Many commentators prefer to take the approach that a solution depends on to which of these two views one gives preference. Excision of one may impinge on the freedom of users, whilst excision of the other may impinge on the interests of the authors. Yet the balance here should not be struck between the interests of the public and those of the authors. In fact, the interests of the authors in not having their work altered unduly seem to coincide with those of the public that has a right to receive authentic and unaltered works. Along these lines of thought the propositions outlined below seem viable.

10.1.4.2.2.3.1 A first solution One idea is to follow the German model on cinematographic works. Article 93 of the German Copyright Act provides that

[t]he authors of a cinematographic work and of works used in its production, [...] may prohibit [...] only *gross distortions or other gross mutilations of their works or of their contributions*, with respect to the production and exploitation of the cinematographic work. Each author and the rightholder shall take the others and the film producer into due account when exercising the right (emphasis added).

According to these terms, a restriction of the right of integrity to only those cases where gross distortions of a multimedia work have taken place (and where in the assessment of these distortions the rights of the other interested parties are also taken into account) might prevent claims of moral rights that are either unjustified or far-reaching. If one wants to restrict the right of integrity even further, one can add the requirement that the author's right of integrity is infringed only if there is damage to the author's honour and reputation. This view is based on the Anglo-Saxon presumption that a distortion or mutilation does not necessarily prejudice the author's honour and reputation.[64] Such an additional requirement

---

[63] 'A large number of parties, notably rightholders and end users, are in favour of strong and coherent moral rights protection across the EU', Commission Communication, COM (96) 568 final, at 28.

[64] The Japanese Report on the new rule on intellectual property for multimedia gives two alternatives (Exposure '94 Report, at 26). One amounts to an integrity right that comes into operation only once the threshold of prejudice to the author's honour and reputation has been passed, whilst the other treats that threshold as a ceiling that cannot be removed and installs a system of contractual waivers which will be 'valid as long as

would, within the scope of normal use of a multimedia work, clearly allow any change of the work that does not go so far as to impinge on the author's honour and reputation.[65] However, this solution is very restrictive since it already gives away a substantial part of the author's integrity right without his consent. That can also be held as retrogression in the law on moral rights. In addition, it should be rejected on the grounds that it allows changes in a work to a degree, which, although not affecting the author's honour and reputation, does nevertheless affect the right and original form of the work. This solution does not satisfactorily address either the concerns of the authors or those of the public on that issue.

10.1.4.2.2.3.2 A second solution   A second proposition that has been put forward is the introduction of a concept of fair use or fair dealing against which the right of integrity will be assessed. Dietz proposes a list of criteria along the lines of the ones provided in §107 of the US Copyright Act that should be taken into account in order for one to determine whether there is an infringement of the right of integrity or not. These criteria can be the

nature and intensity of modifications of or other interference of the work, as well as its reversible or irreversible character; the number of people or the size of the public addressed by the use of the infringing work; whether the author created the work in an employment relationship or as a self-employed author, or whether a commissioning party had or did not have decisive influence on the final result of the creation; also the possible consequences for the professional life of the author, and, of course, for his honour and reputation have to be taken into consideration.[66]

Another criterion that can also be proposed is that the more creative (original) a work is, the more strictly the right of integrity should be applied to it.[67] This proposition might prove to be very important especially in relation to multimedia products and their multifarious nature. Yet if the above proposition applies, any infringement of the right of integrity will

[they] would not prejudice the author's honour or reputation' which is to apply to all other changes. The Report of the Institute of Intellectual Property (February 1994) does not make a final choice between these alternatives. See also notes 66 and 67 below in relation to the point made in this respect by Dietz.

[65] This proposition relates to Gendreau's views on this issue. Y. Gendreau, 'Digital technology and copyright: can moral rights survive the disappearance of the hard copy?' [1995] 6 *Ent LR* 214, at 220.

[66] A. Dietz, 'Legal principles of moral rights in civil law countries' (1993) 11 *Copyright Reporter* 1, at 15; and (1995) 19 *Columbia – VLA of Law and the Arts Journal* 199, at 225.

[67] A. Dietz, 'Authenticity of authorship and work', General Report ALAI Study Days, Amsterdam 4–8 June 1996, in ALAI, *Copyright in cyberspace*, Otto Cramwinckel, Amsterdam, 1996, 165, at 175–6.

only be decided after a litigation process. That means that the context of the right in relation to multimedia works will be determined, formed and standardised through case-law on a case-by-case basis. This, however, does not seem to be a very desirable option on two grounds. First, it would in fact transfer the responsibility for the definition of the content of the right from the legislative arena to the judicial one. Even if such conduct is dictated by the variable nature of multimedia products, it would nevertheless create uncertainty on the market. The more a right is defined at an early stage the better delineated are the obligations and responsibilities of the parties. The court should be there to define the particularities of each case at a second stage only, and with regard to the appreciation of concrete notions, such as honour and reputation, if one opts for that criterion. In addition, such an approach necessarily allows countries substantial discretion to adopt and refer back to their traditional views on this point. If one takes into account that moral rights are perhaps the one issue in copyright which presents the most substantial differences in copyright traditions, one also realises that if we go down the path of the case-by-case approach, it will be extremely difficult at a later stage, should the need arise, to harmonise moral rights protection at European Union or international level. Our moral rights approaches with regard to multimedia works will already be far apart and almost irreconcilable by that time.

10.1.4.2.2.3.3 A third (best) solution

An alternative (third) and more desirable solution seems to be that of the provision of a partial waiver. The Belgian and German copyright law models seem to provide for such a solution. According to the Belgian copyright law, an overall waiver of moral rights for the future is void.[68] Moral rights can be waived in specific cases that are strictly defined in relation to existing works only.[69] Even where the moral right of integrity has been waived in relation to a specific case, the author always retains the right to object to any distortion or mutilation or any other change to the work that damages his honour and reputation.[70] Honour and reputation constitute the ceiling of

---

[68] Art. 1(2)(2) of the Belgian Copyright Act 1994.
[69] Court of Appeal, Brussels, 29 September 1965, *JT* 1965, 561, *La Veuve Joyeuse*: 'a general authorisation to make changes that are desirable to the work is void. But what is acceptable is to conclude an agreement in full knowledge of what the changes are going to be as long as that agreement is given with the explicit consent of the author.' 'For the past, a general waiver is possible but even then it cannot be implied.' Cour de Cassation, 13 November 1973, (1973) 80 *RIDA* 62 and Austrian Supreme Court, 1 July 1986, [1986] *EIPR* D-211.
[70] Art. 1(2) *in fine* of the Belgian Copyright Act 1994. 'Notwithstanding any renunciation, [the author] shall maintain the right to oppose any distortion, mutilation or other alteration to his work or any other prejudicial act to the same work that may damage his honour or reputation.' See in this respect J. Corbet, *Auteursrecht*, Story – Scientia, Brussels, 1997, at 59.

the integrity right, above which no waivability is permitted. The Belgian provision on waivability tries to exclude the risk, clearly present in the CDPA 1988 model, which consists of the request for a general waiver for the future becoming part of the negotiations for the initial publishing contract. Obviously in such a situation the stronger party, i.e. the publisher, can put a large amount of pressure on the author to consent to such a waiver. Such waivers are not possible in the Belgian model, and the specific and partial waivers that are allowed necessarily come into play once a publishing contract has been concluded and the work is subsequently put to another use. At this stage the publisher no longer has the opportunity of making the publication contract subject to the waiver. On the contrary, he is now the party that wants to be allowed to make further use of the work and the author can decide whether or not such use is acceptable, taking into account the type of use and the royalty that is on offer.

German copyright law reaches the same conclusion via another route. According to German copyright law the right of integrity is not an absolute right. It is justified only if the interests of the author are protected.[71] That conclusion can be reached only through a balancing of interests. This technique has been developed in a number of cases.[72] Dietz summarises the outcome of this test as follows:

[C]hanges or modifications in the process of exploitation of a work, which would be solely dictated by artistic and aesthetic convictions and concepts of other persons (especially the user of the work), would not be acceptable, whereas those dictated by the concrete technical, financial and circumstantial conditions of the exploitation of the work would have to be taken into consideration in the process of balancing interests. This is also recognised even in French law in the special case of adaptations of a work, a situation which, under modern conditions, exists more often than one would expect, since adaptation in the technical but not necessarily creational sense of the word appears rather the rule than the exception.[73]

A narrowly construed waiver in relation to certain acts with regard to existing works seems to be the ideal solution for multimedia products. First,

[71] Arts. 39(2) and 14 of the German Copyright Act. See also H. Schack, *Urheber- und Urhebervertragsrecht*, Mohr Siebeck, Munich, 1997, at 158–64.
[72] Bundesgerichtshof, [1982] *GRUR* 107, *Kirchen – Innenraumgestaltung*; BGHZ 55, 1, 3, [1971] *GRUR* 35, *Maske in Blau* (operetta) OLG Frankfurt am Main [1976] *GRUR* 199, at 202, Götterdämmerung.
[73] Dietz, 'Authenticity', at 174. As the Resolution of the Executive Committee of ALAI points out, 'a certain flexibility in the application of copyright law with regard to authors' moral rights...should also permit authors to include certain clauses in the contracts which they enter into with users of their works, regarding the exercise of their moral rights subject to strict limits, in specifically determined cases. A prohibition on assignment of moral rights as well as a global waiver of same must in essence be maintained as the basic corner stone of authors' protection, as guaranteed by the Universal Declaration of Human Rights.' See ALAI, *Le droit moral de l'auteur / The moral right of the author*, Antwerp Congress, 19–24 September 1993, ALAI, Paris, 1995, at 561. See also Stamatoudi, 'Moral rights', at 509.

if it is limited and restricted in scope along the lines of the Belgian model it does not compromise the rights of the authors in any respect. In fact it allows them to consent to particularly defined actions in relation to their work and in most cases after a publication contract has been concluded, which shifts the bargaining power that publishers and producers usually have in the case of global waivers. In addition, whatever is not mentioned in such a contract is presumed not to have been allowed by the author. If the author makes things too difficult for publication and use, he will anyway *de facto* exclude himself from the multimedia market. Such a solution fully respects the choice of the author and gives him the right to restrict his moral right of integrity as much as he wishes, always with the ceiling of the prejudice to honour and reputation. He is also the one to draw the line of protection in a digital environment after having taken all the relevant points and risks into account. This is something that is closely linked to the personality of the author and can never be contracted away. Waivers can also be used at the production level of a multimedia work in order to restrict the moral rights of authors with regard to the necessary changes and adaptations of the work for reasons of its commercialisation.

Limited contractual waivers should also be the practice in relation to employee–authors. Any provision that alienates employee–authors from any moral rights protection altogether is inconsistent with the provisions of the Berne Convention. It also contradicts the need to reinforce moral rights in the digital environment. If no one is to be afforded moral rights protection in relation to a multimedia work that has been created in the course of employment, both authors and producers[74] run the risk of diminished weaponry against the problems of authentication and integrity of the work. This presents both economic and social problems. The moral rights of employee–authors can always be restricted by the application of a waiver reached by common accord between the author and the producer. That, however, has to be limited in scope according to what we have already described.

In this context it is clear that users will be able to use a multimedia product and transform its contents according to the scope of the licence they have acquired, which in most cases will also be the scope technically available in the product. However, one should always bear in mind that the fact that a work is received on-line and that the opportunities offered to users in terms of manipulation of the work are more numerous than those in relation to off-line works by no means diminishes the moral rights of authors. Users have to be equally attentive both with on-line and off-line works.

[74] When it comes to issues of paternity and the integrity of the work, the producers' rights are protected via the rights of the authors.

10.1.4.2.3 An important restriction in relation to moral rights

One clarification should be made regarding the above points, which will put the moral rights issue in its proper context. In practice moral rights of authors are only relevant once the work is communicated to the public. If distorted works are kept within the private sphere of the person initiating them, then the whole moral rights issue becomes irrelevant, i.e. because the honour and reputation of the author exist only in relation to the public and can therefore be destroyed only by a distorted version of the work being communicated to the public. Changes to the work can be taken into account by the public only if the public knows about them. Or as Dietz puts it,

> if the user of an individual copy of a multimedia product is a consumer or end user acting in his private sphere, the problem of the moral rights protection normally does not arise at all, since – apart from the very delicate questions of destruction of unique pieces of art – it was never denied that an end user can dispose, manipulate, modify and destroy his copy of the work as he likes, as long as the results of his activities do not reenter the public sphere.[75]

However, a multimedia work which has been delivered over the Internet and has been fed back to the system after it has undergone alterations amounting to infringing acts can give rise to moral rights claims on the part of the author. At this stage moral rights provisions should be enforced to prevent such situations on three grounds: first for the sake of the author, secondly for the sake of the public that has an interest in receiving authentic and unaltered works, and lastly for the sake of the investment of the producer. Moral rights are supposed to serve only the first and second tasks, especially in copyright regimes that adopt the dualistic approach.[76]

10.1.4.3 Conclusion

According to what we have discussed in the preceding section, an ideal harmonised moral rights regime for multimedia products could be described as follows. The author (editor) of a multimedia product should be granted the rights of divulgation, paternity and integrity. None of these

---

[75] Dietz, 'Authenticity', at 175 (computer programs are a special case).
[76] Almost all copyright regimes recognise that moral rights serve both the interests of authors and those of the public. See, for example, Court of Appeal, Brussels, 8 June 1978, *JT*, 1978, 619, *Tintin*. On occasion it is recognised that this protection can also be extended to producers (i.e. in instances where neither the author nor the producer possesses the economic rights in the work). That, however, can only be the case after purposive interpretation in monistic systems. In dualistic systems such as France this conclusion is impermissible. See the whole discussion on producers' quasi-moral rights in Dietz, 'Authenticity'.

rights should be conditional or subject to additional requirements or formalities. No special provision should be made for employee–authors.

The right of integrity should be waivable in particular cases that must be narrowly construed and in relation to existing works only. Partial waivability should be the only resort for conditioning, regulating or restricting moral rights at a post-production level. Specific provisions in relation to the right of integrity with regard to gross distortions or damage to the author's honour or reputation should not be expressly enshrined in the law. That would unreasonably restrict the choice of the author whether or not to opt for restriction of his moral rights, and it would also fall foul of the need to reinforce moral rights protection (or at least preserve the current level) in the era of ease of digital copying and manipulation of the works. That would undermine the interests of all the parties involved in the creation and use of a multimedia product, i.e. authors, producers and users. However, the requirement of damage to the author's honour or reputation should be introduced in the law as a ceiling/safety net from which an author cannot contract out. Any other solution would impinge on the author's personality rights. In the exercise of the integrity right a balancing test that takes into account both the interests of the other authors or parties involved in the creation and use of a multimedia product and the particular nature of the work, i.e. its originality, the purpose of its use, etc., should also take place. The significance of such a test is particularly great in view of the differing nature of multimedia products. What exactly amounts to a distortion or mutilation, for example, in a multimedia context will have to be defined by the courts in the context of this balancing test which takes due account of all these factors, and the outcome will be influenced by the particular nature of a multimedia product.

Lastly, the issue of moral rights becomes relevant only when a work is communicated to the public. If the work is kept in the private sphere of the person making the alterations, these alterations cannot be held to be infringing acts.

Such a solution seems to reconcile the common law and the continental law traditions on moral rights. That can prove particularly useful in view of a potential harmonisation in the area.

10.1.5 Technical devices

Digitisation and interactivity offer multiple and extensive opportunities for the manipulation and, potentially, the distortion of multimedia works. Whatever goes beyond the limit of changes which have been authorised by reason of a licence or assignment will be held to amount to an

A regime of protection for multimedia products 241

infringement of both the economic and the moral rights of authors in the work, once the altered work is communicated to the public. The introduction of new legislation in the area might draw the line between legitimate and illegitimate use and sanction actions coming within the second case. However, the law is not capable of tracing such infringements or even practically preventing them before they take place. In many cases, after they have taken place, damage might already be irreparable both for the author and producer of the multimedia work and for the public. Problems of both respect for the work and authenticity of the work arise. The answer to the problems of digitisation seems to be found in digitisation. Digitisation allows works to be identified, protected and automatically managed, provided the appropriate systems are installed. In that sense digitisation is both an opportunity and a serious danger.[77]

The fact that many multimedia products consist of pre-existing works and materials and the fact that these materials have to be obtained quickly, efficiently and with certainty as to the rights conferred on the multimedia producers gives rise to problems of clearance and administration of rights too. In fact, co-operation between collecting management societies and, even better, international centralised systems for clearance of rights are two of the options for the future. Technology can also be used for the attainment of these objectives.

In the light of the above, technical devices have been developed to achieve two main aims: to prevent piracy and to facilitate the administration and clearance of intellectual property rights.

10.1.5.1 *Technical devices against piracy*

Technical devices against piracy are usually known as systems of identification of the work. Their task is to embed distinguishable digital marks in the work (tattooing or marking) that are capable of identifying it. These marks also reveal the identity of the rightholders, the use that is licensed and the registration number of the work in a general registry which can provide more information in relation to the work. These systems are equivalent to the systems of identification initially used in analogue works, as for example the ISBN number for books and the ISSN number for journals.

Examples of technical protection devices against piracy are encryption, digital signatures, steganography, Serial Copyright Management System (SCMS), personal authentication procedures and others that are less

---

[77] Commission Green Paper of 19 July 1995 on copyright and related rights in the information society, COM (95) 382 final, at 79.

known or less developed.[78] Encryption is a process that transforms a file that is originally written in a format capable of being manipulated into a 'scrambled' format through the use of mathematical principles. The scrambled file can be restored to an accessible and usable format only through the use of an authorisation that takes the form of a 'key' to unscramble the file. Digital signatures are mathematical algorithms that are used to 'sign' and 'seal' the work. Thus, through the use of digital signatures one will be able to identify the source of the particular work as well as verify whether the original contents of the work have been altered. Digital signatures are essentially a means of authentication of the work. Steganography (or 'digital fingerprinting' or 'digital watermarking') is a method of encoding digitised information with attributes (hidden messages) that cannot be disassociated from the file that contains that information. These attributes do not interfere with the quality of the work but can be detected whenever they are specifically looked for.[79] Lastly, SCMS is a system that prevents a second copy being made privately from the first copy.

All these systems present ample opportunity to keep the access and use of copyright material under control. They also serve as means of authentication of the work so that the public is certain that it is receiving genuine unaltered information. All these systems, of course, can be used only in a digital environment.

The importance of the use of these technical devices for the protection of the rights of authors and the public and eventually those of the producers is expressed in a number of national and international legal instruments. Some examples of these are the US White Paper,[80] the EU Green Paper[81] and the European Commission Communication,[82] the two recent WIPO treaties,[83] and the EU draft Directive.[84] Specifically, the European Union has legitimised the use of such technical devices in article 7.1(c) of the software Directive.[85] This article states that Member States shall provide for appropriate remedies against persons putting into circulation, or possessing for commercial purposes, any means, the sole intended purpose of which is to facilitate the unauthorised removal or circumvention of any technical device which may have been applied

---

[78] See also on this issue T. Roosen, 'L'identification des oeuvres et la communication en ligne' in C. Doutrelepont, P. Van Binst and C. Wilkin (eds.), *Libertés, droits et réseaux dans la société de l'information*, Bruylant and LGDJ, Brussels, Paris, 1996, at 75.
[79] US White Paper, at 185ff.
[80] *Ibid.*, at 177.
[81] Commission Green Paper, COM (95) 382 final, at 79ff.
[82] Commission Communication, COM (96) 568 final, at 15ff.
[83] Art. 11 WCT and art. 18 WPPT.
[84] Art. 6 of the EU draft Directive.
[85] EC software Directive.

to protect a computer program. Article 7.3 adds that Member States may provide for the seizure of any such means. Community law does not require the compulsory introduction of such means. It only protects those who choose to install technical systems for the protection of computer programs systems by making it unlawful to put pirate decoding or other similar equipment into circulation or to possess it for commercial purposes.[86] However, the Community reserves the right to make technical protection devices compulsory in the near future. This, of course, will only take place on a harmonised basis and after these devices have been developed and accepted by the industry.[87] Article 7 of the software Directive has been implemented, for example, by article 10 of the Belgian copyright law. This provision also imposes specific fines on infringers.[88] The WCT and the WPPT require the introduction in national laws of a provision that secures 'adequate legal protection and effective legal remedies against the circumvention of effective technological measures that are used by authors in connection with the exercise of their rights under this Treaty or the Berne Convention and that restrict acts, in respect of their works, which are not authorised by the authors concerned or permitted by law'.[89]

However, the use of any such device has to be under tight control in order for it not to be used to the detriment of the public. That can happen in situations where the access to, and use of, materials is restricted without these materials being subject to any copyright or other protection. In these circumstances the person possessing the technology is usually also the one setting the rules. The laws on free access to information, expression, privacy and abuse of power should assist on this point. This is essential in relation to multimedia works where there is an excessive need for materials and any blockage of information will inevitably result in an obstruction to creation. Perhaps today more than ever before there is increased anxiety concerning the extent to which the right of the public to access to information is preserved. This concern was recently raised in the discussion concerning the right of reproduction and technical protection systems during the drafting of the WCT and the WPPT. The problem of restricting the right of the public was essentially centred on two main issues. The first

---

[86] However, the Internet music recorder was not banned on this basis because it can have a dual function. See *Guardian*, 20 November 1998, at 16. A good example of a provision incorporating the prohibition on the circumvention of copyright protection systems into national law can be found in § 1201 of the US Digital Millennium Copyright Act 1998.
[87] Commission Green Paper, COM (95) 382 final, at 82.
[88] The sanction provided by the Belgian Software Act is a fine of between 100 and 100,000 Belgian francs (obviously to be multiplied by the legal multiplier). Loi transposant en droit belge la directive européenne du 14 mai 1991 concernant la protection juridique des programmes d'ordinateur, 30 June 1994 [1994] BS (*Belgisch Staatsblad–Moniteur belge*) 27 July 1994, 19315.
[89] Art. 11 WCT and see also art. 18 WPPT.

was the issue of blocking access to any kind of information, whether under copyright protection or not, by the extensive use of technical protection systems which may also cover works that are in the public domain. The second issue centred on the potential *de facto* creation of information monopolies which will restrict free access to information to a substantial degree or allow it on the basis of 'take-it-or-leave-it' contracts over the content of which the public has little control or choice. On top of everything, a very extreme right of reproduction coupled with a limited number of exceptions to economic rights will oblige members of the public to pay for every single use of the work even if such use may have been exempted in an analogue environment. In that respect copyright may become a very extensive and powerful right and the balance between rightholders and the public may become distorted in favour of the former.[90]

The other extreme, of course, would be to have multimedia works as a result of mass copying. As Clark points out, 'both mass copying and multimedia [will be] dramatically transformed from copyright infringements to vehicles for the realisation of rights'.[91]

The conclusion should be that the regulated use of technical protection devices is the only way of enforcing the rights of the authors and producers[92] effectively. In addition, the authenticity and integrity of the works are safeguarded for the sake of the public. Yet technical protection devices should not constitute vehicles for abuse of power on the part of those who control them. And in any case they cannot replace the function of law. They serve the needs of copyright protection but there is no way in which they replace copyright protection. Therefore their use should always remain under close scrutiny.

10.1.5.2 *Technical devices for the administration and clearance of rights*

The second aspect of the twofold role of technological devices in the digital era is their use for the administration[93] and clearance of rights.

---

[90] T. Vinje, 'The new WIPO Copyright Treaty: a happy result in Geneva' [1997] 5 *EIPR* 230; A. Mason, 'Developments in the law of copyright and public access to information' [1997] 11 *EIPR* 636.

[91] C. Clark and T. Koskinen-Olsson, 'New alternatives for centralised management: "one-stop-shops"' in *WIPO international forum on the exercise and management of copyright and neighbouring rights in the face of the challenges of digital technology*, Seville, 14–16 May 1997, WIPO, 1998, 227, at 240.

[92] See Dietz, 'Authenticity' at 165, where he argues that technical device protection (authentication) for producers amounts to quasi-moral right protection.

[93] The collecting societies have set up a uniform system to standardise and communicate data in an efficient and integrated way. This system will achieve significant economies of scale whilst creating more efficient mechanisms for exchanging information to support

The need for multimedia producers to clear rights quickly, efficiently and with certainty in a wide range of areas (since all kind of expressions are contained in a multimedia work) has further accentuated the need for such devices.

Technical devices used in this area purport to (a) inform parties as to the details of the work (the identity of the rightholders, the expiry dates of the rights in it, the price for its use, etc.), (b) either refer the parties to the organisations where they can buy licences or conclude transactions themselves, and (c) keep a record of the transaction and the details of the user (known as 'non-repudiation' and 'date stamping').

In order for technical devices to perform such functions there is again a digital mark that has to be embedded in the work and which allows it to be identified and to constitute the object of a transaction. Various initiatives have been taken to this end. Some of them are Cypertech, CITED,[94] COPICAT, DAVID, COPEARMS, IMPRIMATUR, CLARCS and COPYMART. Cypertech is a digital-marking system that allows a digitally distinguished mark to be incorporated in each work. That system determines the time for which a work is used and which receivers can receive and decode it in real time. CLARCS is a transaction-processing system that is based around two databases. One of them consists of works with associated fees and conditions and the other of registered users. Each transaction links a user with a work and the details of each transaction are recorded in a transaction file. IMPRIMATUR identifies works with a unique number and allows the marketing of the works either by sale or by licence with payments being remitted to the copyright owner. Lastly, COPYMART, perhaps the most ambitious one, envisages a central international administration of copyrights (irrespective of the type of expression of the work). COPYMART is an international registry of copyright works and indicates the conditions under which each of the works can be purchased or licensed. Interested parties can conclude transactions over the works that are registered in it, and they obtain their copies and pay their fees on-line directly to the rightholders. The basic idea for this system was first presented in 1989 by Professor Zentaro Kitagawa of the University of Kyoto[95] in a presentation in London on

---

automated transactions for the licensing, tracking and monitoring functions demanded by a dynamic digital trading environment. The system is called the Common Information System (CIS). For further details see D. Yon and K. Hill, 'Collective administration of copyright in cyberspace' in M.-C. Janssens (ed.), *Intellectual property rights in the information society*, Bruylant, Brussels, 1998, at 93.

[94] For further details see CITED (Copyright in Transmitted Electronic Documents) Final Report, CITED Consortium, London, 1994.

[95] On the position in Japan itself, see C. Heath, 'Multimedia und Urheberrecht in Japan' [1995] *GRUR Int* 843, at 844.

'clearance or copysale'. The remainder of the above-mentioned systems also function along the same lines.[96]

Not only is an effective administration of copyrights achieved through the operation of these systems but also control of access to and use of these works. Eventually, uses that go beyond the licensed permission can be detected and either stopped or charged accordingly. In addition, users can rest assured that they are receiving the original unaltered materials that they require. Thus, the on-line collective administration systems incorporate to a certain extent the functions of the first technical protection devices we described.

As far as the producers of multimedia products are concerned, technical devices may alter the method of production. Producers will no longer be the assemblers of the information that constitutes the contents of the works they publish but simply the providers.[97] All materials will be obtained through on-line systems that will allow immediate buying of the work. However, this opportunity should be looked into in further detail and one should determine to what extent it is likely to strengthen the bargaining and marketing power of the organisations of collective administration of rights against authors and users.[98] Both authors and users run the risk of being offered standard-type contracts on a take-it-or-leave-it basis. That will put them in a difficult position since their refusal to sign up to such a deal will practically exclude their works from the market. In the same way users might incur a competitive disadvantage in relation to other users being offered the same terms in licensing contracts.

[96] Clark and Koskinen-Olsson, 'New alternatives'; and R. Oman, 'Moderator's contribution to the fourth panel discussion on technological means of protection and rights management information' in *WIPO international forum*, 55, at 57. If a system such as COPYMART were to be put in place, it is to be anticipated that the need for an international equivalent to the UK's Copyright Tribunal (or an equivalent competition law authority) would also arise. In the framework of INFO 2000 the European Commission supports ten pilot projects concerning multimedia rights clearance systems. These projects (INDECS, EFRIS, TV FILES, PRISAM, ORS, etc.) will finally lead to one system of multimedia rights clearance, the VERDI project (Very Extensive Rights Data Information project), which is designed to cope with the needs and challenges of the information society in the most efficient way. As a first stage the national clearing centres of six different EU Member States will be linked together in a rights information and licensing network. The VERDI project does not aim to develop totally new structures and systems but to connect the existing ones by intelligently combining and linking them together into a new and effective service which will constitute a simple and cost-effective means by which the multimedia producer can obtain exploitation rights under legally secure and reasonable conditions. M. Schippan, 'Purchase and licensing of digital rights: the VERDI project and the clearing of multimedia rights in Europe' [2000] *EIPR* 24, at 24 and 27.

[97] Clark and Koskinen-Olsson, 'New alternatives', at 241.

[98] See I. Stamatoudi, 'The European Court's love–hate relationship with collecting societies' [1997] 6 *EIPR* 289; P. Torremans and I. Stamatoudi, 'Collecting societies: sorry, the Community is no longer interested!' (1997) 22 *EL Rev* 352. The case-law referred to in these articles clearly illustrates the risks involved.

A regime of protection for multimedia products   247

Competition law must regulate such situations thoroughly, especially in cases where the dominant position of on-line clearing systems and the co-operation of powerful copyright management societies is favoured and even facilitated by the European Commission in view of setting up international centralised units for the administration of these rights.[99] In these circumstances it should be guaranteed that adequate flexibility is given to both authors and users[100] and that the public is allowed access to all indispensable information for further use.[101] If seen from the other end of the spectrum, this system will boost the exploitation of their works to a far greater degree with perhaps more favourable terms than before if authors take appropriate immediate steps[102] and in this way they might also avoid the imposition of compulsory licences.[103] Users might be able to save the costs of lengthy, difficult and private negotiations, and secure better prices for protected material.

10.1.5.3 The overall position

The role of technology in assisting the protection of authors' rights and in helping the administration of those rights is indispensable. However,

---

[99] See in this respect the reference in Case T-5/93, *Roger Tremblay and others* v. *EC Commission (Syndicats des exploitants de lieux de loisirs (SELL), intervening)* [1995] ECR II-185, at para. 85 to the statements of a Community official and a representative of SACEM made at a conference on copyright held in Madrid on 16 and 17 March 1992. And see also the Green Paper, COM (95) 382 final, at 27 and 70ff.

[100] This means central rather than collective administration of rights, allowing space and an opportunity for both authors and users to negotiate the terms of their agreement. See the discussion in the next section of this chapter. See also F. Melichar, 'Collective administration of electronic rights: a realistic option?' in P. Hugenholtz (ed.), *The future of copyright in a digital environment*, Kluwer Law International, 1996, 147, at The Hague, Boston, 151.

[101] See I. Stamatoudi, 'The hidden agenda in *Magill* and its impact on new technologies' (1998) 1 *Journal of World Intellectual Property* 153; Joint Cases C-241/91P and C-242/91P, *Radio Telefis Eireann and Independent Television Publications Ltd* v. *Commission* [1995] ECR I-743 and [1995] 4 CMLR 718. In this case the copyright work at issue was considered to be indispensable information and a licence granting access to it could be imposed (cf. the essential facilities doctrine).

[102] Failure to act immediately could be taken as silent consent once a substantial period of time has lapsed. See Melichar, 'Collective administration', at 148.

[103] For details of the circumstances in which compulsory licences can apply see Joint Cases C-241/91P and C-242/91P, *Radio Telefis Eireann and Independent Television Publications Ltd* v. *Commission* [1995] ECR I-743 and [1995] 4 CMLR 718; Stamatoudi, 'Hidden agenda'. See also the reference to compulsory licences in the Commission's Green Paper, COM (95) 382 final, at 72. On the issue of compulsory licensing, especially for the arguments in favour and against, see R. Merges, 'Contracting into liability rules: intellectual property rights and collective rights organisations' (1996) 84 *California Law Review* 1293. The position against compulsory licensing is also set out very clearly by A. Dixon and L. Self, 'Copyright protection for the information superhighway' [1994] 11 *EIPR* 465, at 471. And see also the Commission's Green Paper, COM (95) 382 final, at 77.

it would be a fatal mistake to argue either that technology can replace the function of the law or that copyright has become irrelevant because technology can sort out the problems on its own. The existence of technical devices on the market has to be legitimised, and technical devices do not themselves create exclusive rights. There have to be legitimate rights that technology will set out to protect. The limits of these rights must be delineated in order to avoid the other extreme where those possessing the technology will be able to set the rules. The interests of authors, producers and the public have to be taken into account and the right balance struck. Technical devices can potentially produce any result; therefore copyright law has to balance the interests involved and lay down clear limits to the rights that can be exercised and protected through the use of technical devices. If the law does not strike the right balance, the market and technology will strike it according to their own needs; a situation that society cannot afford.

10.1.6 Term of protection

Affording copyright protection to multimedia products necessarily results in granting them, at least in the EU,[104] a term of protection[105] for the life of the author plus seventy years. Since multimedia products deserve copyright protection on the grounds of their creativity, in the same sense as any other work, they also deserve protection for the life of the author plus seventy years. In this respect multimedia works come under the standard copyright rule. However, multimedia products are in general driven and initiated by the market and industry, just as computer programs and databases are. They are created primarily by or on behalf of companies. It follows that in reality the primary aim of multimedia products is to be marketed and to recoup the investment put into their creation. The marketing of these products takes place immediately therefore, and the investment is either recouped or lost within a short period of time, on most occasions not even as long as the life of the author. The rapid progress of technology, the updating of the information and the fashion of the market renders any multimedia product outdated in a very short period of time.

The creators and exploiters of these types of works and their investment and creation decisions are in the main indifferent to the prospect of copyright protection in the long term. They want to recoup their

---

[104] Article 1 of the EC term Directive, [1993] OJ L290/9. In the Berne Convention and the TRIPs Agreement there are provisions for protection for the life of the author plus a minimum of fifty years.
[105] Both for economic and for moral rights.

investment in the short term and they need a copyright regime that allows them to do so. Long-term copyright protection does not influence their decisions and is therefore rapidly becoming an unnecessary restriction on competition which cannot be justified.[106] However, the issue of whether the seventy-year term of protection is generally too long for copyright works is an issue relating to copyright as a whole, rather than multimedia works specifically. It is also an issue which merits separate consideration and which cannot be addressed fully within the scope of this book.[107] From a purely practical point of view, the issue may not be urgent though, since an outdated work will no longer be used and copyright only requires remuneration to be paid for use. In such a scenario the theoretical ongoing copyright protection becomes an irrelevant detail.

10.2 A 'DATABASE-STYLE' *SUI GENERIS* REGIME OF PROTECTION FOR MULTIMEDIA PRODUCTS

10.2.1 Deficiencies of a copyright-only model

The investments required for the production of a sophisticated multimedia product are often considerably higher than those for the production of any other copyright work, including databases. This is mainly so because in a multimedia product a large number of various kinds of works are put together and are digitised (if they are not already in that format), integrated and made interactive. On most occasions this task is a highly creative one which attracts copyright protection on the basis of the final outcome of the work. However, there can also be cases where multimedia products are not necessarily original. A major aspect of the originality of multimedia products is found in the (complete) integration of their various components. This is in addition to the fact that they are collections of a very high number of works, a characteristic which they often share with databases. The integration, through the use of software tools and advanced levels of interactivity, creates the added value of multimedia products and it also distinguishes them clearly from the category of databases where individual accessibility is the norm. Certain primitive multimedia works may not pass the originality hurdle though, as a result of their extremely low level of integration of components. For example, a

---

[106] R. Bard and L. Kurlantzick, *Copyright duration: duration, term extension, the European Union, and the making of copyright policy*, Austin & Winfield, San Francisco, London, Bethesda, 1999, at 215.
[107] Economists will even argue that intellectual property protection is needed only if market lead time is inadequate to recoup investment. The question whether lead time would be sufficient in relation to multimedia products cannot be answered here completely, but it seems unlikely that lead time on its own would be sufficient in all cases.

CD-ROM-based encyclopaedia may offer the user a combination on the computer screen of a picture of a statue and a bibliographical note in text format on the sculptor. There may be problems in granting copyright to this primitive form of integration, or rather juxtaposition, for the added value of the combination in addition to the rights in the two pre-existing works. However, the works are not individually accessible because they appear only as a combination. A database classification is therefore not appropriate and the 'more-than-one-expression' argument places works of this kind in the multimedia category. Arguably copyright should not be granted here on grounds of lack of originality, especially if the EU criterion of personal expression by the author is used. What remains though is that these primitive non-original multimedia products have rather a lot in common with databases. The potential consequences of these similarities warrant further consideration.

Multimedia products, irrespective of whether they are original or not, require substantial investments for their production. Sometimes the amount of money and effort put into the design, accumulation of the various elements and realisation of a multimedia product (which is not original) can be extremely substantial and can even surpass those for the creation of an original work. The possibility of copying these works in perfect quality at a fraction of the original cost and the marketing of similar or identical products clearly jeopardises the investment put into this domain and greatly discourages future projects in the area. The multimedia industry in this respect runs an important risk that is similar to the one the database industry was confronted with some years ago. Therefore, there is a need for protection even for those multimedia products that do not come under the umbrella of copyright. This need is not based on their creativity or the fact that they offer society a new expression of a concept, but rather on the substantial investment in them.

The same considerations have been taken into account by the European Community in the area of databases. The EU Directive on databases[108] confers a *sui generis* right on a database by reason of the investment put into it, irrespective of whether or not it qualifies for copyright protection. If the maker[109] of a database can prove that he has put a quantitatively and/or qualitatively substantial investment[110] into the obtaining, verification or presentation of the contents of a database, he is granted the

---

[108] EU database Directive.
[109] According to Recital 41 to the database Directive, the 'maker' is the person who takes the initiative and the risk of investing, excluding subcontractors. It is also in this sense that we will use the term in the context of multimedia products.
[110] Recital 40 to the database Directive provides that such an investment may consist of the deployment of financial resources and/or the expenditure of time, effort and energy.

exclusive right of preventing extraction and/or re-utilisation of the whole or a substantial part of the database.[111] The maker of the database is entitled to this right even if his database is copyrightable. In this case the author of the database will have copyright in relation to the structure of the database[112] and the maker a *sui generis* right in relation to the contents of the database.[113] The rights of the authors of the works that constitute the contents of the database are not to be affected.[114]

10.2.2 The difference between databases and multimedia products

The *sui generis* right for databases is a right referring to the contents rather than the structure of the database.[115] The fact that these two forms of protection do not coincide is also the reason why a database that is original can qualify for both copyright and a *sui generis* protection. However, in a multimedia context the distinction between the structure of the work and its contents is not always an easy one to make. First, the structure of a multimedia product does not necessarily translate into the systematic selection and arrangement of its contents, as is the case with databases. If that were the case then the multimedia work would qualify as a database rather than anything else. Selection and arrangement of the contents of a multimedia work is a task which takes place at a pre-production stage or at least at the first stage of production of the multimedia work. After the works or other elements that are to be included in a multimedia product have been selected, they are necessarily arranged[116] in such a way as to enable their integration into the product. Integration takes place to such an extent that the new work that emerges has only little in common with its initial contents. The selection and arrangement of the contents of this new work are no longer apparent. The structure of the multimedia product is in fact the structure that appears on one's screen as a general merged image with which the user can interact. In this sense a reference,

---

[111] Art. 7 of the database Directive.
[112] In fact in relation to the selection and arrangement of its contents. See art. 3.1 of the database Directive.
[113] At the end of the day the maker of the database (the producer) will possess all the economic rights in the work, either as first owner or as assignee of these rights.
[114] Stamatoudi, 'EU database Directive', at 459ff.
[115] The very first case in Europe dealing with the *sui generis* right concerned a non-original database containing a list of self-help groups. This list was copied and re-utilised by the defendant when it launched its own database of self-help groups which was simply wider in territorial coverage. Court of First Instance, Brussels, 16 March 1999, 118 *JT* 1999, 305–7.
[116] Arrangement of the various elements in a multimedia product goes one step further than that in databases since it allows integration.

either to the elements of a multimedia product (after these elements have been incorporated into it) or to the content of the multimedia product, seems to be a reference to one and the same thing. It is this content of the multimedia work that can be considered original and therefore capable of attracting copyright protection.

In the light of the above, any extraction or re-utilisation right in relation to multimedia products, analogous to that for databases, will necessarily refer to the content of the multimedia work rather than its elements, since the elements are no longer distinguishable on screen. In this context if a multimedia product were to attract both copyright and *sui generis* protection, the latter would make no sense since it would be necessarily covered by the former via the rights of reproduction and distribution. One could nevertheless argue that a way of distinguishing the elements of a multimedia product from its content/structure is to imagine a situation where one uses the same elements in order to produce a very different product or even the same product if there are no copyright constraints on it. Nevertheless, this situation would either be rare or of a diminished practical significance. First, in order for one to engage in such a task one would need to be able to copy the initial elements found in the multimedia product and not their blurred version, which is not an easy task. Secondly, multimedia products do not necessarily combine rare, unique or difficult-to-assemble information that would make copying attractive as in the case of databases. Multimedia products essentially aim to produce an overall image in the same way as audiovisual works or films. In that image indispensable information is only a rare or small part. Thirdly, it is not the obtaining, verification and presentation of the elements of a multimedia product that make that product valuable and costly to produce. It is rather the integration and interactive presentation of these elements which at that stage is transformed into the content of the multimedia work.[117] Granting a *sui generis* right of such contents to multimedia works would confer upon their makers exclusive rights that are not indispensable and therefore produce unjustified constraints on the market.[118] In addition, they are likely to cause confusion and bewilderment to third parties as they will add to the existing pile of exclusive rights in relation to the multimedia product, that is copyright and the rights of the authors of the works included in the multimedia product.

---

[117] In other words, one is allowed to copy the elements that make up the original multimedia product as long as the new work has nothing or only a little to do with the original product (i.e. one has borrowed only insubstantial parts).
[118] Cumulation of various rights may potentially upset the balance between the rights of the owners, the rights of the users and those of the public.

What, however, would make sense would be to grant *sui generis* protection to those multimedia products that do *not* attract copyright protection. The makers of such products have no exclusive rights that can restrain third persons from copying their work and invalidating their investment in the new product. Therefore they are in need of an unfair-competition-law-style right. In such cases a *sui generis* protection will confer on them an exclusive right to prevent substantial parts of their product (content) being extracted and/or re-utilised in other productions, similar or non-similar, for private or for commercial use. It is felt that private use should be restricted as well since there are no effective measures yet in place that can control this use.[119] In addition, there is no reason for a multimedia work to be reproduced for private purposes because in this case there is the risk that multimedia products that are transmitted on-line will be copied and therefore their commercial value will be diminished as the user will not in future need to consult them and pay the relevant fee if he has copied their contents first time round. However, the fact that a *sui generis* right is needed only on the basis of unfair competition law, and not as proprietary right, dictates that that right has to be of a limited nature, both in substance and in time, and should not interfere with the right of the authors of the works included in the multimedia product.

10.2.3 A *sui generis* regime of protection for multimedia products

Following on from the preceding discussion, the ideal *sui generis* model of protection for multimedia works, which is heavily inspired by the *sui generis* protection for databases as found in the EU Directive, can be described as follows. It is an unfair-competition-law right designed on the basis of the rights of reproduction and distribution that are found in copyright. The *producer* of the multimedia product who has sunk a qualitatively and/or quantitatively substantial investment into the production of a multimedia product, i.e. *into the bringing together of the various components, combining, integrating them and making them interactive*, will be given a right to prevent extraction[120] and/or re-utilisation[121] of the whole or a substantial part, evaluated qualitatively and/or quantitatively, *of the content* of his multimedia product. There will be no exception for private

---

[119] See art. 6.2(a) of the database Directive.
[120] 'Extraction' shall mean the permanent or temporary transfer of all or a substantial part of the contents of a multimedia product to another medium by any means or in any form.
[121] 'Re-utilisation' shall mean any form of making available to the public all or a substantial part of the contents of a multimedia work by the distribution of copies, by renting, by on-line or other forms of transmission.

copying. That right will be granted only to the publishers of those multimedia works that do not attract copyright protection. The *sui generis* right should be granted for no more than five years, starting from the date of the completion of the multimedia product, without any possibility of renewal.[122] A short term of protection is dictated both by the needs of the public for access to information and by the facilitation of further creation of derivative works. In any case any multimedia work will undoubtedly be outdated within five years. Even if that is not the case, at least the producer of the multimedia work will be able within this time to capture the market and recoup his investment. Whether or not this right can be exhausted internationally is a matter which, from the current EU position, should perhaps be answered in the negative.[123] Yet the right should be exhausted by the first sale of a hard copy of the multimedia product within the Community by the rightholder or with his consent.[124] The remainder of the attributes of this right can follow faithfully the model of the EU Directive on the protection of databases.

The preference for a database-style *sui generis* right is also motivated by the Commission's clear intention to use the database model as a 'cornerstone of intellectual property protection in the new technological environment'[125] and as 'the basis for all complementary future initiatives'[126] in this field.[127] It is submitted though that it would be wrong simply to copy the *sui generis* provisions of the database Directive. The reason for this submission is that in a multimedia context the coverage of a *sui generis* right is necessarily broader than in databases, as explained above.[128] It is also given in most cases to the same person who owns the

---

[122] Due to the fact that it will be a very narrow category it might be considered appropriate, in order not to have an entirely different format, to use the existing database format in an unchanged form. Although this might be attractive to an encyclopaedia/database-like multimedia work that will be updated regularly, it will be obvious that this rationale does not apply to most multimedia works and that the idea therefore needs to be rejected.

[123] See Case C-355/96, *Silhouette International Schmied GmbH & Co. KG v. Hartlauer Handelsgesellschaft mbH* [1998] 2 CMLR 953; Case C-173/98, *Sebago Inc. and Ancienne Maison Dubois et Fils SA v. GB-Unic SA* [1999] 2 CMLR 1317. See also I. Stamatoudi and P. Torremans, 'International exhaustion in the European Union in the light of "Zino Davidoff": contract versus trade mark law?' (2000) 31 *IIC* 123.

[124] On-line transmission is not covered and does not automatically lead to exhaustion.

[125] Commission Communication, COM (96) 568 final.

[126] Green Paper, COM (95) 382 final.

[127] It is always easier to use an existing right than to create an entirely new one.

[128] One could also build upon Gotzen's argument that 'it is important to stress that this new right will be extremely broad as it will allow the maker of the database to prohibit not only the slavish imitation or the manufacture of a parasitic competing product, but also to prevent the making of a derived product that, though looking and feeling quite different from the original database, would nevertheless have relied too heavily on its contents, so as to harm the initial investment' and say that the situation is different in relation to multimedia products in the sense that they are normally derivative products

A regime of protection for multimedia products   255

copyright,[129] whilst in databases the rights are given to different persons. Any overlap between copyright and the *sui generis* right, a problem that does not arise in the database context, should therefore be avoided.[130] The broader scope of the multimedia *sui generis* right also means that it would necessarily cover aspects which are reserved for copyright in a database context. It would not be advisable to grant long-term protection, with an effect similar to copyright, for those aspects in cases where the work itself does not qualify for copyright. Hence the very restricted scope in terms of time of the proposed multimedia *sui generis* right.

Not a lot needs to be said in relation to the issue of compulsory licences for works on which exclusive rights are conferred on the market and that therefore prevent access by third parties to that information by reason of the essential and indispensable nature of their contents. One can only imagine rare cases where multimedia products will present such a problem since, as we explained earlier, their aim is to produce a new image and not to block raw material on the market. If the European Commission decided to omit such a provision from the draft Directive on databases and include it in the final version only as a general clause under which the Commission can take action whenever it feels it is necessary[131] then the need for such a provision in relation to a potential introduction of legislation for multimedia products is even more limited.[132] Yet if such a situation occurs, the European Court of Justice has proved in the *Magill* case that it is capable of coping perfectly well in these situations under the general competition law provisions of the EC Treaty.[133]

10.2.4 Final considerations

A *sui generis* right of protection for multimedia products that are not capable of attracting copyright protection is dictated by the needs of the market and the multimedia industry. The investments sunk into the creation of these products need to be secured. Otherwise the industry will

---

where the major investment lies in the added value rather than in the selection of the underlying database. The conclusion must therefore be that an even broader right can only be accepted if its duration is curtailed substantially. See F. Gotzen, 'Harmonisation of copyright in the European Union' in Janssens, *Intellectual property rights*, 121, at 135.

[129] This would be the case if the model that has been proposed in this chapter is followed.
[130] See the discussion at section 10.2.2 above.
[131] Art. 16(3): '... the Commission shall submit ... a report ... and shall verify especially whether the application of this right has led to abuse of a dominant position or other interference with free competition which would justify appropriate measures being taken, including the establishment of non-voluntary licensing arrangements'.
[132] The same position has also been adopted in TRIPs, and see also art. 16.3 of the EU database Directive.
[133] See Stamatoudi, 'Hidden agenda'.

refrain from investing in such projects especially in an era when copying and trespassing are not entirely controllable.[134] Therefore exclusive rights in this area can boost production and further development. Any arguments in relation to putting too many constraints on the free flow of information cannot overrule these imperative reasons. The public will have more to lose in the long term if production stops than if it cannot copy easily whatever appears on the screen. The *sui generis* right does not extend copyright protection to non-original works by granting unjustifiably non-exclusive rights. Nevertheless, copyright was designed in an era when functional and utilitarian works did not merit exclusive protection on any grounds, not to mention on grounds of investment. Technology has changed this picture and if law is to survive the new reality it should adjust to these needs.

Non-original multimedia products are, after all, extremely similar to databases. It would therefore be unfair to deny *sui generis* protection to these multimedia products that are not copyrightable, but that share with databases the very reasons for which a *sui generis* right for databases was created. In practice these multimedia products form a small niche group that falls outside the scope of copyrightable multimedia products, whilst nevertheless not being relegated entirely to the database category.

10.3 COLLECTIVE ADMINISTRATION AND UNFAIR COMPETITION LAW

In a traditional market, the purchase of a copyright work could be described as follows. The copyright work is displayed in the window of a shop. The customer enters the shop and has a look at the product on offer. This product has on it a price tag and instructions for use. The customer decides whether or not to buy the product and, if he does decide to buy, he proceeds to pay at the till. If such a model of purchase were transposed to a digital environment, the following questions would arise.

- Who is the shopkeeper and should he always be willing to sell?
- Can the product's instructions for use be tailored to the specific needs of the customer, and is its price negotiable?

These questions give rise to a number of problems in relation to the administration and clearance of rights in multimedia products. Some of the issues they touch upon are whether collective administration should be preferred to individual administration and whether it should be optional or compulsory in relation to certain works that either constitute

---

[134] Even if technological measures are put in place they cannot replace the law altogether.

multimedia products or are works that are to be included in multimedia products. They also raise the issue of flexibility in the licensing of works and open the discussion on whether a 'collective' or a 'central' administration of rights is both preferable and feasible in the digital era.

10.3.1 Administration of rights

10.3.1.1 *Individual administration v. collective administration*

10.3.1.1.1 In an analogue environment

The first issue that should be examined is whether there is, realistically speaking, a choice between individual and collective administration in relation to multimedia works.[135] Although individual administration has traditionally been the author's right, during recent decades market conditions have made it difficult for this right to be exercised on an individual basis. The facts that the author of the work is not necessarily its rightholder and the rightholders of a work are not easily traced, as well as the fact that once traced they do not have either the expertise or the bargaining power required to license uses of their works to third parties, have paved the way for a collective administration of intellectual property rights.[136] On the part of the users, it is easier to obtain licences through a central unit which provides you with certainty as to what you are licensed for and what you are allowed to use it for. Any other solution would make the licensing of any works a costly and time-consuming task. This reason has prompted many national systems either to introduce or to provide for collective administration of copyright works.

In the beginning, collective administration of copyright works did not necessarily mean licensing of works under the same conditions through standard-type contracts on a take-it-or-leave-it basis; rather it was done on an individual basis. The change was introduced at a later stage when broadcasts, sound recordings and video recordings appeared. In fact

---

[135] Theoretically there should always be a choice. However, the market is bound to make the choice for the creators.
[136] Ideally there should be one register in which are found the names of the copyright holders, the holders of the *sui generis* rights and the holders of moral rights. The holders of moral rights will have to be contacted on an individual basis. In practice there is already a problem in finding all those who are entitled to royalties after the death of an author: see J. Rayner, 'Who will pay the jazz man?' *Guardian*, 1 July 1996, at 28, and on top of that there are hardly any works to be found in which no rights whatsoever exist. At least in some jurisdictions perpetual moral rights will survive. See G. Vercken, *Guide pratique du droit d'auteur pour les producteurs de multimédia*, commissioned by the European Communities, DG XIII (Translic) from AIDAA, 1994, at 87–8.

what were transferred to collecting societies to manage were the secondary rights in the works and not the primary rights. In other words, the rightholders did not give the collecting societies the right to exploit the original work incorporated in the recordings mentioned above, i.e. the musical work, the audiovisual work, etc., but the right of transmission and public performance of the recording itself. In that sense the rights of exploitation of the original work remained with the initial author or other rightholders. In this context the uses of the work that were licensed to third parties were necessarily the same since the parties were commercial entities aiming at the transmission or public performance of these recordings in order to make a profit. The establishment of standard-type contracts with regard to predefined uses at a set price was dictated by commercial practice. Dealing on an individual basis, meaning providing licences tailored to the specific needs of the customer, was not an option that was commercially viable since it was not cost effective. On the one hand, the needs of the third parties were coming down to almost the same use of the work, with variations only in the frequency of use and the width of the collecting society's repertoire. On the other hand, the real use of the collecting society's repertoire could not realistically be measured, in the sense that collecting societies could not practically employ the personnel that could go round each public house or radio or television station to check what exactly was transmitted and how often in order to ask for the corresponding remuneration. That would undoubtedly be to the detriment of authors since the operation costs would surpass the amount of the remuneration of the authors.[137]

In the light of this, blanket licences had to be given out to third parties which included the use of any work of the collecting society's repertoire for a standard non-negotiable fee. The remuneration of the authors was calculated on the basis of an 'objective possibility of use' drafted on the basis of surveys and questionnaires of popularity for certain works and authors.

In the late 1980s the conduct of the French collecting society of authors, composers and publishers of music (SACEM) relating to its denial of access to part of its repertoire and its refusal to lower its prices was objected to by a number of French discothèques because they felt it was abusing its dominant position in the market. The European Court of Justice, which dealt with this case in the form of a preliminary ruling, ruled in relation to the prices charged that

art. 86 of the Treaty must be interpreted as meaning that a national copyright-management society holding a dominant position in a substantial part of the common market imposes unfair trading conditions where the royalties which it

---

[137] The fact that under this system certain less popular authors were not paid on a basis strictly equal to more popular ones was one of the handicaps of the system.

charges are appreciably higher than those charged in other Member States, the rates being compared on a consistent basis. That would not be the case if the copyright management society was able to justify such a difference by reference to objective and relevant dissimilarities between copyright management in the Member State concerned and copyright management in the other Member States.[138]

In the case at issue all the submissions put forward by SACEM were rejected and it was therefore made clear that any exceptional circumstances in this respect would form the exception rather than the rule.[139] As regards SACEM's refusal to subdivide its repertoire, the Court took account of the practicalities of controlling the use of the works and assembling variable fees adjusted to each use, and ruled that such conduct was justifiable 'unless access to a part of the protected repertoire could entirely safeguard the interests of authors, composers and publishers of music without thereby increasing the costs of managing contracts and monitoring the use of protected musical works'.[140] This meant that in that case any subdivision of the collecting society's repertoire was not a viable option on the market.

Thus, although the Court did not find any excuse for the charging of high royalties on the part of SACEM, it did recognise that SACEM's refusal to subdivide its repertoire was justified due to the increased costs which would result from any other conduct and which would eventually be to the detriment of the authors. In an analogue environment any subdivision of the repertoire was simply not viable and therefore it stayed clear of the net of unfair competition law.

10.3.1.1.2 In a digital environment

The very same reasons that dictated the solution of collective administration of copyrights in an analogue environment are also valid in relation to digital works distributed in a digital environment.[141] In that sense multimedia products do not present any particularities when compared to other digital works. Rightholders are not easily traced, and even when they are traced they might be large in number. Clearance of rights in

---

[138] Case 110/88, *SACEM* v. *Lucazeau*; Case 241/88, *SACEM* v. *Debelle*; Case 242/88, *SACEM* v. *Soumagnac*; Case 395/87, *Ministère Public* v. *Tournier*: all at [1989] ECR 2811, [1991] 4 CMLR 248, at 292.

[139] See Stamatoudi, 'European Court's love–hate relationship', at 294.

[140] Case 110/88, *SACEM* v. *Lucazeau*; Case 241/88, *SACEM* v. *Debelle*; Case 242/88, *SACEM* v. *Soumagnac*; Case 395/87, *Ministère Public* v. *Tournier*: all at [1989] ECR 2811, [1991] 4 CMLR 248, at 292.

[141] On the role of collecting societies in a multimedia context see R. Kreile and J. Becker, 'Multimedia und die Praxis der Lizenzierung von Urheberrechten' [1996] *GRUR Int* 677.

relation to works that are to be included in a multimedia product requires the necessary technical equipment and expertise on the part of the rightholders, especially since it involves digital rights and rights in on-line systems, the status of which is somewhat uncertain. It also requires knowledge, time and investment as well as bargaining power. The administration of the rights in a work makes things easier for both authors and users since there is a central unit with which authors can be registered. They can thus have their works exploited effectively and make a profit, whilst users can effectively trace the works they need and be certain as to the use of the work they are entitled to make. That saves them time, effort and money and boosts production and profitable exploitation.

The additional problems that are introduced by digital works in general and multimedia products in particular are the following. First, many more works are needed in the production of a multimedia work than in the production of any other work. These works are diverse in nature and are intended for various kinds of uses in any part of the world. Second, there is an eminent need for control of these uses in view of the facilities of manipulation a digital environment offers. This is especially so in view of the fact that the same devices used for the licensing of works will also be used to track down potential infringers. Third, there is almost no distinction in a digital environment between primary and secondary exploitation of the work. Almost as soon as a work is put on the system it is communicated to the public without the intermediary stage of a recording or separate distribution process. Thus any distinction between primary and secondary exploitation of the work is blurred.

On the other hand, digitisation facilitates the tracing of the author's identity and in certain cases also the conditions of the licence. Digitised works can carry all the necessary documentation as to the uses allowed, as they have almost no constraints in terms of the potential volume of information that can be carried. Digitisation also offers the possibility for clearance of rights on-line, better control of the uses and control of the real and actual use of each work, as well as the kind of use and the time of use. In addition, it allows collecting societies to join their efforts through central on-line systems where, even in cases where they are not allowed to clear rights themselves and conclude transactions, they can refer clients to the appropriate units that are allowed to license rights in certain works. Because digitisation removes practically all limits of space, all this information can be carried with the work at any time, and on top of that, when one concludes a transaction over a work on a net one can also immediately acquire the content of the work which can be kept in an on-line registry. Details that are registered include the identity of the parties concluding the transaction, the date of the transaction, the content of the contract, etc. The technical systems that allow for all these facilities have been analysed in the section on technical devices.[142]

Consequently, there is without doubt a need for the administration of copyrights of multimedia products by copyright management societies. This is particularly so in an era when there are a large number of different kinds of works involved in the production of a multimedia work for various extended uses, and when many multimedia works will be derivative works or works which depend heavily on pre-existing materials. However, the current copyright management societies' conduct, which involves standard practices and contracts, is not necessarily the best solution possible. The potential offered by digitisation is for more flexibility, personalisation of the procedures through a more stringent control of the licensing and use of the work, and perhaps somehow a return to the primary objectives of the administration of intellectual property rights.

10.3.1.2 Collective administration v. central administration

The possible models of administration of rights by copyright management societies can be described as follows:

> – The current model (or model of 'collective administration') where an author who wants to accede to the collecting society at issue has to accept that his work will be licensed for certain uses at a certain price, a predefined share of which he has to accept. On the other hand, users of the work are offered standard-type contracts (in the form of blanket licences or packages of works) on a 'take-it-or-leave-it' basis. Subdivision of these packages or negotiation of the price is not an option.

This model is the most inflexible one, but at the same time it is the most cost-effective one. It takes no account of special cases; thus administrative and operation costs are kept to a minimum. On the other hand, it takes no account of the specific desires of the authors with the result that it either excludes their works from the system or puts pressure on them to allow their works to be subject to uses to which they do not initially agree. On the part of the users, it allows collecting societies to enforce their bargaining power on users by making them buy packages that they will not use in their entirety and that therefore put them at a competitive

---

[142] See section 10.1.5 above.

disadvantage in relation to their potential large-scale competitors on the market.[143]

> – The model of 'central administration' allows both authors and users to define the use of the works the former wish to license and the latter wish to purchase. The remuneration of the authors and the licences of the users are calculated and priced according to the content of each licence.

This is the most flexible model in so far as it takes into account both the desires of the authors (respecting also their moral rights) as well as the needs of the users. What, however, has to be secured is that any rights in any work should be offered to all third parties on an equal basis or they should not be offered at all. Variations in licensing procedures are justified only if there is good reason for them if one starts from a dominant position.[144] Although this model takes into account any possible particularity of the parties involved in a licensing transaction, its costs are not substantially or prohibitively higher than those of the previous model, since the system operates in a digital on-line environment with pre-programmed automatic technical devices that can cope with these variations in circumstances. No additional costs are required in terms of expertise and personnel. In that sense this model is almost as cost-effective as the previous one.

In view of the pros and cons of the two above models, it is clear that the balance tends to favour the second solution as the fairest one and the one that is closer to the principles of copyright. In the light of digitisation, it is very likely that if the *Lucazeau* and *Tournier* cases[145] were to be decided in relation to digitised works, whose rights could be cleared on-line, the European Court would have reached an entirely different decision, probably favouring the subdivision of SACEM's repertoire.[146] Yet even if one opts for the system of central administration there are some important questions to be answered. First, should there always be a society that receives the royalties of a licence, or could it also be the rightholder himself who receives it directly? And secondly, is consent for the particular uses of one's work presumed as long as one registers one's

---

[143] As could arguably be the case with TV stations and discos.
[144] I.e. in cases where one does not provide the guarantees of use in relation to a particular work. See in this respect Case 238/87, *Volvo* v. *Erik Veng* [1988] ECR 6211, [1989] 4 CMLR 122.
[145] Case 110/88, *SACEM* v. *Lucazeau*; Case 395/87, *Ministère Public* v. *Tournier*: both at [1989] ECR 2811, [1991] 4 CMLR 248, at 292.
[146] See the reservation put forward by the court in these cases: 'unless access to a part of the protected repertoire could entirely safeguard the interests of authors, composers and publishers of music without thereby increasing the costs of managing contracts and monitoring the use of protected musical works', [1991] 4 CMLR 248, at 292.

work with a collecting society's databases, or does it have to be certified on each occasion?

It is true that digitisation offers the opportunity for authors to collect their royalties immediately by automatic transfer to their accounts even if the collecting society acts as an intermediary. Alternatively, the collecting society can hold onto the authors' royalties and transfer them only at a second stage. This can also be done where the collecting society is no more than an agent for the various collecting societies that possess the various kinds of works. Both systems can still operate in this case. Yet in a multimedia context where everything has to be efficient and cost-effective, direct transactions, either through a collecting society which administers rights for all kinds of works or through a collecting society agent, represent the best possible solution.[147]

In relation to the second question, three solutions are possible. The author's consent can be presumed by the fact that he allows the administration of his rights in his work. Even before he allows the collecting society to administer those rights, he has specified the uses to which his work can be subjected. The second alternative is that as soon as a user shows an interest in a particular work, the collecting society acts as an intermediary in order to obtain the author's accord. Lastly, the society allows the use of the work and is responsible for acquiring the consent of the author only after the transaction has been concluded.

Although the first solution is the simplest and the most efficient one in terms of administration, it puts some constraints on both authors and users. First, authors have to accept in advance a package of predefined uses. Even if they have the right to determine these uses themselves, it is still difficult for them to go back later and withdraw some of them. In fact they lose control over who gets a licence for their work and what use is made of it. Although this might be desirable in the sense that a work is licensed to everyone under the same terms and conditions, it does not allow the author to receive information about and to take account of the particularities of each case and the identity of the user. In this sense, his moral rights protection becomes invalid and his copyright in the work becomes the provision of a work against a fee. On the other hand, third parties will not be able to negotiate further uses of the work with the author if he has not permitted these uses in the first place or if he did not know about these uses at the stage when he commissioned the collecting society to administer the rights in his work.

The second solution takes into account the particularities of each case by allowing the rightholder to assess each situation and to decide either to license or not to license his work. Each refusal, of course, must be justified

---

[147] US White Paper, at 191.

(at least on moral grounds),[148] otherwise competition law issues come into play in cases where the rightholder possesses a dominant position in the market.[149]

The third solution is as problematic as the first one in the sense that, although it allows some control on the part of the author, that control comes at a late stage when in most situations damages by way of remedy are the only possible result. It is efficient only in the sense that the user of the work can immediately proceed with his production without risking delays by the author. However, these delays need not be substantial, if they are well moderated. And in a balancing of interests, what outweighs everything is not the production of the new work but the certainty of the clearance of rights in the works that are to be included in the new production.

The best possible solution seems to be a mixture of the first and second solutions with the opportunity for the author to receive his share for the use of his work directly. In that sense the author can decide himself whether he wants to give blanket authorisation to a collecting society to use his work as it wishes or whether he wants to be asked before any use takes place. That allows the author to evaluate the particularities of each case and also allows the users to negotiate further deals with the rightholders since the personalisation of the rights in the work is not totally lost through the operation of a collecting society. The parties themselves can continue to play a substantive role.

10.3.2 Unfair competition law considerations

The new picture in relation to collecting societies in the digital era brings in a number of unfair competition law considerations. First, the dominant position of these societies is strengthened by reason of their collaboration in order to be able to deal with more kinds of works in ever larger territories. That means that dominant undertakings are more prone to abuse their position by imposing unilateral rules to which other parties have no option but to accede if they do not want to be left out of the market. Second, copyright in certain works produced today, whose utilitarian and functional nature is prominent, might cause trouble by blocking raw materials for the creation of further works and for the access to information by the public.[150]

---

[148] This issue is not entirely resolved in an EU competition law context, since European law does not immediately take moral rights protection into account.
[149] See *Volvo v. Veng* [1988] ECR 6211, [1989] 4 CMLR 122.
[150] The fact that copyright affords its holder an exclusive right makes it more prone to create a monopoly, depending, of course, on how narrowly one defines the market.

10.3.2.1 *Abuses by dominant copyright management societies*

In a series of cases on collecting societies the European Commission and the Court of Justice have already provided some answers to, and guidelines for, some of the issues involved. Dominance as such is not an infringement.[151] Infringement starts when one abuses one's dominant position by imposing unfair and discriminatory conditions on others. A number of such infringements were found by the European Commission in *GEMA*[152] and concerned discrimination on grounds of nationality and excessive obligations towards members such as excessive assignment periods, assignment of future works, long waiting periods for the acquisition of benefits under the social fund, no right of judicial recourse, etc. These infringements were swiftly redressed. A second issue which came under scrutiny, this time related to the users, was whether collecting societies were charging excessive royalties. The ECJ's view in this respect was favourable to the users. It found that any substantial difference in royalties between Member States had to be justified by reference to objective and relevant dissimilarities between the situation of the collecting societies of the various Member States after a comparison on a consistent basis had taken place. Yet, in its judgment it made it clear that such particularities would be the exception rather than the rule. The third issue referred to the ECJ was whether the collecting societies' refusal to subdivide part of their repertoire was an infringement under article 82EC (ex 86EC). The Court took into account the interests of the authors and the impossibility of the collecting societies checking what exactly a disco (the plaintiff in the case at issue) was playing and for how long, since that would involve excessive administrative costs. They came to the conclusion that such conduct was not abusive. However, that would not be the case if a potential subdivision of the repertoire could entirely safeguard the interests of the authors without thereby increasing the costs of managing contracts and monitoring the use of protected musical works. Although all these judgments which were based on preliminary rulings made it look as if

---

That will be the case particularly for content providers in the multimedia era when large companies acquire many copyrights and rights in non-copyrightable materials or materials in which copyright has expired in order to use them either to produce multimedia products themselves or to license them out for that use. See M. Berlins 'The image brokers' (1997) *HotAir* 15 (February) (Virgin Atlantic's inflight magazine), where it is explained how Bill Gates, Ted Turner and Mark Getty acquire rights to great art and how they plan to charge for access to the world's visual history. See also W. Schwartz, 'Legal issues raised by strategic alliances involving multimedia' (1993) 10 *Computer Lawyer* (no. 11), 19.

[151] *Volvo v. Veng* [1988] ECR 6211, [1989] 4 CMLR 122.
[152] *GEMA* decision (1971) OJ L134/15.

the European Union intended to take substantive steps to control the conduct of collecting societies in Europe, a last decision in the *Tremblay* case[153] reversed any expectations in this respect. In this last case the ECJ did not get into the substance of the issue by reason of lack of Community interest.[154] The decision was left to the national courts.

As we explained earlier, the circumstances have changed dramatically in the digital era. The impact, however, is prominent on the second and third issues that we discussed in the previous paragraph. The automatic functioning of the various administration systems on-line has decreased the costs of administration even more, and therefore calculation of the various royalties might need to take place on an individual basis. In relation to the subdivision of a collecting society's repertoire, it is fairly clear that it is no longer a justifiable solution to ask users to purchase blanket licences for all the works administered by the collecting society. This is so, first because collecting societies in a multimedia context administer works of various kinds and not only musical, audiovisual or other works, and secondly, even if the price for a blanket licence of this nature were low, if one needed only a tiny part of the repertoire it would still be unfair to pay the same price as a large-scale user in whose interest it is to pay a low price for all the works, or works in a package, if he intends to use all or most of them. Offering licences for separate works no longer incurs high administrative costs in view of the fact that the use of these works can be controlled through the use of technical devices. In addition, the internationalisation of the operation of such central units of administration of copyrights, or even works out of copyright[155] (where competition law should be applied even more strictly), will no longer be a matter that is only of national significance. It is evident that in that context arguments of 'no Community interest' are no longer viable.

10.3.2.2 *Copyright in small amounts of information*

The second problem we identified above was that of copyright in small amounts of information. Only rarely will a multimedia work be regarded as information or indispensable material for the creation of further works.

---

[153] Case T-5/93, *Roger Tremblay* v. *EC Commission* (*Syndicat des Exploitants de Lieux de Loisirs (SELL) intervening*) [1995] ECR II-185, [1996] 4 CMLR 305; Case C-91/95, *Roger Tremblay* v. *EC Commission* [1996] ECR I-5547, [1997] 4 CMLR 211; Case T-114/92, *Bureau Européen des Médias de l'Industrie Musicale (BEMIM)* v. *EC Commission* [1995] ECR II-147, [1996] 4 CMLR 305. See also Torremans and Stamatoudi, 'Collecting societies'.

[154] Presumably because of the role collecting societies are bound to play in the information society.

[155] Either works that do not attract copyright protection or those in which copyright protection has expired. However, they might attract *sui generis* protection.

A regime of protection for multimedia products   267

As we explained in earlier chapters, multimedia works are usually highly creative works attracting copyright protection on this basis. Yet we cannot exclude altogether the case of a work that is utilitarian in nature but which would nevertheless attract copyright on the basis of a UK criterion of originality that involves only skill and labour. This can also be the case with functional or utilitarian works that are to be included in a multimedia product.

A very interesting case came before the European Court of Justice in relation to copyright protection in TV programme listings. Magill, an Irish publisher, wanted to publish a comprehensive weekly television guide, containing the forthcoming television programmes of BBC, RTE and ITV, the channels received in Ireland and Northern Ireland. However, Magill was prevented from doing so on the basis that the broadcasting companies involved had copyright in these TV programme listings. The Court came to the conclusion that these companies had both a factual and a legal monopoly over the production and first publication of their weekly listings. In the case at issue, the companies abused this monopoly position by denying licences to Magill on the basis of the presence of 'exceptional circumstances'. Three exceptional circumstances were found in this case. First, the Court estimated that there was no substitute for that kind of product on the market, although there was a specific, constant and regular potential demand on the part of consumers. The broadcasting companies were the only source of this information and, by refusing to supply the raw material, they prevented the emergence of a new product (i.e. the essential facilities doctrine). Second, the broadcasters' refusal to supply was not justified by virtue either of the activity of television broadcasting or that of publishing television guides. And third, the broadcasters' refusal to supply Magill with their programme listings was in fact a denial of access to basic information, which was indispensable for the creation of a comprehensive weekly TV guide. In that way they reserved for themselves a secondary market, excluding from that market all other competition.[156]

---

[156] See Joint Cases C-241/91P and C-242/91P, *Radio Telefis Eireann and Independent Television Publications Ltd* v. *Commission* [1995] ECR I-743, [1995] 4 CMLR 718. See also for a very similar set of facts and for a similar legal analysis *CMS* v. *France Télécom*, Cour d'Appel de Paris, 1ère Chambre section A, 7 February 1994. The crucial point of the latter judgment was summarised by Muenchinger as meaning 'that when an entity (in this case France Telecom) collects and commercialises data within the scope of a public service "mission" (in this case, nominative data concerning its "orange list" of subscribers), it benefits from a competitive advantage which generally places it in a dominant position and it does not have the right to refuse to communicate such data to a competitor without being vulnerable to a claim of abuse of that position'. N. Muenchinger, 'French law and practice concerning multimedia and telecommunications' [1996] 4 *EIPR* 186, at 193.

There has been much criticism of this decision and fear as to how far this case and the 'exceptional circumstances' device would go in order to eliminate exclusive rights in copyright material which in the view of the Court did not deserve copyright protection. Of course, such a declaration would supersede the Court's competence. The reality, however, was that this judgment managed to annul the specific subject matter in a work which was highly utilitarian and functional. The *Ladbroke* case[157] which followed indicated that *Magill* is to be used narrowly and only in exceptional cases. In the case of multimedia works one has to prove, first, that the work constitutes basic information indispensable for the creation of a new product, and second, the prevention of the emergence of that new product results in the prevention of the emergence of a secondary market that is not part of the licensor's main activity. All these circumstances have to exist cumulatively.

In *Volvo* v. *Veng*[158] it was also made clear that a refusal to license one's rights comes squarely within the specific subject matter of one's intellectual property right. Yet problems arise when one decides to license one's rights on a discriminatory basis without any justifiable reason. Such conduct is likely to fall foul of article 82EC (ex 86EC) if it is proved that the rightholder holds a dominant position. The conclusion that anyone holding an intellectual property right is in possession of a legal monopoly and therefore is in a factually dominant position, though tempting, is not the right conclusion. Considerations as to the market share have also to be taken into account. Yet how narrowly or how widely we define the market is another issue and, indeed, we might find ourselves in situations where the market will have to be defined so narrowly that an intellectual property right-holder will be *de facto* a holder of a dominant position.

Compulsory licences in these circumstances might be a solution as long as they do not clash with the essence of the intellectual property right itself if that right is derived from a work that deserves copyright protection on grounds of originality. Many will agree that this is initially an issue for the national law to regulate, whilst the role of competition law is to block excesses in this area as well as abusive use of the national rights. Lines should therefore be drawn so as not to make multimedia products, or any other work, vehicles of undeserved exclusive rights that result in monopolies blocking further evolution and creation in the area. That is increasingly so for multimedia products that are essentially derivative

---

[157] Case T-504/93, *Tiercé Ladbroke SA* v. *European Commission* (*Société d'Encouragement et des Steeple-Chases de France intervening*) [1997] 5 CMLR 309. See also Case C-7/97, *Oscar Bronner GmbH & Co. KG* v. *Mediaprint Zeitungs- und Zeitschriftenverlag GmbH & Co. KG and others* [1999] 4 CMLR 112.

[158] Case 238/87, *Volvo AB* v. *Erik Veng* [1988] ECR 6211, [1989] 4 CMLR 122.

works or works depending on pre-existing materials. The rights in the investment and those in the creation should be distinguished and protected accordingly, as is the case with databases and their copyright and *sui generis* protection.

10.3.3 Conclusion

The conclusion is that, in a multimedia context, the shopkeeper of our initial example should ideally be a central unit acting as an agent or a principal that provides information on works that can be licensed. The tag on every single work should contain the uses allowed by the rightholder of the work subject to his prior consent. The client should be able to choose amongst these uses and pay a price that is calculated on the basis of the uses he purchases. If the work is not on offer for a particular use, either he has to move on to another work or, if that work is indispensable to him, he has to prove that refusal by the author constitutes an infringement of his dominant position. In this exceptional case, however, he has to prove first of all that the author holds a dominant position in the market in relation to that work, which is considered to be indispensable information for the creation of a new product which does not come within the sphere of activity of the licensor and for which there is a constant demand on the part of the consumers. He also has to prove that a refusal to license this product necessarily results in the prevention of the emergence of a secondary market. If the author has already licensed his product for similar uses to other parties, he has to have a good reason for not licensing it to the next applicant. The fact that the investment put into the creation of a product has to be taken into account even in these situations where the product is not capable of attracting copyright protection is a separate issue that has been considered in the previous section of this chapter.

11 Conclusions

In this book I have shown that most sophisticated multimedia works do not fit in easily with the existing copyright works' regimes of protection. Before I go any further and discuss the ideal regime of protection for multimedia works, it is interesting to consider a recent French case which confirms the point that the existing copyright regimes of protection are not suitable for multimedia works.[1] The Court of Appeal in Paris, in a case concerned with an encyclopaedia on CD-ROM, came to the conclusion that the multimedia work at issue[2] could not come within the categories of audiovisual works, collective works or collaborative works.[3] It could not qualify as an audiovisual work on two grounds. First, it did not present a linear unfolding of sequences of images since the user could intervene and modify the order of sequences by means of interactivity. Secondly, the encyclopaedia did not contain a succession of moving images but only fixed sequences, which could contain moving images. These two points seemed to lie outside the notion of audiovisual works under art. L112-2 of the French Copyright Act. The multimedia work was also found not to be a collective work on the basis that the person who published and disclosed the work was not the person who initiated its creation nor the person who was responsible for the scenario, direction and organisation of the work's interactivity. The publication of a work by a publisher alone does not suffice to render it a collective work. The multimedia work also did not qualify as a collaborative work since in essence it was one person only who was responsible for its creation (assisted by a technical team) rather than several persons.

---

[1] Sté Havas Interactive v. Françoise Casaril, Court of Appeal (Paris), 4e Chambre, 28 April 2000, [2001] 187 RIDA 314.

[2] The court defined multimedia works as 'works including text, sounds and images, which are linked with each other by means of software on one medium (CD-Rom) with a view to being communicated simultaneously in an interactive manner'. *Ibid.*

[3] The Court considered these categories as being the closest ones to the multimedia work at issue.

11.1 A REGIME OF PROTECTION FOR MULTIMEDIA PRODUCTS: A MIXTURE OF THE REGIME FOR FILMS AND THE *SUI GENERIS* RIGHT FOR DATABASES

Multimedia products have successfully captured the international market.[4] They have managed to introduce new methods in education, information, trade, security and entertainment.[5] They have redefined the notion of communication. However, their economic growth and further success on the market requires rapid and efficient action as regards their legal status and protection.

Since multimedia products can be considered 'creative' works of the mind and since they do incorporate traditional types of works, such as images, text, sound, etc., copyright seems to be the appropriate means for their protection.[6]

This book has tried to show that the modern and more advanced version of multimedia works, otherwise known as the second generation of multimedia products, cannot always be adequately accommodated by the current copyright legislation either because we are confronted with cumulative qualifications or because we are faced with a legal gap (*vide juridique*) where no protection is suitable or available.[7] Their effective protection requires the introduction of new legislation,[8] which will preferably

---

[4] The multimedia market saw an exponential growth in terms of turnover in the first half of the 1990s. Various estimates are available, and whilst all of them show huge growth on average, one found that the figures for 1995 and 1996 ($12.5 to $17 billion) were between five and ten times higher than those for 1989 and 1992 ($1.2 to $3.2 billion). For further details see G. Vercken, *A practical guide to copyright for multimedia producers*, European Commission, DG XIII, 1996, at 16 ff. Other sources indicated that the growth in turnover was expected to continue and that by 1997 it may have reached $23.9 billion, excluding video games. See Interactive Multimedia Association (Annapolis, USA), as referred to by M. Radcliffe, 'Legal issues in new media technologies' (1995) 12 *Computer Lawyer* (no. 12), at 2.

[5] 'The CIA uses it for language training; InterOptica, for travel guides to foreign destinations; Sony, for a press release; Time magazine, for a history of the Desert Storm invasion; the state of California, for kiosks at which residents eventually will be able to pay traffic tickets and renew drivers' licenses; and the America Media Center in Denver, to provide information on cancer treatment to nonliterate people.' J. Eckhouse, 'Multimedia is electronics megatrend blend of art with high-tech promises to change the world', *San Francisco Chronicle*, 7 December 1992, at B1, available in Lexis, Nexis Library, Papers file.

[6] Since computer programs are protected by copyright, multimedia products, which are often more creative works, should be protected as well.

[7] Ginsburg alleges that in the USA a multimedia work may be considered as either an audiovisual work or a compilation or both. It is interesting to note that the USA does not seem to draw strict borderlines between the various categories of copyright works. J. Ginsburg, 'Domestic and international copyright issues implicated in the compilation of a multimedia product' (1995) 25 *Seton Hall Law Review* 1397, at 1399.

[8] Wei argues that 'for these reasons, it may be desirable to consider creating a new category of copyright subject-matter to specifically protect multimedia databases. The

have to draw upon the paradigms of two essential categories of copyright works, i.e. films and databases.[9] This legislation should provide for copyright protection, along the lines of films,[10] for those multimedia works that are creative as well as for *sui generis* protection, along the lines of databases, for those multimedia works that are not capable of attracting copyright protection in the first place.

The need to introduce a separate category of copyright works to accommodate multimedia products is dictated by the fact that multimedia products are 'different' from existing copyright works. What makes them different is the fact that the vast amounts of various expressions that are contained in a multimedia product are integrated. Integration is made possible because of digitisation. However, integration rather than digitisation is the key concept, because 'the digitisation of works does not originate a new kind of object of protection – it rather transforms the well-known kind of literary works, musical works and the like into a new format, into a binary, machine-readable code. This is in principle not unusual for copyright; the recording of musical works onto tapes and the transformation of sound into magnetic signals generated thereby is a famous example.'[11] Although various expressions were combined in the

> advantages of such an approach include the following points:
>> Direct protection is given to the efforts of the multimedia database producer in selecting the material for compilation into the multimedia application.
>> It will not be necessary to stretch existing copyright categories to cover what is essentially a new media for presentation of information.
>> It will more easily enable policy makers to determine the scope of the protection, including available defences, without affecting established copyright principles for existing categories of copyright subject-matter.
>> It will more easily enable policy makers to tailor the new category to suit the needs of the industry and the public at large. For example, it may be thought desirable that any new multimedia copyright category should place primary emphasis on protecting the investment of the "entrepreneur" behind the development of a multimedia package. That being so, the copyright in "multimedia works" may more appropriately be conferred on the person who made the arrangements to produce the multimedia work rather than on the "author" of the multimedia work. Other specific issues such as the question of whether networking rights are to be conferred in respect of multimedia works could also be addressed.'

G. Wei, 'Multimedia and intellectual and industrial property rights in Singapore' (1995) 3 *IJLIT* 214, at 244–5.

[9] As discussed in previous chapters, the introduction of legal rules is dictated by the needs of the market, i.e. when the balance between innovation–production–consumption is not the right one.

[10] With various adaptations, though.

[11] U. Loewenheim, 'Multimedia and the European copyright law' (1996) 27 *IIC* 41, at 44. There seems to be a lot of exaggeration when the issue of digitisation is discussed. Digitisation does not transform a work. A literary work remains a literary work and a musical work remains a musical work. However, digitisation enables certain things to happen, such as easy copying and manipulation of works.

Conclusions

past in an analogue environment, there was never integration, or at least, not to the extent that a result was produced that was substantially (qualitatively) different from the elements initially combined. It is integration and interactivity, provided by a software tool, which form the added value of a multimedia product. This added value[12] renders multimedia works a new species of work.

At an earlier stage we reached the conclusion that multimedia works have certain features in common with films, especially as regards their looks and process of creation. We have, however, explained in chapter 6 that these apparent similarities cannot take us as far as allowing a multimedia work to qualify as a film and applying *per se* the corresponding regime of protection.[13] Since the regime of protection for films seems to take into account the audiovisual effects of films, the investment of the producer and the creative role of the editor, these are also features that can be used in the context of the protection of a multimedia work.

In an ideal regime of protection for multimedia works, the publisher/producer and the editor of the multimedia work play a very important, if not the most important, role in the realisation of the project. The publisher conceives the idea and sinks the necessary investments into it, whilst the editor undertakes to create the final image of the product. If one takes into account how multimedia works are produced today, one realises that investment can be as significant as creation, and creation is heavily assisted by teamwork, whilst aided by information technology and software tools that again require substantial sums of money. From this point of view, both the producer of the multimedia work and the editor should be vested with the necessary rights in order for the former to recoup his investment and the latter to be compensated for his creative labour. If the UK model on films is to be followed both the publisher and the editor of a multimedia work should be afforded authorship. In a continental context, where only natural persons can qualify as authors, the editor should be the author and the first owner of the rights in the work. At a second stage, by the operation of the law and by reason of a legal presumption, these rights should be automatically transferred to the publisher. Of course, the moral rights will remain with the editor.

Since multimedia products are to be protected by copyright the same exclusive rights that are afforded to the authors of any copyright work will also be afforded to the author or authors of multimedia products. It

---

[12] See also the strong views expressed by M. Scott, 'Pre-existing content: the "emperor's new clothes" of the multimedia "kingdom". "It's the content, stupid!"' [1995] 11 *Computer Law and Security Report* 255.

[13] Unless, of course, the particular multimedia product possesses all the characteristics of a film.

is interesting to note though that the new WIPO treaties make it clear that the temporary reproduction of a work also comes within the scope of the right of reproduction. In that sense a wider right of reproduction is afforded to authors, but it might need to be accompanied by a limited set of exceptions.[14] In the light of this, private copying should not be allowed,[15] whilst the fair dealing provisions might have to be limited significantly in the future.[16] However, the issues just mentioned do not relate particularly to multimedia products. They are considerations relating to all digitised works and will have to be the subject of separate scrutiny by the international and EU working parties in this area.[17]

The existing moral rights provisions do not seem to create insurmountable problems. However, in an ideal regime of protection the UK provisions on moral rights might prove to fall foul of the effective protection of the works in the digital era. It is also interesting to note that even entrepreneurs are favourable towards a revision of the moral rights provisions in view of the tremendous opportunities of manipulation that digital technology provides.[18] Perhaps this time both entrepreneurs and authors will find themselves working on the same side. Possible changes in the UK law might need to take place as regards the provisions on waivability. Waivers might need to be restricted along the lines of the 1994 Belgian Copyright Act where waivability is allowed only in relation to specifically designated acts as regards existing works only and never by means of a blanket waiver. On the other hand, France and countries that

---

[14] It is at least arguably the case that 'rights and exceptions are intertwined; if the scope of rights increases, exceptions must be widened accordingly'. 'The EC Legal Advisory Board's reply to the Green Paper on Copyright and Related Rights in the Information Society' [1996] 12 *Computer Law and Security Report* 143, at 147. See also in this respect the Commission's amended proposal for a European Parliament and Council Directive on the harmonisation of certain aspects of copyright and related rights in the information society, available on-line at http://www.europa.eu.int.

[15] In the same way it is not allowed in relation to electronic databases. See art. 6.2(a) of the database Directive, [1996] OJ L77/20.

[16] See in this respect the provisions on exceptions to restricted acts in the WIPO treaties. See also J. Cohen's comments on the future of the fair use exception in the USA in 'WIPO Treaty implementation in the United States: will fair use survive?' [1999] 5 *EIPR* 236; J. Goldberg, 'Now that the future has arrived, maybe the law should take a look: multimedia technology and its interaction with the fair use doctrine' (1995) 44 *American University Law Review* 919.

[17] It is interesting to note that the notion of 'public' in the context of public performance, display or transmission has also taken on a wider meaning since it includes transmission into the private sphere of a person, i.e. on his computer at his home as long as he is a subscriber to that service or that service is made available to a considerable number of persons.

[18] Producers might persuade authors to use their moral rights protection in order to block unauthorised use of their works if the producers themselves have already transferred the economic rights in the work.

follow its paradigm might need to reconsider the sustaining of certain of their moral rights provisions, such as the right of withdrawal and the lack of any provisions on waivability, which place unnecessary constraints on the publishers of multimedia works. This might be especially so given the fact that multimedia works are derivative works being often based on adaptations of pre-existing works.

Apart from copyright protection, there should also be a provision for *sui generis* protection along the lines of databases. Copyright and *sui generis* protection should not be given cumulatively, since, as we discussed in chapter 10, they seem to amount to the same thing (i.e. they would grant a right of reproduction twice) in view of the inability to assess the originality of a multimedia work on the merits of the selection and arrangement of its content. In cases where multimedia products will not attract copyright protection but substantial investments are made for their realisation, they should not fall prey to potential infringers. This role can be undertaken by a *sui generis* right which in reality will be a form of limited unfair competition law protection. Makers of 'unoriginal' multimedia products that required a qualitatively and/or quantitatively substantial investment for their realisation will be given the exclusive right to prevent extraction and/or re-utilisation of the whole or of a substantial part of their product for five years.

No special provisions for compulsory licensing should be introduced. Compulsory licensing seems to contradict the principles of copyright, especially in those countries that hold a strong attitude towards the work as being an extension of the author's personality. In that sense, compulsory licensing would undermine the provisions on moral rights protection. In any case, the traditional provisions on competition law can put right those situations that go beyond the boundaries of a well-intended copyright and abuse its rights. *Magill* forms a characteristic example in this respect.

Authors should also be given the choice between individual and collective administration of their rights. However, there has to be a platform for collective administration for those that opt for such a system, preferably along the lines of the model of central administration of copyrights, as described in chapter 10. Initiatives on central globalised systems of one-stop shops should be encouraged and brought to completion sooner rather than later in order to facilitate clearance of rights and boost production further.

The task of clearance of rights can also be assisted by technical devices. In any case, technical protection devices should be introduced and perhaps imposed in order to assist the law to track down trespassers and prevent unauthorised copying. In the same context, copying devices that circumvent the law might need to be outlawed along the lines of article 7 of the software Directive.[19]

What, however, has been prevalent in our discussions so far is the international character of multimedia products and the fact that the problems they present are necessarily problems felt almost round the globe. National solutions in the area of multimedia can bring only a limited benefit to the nationals of that state or to the products marketed therein but will definitely not solve the multimedia issue within the EU.[20] It is also apparent that multimedia products may qualify as different things in different countries. That, of course, is bound to cause confusion and uncertainty on the market. It goes without saying that a harmonised approach on the issue would form the most effective solution regarding also the impact that multimedia works have in the Single Market. It is also submitted that the effects of intellectual property in the Single Market, because of its increasing significance, are such that even those areas that were traditionally left to the Member States' discretion, such as moral rights, compulsory licensing, technical devices and collective administration, should also be considered carefully and a harmonised position should be envisaged. New technology creations are no longer problems on a national scale. Their international marketing and subsequently their impact therefrom dictates action at a European, if not at an international level.[21] Obviously, a global solution is to be preferred, but if such a solution cannot be achieved, an EU solution will be a good second-best alternative.

11.2 WIDER IMPLICATIONS FOR COPYRIGHT

Although in the past copyright has managed to cope with technical and economic evolution, and has as a result been able to incorporate new categories of works, such as broadcasts, films, computer programs and so on, within its scope of protection, multimedia products represent a challenge to it like no other work ever before. The question of incorporating

---

[19] Art. 7.1(c): '... Member States shall provide, in accordance with their national legislation, appropriate remedies against a person committing... any act of putting into circulation, or the possession for commercial purposes of, any means the sole intended purpose of which is to facilitate the unauthorised removal or circumvention of any technical device which may have been applied to protect a computer program', EC software Directive, [1991] OJ L122/42. See also art. 11 WCT and art. 18 WPPT.

[20] 75 per cent of CD-ROMs are marketed on an international basis from their initial release. D. Werbner, 'The multimedia environment: the broadcasters' perspective' in C. Van Rij and H. Best, *Moral rights*, reports presented at the meeting of the International Association of Entertainment Lawyers, MIDEM 1995, Cannes, MAKLU Publishers, Apeldoon, Antwerp, 1995, 225, at 236.

[21] It is easier to reach a solution at EU level than at a national level since most Member States are not prepared to depart from their traditional views on copyright. But even if they did so, disparities would be created which would be difficult to reconcile in the future when there is likely to be a need for harmonisation.

multimedia within its scope of protection is not only a question of adaptation for copyright. It is more a question of *change* that started modestly with the inclusion of computer programs. It is that question that puts under close scrutiny and revision copyright's primary principles and rationale (*raison d'être*) and might perhaps lead to the redefinition of the notions of authorship, creation, moral rights and so on. Changes in copyright at that stage are not only of a quantitative but also of a qualitative nature. It is felt that copyright is somehow reconceptualised.

The changes so far are the result of four essential trends in the area. First, works are no longer created according to the traditional process whereby a sole author, usually lacking financial means, was trying to put on a piece of paper or on a canvas the expression of his personal ideas and ideals. Today the creation of a work resembles more an industrial activity. Many works are commissioned, put together by a number of 'experts' in various areas, require huge investments, and their creation is aided by information and software tools. Second, 'original creation' increasingly loses ground as new works are largely based on pre-existing materials that are either reconstructed or adapted in order to achieve a new result. Third, the incentive for the creation of a work is no longer the author's personal desire and inspiration but there are commercial and market needs that also dictate the final content and outcome of the work. Lastly, the increasing provision of on-line services and the digitisation of the various expressions has dematerialised the notion of a work. The work is distinguished and separated from its material support.

The results of this new reality can be summarised as follows:

In relation to the first trend,

- Works today increasingly resemble products and occasionally they can be bundled together with 'copper, soya beans and livestock'.[22]
- Creations are replaced by technical, utilitarian and functional works that are also used as tools for the further creation of new productions.
- As authors are increasingly replaced by producers, the weight of originality is accordingly replaced by the weight of investment.[23] Sources

---

[22] T. Dreier, 'Authorship and new technologies from the viewpoint of civil law traditions' (1995) 26 *IIC* 989, at 998.

[23] At EU level some radically new rights have been introduced that show clearly the shift towards a more entrepreneurial approach. These rights are (1) the right of protection of previously unpublished works. 'Any person who, after the expiry of copyright protection, for the first time lawfully publishes or lawfully communicates to the public a previously unpublished work, shall benefit from a protection equivalent to the economic rights of the author. The term of protection of such rights shall be 25 years from the time when the work was first lawfully published or lawfully communicated to the public' (art. 4 of the EC term Directive, [1993] OJ L290/9). (2) The right of protection for critical and scientific publications. 'Member States may protect critical and

capable of providing this investment are no longer poor natural persons but rather multi-billion multinational undertakings.
- Moral rights protection loses its significance when alienated from the notion of the traditional author and either becomes irrelevant or is used as a tool to increase financial gain.
- The more investment is rewarded the less copyright is needed to perform its traditional functions.
- Neighbouring and *sui generis* rights seem to replace copyright in those areas where originality is absent. However, the limitation of copyright signifies a shift from property rights to unfair competition law.

In relation to the second trend,

- Works that are increasingly the result of teamwork render authors contributors.
- Copyright protection is shifted from original works to compilations, databases and derivative works. That is perhaps the most important alienation of copyright.
- The notion of authorisation solely on the part of the author without other criteria being taken into account weakens in view of potential compulsory licensing, collective administration and competition law considerations.
- The increasing need for the introduction of collective administration of intellectual property rights schemes and the fact that copyright can only be enforced with difficulty in the digital era turn copyright into a right of authoring against a fee, diminishing substantially the value of moral rights protection.
- The role of moral rights is redefined by including both the need of authors to protect their personal interests in the work and the public's need to ensure that what it receives on its screens is the authoritative version of the author's original work.[24]

scientific publications of works which have come into the public domain. The maximum term of protection of such rights shall be 30 years from the time when the publication was first published' (art. 5 of the same Directive). And (3) the *sui generis* right for databases (art. 7 of the EU database Directive). See also M. Vivant, 'L'incidence de l'harmonisation communautaire en matière de droits d'auteur sur le multimédia', European Commission, DG XIII, Brussels, Luxembourg, 1995 (vol. 3, Copyright on electronic delivery services and multimedia products series, EUR 16068 FR), at 33–4.

[24] 'In the future moral rights will be less about straightforward waiver and more about the appropriate payment to the author in compensation for new derivative products which use content from the original program ... An indication that moral rights are merging into the economic arena is that collecting societies normally solely licensed to represent copyright interests have in certain circumstances purported to represent an author's moral rights. If these rights are purely personal then a third party should not be able to represent the author's interests.' Werbner, 'Multimedia environment', at 230.

In relation to the third trend,

- Creations are made to be user-friendly and consumer-attractive. Originality is based on financial considerations and it reflects the market needs rather than the personality of the author.
- The content of the work is approached as data rather than original creations.[25] Original creations are losing ground to information.
- In the light of the above, any balance of interests between the author and the public might need to be reconsidered.[26] Extensive protection of information is likely to impede the public's right for access to information unjustifiably.[27]
- In the main, considerations on monopolies and joint ventures come more easily into play by reason of the significance of the content of the works in which there is copyright protection. Information can also be blocked more easily because of the granting of exclusive rights in new creations.[28]

In relation to the fourth trend,

- Information is valuable *per se* and is distinguished from the medium on which it is carried.[29]

---

[25] The traditional classification of works in work categories is losing some of its former significance in the multimedia environment. They are all stored in the same bitmap file, forming part of a homogeneous product, where distinction between different work categories seems to make little sense. Loewenheim, 'Multimedia' (*IIC*), at 45.

[26] Any new legislation has first of all to be flexible enough to accommodate the interests of the parties involved and all future technological developments in the area. The basic interest groups involved are (1) the deviser(s) of the product, (2) the competitors, (3) the consumers, (4) the general public and (5) the interests of the developing world. M. Pendleton, 'Intellectual property, information-based society and a new international economic order – the policy options?' [1985] 2 *EIPR* 31, at 32.

[27] The balance in the triptych innovation–production–consumption might need to be reconsidered.

[28] An example in this respect is the First Cities Group of twelve multimedia companies which include Apple, Bellcore, Kodak, Daleida and Tandem among others. See also Bell Atlantic's attempted merger with Tele-Communications Inc., AT&T's proposed acquisition of McCaw Cellular Communications Inc., the deal between QVC and the Home Shopping Network, and Viacom's victory over QVC ending a controversial bidding war for Paramount Communications. J. Choe, 'Interactive multimedia: a new technology tests the limits of copyright law' (1994) 46 *Rutgers Law Review* 929, at 937–8. Interesting also in this respect will be the results of the intended joint venture between BT and AT&T.

[29] This separation is made possible because of digitisation. Digitisation can arguably be considered as a fifth trend which enables easy copying and manipulation of works, leads to difficulties in distinguishing between the various categories of works and abolishes any physical constraints of time and space. However, in reality digitisation is a tool that gives rise to quantitative rather than qualitative changes. See the reference to P. Samuelson's list of characteristics of digitally based works in G. Davis III, 'The digital dilemma: coping with copyright in a digital world' [1993] 27 *Copyright World* 18, at

- Manipulation is easier since the potential hurdles that material supports set are removed.
- The right of reproduction has been widened in order to include temporary copies and on-line transmission of works.[30]
- The notion of 'public' has been stretched to include even communication to private parties as long, of course, as these parties form part of a wider abstract 'public'.[31]

The current role of copyright is restricted in the digital era as regards the protection of authors and its emphasis is shifted to the protection of works and investors. A more entrepreneurial approach is followed. This shift is bound to be felt more strongly on the continent than in the UK, since the latter has, right from the start, regarded intellectual property rights as proprietary rights and has given priority to economic considerations.

This shift also signifies a move towards narrowing the gap between the civil law and the common law traditions.[32] Member States may feel reluctant to make that move since it will impinge on well-established traditional principles in copyright. Analogy is always an option, though a poor one. What might perhaps assist this move is the introduction of harmonised legislation at either EU or international level.[33] It is also easier for the EU to introduce new legislation since it is in the process of doing so in order to harmonise essential aspects of copyright. The EU

19–20: '(1) Ease of copying or capturing the data from any work, (2) ease of distribution or transmission of the captured idea, (3) ease of manipulation or editing the captured data, (4) ease of storage of the data because of digital compaction, (5) ease of searching and linking of such digital data and (6) equivalence of digital works creates classification problems under the copyright laws, which laws provide different rights for different types of works and media.'

[30] For example, 'browsing' is also included. See art. 7 WCT and M. Ficsor, 'The spring 1997 Horace S. Manges Lecture – copyright for the digital era: the WIPO "Internet" Treaties' (1997) 21 *Columbia – VLA of Law and the Arts Journal* 197, at 203.

[31] This includes the phenomena of 'pay-per-view', 'pay-on-demand', etc. Public communication traditionally means communication to a large number of people at the same time. It is also important to note that, as Christie points out, 'with the advent of communications networking, transmission of data is no longer limited to that which occurs on a one-to-one basis (as is the case with standard telephone communication) or on a one-to-many basis (which is "broadcasting"). The networking of communications facilities allows transmission of data on a many-to-many basis, or indeed on an all-to-all basis': A. Christie, 'Reconceptualising copyright in the digital era' [1995] 11 *EIPR* 522, at 523.

[32] 'Copyright systems would give up the search for a human author much earlier and grant protection to the producer responsible for the investment made much faster, than any of the *droit d'auteur* systems': Dreier, 'Authorship and new technologies', at 996.

[33] See the views of R. Sherwood, 'Why a uniform intellectual property system makes sense for the world' in M. Wallerstein, M. Mogee and R. Schoen (eds.), *Global dimensions of intellectual property rights in science and technology*, National Academy Press, Washington D.C., 1993, at 68.

Conclusions

originality criterion is a characteristic example of the reconciliation of the two traditions.

In an era of globalisation of communication and trade, any attempt to introduce national intellectual property solutions severely disregards the new reality and loses sight of the precise scope of the problems that are emerging. National solutions can serve only as stopgap solutions. Especially in the light of the Internet and other on-line services, the interests of the authors are necessarily their interests around the globe. A coherent copyright approach needs to have both an international impact and a harmonised 'international copyright' as its principal aim. Such an 'international copyright' will necessarily be inspired by national practices, but it has to go way beyond these practices to achieve its aim. As Ginsburg put it in her paper on the 'Role of national copyright in an era of international copyright norms' at the 1999 ALAI Conference in Berlin,[34]

> 'International copyright' can no longer accurately be described as a 'bundle' consisting of many separate sticks, each representing a distinct national law, tied together by a thin ribbon of Berne Convention supranational norms. Today's international copyright more closely resembles a giant squid, whose many national law tentacles emanate from but depend on a large common body of international norms. (At the risk of excessively pursuing this molluskular metaphor, I would further note that the squid's body houses its ink; since we all know what happens when a squid releases its ink, we shall hope that this does not foretell an obscure future for international norms.)

The introduction of an 'international copyright' will not be enough to solve all our problems though. Common law and continental law traditions will still keep some of their particularities. Or, as the Chinese say in relation to Hong Kong, 'one law two systems'. Arguably these variations will not go so far as to jeopardise international trade in intellectual property and create uncertainty as to the status of the same author in various countries. For example, works that are put on the Internet have to be legitimate or illegitimate throughout the whole geographical sphere in which they are received. And for clearance of rights to be facilitated, they consistently have to be films or databases in every country, etc. In this respect 'harmonisation' seems to be the magic word and the one inviting us to look into what can bring us together instead of what takes us apart.

---

[34] ALAI Conference on 'Enforcement of copyright. The role of national legislation in copyright law', Berlin, 16–19 June 1999, ALAI, Munich, 2000.

Postscript

Looking into multimedia is in fact like looking into the basic notions and principles of copyright.

The fact that copyright has recently undergone a process of change does not necessarily imply that it has been either invalidated or diminished in significance. It rather means that it is in the process of being transformed and therefore adaptations might need to be more radical than before.

In order for one to deal with potential new legislation on multimedia, one has necessarily to look back and base this new legislation on existing provisions in relevant areas. In that sense our legal past is both valuable and indispensable for the future. However, depending on the past does not necessarily mean that one should not look to the future. The future, however, brings with it bewilderment and confusion. It represents the threat (and challenge at the same time) of the unknown and the new. Once one has to depart from long and well-established principles for something new one feels rather uncomfortable. Yet, the ultimate role of law is to catch up with the developments in society if not to transform society itself. Law is there to serve people and their needs and both people and their needs are subject to development. In that sense the law needs to be revised if it is to survive the test of time.

It is in relation to multimedia that copyright is called upon now to pass the test of time.

By the time this book reaches its audience technology might have progressed further and the technological basis of my legal thoughts might already be outdated. But if that were not true for many areas of law then legal research would find no reason for its existence. 'For last year's words belong to last year's language, and next year's words await another voice' (T. S. Eliot, 'Little Gidding', in *Four Quartets*, 1944, 35, 39).

Bibliography

ACM, Proceedings, *ACM Multimedia 96*, Boston, Mass., 18–22 November 1996

Adams, J., R. Brownsword and D. Beyleveld, 'Privity of contract – the benefits and burdens of law reform' [1997] *MLR* 238

AFTEL, *Le droit du multimédia: de la télématique à Internet*, Les Editions du Téléphone, Paris, 1996

Agnola, M., *Passeport pour le multimédia*, CFPJ, 1996

ALAI, *Le droit moral de l'auteur / The moral right of the author*, Antwerp Congress, 19–24 September 1993, ALAI, Paris, 1995

  Audiovisual works and literary and artistic property, ALAI, Paris, 1995

  Copyright in cyberspace, Otto Cramwinckel, Amsterdam, 1996

  Protection of authors and performers through contracts, Les Editions Yvon Blais, Paris, 1998

Alben, A., 'What is an on-line service? (In the eyes of the law)' (1996) 13 *Computer Lawyer* 1

Anderman, S., *EC competition law and intellectual property rights*, Clarendon Press, Oxford, 1998

Aplin, T., 'Not in our galaxy: why "film" won't rescue multimedia' [1999] *EIPR* 633

Appleton, J. and R. Hart, 'Comments on the EC Green Paper on copyright and the challenge of technology' [1988] 10 *EIPR* 287

Armitage, E., 'The changing face of intellectual property' [1987] 7 *EIPR* 191

van Arsdale, C., 'Needs and problems of multimedia producers' in K. Hill and L. Morse (eds.), *Emerging technologies and intellectual property: multimedia, biotechnology and other issues*, Atrip and Casrip Publication Series, Washington D.C., 1996 (No. 2), 26

ASLIB, *Copyright in multimedia (conference papers)*, ASLIB, London, 1995

Australian Copyright Law Review Committee, *Final report on computer software protection*, Attorney-General's Department, Canberra, April 1995

  Simplification of the Copyright Act 1968, Part 2: Categorisation of subject-matter and exclusive rights, and other issues, AGPS, Canberra, 1999

Band, J. and L. McDonald, 'The proposed EC database directive: the "reversal" of *Feist* v *Rural Telephone* (111 S. Ct. 1282 (1991))' (1992) 9 *Computer Lawyer* 19

Banki, P., *Multimedia and copyright in business*, BLEC Books, Melbourne, 1995

Bard, R. and L. Kurlantzick, *Copyright duration: duration, term extension, the European Union, and the making of copyright policy*, Austin & Winfield, San Francisco, London, Bethesda, 1999

Barendt, E. (gen. ed.), *The yearbook of media and entertainment law 1995*, Clarendon Press, Oxford, 1995

Barlas, C., 'The IMPRIMATUR project' in ASLIB, *Copyright in multimedia (conference papers)*, ASLIB, London, 1995

Barrington, L. (ed.), *New technologies: their influence on international audiovisual law*, ICC Dossiers, Paris, 1994

Barrow, E., 'Licensing towards solutions' in ASLIB, *Copyright in multimedia (conference papers)*, ASLIB, London, 1995

Barton, J., 'Adapting the intellectual property system to new technologies' in M. Wallerstein, M. Mogee and R. Schoen (eds.), *Global dimensions of intellectual property rights in science and technology*, National Academy Press, Washington D.C., 1993, 256

Battcock, R., 'Data protection: where next?' (1995) 3 *International Journal of Law and Information Technology* 156

Battersby, G. and C. Grimes, *A primer on technology licensing*, Kent Press, Stamford, Conn., 1996

Bechtold, S., 'Multimedia und Urheberrecht – einige grundsätzliche Anmerkungen' [1998] 1 *GRUR* 18

Beck, H., 'Copyright protection for compilations and databases after Feist (*Feist Publications, Inc. v. Rural Telephone Service Co., Inc.*, 111 S. Ct. 1282)' (1991) 8 *Computer Lawyer* 1

Benabou, V., *Droits d'auteur, droits voisins et droit communautaire*, Bruylant, Brussels, 1997

Bennet, S., 'Copyright and intellectual property – portions of video games may constitute protected property' (1983) 66 *Marquette Law Review* 817

Bently, L. and R. Burrell, 'Copyright and the information society in Europe: a matter of timing as well as content' (1997) 34 *CML Rev* 1197

Bercovitz, A., 'La titularité des droits de propriété intellectuelle relatifs aux oeuvres audiovisuelles: le plan législatif' in Congrès de L'ALAI, *Audiovisual works and literary and artistic property*, ALAI, Paris, 1995, 204

'Vermögensrechte in den Informationsautobahnen' [1996] 10 *GRUR Int* 1010

Berenboom, A., *Le nouveau droit d'auteur et les droits voisins*, Larcier, Paris, 1995

Berkvens, J., 'Data regulation in copyright law: will the problem of software ever be solved?' [1993] 3 *EIPR* 79

Berlins, M., 'The image brokers' (1997) *HotAir* 15 (February) (Virgin Atlantic's inflight magazine)

Berman, A., 'Into the great wide open: performance licenses on the Internet', http://www.degrees.com/melon/archive/101/into.html

'Picture this: the licensing of graphic art images for an enhanced CD', http://www.degrees.com/melon/archive/205/pictures.html

Bertrand, A., 'La protection des jeux video', *Expertises* 1983, no. 56

Le droit d'auteur et les droits voisins, Masson, Paris, 1991

Besek, J., 'Copyright law and multimedia works: initiatives to change national laws and international treaties to better accommodate works of new technologies' in M. Radcliffe and W. Tannenbaum, *Multimedia and the law 1996. Protecting your clients' interests*, Practicing Law Institute, New York, 1996, 69

Beutler, S., 'The protection of multimedia products through the European Community's Directive on the legal protection of databases' [1996] 8 *Ent LR* 317

Bicknell, M., 'Direct to home satellite television: the digital era' in L. Barrington (ed.), *New technologies: their influence on international audiovisual law*, ICC Dossiers, Paris, 1994, 15

Birch, D. and P. Buck, 'What is cyberspace?' [1992] 8 *Computer Law and Security Report* 74

Bitan, H., 'Les rapports de force entre la technologie du multimédia et le droit' [1996] *Gaz Pal* (26 January 1996) 12

Bizer, J., V. Hammer, U. Pordesch and A. Rossnagel, 'Entwurf gesetzlicher Regelungen zum Datenschutz und zur Rechtssicherheit in Online-Multimedia-Anwendungen', Opinion prepared for the Bundesministerium für Bildung, Wissenschaft, Forschung und Technologie, 1996, http://www.uni-muester.de/jura.itm.hoeren/materialen/njw.pdf

'Entwurf gesetzlicher Regelungen zum Datenschutz und zur Rechtssicherheit in Online-Multimedia-Anwendungen – Gesetzesbegründung', Provet – Publikationen (available on the Internet)

Blakemore, F., 'The economic importance of multimedia' in ASLIB, *Copyright in multimedia (conference papers)*, ASLIB, London, 1995

Blumberg, D. 'Assessment of the legal issues and conflicts in the information technology service market' (1992) 9 *Computer Lawyer* 14

Blume, P., 'Practical data protection' (1994) 2 *International Journal of Law and Information Technology* 194

Boyle, J., 'Aspects contractuels relatifs à l'informatisation' in *Droit de l'informatique, enjeux, nouvelles responsabilités*, Jeune Barreau, Paris, 1993

Brennan, L., 'International copyright conflicts' (1995) 17 *Whittier Law Review* 203

Brenner, D., 'In search of the multimedia grail' (1994) 47 *Federal Communications Law Journal* 197

Brinson, D. and M. Radcliffe, *Multimedia law handbook. A practical guide for developers and publishers*, Ladera Press, California, 1994

Multimedia law and business handbook, Ladera Press, California, 1996

British Copyright Council, 'Submission of the British Copyright Council to the Commission of the European Communities concerning the issues raised by digital technology in the field of copyright and related rights' [1995] 11 *Computer Law and Security Report* 115 and [1996] 1 *EIPR* 52

Brown, R., 'Copyright and computer databases: the case of the bibliographical utility' (1985) 20 *Rutgers Computer and Technology Law Journal* 17

Brueckmann, W., 'Intellectual property protection in the European Community' in F. Rushing and C. Ganz Brown (eds.), *Intellectual property rights in science, technology, and economic performance*, Westview Press, Boulder, San Francisco, London, 1990

Bull, G., 'Hard and soft machines' [1993] 9 *Computer Law and Security Report* 149

Bullinger, M. and E.-J. Mestmäcker, 'Multimediadienste – Aufgabe und Zuständigkeit von Bund und Ländern – Rechtsgutachten', Opinion prepared for the Bundesministerium für Bildung, Wissenschaft, Forschung und Technologie, 1996, http://www.pitt.edu/~wwwes/teu.mspr-ge-b.html

Burk, D., 'Trade marks along the Infobahn: a first look at the emerging law of cybermarks' (10 April 1995) *Richmond Journal of Law and Technology* (available on the Internet)

Burr, J., 'Competition policy and intellectual property in the information age' (1996) 41 *Villanova Law Review* 193

Caden, M. and S. Lucas, 'Accidents on the information superhighway: on-line liability and regulation' (13 February 1996) *Richmond Journal of Law and Technology* (available on the Internet)

Cameron, J., 'Approaches to the problems of multimedia' [1996] 3 *EIPR* 115

Campbell, C. *Data processing and the law*, Sweet & Maxwell, London, 1984

Campbell, D. and S. Cotter (eds.), *International intellectual property law. New developments*, J. Wiley & Sons, Chichester, 1995

Caron, C., *Abus de droit et droit d'auteur*, Litec, Paris, 1998

Carr, H. and R. Arnold, *Computer software: legal protection in the UK*, 2nd edn, Sweet & Maxwell, London, 1992

Castell, S., 'Computers trusted, and found wanting' [1993] 9 *Computer Law and Security Report* 155

Cerina, P., 'The originality requirement in the protection of databases in Europe and the United States' (1993) 24 *IIC* 579

Chafee, Z., 'Reflexions on the law of copyright: I' (1945) 45 *Col LR* 503
'Reflexions on the law of copyright: II' (1945) 45 *Col LR* 719

Chalton, S., 'The criterion of originality for copyright in computer programs and databases: a galloping trojan horse', [1993] 9 *Computer Law and Security Report* 167
'The amended database Directive proposal: a commentary and synopsis' [1994] 3 *EIPR* 94
'The legal protection of databases in Europe: the common position on the proposal for a directive' [1995] 11 *Computer Law and Security Report* 295
'The effect of the EC database Directive on United Kingdom copyright law in relation to databases: a comparison of features' [1997] 6 *EIPR* 278

Choe, J., 'Interactive multimedia: a new technology tests the limits of copyright law' (1994) 46 *Rutgers Law Review* 929

Christie, A., 'Reconceptualising copyright in the digital era' [1995] 11 *EIPR* 522

Christie, A. and K. Fong, 'Copyright protection for non-code elements of software' (1996) 6 *Journal of Law and Information Science* 149

CITED (Copyright in Transmitted Electronic Documents) Final Report, CITED Consortium, London, 1994

Clark, C. 'The copyright environment for the publisher in the digital world' in *WIPO Worldwide Symposium on the Future of Copyright and Neighbouring Rights*, Louvre, Paris, 1994
'An investigation of current practice with contractual arrangements and copyright clearing services', Commission of the European Communities, Brussels

and Luxembourg, 1995 (vol. 2, *Copyright on electronic delivery services and multimedia products* series, EUR 16067 EN)

'Publishers and publishing in the digital era' in *WIPO Worldwide Symposium on Copyright in the Global Information Infrastructure*, Mexico City, 22–24 May 1995, 342

'The answer to the machine is the machine' in B. Hugenholtz (ed.), *The future of copyright in a digital environment*, Kluwer Law International, The Hague, London, Boston, 1996, 139

Clark, C. and T. Koshinen-Olsson, 'New alternatives for centralised management: "one-stop shops"' in *WIPO international forum on the exercise and management of copyright and neighbouring rights in the face of the challenges of digital technology*, Seville, 14–16 May 1997, WIPO, 1998, 227

Claverie, A., 'Minutes', paper presented at the European Commission Legal Advisory Board Conference on the Information Society: Copyright and Multimedia, Luxembourg, 26 April 1995

Clifford, R., 'Intellectual property in the era of the creative computer program: will the true creator please stand up?' (1997) 71 *Tulane Law Review* 1675

de Cock Buning, M. and J. Haeck, 'Colloquium discussions' in P. Hugenholtz (ed.), *The future of copyright in a digital environment*, Kluwer Law International, The Hague, London, Boston, 1996, 221

Cohen, B., 'A proposed regime for copyright protection on the Internet' (1996) 22 *Brooklyn Journal of International Law* 401

Cohen, J., 'A right to read anonymously: a closer look at "copyright management" in cyberspace' (1996) 28 *Connecticut Law Review* 981

'WIPO Treaty implementation in the United States: will fair use survive?' [1999] 5 *EIPR* 236

Colombet, C., *Grands principes du droit d'auteur et les droits voisins dans le monde, approche de droit comparé*, 2nd edn, Litec, Paris, 1992

Commission of the European Communities, 'Statement accompanying the Green Paper on copyright and related rights in the information society' [1995] 11 *Computer Law and Security Report* 331

Commission of the European Communities (DG XIII), 'Strategic developments for the European publishing industry towards the year 2000: Europe's multimedia challenge', http://www.europa.eu.int

Common Law Institute of Intellectual Property, *Databases: the EC's latest proposals*, Seminar Report, London, 20 January 1994

Conley, J., 'Editorial' (1997) 6 *Information and Communications Technology Law* 99

Conley, J. and K. Bemelmans, 'Intellectual property implications of multimedia products: a case study' (1997) 6 *Information and Communications Technology Law* 3

Cook, F., 'How to choose a good multimedia lawyer' in L. Barrington (ed.), *New technologies: their influence on international audiovisual law*, ICC Dossiers, Paris, 1994, 65

Cook, T., 'The current status of the EC database Directive' [1995] 52 *Copyright World* 27

Cookson, B., 'The progress of European harmonisation' [1997] 8 *EIPR* 462
Cooper, J., 'Moral rights in the United States and multimedia contractual issues' in L. Barrington (ed.), *New technologies: their influence on international audiovisual law*, ICC Dossiers, Paris, 1994, 93
  'Licensing and cross-licensing of characters, names and persons in the multimedia context: publicity, contract rights, descendability, scope of rights, clearances', paper delivered at the conference on 'Making international multimedia deals in the interactive age', Cannes, 21–22 May 1995
Copyright Symposium, 'Copyright protection for computer databases, CD-ROMs and factual compilations' (1992) 17 *University of Dayton Law Review* 323
Corbet, J., *Auteursrecht*, Story – Scientia, Brussels, 1997
Cornish, W., '1996 European Community Directive on database protection' (1996) 21 *Columbia – VLA of Law and the Arts Journal* 1
  'Protecting databases: the EC Directive' based on the General Report for Netherlands National Group of ALAI, Amsterdam Conference, 5–8 June 1996, paper supplied by the author
  'Protection of and vis-à-vis databases' in ALAI, *Copyright in cyberspace*, Otto Cramwinckel, Amsterdam, 1996, 435
  Intellectual property: patents, copyright, trade marks and allied rights, 4th edn, Sweet & Maxwell, London, 1999
Cross, J., 'Revisiting the "shrinkwrap license": *ProCD Inc.* v *Zeidenberg*' (1997) 6 *Information and Communications Technology Law* 71
Crowther, P., 'Compulsory licensing of intellectual property rights' (1995) 32 *CML Rev* 521
Culler, M.-P., 'Copyright protection for video games: the courts in the *Pac-Man* maze' (1983–84) 32 *Cleveland State Law Review* 521
Dalton, L., 'Intellectual property: striking a balance' (1995) 69 *Law Institute Journal* 1125
Daun, F., 'The content shop: towards an economic legal structure for clearing and licensing multimedia content' (1996) 30 *Loyola of Los Angeles Law Review* 215
Davies, C., 'WIPO Treaties – the new framework for the protection of digital works' (1997) 2 *Communications Law* 46
Davies, G., 'New technology and copyright reform' [1984] 12 *EIPR* 355
  'A technical solution to private copying: the case of digital audio tape' [1987] 6 *EIPR* 155
Davis III, G., 'The digital dilemma: coping with copyright in a digital world' [1993] 27 *Copyright World* 18
Davison, M., 'Geographical restraints on the distribution of copyright material in a digital age: are they justified?' [1996] 9 *EIPR* 477
Denicola, R., 'Copyright in collections of facts: a theory for the protection of nonfiction literary works' (1981) 81 *Col LR* 576
Deprez, P. and V. Fauchoux, *Lois, contrats et usages du multimédia*, Dixit, Paris, 1997
Desbois, H., A. Françon and A. Kerever, *Les conventions internationales du droit d'auteur et des droits voisins*, Dalloz, Paris, 1976

Desjeux, X., 'From design to software: software, video games and copyright, the analytical method in the test of technology' (1986) 2 *Journal of Law and Information Science* 18

Desurmont, T., 'Qualification juridique de la transmission numérique' (1996) *RIDA* 55

'La position de sociétés de gestion sur la proposition de directive relative au droit d'auteur et aux droits voisins dans la société de l'information' [1998] *Auteurs & Media* 319

Dietz, A., 'Legal principles of moral rights in civil law countries' (1993) 11 *Copyright Reporter* 1 and (1995) 19 *Columbia – VLA of Law and the Arts Journal* 199

Dixon, A. and N. Hansen, 'The Berne Convention enters the digital age' [1996] 11 *EIPR* 604

Dixon, A. and L. Self, 'Copyright protection for the information superhighway' [1994] 11 *EIPR* 465

Doane, M., 'TRIPS and international intellectual property protection in an age of advancing technology' (1994) 9 *American University Journal of International Law and Policy* 465

Dommering, E., 'An introduction to information law works of fact at the crossroads of freedom and protection' in E. Dommering and P. Hugenholtz (eds.), *Protecting works of fact*, Kluwer Law and Taxation Publishers, Deventer, Boston, 1991, 1

Dommering, E. and P. Hugenholtz (eds.), *Protecting works of fact*, Kluwer Law and Taxation Publishers, Deventer, Boston, 1991

Doutrelepont, C., *Le droit moral de l'auteur et le droit communautaire*, Bruylant, Brussels, 1997

Doutrelepont, C., P. Van Binst and C. Wilkin (eds.), *Libertés, droits et réseaux dans la société de l'information*, Bruylant and LGDJ, Brussels, Paris, 1996

Downing, R., *EC information technology law*, J. Wiley & Sons, Chichester, 1995

Drakulic, M., 'Towards the legal literacy of information system designers' [1990–91] 7 *Computer Law and Security Report* 63

Dreier, T., 'Copyright in the age of digital technology' (1993) 14 *IIC* 481

'Authorship and new technologies from the viewpoint of civil law traditions' in *WIPO Worldwide Symposium on the Future of Copyright and Neighbouring Rights*, Louvre, Paris, 1–3 June 1994, 51 and (1995) 26 *IIC* 989

'L'analogue, le digital et le droit d'auteur' in *Propriétés intellectuelles: mélanges en l'honneur de André Françon*, Dalloz, Paris, 1995, 119

'Der französische "Rapport Sirinelli" zum Urheberrecht und den neuen Technologien' [1995] *GRUR Int* 840

Drexl, J., 'What is protected in a computer program?' (1994) 15 *IIC Studies* 33

Dries, J. and R. Woldt, *The role of public service broadcasting in the information society*, European Institute for the Media, Düsseldorf, February 1996

DTI, *Development of the information society: an international analysis*, Department of Trade and Industry, London, 1996

Duant, J. and G. von Gehr, 'Corporate partnering: a strategy for high technology companies' [1992] 8 *Computer Law and Security Report* 50

Durdik, P., 'Ancient debate, new technology: the European Community moves to protect computer databases' (1994) 12 *Boston University International Law Journal* 153

Dworkin, G., 'Understanding the new copyright environment: an assessment of the state of copyright law – from Whitford to multimedia' in E. Barendt (gen. ed.), *The yearbook of media and entertainment law 1995*, Clarendon Press, Oxford, 1995, 161

Eckhouse, J., 'Multimedia is electronics megatrend blend of art with high-tech promises to change the world', *San Francisco Chronicle*, 7 December 1992, B1

Edelman, B., *Droits d'auteur droits voisins: droit d'auteur et marché*, Dalloz, Paris, 1993

'L'oeuvre multimédia, un essai de qualification' [1995] 15 *Recueil Dalloz Sirey (Chronique)* 109

Edwards, C. and N. Savage, *Information technology and the law*, 2nd edn, Macmillan, London, 1990

Engelmann, M., *How to draft, negotiate and enforce licensing agreements 1997. A satellite program*, Practicing Law Institute, New York, 1997

Epstein, M., *Modern intellectual property*, 3rd edn, Aspen Law and Business, New York, 1995

Epstein, M. and F. Politano, *Current issues in multimedia licensing*, Prentice Hall Law and Business, New Jersey, 1994

Estève, A., 'Das Multimediawerk in der spanischen Gesetzgebung' [1998] *GRUR Int* 1

Fakes, A., 'The EEC's Directive on software protection and its moral rights loophole' (1992) 5 *Software Law Journal* 531

Fawcett, J. and P. Torremans, *Intellectual property and private international law*, Clarendon Press, Oxford, 1998

Feldman, T., *Multimedia in the 1990s. BNB Research Fund Report*, British Library, 1991

Ferné, G., 'The economic stakes in computer standardisation' [1990–91] 6 *Computer Law and Security Report* 2

Ficsor, M., 'New technologies and copyright: need for change, need for continuity' in *WIPO Worldwide Symposium on the Future of Copyright and Neighbouring Rights*, Louvre, Paris, 1–3 June 1994, 209

'International harmonisation of copyright and neighbouring rights' in *WIPO Worldwide Symposium on Copyright in the Global Information Infrastructure*, Mexico City, 22–24 May 1995, 369

'The spring 1997 Horace S. Manges lecture – copyright for the digital era: the WIPO "Internet" Treaties' (1997) 21 *Columbia – VLA of Law and the Arts Journal* 197

Fitzgerald, A. and C. Cifuentes, 'Copyright protection for digital multimedia works' [1999] *Ent LR* 23

Fitzgerald, J., 'Licensing content for multimedia' (1998) 84 *Copyright World* 23

Flint, M., *A user's guide to copyright*, 4th edn, Butterworths, London, 1997

Flint, M., for the Intellectual Property Institute, 'Digitisation', Seminar Report, 28 April 1994

Fordham Conference on International Intellectual Property Law and Policy, special issue (1993) 4 *Fordham Intellectual Property, Media and Entertainment Law Journal* 1

Franzosi, M. and G. de Sanctis, 'Moral rights and new technology: are copyright and patents converging?' [1995] 2 *EIPR* 63

Freed, R., 'Comments on the Green Paper entitled "Intellectual property and the national information infrastructure"' [1995] 11 *Computer Law and Security Report* 234

Freedman, J., *Where worlds collide: music, film and multimedia*, UCLA, Los Angeles, 1995

Friedman, B., 'Note: from deontology to dialogue: the culture consequences of copyright' (1994) 13 *Cardozo Arts and Entertainment Law Journal* 157

Frischtak, C., 'Harmonisation versus differentiation in intellectual property right regimes' in M. Wallerstein, M. Mogee and R. Schoen (eds.), *Global dimensions of intellectual property rights in science and technology*, National Academy Press, Washington D.C., 1993, 89

Frome, N. and H. Rowe, 'The legal protection of databases under English law' [1990-91] 7 *Computer Law and Security Report* 117

Frost, D., 'Key questions to ask your client about a proposed license or development deal for a "multimedia" product' in M. Radcliffe and W. Tannenbaum (ed.), *Multimedia and the law 1996. Protecting your clients' interests*, Practicing Law Institute, New York, 1996, 359

Fuller, M., 'Hollywood goes interactive: licensing problems associated with re-purposing motion pictures into interactive multimedia' (1995) 15 *Loyola of Los Angeles Entertainment Law Journal* 599

Garnett, K., J. Rayner James and G. Davies, *Copinger and Skone James on Copyright*, 14th edn, Sweet & Maxwell, London, 1999

Garrigues, C., 'Databases: a subject-matter for copyright or for a neighbouring rights regime' [1997] 1 *EIPR* 3

Gaster, J., 'Authors' rights and neighbouring rights in the information society' in ASLIB, *Copyright in multimedia (conference papers)*, ASLIB, London, 1995

'The EU Council of Ministers' common position concerning the legal protection of databases' [1995] 7 *Ent LR* 258

'Urheberrecht und verwandte Schutzrechte in der Informationsgesellschaft' [1995] 11 *ZUM* 740

'La protection juridique des bases de données à la lumière de la discussion concernant le droit d'auteur et les droits voisins dans la société de l'information' in C. Doutrelepont, P. Van Binst and C. Wilkin (eds.), *Libertés, droits et réseaux dans la société de l'information*, Bruylant and LGDJ, Brussels, Paris, 1996, 27

Gaster, J. and M. Powell, *Legal protection of databases in Europe – a guide to the Directive*, Butterworths, London, 1997

Gautier, P.-Y., 'Les oeuvres "multimédia" en droit français' (1994) 160 *RIDA* 91

Geller, P., 'Copyright in factual compilations: US Supreme Court decides the *Feist* case' (1991) 22 *IIC* 802

'Neue Triebkräfte im internationalen Urheberrecht' [1993] *GRUR Int* 526

'Conflicts of law in cyberspace: international copyright in a digitally networked world' in P. Hugenholtz (ed.), *The future of copyright in a digital environment*, Kluwer Law International, The Hague, London, Boston, 1996, 27

Gendreau, Y., 'Digital technology and copyright: can moral rights survive the disappearance of the hard copy?' [1995] 6 *Ent LR* 214

Genton, F., 'Multimedia im französischen Urheberrecht: der zweite Sirinelli-Bericht' [1996] 6 *GRUR Int* 693

Gilligan, M., 'The multimedia maze – an illustration of the legal rights in multimedia products' (1997) 2 *Communications Law* 49

Gilson, H., 'La transmission et la gestion de savoir à l'ère electronique' in C. Doutrelepont, P. Van Binst and C. Wilkin (eds), *Libertés, droits et réseaux dans la société de l'information*, Bruylant and LGDJ, Brussels, Paris, 1996, 321

Ginsburg, J., 'Creation and commercial value: copyright protection of works of information' (1990) 90 *Col LR* 1865

'Creation and commercial value: copyright protection of works of information in the United States' in E. Dommering and P. Hugenholtz (eds.), *Protecting works of fact*, Kluwer Law and Taxation Publishers, Deventer, Boston, 1991, 41

'L'exploitation internationale de l'oeuvre audiovisuelle: France/Etats-Unis' [1994] 4 *La Semaine Juridique* 49 (*Doctrine*)

'Surveying the borders of copyright' in *WIPO Worldwide Symposium on the Future of Copyright and Neighbouring Rights*, Louvre, Paris, 1–3 June 1994, 221

'Domestic and international copyright issues implicated in the compilation of a multimedia product' (1995) 25 *Seton Hall Law Review* 1397

'Global use, territorial rights, private international law questions of the global information infrastructure' in *WIPO Worldwide Symposium on Copyright in the Global Information Infrastructure*, Mexico City, 22–24 May 1995, 382

'Putting cars on the "information superhighway": authors, exploiters, and copyright in cyberspace' (1995) 95 *Col LR* 1466

'Digital libraries and some of the copyright issues they raise' (1996) 169 *RIDA* 4

'Copyright without borders? Choice of forum and choice of law for copyright infringement in cyberspace' (1997) 15 *Cardozo Arts and Entertainment Law Journal* 153

Ginsburg, J. and P. Sirinelli, 'Auteur, création et adaptation en droit international privé et en droit interne français. Réflexions à partir de l'affaire Huston' (1991) 150 *RIDA* 3

'Les difficultés rencontrées lors de l'élaboration d'une oeuvre multimédia. Analyse de droits français et américain' [1996] *La Semaine Juridique* 65

Glick, M. and M. Page, 'Copyright protection of video games in the United States: *Galoob* v *Nintendo*' [1992] 1 *EIPR* 24

Goldberg, J., 'Now that the future has arrived, maybe the law should take a look: multimedia technology and its interaction with the fair use doctrine' (1995) 44 *American University Law Review* 919

Goldstein, P., 'Copyright and author's right in the twenty-first century' in WIPO *Worldwide Symposium on the Future of Copyright and Neighbouring Rights*, Louvre, Paris, 1–3 June 1994, 261

'The future of copyright in a digital environment' in P. Hugenholtz (ed.), *The future of copyright in a digital environment*, Kluwer Law International, The Hague, London, Boston, 1996, 241

Golvers, L., 'La société de l'information: sécurité et insécurité' in C. Doutrelepont, P. Van Binst and C. Wilkin (eds.), *Libertés, droits et réseaux dans la société de l'information*, Bruylant and LGDJ, Brussels, Paris, 1996, 155

Gordon, M., D. McKenzie and M. Jacobs, 'Data deals: the essence of multimedia transactions' (1993) 10 *Computer Lawyer* 10

Gordon, S., 'The very idea!: Why copyright law is an inappropriate way to protect computer programs' [1998] 1 *EIPR* 10

Gorman, R. and J. Ginsburg, *Copyright. Cases and materials*, 5th edn, Lexis Law Publishing, Charlottesville, Va., 1999

Gotzen, F., 'Harmonisation of copyright in the European Union' in M.-C. Janssens (ed.), *Intellectual property rights in the information society*, Bruylant, Brussels, 1998, 121

(ed.), *Le renouveau du droit d'auteur en Belgique*, Bruylant, Brussels, 1996

Gotzen, M., *Het bestemmingsrecht van de auteur*, Larcier, Brussels, 1975

Govaere, I., *The use and abuse of intellectual property rights in EC law*, Sweet & Maxwell, London, 1996

Greguras, F., M. Egger and S. Wong, 'Multimedia and the superhighway: rapid acceleration or foot on the brake?' (1994) 11 *Computer Lawyer* 12

Gringras, C., 'Competition in cyberspace' [1996] 2 *ECLR* 71

Grogan, A., 'Licensing for next generation new media technology' (1993) 10 *Computer Lawyer* 1

Grosheide, F., 'Copyright and publishers' rights: exploitation of information by a proprietary right' in W. Korthals Altes, E. Dommering, B. Hugenholtz and J. Kabel (eds.), *Information law towards the 21st century*, Kluwer Law and Taxation Publishers, Deventer, Boston, 1992, 295

'When ideas take the stage' [1994] 6 *EIPR* 219

Groupe Audiovisuel et Multimédia de l'Edition, *Questions juridiques relatives aux oeuvres multimédia* (Livre Blanc), Paris, 1994

Groves, P., 'Copyright in a digitized typography' [1992] 8 *Computer Law and Security Report* 125

'Copyright on the Internet (reprise)' [1997] *Student Law Review* 41

Guédon, L., 'International identification of computer programs and information technology products' in *WIPO Worldwide Symposium on the Impact of Digital Technology on Copyright and on Neighbouring Rights*, Harvard University, 31 March – 2 April 1993, 171

Gyertyanfy, P., 'Conflicts and changes. The new technologies in the protection and administration of copyright' in *WIPO Worldwide Symposium on the Impact of Digital Technology on Copyright and on Neighbouring Rights*, Harvard University, 31 March – 2 April 1993, 157

Haesner, C., 'The German legal reaction to multimedia' in L. Barrington (ed.), *New technologies: their influence on international audiovisual law*, ICC Dossiers, Paris, 1994, 81

Hails, R., 'Liability of on-line service providers resulting from copyright infringement performed by their subscribers: *Religious Technology Center* v *Netcom On-line Communication Services Inc.*' [1996] 5 *EIPR* 304

Halpern, S., C. Nard and K. Port, *Fundamentals of United States intellectual property law: copyright, patents and trade marks*, Kluwer Law International, The Hague, Boston, London, 1999

Hamilton, M., 'The TRIPS agreement: imperialistic, outdated and overprotective' (1996) 29 *Vanderbilt Journal of Transnational Law* 613

Hammond, G., 'The legal protection of ideas – part I' [1992] 8 *Computer Law and Security Report* 111

'The legal protection of ideas – part II' [1992] 8 *Computer Law and Security Report* 155

Hardy, T., 'Contracts, copyright and preemption in a digital world' (17 April 1995) *Richmond Journal of Law and Technology* (available on the Internet)

Harper, G., 'The university community: pursuit of the promise of the new media' (The Herbert Tenzer Memorial Conference: copyright in the twenty-first century information superhighway: the challenge of multimedia technology), (1995) 13 *Cardozo Arts and Entertainment Law Journal* 447

Hart, M., 'The proposed directive for copyright in the information society: nice rights, shame about the exceptions' [1998] 5 *EIPR* 169

Hart, R., 'Author's own intellectual creation – computer generated works' [1993] 9 *Computer Law and Security Report* 164

'A voluntary international numbering system – the latest WIPO proposals' [1995] 11 *Computer Law and Security Report* 127

Hayden, J., 'Copyright protection of computer databases after *Feist*' (1991) 5 *Harvard Journal of Law and Technology* 215

Heath, C., 'Multimedia und Urheberrecht in Japan' [1995] *GRUR Int* 843

Heker, H., 'The publisher in the electronic age: caught in the area of conflict of copyright and competition law' [1995] 2 *EIPR* 75

Henry, M., *Publishing and multimedia law*, Butterworths, London, Dublin, Edinburgh, 1994

Hibbitts, B., 'Last writes? Reassessing the law review in the age of cyberspace' (1996) 71 *New York University Law Review* 615

Hicks, J., 'Copyright and computer databases: is traditional compilation law adequate?' (1990) 37 *Copyright Law Symposium* 85

Higham, N., 'The new challenges of digitisation' [1993] 10 *EIPR* 355

'The new challenges of digitisation' (1994) 2 *International Computer Lawyer* 14

Hill, R., 'What is the smallest copyrightable element in a multimedia world?' (1995) *Computers and Law* 15

Hodac, I., 'The reaction of the market' in L. Barrington (ed.), *New technologies: their influence on international audiovisual law*, ICC Dossiers, Paris, 1994, 57

van Hoecke, M. (ed.), *The socio-economic role of intellectual property rights*, Story-Scientia, Brussels, 1991

Hoeren, T., 'An assessment of long-term solutions in the context of copyright and electronic delivery services and multimedia products', European

Commission, Brussels, Luxembourg, 1995 (vol. 4, *Copyright on electronic delivery services and multimedia products* series, EUR 16069 EN)

'Some considerations on Multisolution/94', paper delivered at the European Commission Legal Advisory Board Conference on the Information Society: Copyright and Multimedia, Luxembourg, 26 April 1995 (available on the Internet)

'Legal aspects of multimedia. Long term solutions', European Commission Legal Advisory Board (available on the Internet)

Holleyman, R. and J. Steinhardt, 'Multimedia in the global information infrastructure' in *WIPO Worldwide Symposium on Copyright in the Global Information Infrastructure*, Mexico City, 22–24 May 1995, 55

Huber, W., 'Sinking the data pirates' [1993] 9 *Computer Law and Security Report* 2

Huet, J., 'Aspects juridiques des nouvelles techniques d'information' in L. Barrington (ed.), *New technologies: their influence on international audiovisual law*, ICC Dossiers, Paris, 1994, 73

'Rapport de synthèse' in L. Barrington (ed.), *New technologies: their influence on international audiovisual law*, ICC Dossiers, Paris, 1994, 123

Huet, P., *Le droit du multimédia. De la télématique à Internet*, AFTEL, Les Editions du Téléphone, Paris, 1996

Hugenholtz, P., 'Protection of compilation of facts in Germany and the Netherlands' in E. Dommering and P. Hugenholtz (eds.), *Protecting works of fact*, Kluwer Law and Taxation Publishers, Deventer, Boston, 1991, 59

'Convergence and divergence in intellectual property law: the case of the software Directive' in W. Korthals Altes, E. Dommering, B. Hugenholtz and J. Kabel (eds.), *Information law towards the 21st century*, Kluwer Law and Taxation Publishers, Deventer, Boston, 1992, 319

Copyright in information, English translation, Deventer, Kluwer, 1992

'Copyright problems of electronic document delivery', European Commission, Brussels, Luxembourg, 1995 (vol. 1, *Copyright on electronic delivery services and multimedia products* series, EUR 16056 EN)

'Licensing rights in a digital multimedia environment', paper presented at the European Commission Legal Advisory Board Conference on the Information Society: Copyright and Multimedia, Luxembourg, 26 April 1995

'Adapting copyright to the information superhighway' in P. Hugenholtz, *The future of copyright in a digital environment*, Kluwer Law International, The Hague, London, Boston, 1996, 81

(ed.), *The future of copyright in a digital environment*, Kluwer Law International, The Hague, London, Boston, 1996

Hughes, P., 'A common information market for Europe – what are the legal barriers to success?' [1986] 9 *EIPR* 275

Hughes, G. and D. Cosgrove, 'Legal questions involving the Internet' [1995] 11 *Computer Law and Security Report* 321

Hughes, J. and E. Weightman 'EC database protection: fine tuning the Commission's proposal' [1992] 5 *EIPR* 147

Institute of Intellectual Property, *A proposal of the new rule on intellectual property for multimedia*, Japan, February 1994

'Proposed rules for administering IP rights in multimedia society' [1995] 4 *Patents and Licensing* 23

Intellectual Property Institute, *Digitisation*, Seminar Report, 28 April 1994
Intellectual Property Rights Sub-Group Report, National Computer Board, Singapore 1996 (available on the Internet)
International Chamber of Commerce, 'ICC statement on the global information infrastructure' [1995] 11 *Computer Law and Security Report* 333
Isaac, B., 'Intellectual property and multimedia: problems of definition and enforcement' [1995] 12 *Canadian Intellectual Property Review* 47
Janssens, M.-C. (ed.), *Intellectual property rights in the information society*, Bruylant, Brussels, 1998
Jeffcoate, J., 'Publishing multimedia: is there a market?' in ASLIB, *Copyright in multimedia (conference papers)*, ASLIB, London, 1995
Jenkins, G., 'Help or hindrance – the legislative framework: the UK perspective' in ASLIB, *Copyright in multimedia (conference papers)*, ASLIB, London, 1995
John, S., 'What rights do record companies have on the information superhighway?' [1996] 2 *EIPR* 74
Johns, M., 'The first amendment and cyberspace: trying to teach old doctrines new tricks' (1996) 64 *University of Cincinnati Law Review* 1383
Jones, S., 'Multimedia and the superhighway: exploring the rights minefield' (1996) 1 *Communications Law* 28
Jouët, J. and S. Coudray, 'New communication technologies: research trends', UNESCO Paper, 1991
Kallinikou, D., *Principal issues of the 2121/1993 law of intellectual property and related rights*, P. N. Sakkoulas, Athens, 1994
Pnevmatiki idioktissia kai syggenika dikaiomata, P. N. Sakkoulas, Athens, 2000
Karjala, D., 'Protection of computer databases under Japanese law' [1986] 9 *EIPR* 267
Karnell, G., 'The idea/expression dichotomy – a conceptual fallacy' (1989) 7 *Copyright World* 16
'The Nordic catalogue rule' in E. Dommering and P. Hugenholtz (eds.), *Protecting works of fact*, Kluwer Law and Taxation Publishers, Deventer, Boston, 1991, 67
Kassel, M. and J. Kassel, 'Don't get caught in the Net: an intellectual property practitioner's guide to using the Internet' (1995) 13 *John Marshall Journal of Computer and Information Law* 373
Katsh, M., 'Dispute resolution in cyberspace' (1996) 28 *Connecticut Law Review* 953
Katzenberger, P., 'Copyright law and databanks' (1990) 21 *IIC* 310
Kaufmann, T., 'Competition issues relevant to copyright and the information society', paper presented at the European Commission Legal Advisory Board Conference on the Information Society: Copyright and Multimedia, Luxembourg, 26 April 1995
Kaye, L., 'The proposed EU Directive for the legal protection of databases: a cornerstone of the information society?' [1995] 12 *EIPR* 583
Kelly, D. and K. Kumor, 'Trade marks: intellectual property protection on the information superhighway' [1995] 10 *EIPR* 481
Kelman, A., 'Certainty of rights in the information society – a discussion paper on potential barriers to the creation of the information society' [1996] 12 *Computer Law and Security Report* 294

van Kerckhove, M., 'The Advocate General delivers his opinion in *Magill*' (1994) 5 *ECLR* 276

Kerever, A., 'Gestion collective des oeuvres audiovisuelles in nouvelles technologies' in ALAI, *Audiovisual works and literary and artistic property*, ALAI, Paris, 1996, 399

'La problemática de la adaptación del derecho de reproducción y del derecho de representación pública en el ámbito numérico de los multimedia' (1997) 31 *Boletin de Derecho de Autor (Multimedia, Reproducción y Representación Pública)* 4

Keustermans, J., 'The intellectual effort requirement in chip protection laws compared to the originality requirement in copyright law' in W. Korthals Altes, E. Dommering, B. Hugenholtz and J. Kabel (eds.), *Information law towards the 21st century*, Kluwer Law and Taxation Publishers, Deventer, Boston, 1992, 309

'Software, chips en databanken' in F. Gotzen (ed.), *Le renouveau du droit d'auteur en Belgique*, Bruylant, Brussels, 1996, 447

Kirby, M., 'The law and information: data protection laws' [1987] 3 *Computer Law and Security Report* 2

'Informatics, transborder data flows and law – the new challenges' [1989–90] 4 *Computer Law and Security Report* 2

'Information security – OECD initiatives' [1992] 8 *Computer Law and Security Report* 102

Kirchhoefer, G., 'Acquiring rights in software, documentation and databases' (1993) 6 *Software Law Journal* 83

Kirchner, J., 'The search for new markets: multimedia and digital television under German broadcasting and copyright law' [1995] 6 *EIPR* 269

Kitagawa, Z., 'Copymart: a new concept – an application of digital technology to the collective management of copyright' in *WIPO Worldwide Symposium on the Impact of Digital Technology on Copyright and on Neighbouring Rights*, Harvard University, 31 March – 2 April 1993, 139

'Computers, digital technology and copyright' in *WIPO Worldwide Symposium on the Future of Copyright and Neighbouring Rights*, Louvre, Paris, 1–3 June 1994

Knight, P., 'The impact of copyright law on the use of new multimedia technology' (1994) 2 *International Computer Lawyer* 2

Knopf, H., 'The role of law in dealing with technological solutions to copyright problems created by technology' in *WIPO Worldwide Symposium on Copyright in the Global Information Infrastructure*, Mexico City, 22–24 May 1995, 205

Koboldt, C., 'The EU Directive on the legal protection of databases and the incentives to update: an economic analysis' (1997) 17 *International Review of Law and Economics* 127

Koch, F., 'Software – Urheberrechtsschutz für Multimedia – Anwendungen' [1995] *GRUR* 459

Koopmans, T., 'Information monopolies in European Community law' in E. Dommering and P. Hugenholtz (eds.), *Protecting works of fact*, Kluwer Law and Taxation Publishers, Deventer, Boston, 1991, 83

Korthals Altes, W., E. Dommering, B. Hugenholtz and J. Kabel (eds.), *Information law towards the 21st century*, Kluwer Law and Taxation Publishers, Deventer, Boston, 1992

Koumantos, G., 'Copyright and private international law in the face of the international diffusion of works' in *WIPO Worldwide Symposium on the Future of Copyright and Neighbouring Rights*, Louvre, Paris, 1–3 June 1994, 233

'Les aspects de droit international privé en matière d'infrastructure mondiale d'information' [1996] *Koinodikion* 2.B, 241

'Les bases de données dans la directive Communautaire' (1997) 171 *RIDA* 78

'Reflexions on the concept of intellectual property' in J. Kable and G. Mom (eds.), *Intellectual property and information law, essays in honour of Herman Cohen Jehoram*, Kluwer Law International, The Hague, London, Boston, 1997, 39

Pnevmatiki idioktissia, 7th edn, Ant. N. Sakkoulas, Athens, 2000

Kounoupias, N. and K. Hill, 'Online distribution: mechanical right, performing right, or both' [1996] 12 *Computer Law and Security Report* 226

Kreile, R. and J. Becker, 'Multimedia und die Praxis der Lizenzierung von Urheberrechten' [1996] *GRUR Int* 677

Kreile, R. and D. Westphal, 'Multimedia und das Filmbearbeitungsrecht' [1996] *GRUR* 254

Kreiss, R., 'Introduction' in the Copyright Symposium Part I, Copyright Protection for Computer Databases, CD-ROMs and Factual Compilations (1992) 17 *University of Dayton Law Review* 323

Kunzlik, P., 'Proposed EC Council Directive on the legal protection of databases' [1992] 8 *Computer Law and Security Report* 16

Kurtz, L., 'Copyright and the National Information Infrastructure in the United States' [1996] 3 *EIPR* 120

Kyer, C., 'Information technology law: what does the future hold?' [1995] 11 *Computer Law and Security Report* 140

Kyer, C. and S. Moutsatsos, 'Database protection: the old world heads off in a new direction' [1993] 9 *Computer Law and Security Report* 11

Laddie, H., 'Copyright: over-strength, over-regulated, over-rated?' [1996] 5 *EIPR* 253

Laddie, H., P. Prescott and M. Vitoria, *The modern law of copyright and designs*, 2nd edn, Butterworths, London, Dublin, Edinburgh, 1995

Lai, S., 'The American perspective: the NII White Paper and subsequent draft legislation', National Computer Board, Singapore, 1996, http://www.ncb.gov.sg/nii/96scan6/uswhite.html

'Copyright initiatives in multimedia and cyberspace' [1996] 6 *NII San Current Issue*, http:// www. ncb.gov.sg/nii/current.html

'The EC directive on the legal protection of databases', National Computer Board, Singapore, 1996, http://www.ncb.gov.sg/nii/96scan6/ecdir.html

'The European perspective: the EC Green Paper and related rights in the information society', National Computer Board, Singapore, 1996, http://www.ncb.gov.sg//nii/96scan6

'Specific rights in the basket of copyrights', National Computer Board, Singapore, 1996, http://www.ncb.gov.sg/nii/96scan6/rights2.html

Bibliography

'Database protection in the United Kingdom: the new deal and its effects on software protection' [1998] 1 *EIPR* 32

Lamoree, P., 'Expanding copyrights in software: the struggle to define the "expression" begins' (1988) 4 *Santa Clara Computer and High Technology Law Journal* (No. 1) 49

Landes, W. and R. Posner, 'An economic analysis of copyright law' (1989) 18 *Journal of Legal Studies* 325

Lange, D., 'Sensing the constitution in *Feist*' (1992) 17 *University of Dayton Law Review* 367

Latreille, A., 'La création multimédia comme oeuvre audiovisuelle' [1998] *JCP* (édition générale) I, 156

Laundy, D., 'Revising the copyright law for electronic publishing' [1995] 1 *John Marshall Journal of Computer and Information Law* 1

Law, C., 'Is there a need for a digital diffusion right?', 15 March 1996, http://www.gold.net/users/af82/digdif.html

Lea, G., 'Databases and copyright part I – the problems' [1993] 9 *Computer Law and Security Report* 68

'Database law – solutions beyond copyright part II – the solutions' [1993] 9 *Computer Law and Security Report* 127

'Program copyright and moral rights: a cultural clash?' [1994] 10 *Computer Law and Security Report* 304

Leaffer, M., 'Protecting authors' rights in a digital age' (1995) 27 *University of Toledo Law Review* 1

Legal Advisory Board, 'The Legal Advisory Board on the information market – a progress report' [1988–89] 4 *Computer Law and Security Report* 11

'Comments sent in following meeting' presented at the Conference of 26 April 1995, Luxembourg

'The EC Legal Advisory Board's reply to the Green Paper on copyright and related rights in the information society' [1996] 12 *Computer Law and Security Report* 143

Lehman, B., 'Intellectual property and the national and global information infrastructure' in *WIPO Worldwide Symposium on Copyright in the Global Information Infrastructure*, Mexico City, 22–24 May 1995, 75

Lehman, B. and R. Brown, 'Intellectual property and the National Information Infrastructure', *Report of the Working Group on Intellectual Property Rights*, US Patent and Trademark Office, Washington D.C., September 1995

Lehman, M. (ed.), *Internet – und Multimediarecht (cyberlaw)*, Schäffer Poeschel, Stuttgart, 1997

Lehrberg, R., 'Blind men and the elephant: what does multimedia really mean?' in L. Barrington (ed.), *New technologies: their influence on international audiovisual law*, ICC Dossiers, Paris, 1994, 7

Lemley, M., 'Intellectual property and shrinkwrap licences' (1995) 68 *Southern California Law Review* 1239

von Lewinski, S., 'Adaptation of the legal framework to new technologies' in L. Barrington (ed.), *New technologies: their influence on international audiovisual law*, ICC Dossiers, Paris, 1994, 107

'Das Europäische Grünbuch über das Urheberrecht und neue Technologien' [1995] *GRUR Int* 831

'WIPO Diplomatic Conference in two new treaties' (1997) 28 *IIC* 203

'Die multimedia-Richtlinie. Der EG-Richtlinienvorschlag zum Urheberrecht in der Informationsgesellschaft' [1998] 3 *Multimedia und Recht* 115

Lewis, G., 'Copyright protection for purely factual compilations under *Feist Publications, Inc. v. Rural Telephone Service Co.*: how does *Feist* protect electronic databases of facts?' (1992) 8 *Santa Clara Computer and High Technology Journal* (No. 1) 169

Liedes, J., 'Le soeur de droit de propriété intellectuelle dans le cadre des nouvelles techniques de diffusion' in ALAI, *Audiovisual works and literary and artistic property*, ALAI, Paris, 1996, 339

Lim, Y., 'Multimedia: authorisers of copyright infringement?' (1994) 5 *Journal of Law and Information Science* 306

Lindsay, D., 'Copyright protection of electronic databases' (1993) 4 *Journal of Law and Information Science* 287

Litman, J., 'After *Feist*' (1992) 17 *University of Dayton Law Review* 607

Litwak, M. 'Entertainment law resources: for film, TV and multimedia producers. Legal roadmap for multimedia producers' (available on the Internet)

'Potholes on the information superhighway: a road map to legal issues in multimedia productions' in R. Thorne and J. Viera (eds.), *Entertainment, publishing and the arts handbook* (1995–96 edn), Clark Boardman Callaghan, N.Y., 1996, 199

'Publication and distribution of multimedia programs' in R. Thorne and J. Viera (eds.), *Entertainment, publishing and the arts handbook* (1997–98 edn), Clark Boardman Callaghan, N.Y., 1998, 63

Lloyd, I., *Information technology law*, 3rd edn, Butterworths, London, 2000

Lloyd, I., and M. Simpson, *Law on the electronic frontier*, Edinburgh University Press, Edinburgh, 1994

Loewenheim, U., 'Multimedia and the European copyright law' (1996) 27 *IIC* 41

'Multimedia and the European copyright law' in K. Hill and L. Morse (eds.), *Emerging technologies and intellectual property: multimedia, biotechnology and other issues*, Atrip and Casrip Publication Series, Washington D.C., 1996 (No. 2), 13

'Urheberrechtliche Probleme bei Multimediaanwendungen' [1996] *GRUR* 830

Losey, R., 'Practical and legal protection of computer databases', 1995, http://www.eff.org/pub/intellectual_property/database_protection.paper

Lucas, A., 'Copyright and the new technologies in French law' [1987] 2 *EIPR* 42

Le droit informatique, PUF, Paris, 1987.

'The Council Directive of 14 May 1991 concerning the legal protection of computer programs and its implications in French law' [1991] 1 *EIPR* 28

'Summary of the proceedings of the symposium' in *WIPO Worldwide Symposium on the Future of Copyright and Neighbouring Rights*, Louvre, Paris, 1–3 June 1994, 269

'Droit d'auteur et multimédia' in *Propriétés intellectuelles, mélanges en l'honneur de André Françon*, Dalloz, Paris, 1995, 325

'Les oeuvres multimédias en droit belge et en droit français' in C. Doutrelepont, P. Van Binst and C. Wilkin (ed.), *Libertés, droits et réseaux dans la société de l'information*, Bruylant and LGDJ, Brussels, Paris, 1996, 55

'Multimédia et droit d'auteur' in AFTEL, *Le droit du multimédia: de la télénatique à Internet*, Les Editions du Téléphone, Paris, 1996, 113

Lucas, A. and H. Lucas, *Traité de la propriété littéraire et artistique*, Litec, Paris, 1994

MacDonald, J., 'The search for certainty' (1992) 17 *University of Dayton Law Review* 521

Macfarlane, N., C. Wardle and J. Wilkinson, 'The tension between national intellectual property rights and certain provisions of the EC law' [1994] 12 *EIPR* 525

Mackaay, E., 'Economic incentives in markets for information and innovation' (1990) 13 *Harvard Journal of Law and Public Policy* 867

'Economisch-filosofische aspecten van de intellectuele rechten' in M. van Hoecke (ed.), *The socio-economic role of intellectual property rights*, Story – Scientia, Brussels, 1991, 1

'An economic view of information law' in W. Korthals Altes, E. Dommering, B. Hugenholtz and J. Kabel (eds.), *Information law towards the 21st century*, Kluwer Law and Taxation Publishers, Deventer, Boston, 1992, 43

Mackaay, E., D. Poulin and P. Trudel (eds.), *The electronic superhighway. The shape of technology and law to come*, Kluwer Law International, The Hague, London, Boston, 1995

MacQueen, H., 'Copyright and the Internet' in L. Edwards and C. Waelde (eds.) *The law of the Internet: regulating cyberspace*, Hart Publishing, London, 1997

Mahon, J., 'A commentary on proposals for copyright protection on the National Information Infrastructure' (1996) 22 *Rutgers Computer and Technology Law Journal* 233

Maicher, K., 'Copyrightability of video games: *Stern* and *Atari*' (1983) 14 *Loyola University Law Journal* 391

Maier, P.-A., 'Intellectual property rights and the role of collecting societies', paper presented at the European Commission Legal Advisory Board Conference on the Information Society: Copyright and Multimedia, Luxembourg, 26 April 1995

Mallet-Poujol, N., 'Marché de l'information: le droit d'auteur injustement "tourmenté" ...' (1996) 168 *RIDA* 92

Mansfield, E., 'Unauthorized use of intellectual property: effects on investment, technology transfer, and innovation' in M. Wallerstein, M. Mogee and R. Schoen (eds.), *Global dimensions of intellectual property rights in science and technology*, National Academy Press, Washington D.C., 1993, 107

Marchant, B., 'On-line on the Internet: first amendment and intellectual property uncertainties in the on-line world' (1996) 39 *Howard Law Journal* 477

Marinos, M., *Logismiko (software). Nomiki prostassia kai simvassis*, 2 vols., Kritiki, Athens, 1992

'Provlimata pnevmatikis idioktissias apo tin ekmetallevsi ergon logou se psifiakes vasis dedomenon' (1996) 37 *Elliniki Dikaiossini* 1222

'Nomiki prostassia vasseon dedomenon. To idiaitero (*sui generis*) dikaioma tis odigias 96/9/EOK' [1997] 2 *DEE* 128

Pnevmatiki idioktissia, Ant. N. Sakkoulas, Athens, 2000

Marsland, V. and A. Robertson, 'Sex, violence, and multimedia – European regulation of digital products' (1994) 2 *International Computer Lawyer* 2

Martin, G., 'Online fair use of copyrighted material: issues and concerns', http://www.ncsa.uiuc.edu/sdg/it94/proceedings/pub/martin/www-online-essay.html

Martin, P., 'Digital law: some speculations on the future of legal information technology' NCAIR Sponsored Program on the Future of Legal Information Technology, May 1995, http://www.law.cornell.edu/papers/fut95fnl.html

Martindale, A., 'The impact of competition law' in ASLIB, *Copyright in multimedia (conference papers)*, ASLIB, London, 1995

Mason, Sir A., 'Developments in the law of copyright and public access to information' [1997] 11 *EIPR* 636

McCoy, M. and N. Boddie, 'Cybertheft: will copyright law prevent digital tyranny on the superhighway?' (1995) 30 *Wake Forest Law Review* 169

McKenna, P., 'Copyrightability of video games: *Stern* and *Atari*' (1983) 14 *Loyola University Law Journal* 391

McKnight, S., 'Substantial similarity between video games: an old copyright problem in a new medium' (1983) 36 *Vand LR* 1277

McManis, C., 'Taking trips on the information superhighway: international intellectual protection and emerging computer technology' (1996) 41 *Villanova Law Review* 207

Meade, T., 'Ex-post *Feist*: applications of a landmark copyright decision' (1994) 1 *Journal of Intellectual Property Law University of Georgia School of Law* 245

Meeker, H., 'Multimedia and copyright' (1994) 20 *Rutgers Computer and Technology Law Journal* 375

Melichar, F., 'Collective administration of electronic rights: a realistic option?' in P. Hugenholtz (ed.), *The future of copyright in a digital environment*, Kluwer Law International, The Hague, London, Boston, 1996, 147

Melnik, J., 'A comparative analysis of proposals for the legal protection of computerized databases: NAFTA vs. the European Communities' (1994) 26 *Case Western Reserve Journal of International Law* 57

Mendonsa, P., 'Patent protection for multimedia products' in M. Radcliffe and W. Tannenbaum, *Multimedia and the law 1997. Protecting your clients' interests*, Practicing Law Institute, New York, 1997, 235

Merges, R., 'Contracting into liability rules: intellectual property rights and collective rights organisations' (1996) 84 *California Law Review* 1293

Merians, J., 'An overview of new technology and the entertainment industry' in L. Barrington (ed.), *New technologies: their influence on international audiovisual law*, ICC Dossiers, Paris, 1994; and in R. Thorne and J. Viera (eds.), *Entertainment, publishing and the arts handbook* (1995–96 edn), Clark Boardman Callaghan, New York, 1996, 241

'Actors, factors and privacy issues', paper delivered at the conference on 'Making international multimedia deals in the interactive age', Cannes, 21–22 May 1995

Messanger, G., 'The challenges of collective administration in the world of digital technology' in *WIPO Worldwide Symposium on the Impact of Digital Technology on Copyright and on Neighbouring Rights*, Harvard University, 31 March – 2 April 1993, 149

Metalitz, S., 'The database Directive and the EC's "direction" on copyright: some reflections' (1993) 4 *Fordham Intellectual Property, Media and Entertainment Journal* 33

'The National Information Infrastructure', the Herbert Tenzer Memorial Conference: copyright in the twenty-first century information superhighway: the challenge of multimedia technology (1995) 13 *Cardozo Arts and Entertainment Law Journal* 465

Metaxas, G., 'Protection of databases: quietly steering in the wrong direction?' [1990] 7 *EIPR* 227

Middelhoff, T., 'Wer bestimmt die Wertschöpfungskette von Multimedia' [1998] 2 *Multimedia und Recht* 1

Mikkelsen, K., 'Finding a balance: computer software, intellectual property and the challenge of technology' [1993] 9 *Computer Law and Security Report* 123

Mileson, C., 'The multimedia challenge' (1995) 69 *Law Institute Journal* 127

Mille, A., 'Copyright in the cyberspace era' [1997] 10 *EIPR* 570

Millé, A., 'Status juridico de las "ombras multimedia"' (1997) 31 *Boletin de Derecho de Autor (Multimedia, Reproducción y Representación Pública)* 26

Miller, A., 'Copyright and digital technology: continuity and progress' in *WIPO Worldwide Symposium on the Impact of Digital Technology on Copyright and on Neighbouring Rights*, Harvard University, 31 March – 2 April 1993, 239

'Copyright protection for computer programs, databases, and computer-generated works: is anything new since CONTU?' (1993) 106 *Harvard Law Review* 981

Miller, P., 'Life after *Feist*: facts, the First Amendment, and the copyright status of automated databases' (1991) 60 *Fordham Law Review* 507

Milrad, L. and A. Rush, 'Multimedia big deal' [1994] 43 *Managing Intellectual Property* 36

Modot, A., 'L'évolution du marché et la mutation des entreprises' in L. Barrington (ed.), *New technologies: their influence on international audiovisual law*, ICC Dossiers, Paris, 1994, 49

Möller, M., 'Copyright and the new technologies – the German Federal Republic's solution' [1988] 2 *EIPR* 42

Monet, D., *Le multimédia*, Flammarion, Paris, 1995

Monotti, A., 'The extent of copyright protection for compilations of artistic works' [1993] 5 *EIPR* 156

'Works stored in computer memory: databases and the CLRC draft report' (1993) 4 *Journal of Law and Information Science* 265

Muenchinger, N., 'French law and practice concerning multimedia and telecommunications' [1996] 4 *EIPR* 186

Myric, R., 'Will IP technology still be viable in a unitary market?' [1992] 9 *EIPR* 298

Napier, B., 'The future of information technology law' (1992) 51 *Cambridge Law Journal* 46

Narayanan, A., 'Standards of protection for databases in the European Community and the United States: *Feist* and the myth of creative originality' (1993–94) 27 *George Washington Journal of International Law and Economics* 457

Nash, G., 'Copyright protection on the global information infrastructure' (1994) 2 *International Computer Lawyer* 2

Newman, S., *Report on moral rights and adaptation rights in phonograms*, Intellectual Property Institute, London, 1996

Nielsen, J., *Multimedia and hypertext, the Internet and beyond*, AP Professional, Boston, 1995

Nimmer, D., *Nimmer on Copyright*, Matthew Bender, New York, 1995

Nordemann, W., K. Vinck and P. Hertin, *Urheberrecht*, Kohlhammer, Munich, 1994

Norris, P. and M. Bolender, 'Potential pitfalls in multimedia media product development: clearing the necessary content rights', 1996 (available on the Internet)

Nunn-Price, N., 'The link between CD-ROM and online' (1993) 2 *Law Technology Journal* 13

Ocampo, R. and D. Schellhase, 'The multimedia marketplace: a proposal for handling rights in the digital age' (1994) 14 *California Lawyer* 70

Odozynski, J., 'Infringement of compilation copyright after *Feist*' (1992) 17 *University of Dayton Law Review* 457

Okamoto, K., 'Multimedia and copyright' in *WIPO Worldwide Symposium on Copyright in the Global Information Infrastructure*, Mexico City, 22–24 May 1995, 105

Olivier, F. and E. Barbry, 'Le multimédia à l'épreuve du droit français' [1995] *La Semaine Juridique* (No 43) 421 (*Doctrine* 3879)

Olswang, S., 'Accessright: an evolutionary path for copyright into the digital era?' [1995] 5 *EIPR* 215

Oman, R., 'Moderator's contribution to the fourth panel discussion on technological means of protection and rights management information' in *WIPO International Forum on the Exercise and Management of Copyright and Neighbouring Rights in the Face of the Challenges of Digital Technology*, Seville, 14–16 May 1997, WIPO, 1998, 55

Oppenheim, C., *The legal and regulatory environment for electronic information*, Infonortics, Wiltshire, 1995

'Ethics on the Internet' (1996) 20 *Online and CD-ROM Review* 36

'Copyright in the electronic age' in P. Parrinder and W. Chernaik (eds.), *Textual monopolies, literary copyright and the public domain*, Office for Humanities Communications, London, 1997, 97

Palmer, J., 'Copyright and computer databases' (1983) 14 *IIC* 190

Pasgrinaud, H., 'La qualification juridique de la création multimédia: termes et arrière-pensées d'un vrai-faux débat' [1995] *Gaz Pal* (11 October 1995)

Patterson, R., 'Copyright overextended: a preliminary inquiry into the need for a Federal Statute of Unfair Competition' (1992) 17 *University of Dayton Law Review* 385

Pattison, M., 'The European Commission's proposal on the protection of computer databases' [1992] 4 *EIPR* 113

Pearce, P., 'Directories to databases: bringing the law into the information age', paper presented at the 8th BILETA Conference, April 1993, http://ltc.law.warwick.ac.uk/publications/ltj/v2n2/ltj2-2a.htlm

Pearson, H., 'Information in a digital age – the challenge to copyright' [1996] 12 *Computer Law and Security Report* 90

Pedde, G., 'Multimedia works under Italian copyright law and contractual practice' [1998] 2 *Ent LR* 39

Pendleton, M., 'Intellectual property, information-based society and a new international economic order – the policy options?' [1985] 2 *EIPR* 31

Pepe, S., 'Multimedia computing: copyright law's "last stand"' (1995) 12 *Touro Law Review* 143

Perritt, H., *Law and the information superhighway*, J. Wiley & Sons, New York, Chichester, Brisbane, Toronto, Singapore, 1996

Peters, P., 'La protection des jeux-vidéo électroniques' [1984] 2 *Dr. Inform.* 11

Poullet, Y., 'Information market or information society. Beyond a terminology, the stakes of a choice and the conditions of success of an information society', Legal Advisory Board (available on the Internet)

Power, T., 'Digitisation of serials and publications: the seminal objective of copyright law' [1997] 8 *EIPR* 444

Puri, K., 'The term of copyright protection – is it too long in the wake of new technologies?' [1990] 1 *EIPR* 12

Quaedvlieg, A., 'The economic analysis of intellectual property law' in W. Korthals Altes, E. Dommering, B. Hugenholtz and J. Kabel (eds.), *Information law towards the 21st century*, Kluwer Law and Taxation Publishers, Deventer, Boston, 1992, 379

Radcliffe, M., 'The future of computer law: ten challenges for the next decade' [1991] 10 *EIPR* 358

'Legal issues in new media: multimedia for publishers' in D. Campbell and S. Cotter (eds.), *International intellectual property law. New developments*, J. Wiley & Sons, Chichester, 1995, 181

'Legal issues in new media technologies' (1995) 12 *Computer Lawyer* 1

'On-line rights: how to interpret pre-existing agreements' [1996] 9 *EIPR* 494

Radcliffe, M. and W. Tannenbaum (eds.), *Multimedia and the law 1996. Protecting your clients' interests*, Practicing Law Institute, New York, 1996

Multimedia and the law 1997. Protecting your clients' interests, Practicing Law Institute, New York, 1997

van Raden, L., 'Technology dematerialised: another approach to information-related inventions' [1996] 7 *EIPR* 384

Raskind, L., 'Assessing the impact of *Feist*' (1992) 17 *University of Dayton Law Review* 331

Raubenheimer, A., 'The new copyright provisions for the protection of computer programs in Germany' (1995) 4 *Law, Computers and Artificial Intelligence* 5

'Germany: recent decisions on database protection under copyright law and unfair competition rules' (1996) 1 *Communications Law* 123

Rayner, J., 'Who will pay the jazz man?' *Guardian*, 1 July 1996

Raysman, R., P. Brown and J. Neuburger, *Multimedia law: forms and analysis*, Law Journal Seminars-Press, New York, 1996

Reed, C. and J. Angel (eds.), *Computer law*, 4th edn, Blackstone Press Ltd, London, 2000

Rehbinder, M., 'Multimedia und das Urheberpersönlichkeitsrecht' [1995] *ZUM* 684

Reichman, J., 'Legal hybrids between the patent and copyright paradigms' in W. Korthals Altes, E. Dommering, B. Hugenholtz and J. Kabel (eds.), *Information law towards the 21st century*, Kluwer Law and Taxation Publishers, Deventer, Boston, 1992, 325

 'Electronic information tools – the outer edge of world intellectual property law' (1993) 24 *IIC* 446

 'Legal hybrids between the patent and copyright paradigms' (1994) 94 *Col LR* 2432

 'Charting the collapse of the patent–copyright dichotomy: premises for a restructured international intellectual property system', the Herbert Tenzer Memorial Conference: copyright in the twenty-first century information super-highway: the challenge of multimedia technology (1995) 13 *Cardozo Arts and Entertainment Law Journal* 475

Reinbothe, J., 'The European Union's approach to copyright regarding the global information infrastructure' in ALAI, *Copyright in cyberspace*, Otto Cramwinckel, Amsterdam, 1996, 35

Reinbothe, J., M. Martin-Pratt and S. von Lewinski, 'The new WIPO treaties: a first résumé' [1997] 4 *EIPR* 171

Richardson, M., 'Intellectual property protection and the Internet: Trumpet Software Pty v OzEmail Pty Ltd' [1996] 12 *EIPR* 669

Richetson, S., 'Reaping without sowing' [1984] *UNSW Law Jo* (special issue) 1

 The Berne Convention for the protection of literary and artistic works: 1886–1986, Kluwer, Deventer, 1988

 'The use of copyright works in electronic databases' (1989) 63 *Law Institute Journal* 480

Ritscher, M. and A. Vogel, 'The "origin" of products of multinational enterprises' [1993] 5 *EIPR* 171

Robertson, A., 'The existence and exercise of copyright: can it bear the abuse?' (1995) 111 *LQR* 588

Roos, W., and J. Seignette, *Multimedia deals in the music industry* (reports presented at the meeting of the International Association of Entertainment Lawyers, MIDEM, Cannes 1996), Maklu, Apeldoorn, Antwerp, 1996

Roosen, T., 'L'identification des oeuvres et la communication en ligne' in C. Doutrelepont, P. Van Binst and C. Wilkin (eds.), *Libertés, droits et réseaux dans la société de l'information*, Bruylant and LGDJ, Brussels, Paris, 1996, 75

Rose, L., 'Is copyright dead on the Net?', http://www.eff.org/pub/intellectual_property/is_copyright_dead.paper

Rosenoer, J., *Cyberlaw. The law of the Internet*, Springer, New York, 1997

Rosenzweig, S., 'Don't put my article on line!: Extending copyright's new-use doctrine to the electronic publishing media and beyond' (1995) 143 *University of Pennsylvania Law Review* 899

Roudard, I., 'Special supplement on European information technology law' [1993] 9 *Computer Law and Security Report* 1

Rowland, D., 'The EC database Directive: an original solution to an unoriginal problem?' [1997] 5 *Web Journal of Current Legal Issues*, http://webjcli.ncl.ac.uk/1997/issue5/rowland5.html

Rudell, M., 'Music in multimedia: *Frank Music Corporation* v *Compuserve*' in M. Radcliffe and W. Tannenbaum, *Multimedia and the law 1996. Protecting your clients' interests*, Practicing Law Institute, New York, 1996, 455

Rumphorst, W., 'Fine-tuning copyright for the information society' [1996] 2 *EIPR* 79

Saez, C., 'Enforcing copyrights in the age of multimedia' (1995) 21 *Rutgers Computer and Technology Law Journal* 351

Sakkers, H., 'Licensing and exploiting rights in multimedia products' [1995] 11 *Computer Law and Security Report* 244

Salokannel, M., *Ownership of rights in audiovisual productions. A comparative study*, Kluwer Law International, London, The Hague, 1997

Samuelson, P., 'Creating a new kind of intellectual property: applying the lessons of the chip law to computer programs' (1985) 70 *Minnesota Law Review* 471

'Digital media and the changing face of intellectual property law' (1990) 16 *Rutgers Computer and Technology Law Journal* 323

'Digital media and the law', 1991, http://www.eff.org/pub/intellectual_property/digital_media_and_law.paper

'Is information property?', 1991, http://www.eff.org/pub/intellectual_property/is_info_property.paper

Sandison, H., 'Can copyright survive the multimedia regulation?' in ASLIB, *Copyright in multimedia (conference papers)*, ASLIB, London, 1995

Schack, H., *Urheber- und Urhebervertragsrecht*, Mohr Siebeck, Munich, 1997

Schardt, A., 'Multimedia – Fakten und Rechtfragen' [1996] 11 *GRUR* 827

Schatz, J., B. Anderson and H. Langworthy, 'What's mine is yours? The dilemma of a factual compilation' (1992) 17 *University of Dayton Law Review* 423

Schippan, M., 'Purchase and licensing of digital rights: the VERDI project and the clearing of multimedia rights in Europe' [2000] *EIPR* 24

Schønning, P., 'Applicable law in transfrontier on-line transmissions' (1996) *RIDA* 21

Schricker, G., *Urheberrecht. Kommentar*, 2nd edn, C. H. Beck, Munich, 1999

(ed.), *Urheberrecht auf dem Weg zur Informationsgesellschaft*, Nomos, Baden-Baden, 1997

Schuyler, N., *The business of multimedia*, Allworth Press, New York, 1995

Schwab, A., 'Multimedia litigation' in M. Epstein and F. Politano, *Current issues in multimedia licensing*, Prentice Hall Law and Business, New Jersey, 1994, 309

Schwartz, W., 'Legal issues raised by strategic alliances involving multimedia' (1993) 10 *Computer Lawyer* 19

'Intellectual property and licensing issues raised by strategic alliances involving multimedia' in ASLIB, *Copyright in multimedia (conference papers)*, ASLIB, London, 1995

Schwarz, M., 'Copyright in compilations of facts: *Feist Publications, Inc.* v *Rural Telephone Service Co., Inc.*' [1991] 5 *EIPR* 178

'Copyright protection is "not on the menu"' [1995] 7 *EIPR* 337

'Urheberrecht und unkörperliche Verbreitung multimedialer Werke' [1996] *GRUR* 836

Schweighofer, E., 'Downloading, information filtering and copyright' (1997) 6 *Information and Communications Technology Law* 121

Scott, M., 'Frontier issues: pitfalls in developing and marketing multimedia products' (1995) 13 *Cardozo Arts and Entertainment Law Journal* 413

'Pre-existing content: the "emperor's new clothes" of the multimedia "kingdom". "It's the content, stupid!"' [1995] 11 *Computer Law and Security Report* 255

Scott on multimedia law, Aspen Law and Business, New York, 1997

Scott, M. and J. Talbott, 'Interactive multimedia: what is it, why is it important and what does one need to know about it?' [1993] 8 *EIPR* 284

'Content and licensing issues in multimedia agreements' [1995] 11 *Computer Law and Security Report* 250

Seitel, O. and A. Berman, 'The Internet: law, policy and custom', http://www.degrees.com./melon/internet.html

Selin, S., 'Governing cyberspace: the need for an international solution' (1996–97) 32 *Gonzaga Law Review* 365

Sénat, *Les nouveaux services de communication audiovisuelle et l'industrie multimédia* (Document Sénat No. 245, Paris, 1995)

Sharmon, J., 'Encryption for exploiting copyright' in ASLIB, *Copyright in multimedia (conference papers)*, ASLIB, London, 1995

Sheils, P. and R. Penchina, 'What's all the fuss about *Feist*? The sky is not falling on the intellectual property rights of online database proprietors' (1992) 17 *University of Dayton Law Review* 563

Sherwood, R., 'Why a uniform intellectual property system makes sense for the world' in M. Wallerstein, M. Mogee and R. Schoen (eds.), *Global dimensions of intellectual property rights in science and technology*, National Academy Press, Washington D.C., 1993, 68

Sherwood-Edwards, M. and J. Dickens, 'Legal developments in multimedia in 1994' in E. Barendt (gen. ed.), *The yearbook of media and entertainment law 1995*, Clarendon Press, Oxford, 1995, 457

Shinas, I., 'I vassi dedomenon os antikimeno pnevmatikis idioktissias' (1996) 37 *Elliniki Dikaiossini* 1216

Simonds Lamarre, S., 'Expansion of "fair use" doctrine poses dangers for copyright holders' (1996) 13 *Computer Lawyer* 23

Sirinelli, P., 'Le multimédia' in P. Gavalda and N. Piakowski (eds.), *Droit de l'audiovisuel*, Lamy, Paris, 1995, 511

'The adaptation of copyright in the face of new technology' in *WIPO Worldwide Symposium on the Future of Copyright and Neighbouring Rights*, Louvre, Paris, 1–3 June 1994, 31

Sirinelli Report on multimedia and new technologies, France, Ministère de la culture et de la Francophonie, Paris, 1994

Second Sirinelli Report, *Le régime juridique et la gestion des oeuvres multimédias*, CERDI, Paris, 1996

'Intervention au premier forum de la propriété industrielle et artistique, colloque du 2 et 3 avril 1996' [1996] 183 *Revue Internationale de la Propriété Industrielle et Artistique* 147

Smedinghoff, T., *Multimedia legal handbook*, A guide from the Software Publishers Association, 2nd edn, vol. I, Wiley Law Publications, Chichester, 1996

(ed.), *Online law*, Thomas Addison-Wesley Developers Press, Harlow, 1996

Smith, G., R. Graham and M. Macdonald, 'Doing business on the Internet: the legal issues' [1996] 12 *Computer Law and Security Report* 202

Spoor, J., 'Protecting expert systems, in particular expert systems knowledge: a challenge for lawyers' [1992] 1 *EIPR* 9

Sprague, R., 'Multimedia: the convergence of new technologies and traditional copyright issues' (1994) 71 *Denver University Law Review* 635

Srikantiah, J., 'The response of copyright to the enforcement strain of inexpensive copying technology' (1996) 71 *New York University Law Review* 1634

Stamatoudi, I., 'The EU database Directive: reconceptualising copyright and tracing the future of the *sui generis* right' (1997) 50 *Revue Hellénique de Droit International* 436

'The European Court's love–hate relationship with collecting societies' [1997] 6 *EIPR* 289

'Moral rights of authors in England: the missing emphasis on the role of creators' [1997] 4 *IPQ* 478

'The hidden agenda in *Magill* and its impact on new technologies' (1998) 1 *Journal of World Intellectual Property* 153

'"Joy" for the claimant; can a film also be protected as a dramatic work?' [2000] *IPQ* 117

Stamatoudi, I. and P. Torremans (eds.), *Copyright in the new digital environment*, Sweet & Maxwell, London, 2000

'International exhaustion in the European Union in the light of "Zino Davidoff": contract versus trade mark law?' (2000) 31 *IIC* 123

Sterk, S., 'Rhetoric and reality in copyright law' (1996) 94 *Michigan Law Review* 1197

Sterling, J., *World copyright law*, Sweet & Maxwell, London, 1998

Stintzing, H., 'Moderne Informationsdienste als Herausforderung an das Urheber- und Wettbewerbsrecht – Erörterung als Anlass des Urteils des LG Köln v. 1.12.1992, AZ 31 O 283/92' [1994] *GRUR* 871

Strong, W., 'Database protection after *Feist* v *Rural Telephone Co.*' [1994] *Journal of the Copyright Society of the USA* 39

Strowel, A., *Droit d'auteur et copyright. Divergences et convergences. Etude de droit comparé*, Bruylant and LGDJ, Brussels, Paris, 1993

'La loi du 31 août 1991 concernant la protection des bases des données' (1999) 118 *Journal des Tribunaux* 297

Strowel, A. and J.-P. Triaille, *Le droit d'auteur, du logiciel au multimédia (Copyright, from software to multimedia)*, Bruylant, Brussels, 1997

Stuckey, K., *Internet and online law*, Law Journal Seminars-Press, New York, 1996
Stuurman, K., 'Legal aspects of standardisation of information technology and telecommunications: an overview' [1992] 8 *Computer Law and Security Report* 2
Taebi, A., 'Impact of information superhighway on non-economic rights' [1995] 11 *Computer Law and Security Report* 327
  'Impact of online computer services on copyright law' [1995] 11 *Computer Law and Security Report* 37
  '"Self regulation" on the Internet' [1995] 11 *Computer Law and Security Report* 202
Talbott, J., *New media. Intellectual property, entertainment and technology law*, Clark Boardman Callaghan, New York, 1997
Tannenbaum, W., 'Intellectual property due diligence for multimedia strategic alliances' (1994) 11 *Computer Lawyer* 1
Tapper, C., 'Genius and Janus: information technology and the law' (1985) 11 *Monash University Law Review* 75
  Computer law, 4th edn, Longman, London and New York, 1989
Tarjanne, P., 'The Internet and the information infrastructure: what's the difference?' speech delivered at the Pacific Telecommunications Council 18th Annual Conference, 'The information infrastructure: users, resources and strategies', Honolulu, 1996, http://www.ncb.gov.sg/nii/96 scan2/itu.html
Temple Lang, J., 'Media, multimedia, and the European Community anti-trust law' (1998) 21 *Fordham International Law Journal* 1296
Thorne, C., 'The infringement of database compilations: a case for reform?' [1991] 9 *EIPR* 331
  'Copyright and multimedia products – fitting a round peg in a square hole?' [1995] 49 *Copyright World* 18
Thorne, R. and J. Viera (eds.), *Entertainment, publishing and the arts handbook*, (1995–96 edn), Clark Boardman Callaghan, New York, 1996
Times, The, 'Copyright breach in Internet headline', 21 January 1997
Tonnellier, M.-H. and S. Lemarchand, 'Droit d'auteur reconnue sur le Net: première poursuite, première décision, première analyse' (available on the Internet)
Torremans, P., 'Copyright infringement and private international law', paper delivered at the Law Society of Scotland's Copyright Seminar, Stirling, 4 November 1997
Torremans, P. and J. Holyoak, *Butterworths' student statutes, intellectual property law*, 2nd edn, Butterworths, London, Dublin, Edinburgh, 1998
  Holyoak and Torremans' intellectual property law, 2nd edn, Butterworths, London, Dublin, Edinburgh, 1998
Torremans, P. and I. Stamatoudi, 'Collecting societies: sorry, the Community is no longer interested!' (1997) 22 *EL Rev* 352
Tournier, J.-L., 'The future of collective administration of authors' rights', paper presented at the European Commission Legal Advisory Board Conference on the Information Society: Copyright and Multimedia, Luxembourg, 26 April 1995
  'L'avenir des sociétés d'auteurs' (1996) *RIDA* 91

Traphagen, M., 'Legal issues in creating and protecting new media' in R. Thorne and J. Viera (eds.), *Entertainment, publishing and the arts handbook* (1995–96 edn), Clark Boardman Callaghan, New York, 1996, 233

Tritton, G., *Intellectual property in Europe*, Sweet & Maxwell, London, 1996

Tucker, E., 'Copyright plans win backing', *Financial Times* 11 February 1999

Turner, M., 'Do the old legal categories fit the new multimedia products? A multimedia CD-ROM as a film' [1995] 3 *EIPR* 107

Ulmer, E., 'Copyright protection of scientific works' (1972) 2 *IIC* 56

US Congress, Office of Technology Assessment, *Intellectual property rights in an age of electronics and information*, Washington D.C., 1986

Vandoren, P., 'Copyright and related rights in the information society' in *WIPO Worldwide Symposium on Copyright in the Global Information Infrastructure*, Mexico City, 22–24 May 1995, 83

'Droit d'auteur et droits voisins dans la société de l'information' in ALAI, *Audiovisual works and literary and artistic property*, ALAI, Paris, 1995, 361

Vercken, G., *Guide pratique du droit d'auteur pour les producteurs de multimédia*, commissioned by the European Communities, DG XIII (Translic) from AIDAA, 1994

'Les contrats des oeuvres multimédia' in *Guide de la nouvelle loi sur le droit d'auteur*, SACD–SGDL, Brussels, 1995, 45

'Practical guide to copyright and authors' societies for the use of multimedia producers', paper presented at the European Commission Legal Advisory Board Conference on the Information Society: Copyright and Multimedia, Luxembourg, 26 April 1995

A practical guide to copyright for multimedia producers, European Commission, DG XIII, 1996

Verstrynge, J., 'Copyright in the European Economic Community' (1993) 4 *Fordham Intellectual Property, Media and Entertainment Journal* 5

Viera, J. and R. Thorne (eds.), *Entertainment, publishing and the arts handbook* (1996–97 edn), Clark Boardman Callaghan, New York, 1997

Villeneuve, T., and D. Kaufman, 'Multimedia success will require inter-industry understanding' (1993) 10 *Computer Lawyer* 27

Vincent, A., 'Droit d'auteur; droit des auteurs et multimédia', interview by F. Dooghe, *La Vie Judiciaire*, 22–6 May 1995

Vinje, T., '*Magill*: its impact on the information technology industry' [1992] 11 *EIPR* 397

'The final word on *Magill*' [1995] 6 *EIPR* 297

'Harmonising intellectual property laws in the European Union: past, present and future' [1995] 8 *EIPR* 361

'A brave new world of technical protection systems: will there still be room for copyright?' [1996] 8 *EIPR* 431

'The new WIPO Copyright Treaty: a happy result in Geneva' [1997] 5 *EIPR* 230

Vivant, M., 'Protection of raw data and data banks in France' in E. Dommering and P. Hugenholtz (eds.), *Protecting works of fact*, Kluwer, Deventer, 1991, at 73

'L'incidence de l'harmonisation communautaire en matière de droits d'auteur sur le multimédia', European Commission, Brussels, Luxembourg, 1995 (vol. 3, *Copyright on electronic delivery services and multimedia products* series, EUR 16068 FR)

'Pour une épure de la propriété Intellectuelle' in *Propriétés intellectuelles, Mélanges en l'honneur de André Françon*, Dalloz, Paris, 1995

'The impact of community harmonisation of copyright on multimedia', Legal Advisory Committee (available on the Internet)

Wachter, T., 'Multimedia und Recht' [1995] *GRUR Int* 860

Wallerstein, M., M. Mogee and R. Schoen (eds.), *Global dimensions of intellectual property rights in science and technology*, National Academy Press, Washington D.C., 1993

Walter, P., 'Databases: protecting an asset; avoiding a liability' (1991) 8 *Computer Lawyer* 10

Wangermée, R., 'La notion de radiodiffusion dans les autoroutes de la communication' in C. Doutrelepont, P. Van Binst and C. Wilkin (eds.), *Libertés, droits et réseaux dans la société de l'information*, Bruylant and LGDJ, Brussels and Paris, 1996, 13

Wasoff, L., and B. Zimmerman, 'Clearing permissions for multimedia works: general guidelines' in M. Engelmann, *How to draft, negotiate and enforce licensing agreements 1997. A satellite program*, Practicing Law Institute, New York, 1997, 447

Wei, G., 'Multimedia and intellectual and industrial property rights in Singapore' (1995) 3 *IJLIT* 214

Weiss, J., 'Digital copyright: who owns what?' [1995] 9 *New Media* 38

Werbner, D., 'The multimedia environment: the broadcasters' perspective' in C. van Rij and H. Best, *Moral rights*, reports presented at the meeting of the International Association of Entertainment Lawyers, MIDEM, 1995, MAKLU Publishers, Apeldoorn, Antwerp, 1995, 225

Werra, D. de, 'Le multimédia en droit d'auteur' (1995) 1 *Revue Suisse de la Propriété Intellectuelle* 237

Westerdijk, R., 'The IT industry and the EC proposal for a directive concerning liability for suppliers of services' [1992] 8 *Computer Law and Security Report* 121

Wiebe, A., 'Information als Naturkraft – Immaterialgüterrecht in der Informationsgesellschaft' [1994] *GRUR* 233

Wiebe, A., and D. Funkat, 'Multimedia-Anwendungen als Urheberrechtlicher Schutzgegenstand' [1998] 2 *Multimedia und Recht* 69

Wienand, J., 'Museums as international copyright owners: use and abuse of images; multimedia problems; the Internet' (1997) 2 *Art, Antiquity and Law* 35

Wilkins, J., 'Protecting computer programs as compilations under *Computer Associates* v *Altai*' (1994) 104 *Yale Law Journal* 435

Williams, A., D. Calow and A. Lee, *Multimedia: contracts, rights and licensing*, FT Law and Tax, London, 1996

Winick, R., 'Intellectual property, defamation and the digital alteration of visual images' (1997) 21 *Columbia – VLA of Law and the Arts Journal* 143

WIPO Diplomatic Conference on certain copyright and neighboring rights questions, Basic Proposal for the substantive provisions of the Treaty on certain questions concerning the protection of literary and artistic works to be considered by the Diplomatic Conference, Geneva, 2–20 December 1996, 'Draft Treaty on Certain Questions concerning the Protection of Literary and Artistic Works dated 30 August 1996', http://www.wipo.org/eng/diplconf/4dc_star.html

WIPO Diplomatic Conference on certain copyright and neighboring rights questions, Basic Proposal for the substantive provisions of the Treaty on Intellectual Property in respect of databases to be considered by the Diplomatic Conference, Geneva, 2–20 December 1996, 'Memorandum Prepared by the Chairman of the Committees of Experts dated 30 August 1996', http://www.wipo.org/eng/diplconf/6dc_all.html

WIPO Diplomatic Conference on certain copyright and neighboring rights questions, Basic Proposal for the substantive provisions of the Treaty for the Protection of the Rights of Performers and Producers of Phonograms to be considered by the Diplomatic Conference, Geneva, 2–20 December 1996, 'Memorandum Prepared by the Chairman of the Committees of Experts dated 30 August 1996', http://www.wipo.org/eng/diplconf/4dc_star.html

WIPO Diplomatic Conference on certain copyright and neighboring rights questions, Geneva, 2–20 December 1996. WIPO Copyright Treaty adopted by the Diplomatic Conference on 20 December 1996, http://www.wipo.org/eng/diplconf/distrib/94dc.html

WIPO Diplomatic Conference on certain copyright and neighboring rights questions, Geneva, 2–20 December 1996. WIPO Performances and Phonograms Treaty adopted by the Diplomatic Conference on 20 December 1996, http://www.wipo.org/eng/diplconf/distrib/95dc.html

WIPO Press Release No. 106, Geneva, 20 December 1996, http://www.wipo.org/eng/diplconf/distrib/press106.html

WIPO International Forum on the Exercise and Management of Copyright and Neighbouring Rights in the Face of the Challenges of Digital Technology, Seville, 14–16 May 1997

WIPO World Forum on the Protection of Intellectual Creations in the Information Society, Naples Palazzo Reale, 18–20 October 1995

WIPO Worldwide Symposium on the Impact of Digital Technology on Copyright and on Neighbouring Rights, Harvard University, 31 March – 2 April 1993

WIPO Worldwide Symposium on the Future of Copyright and Neighbouring Rights, Louvre, Paris, 1–3 June 1994

WIPO Worldwide Symposium on Copyright in the Global Information Infrastructure, Mexico City, 22–24 May 1995

Wittweiler, B., 'Produktion von Multimedia und Urheberrecht aus schweizerischer Sicht' (1995) 128 *UFITA* 5

Worthy, J., 'Creating a secondary market in software and databases?' [1992] 8 *Computer Law and Security Report* 256

Worthy, J., and E. Weightman, 'Exploiting commercial information: a legal status report' [1996] 12 *Computer Law and Security Report* 5

Wyatt, D., and A. Dashwood, *European Community law*, 3rd edn, Sweet & Maxwell, London, 1993

Wylie, I., 'Curbing the copyright copy-cats' *Guardian*, 23 November 1996, 2

Yon, D. and Hill, K., 'Collective administration of copyright in cyberspace' in M.-C. Janssens (ed.), *Intellectual property rights in the information society*, Bruylant, Brussels, 1998

Index

Access to information, 3, 243, 244, 247, 254, 255, 264, 267, 279
Adaptation
  generally, 48, 61, 112, 128, 130–1, 275
  in computer programs, 158–9
  right of, 216
Administration of rights
  central, 261–4
  collective, 257–64
  generally, 9, 244–7, 256–7, 266, 275, 277
  individual, 257–61
Artistic works
  compilations of, 76ff., 90
  distinction from moving images, 113, 128, 134
  generally, 233
  notion, 187–9
  originality, 190
Audiovisual works
  as collaborative works, 122, 199, 202
  authorship/ownership, 119–23, 222–3, 230
  comparison with other works, 116–19
  economic rights, 124–5
  fixation, 114–16, 141–3
  generally, 7, 12, 21, 28, 91, 103, 204–5, 270–1
  (sequences of) images, 111–14, 129–41
  moral rights, 123–4, 163, 227–32, 234
  multimedia works as, 126–43, 145–51
  notion, 104–10, 116
  originality, 119, 213, 224–6
  term of protection, 125–6
  video games as, 168–9, 173ff.

Berne Convention, 5, 10–12, 43, 48, 51, 52, 71–3, 77–82, 88, 105–9, 133, 161, 186, 187, 194, 220, 233, 238, 243, 281

Cinematographic works. *See* Audiovisual works
Classification of works. *See* Qualification
Collecting societies, 241, 247, 257–61, 264, 265–6
Collections. *See* Compilations
Communication
  medium of, 132, 169
  notion, 45, 270, 279
  right of, 43, 124, 126, 216, 219, 231
  types of, 3–4, 6, 9, 16–18, 22–3, 36, 38
Competition
  generally, 9, 30, 50, 57, 58, 95, 96, 206–9, 214, 247, 249, 253, 255, 256ff., 264ff., 275, 278
  unfair, 53, 54
Compilations
  components of, 79–80
  differences with multimedia products, 82–7, 102–3
  differences with traditional literary works, 47–9, 80–2
  generally, 117
  of artistic works, 76ff., 90
  notion, 71–8
Compulsory licences, 58, 247, 255, 268, 275, 276, 278
Computer programs
  adaptations, 158–9
  as literary works, 44–7, 49, 55
  back-up copies, 158–9
  comparison with other works, 116–18
  employee-authors, 68, 159–60, 226, 229
  errors, 159
  generally, 10–12, 14, 27, 38, 50, 51, 60, 91, 97
  in multimedia products, 152–6, 164–5, 204, 250
  interactive, 97, 100
  in video games, 144, 168, 174ff.
  moral rights, 160–4, 227, 229–30
  notion, 92

315

Computer programs (*Cont.*)
  operating, 25, 28–31, 35, 89, 93, 97, 98, 100
  originality, 59–61, 213–14
  reverse engineering, 55, 157–8
  right of reproduction, 218–19
    exceptions to the, 157–9
Copyright Act
  Belgian, 42, 52, 60, 78, 92, 105, 120, 123, 126, 147, 150, 187, 201, 236, 243, 274
  French, 33, 42, 52, 60, 74, 75, 104, 113, 120, 121, 122, 123, 124, 125, 132, 146, 147, 150, 174, 188, 196–8, 216, 224, 226, 229
  German, 42, 53, 66, 68, 73, 74, 79, 104, 112, 113, 120, 123, 124, 135, 150, 188, 234, 237
  Greek, 42, 53, 61, 72, 73, 79, 110, 120, 121, 122–4, 132, 150, 188, 201
  Swiss, 42
  United Kingdom, 53, 54, 58, 59, 64, 67, 69, 76, 77, 94, 108, 112, 114, 117, 119, 120, 121, 122, 123, 124, 128, 130, 134, 135, 136, 140, 142, 143, 144, 159, 161, 189, 190, 194, 201, 213, 216, 223, 224, 225, 227, 228, 237
  United States, 54, 67, 73, 74, 105, 112, 113, 115, 117, 120, 125, 133, 134, 135, 138, 154, 168, 169, 170, 173, 176, 179, 188, 190, 201, 235

Databases
  differences with audiovisual works, 117–18
  differences with multimedia products, 96–102, 251–3
  generally, 49–50, 88–90
  independent contents, 90
  individually accessible contents, 90–2, 97–100
  sui generis right, 94–6, 251–3, 270–6
  systematic/methodical arrangement of contents, 93–4
Digitisation, 21–4, 25, 83, 84, 90, 112, 131, 142, 208, 240–1, 260, 261, 263, 272, 276ff.
Distribution
  generally, 22, 23, 29, 34, 147, 218
  right of, 124, 216, 218, 252, 253
Dominant position, 247, 255, 258, 262, 264, 265–6, 268, 269
Dramatic works, 75, 89, 144, 189–90

EU legislation
  Directive
    Copyright and related rights (draft), 39, 41, 217, 218, 219, 220, 242, 274
    Database, 5, 31, 56, 59, 60, 88ff., 117, 118, 136, 155, 158, 205, 207, 214, 218, 219, 250, 251, 253, 254, 255
    Rental and lending, 110, 121
    Software, 30, 59, 60, 92, 89, 150ff., 214, 218, 219, 242, 243, 276
    Term, 110, 125, 126, 149, 223, 248
  Green Paper on copyright and related rights, 20, 139, 231, 241, 242, 243, 247, 254, 274

Films. *See* Audiovisual works
Fixation
  generally, 8, 13, 22, 23, 33, 38–40, 43, 64, 65, 75
  of audiovisual works, 106–10, 112, 114, 141–3
  of literary works, 63
  of video games, 168–71

Interactivity
  generally, 3, 21, 87, 171, 204, 210, 230, 233–4, 272
  in audiovisual works, 136–40, 141, 145
  in databases, 97–8, 215
  in video games, 178, 180–2, 183–4
  notion, 24–6, 209
Internet, 14, 16, 22, 62, 84, 281

Literary works
  depurification, 45–51
  differences with audiovisual works, 116–17
  differences with compilations, 80–2
  differences with multimedia products, 64–70
  fixation, 63
  generally, 203–4
  notion, 42–5
  originality, 51–62

Magill, 88, 255, 267, 268
Management societies. *See* Collecting societies
Moral rights
  access to the work, 228–30, 232–3
  divulgation, 43, 228–30, 232–3, 239–40
  harmonisation, 230–1

Index

generally, 33, 34, 40–1, 54, 55, 62, 64, 198, 201, 223, 224, 225, 226, 263, 273–6
in audiovisual works, 123–4
in computer programs, 160–4
in multimedia products, 226–40
integrity, 149, 162, 227–8, 233–40
paternity, 124, 161, 227–8, 233, 239–40
withdrawal, 228–30, 232–3
Musical works, 75, 86, 89, 118, 144, 190, 212, 258, 259, 265, 272

Originality
generally, 8–9, 13, 38, 48–9, 51–6, 58, 59, 61, 65, 78, 95, 254, 278, 279
in audiovisual works, 119
in multimedia products, 186ff., 190, 213–15, 248–9
in video games, 171–4

Patents, 10–13, 27, 33, 46–7, 50, 54, 157

Qualification
of multimedia, 196–210
of works, 24, 31, 112, 143, 144, 186–96, 271

Reproduction, right of, 39, 61, 125, 170, 216–18, 252, 253
exceptions, 219, 243–4

Software. *See* Computer programs

Technical devices
against piracy, 241–4
for the administration of rights, 244–7. *See also* Administration of rights
generally, 240–1, 247–8
Term of protection
generally, 92, 126, 149, 248–9
in audiovisual works, 125–6
Trade marks, 2
TRIPs Agreement, 8, 10, 11, 71, 88, 89, 105, 153, 248, 255

Unfair competition. *See* Competition, unfair
US White Paper, 188, 193, 217, 242, 263

WIPO Copyright Treaty, 8, 10, 11, 89, 153, 243, 244, 274, 281
WIPO Performances and Phonograms Treaty, 217, 218, 220, 242, 243
Works
collaborative, 121–2, 146, 196–9, 201, 202
collective, 73–4, 91, 121–2, 147, 149, 197, 200–1, 202, 224
composite, 27, 122, 146, 197, 199, 202, 224
of joint authorship. *See* collaborative *above*

For EU product safety concerns, contact us at Calle de José Abascal, 56–1°,
28003 Madrid, Spain or eugpsr@cambridge.org.

www.ingramcontent.com/pod-product-compliance
Ingram Content Group UK Ltd.
Pitfield, Milton Keynes, MK11 3LW, UK
UKHW011323060825
461487UK00005B/311